THE HISTORY OF
THE NORMAN PEOPLE

WACE'S *ROMAN DE ROU*

THE HISTORY OF
THE NORMAN PEOPLE

WACE'S *ROMAN DE ROU*

Translated by
GLYN S. BURGESS

with notes by
Glyn S. Burgess and Elisabeth van Houts

THE BOYDELL PRESS

First published 2004
The Boydell Press, Woodbridge

ISBN 1 84383 007 8

⁊

The Boydell Press is an imprint of Boydell & Brewer Ltd
PO Box 9, Woodbridge, Suffolk IP12 3DF, UK
and of Boydell & Brewer Inc.
PO Box 41026, Rochester, NY 14604–4126, USA
website: www.boydellandbrewer.com

A catalogue record for this book is available
from the British Library

Library of Congress Cataloging-in-Publication Data

Wace, ca. 1100–ca. 1175.
  [Roman de Rou. English & French (Old French)]
  The History of the Norman people: Wace's Roman de Rou/Wace;
translated by Glyn S. Burgess; with notes by Glyn S. Burgess and
Elisabeth M.C. van Houts.
      p. cm.
Includes bibliographical references and indexes.
  ISBN 1–84383–007–8 (pbk.: alk. paper)
  I. Burgess, Glyn S. (Glyn Sheridan) II. Van Houts, Elisabeth M. C. III. Title.
PQ1545.W2A713 2004
841′.1 – dc22   2003018403

This publication is printed on acid-free paper

Printed in Great Britain by
Athenaeum Press Ltd., Gateshead, Tyne & Wear.

CONTENTS

ILLUSTRATION

For Janet

FOREWORD

In May 2002 the Société Jersiaise published a translation of the *Roman de Rou* of Wace by Glyn Burgess together with a reprint of the original text as edited by A. J. Holden. The present volume provides a revised version of the translation alone, but with a reprint of the article by Elisabeth van Houts entitled 'Wace as Historian'.

Glyn Burgess would like to thank Jean Blacker, Andrew Bridgeford, Valentine Fallan and Anthony Holden for help with the revision of the translation and accompanying material.

INTRODUCTION

The *Roman de Rou*: text and patronage

The *Roman de Rou* is a long verse chronicle which narrates the history of the first dukes to rule over Normandy; for the period after 1066 it also provides an account of the first Norman kings of England.[1] The work covers the period from the origins of Normandy, i.e. the time of Hasting and Rollo (Rou), up to the battle of Tinchebray in 1106, the year in which Henry I annexed Normandy by defeating his brother Robert Curthose.[2] The *Rou* was seemingly commissioned, or at least encouraged, by Henry II, who presumably wanted Wace to compose a work of similar scope to his earlier vernacular history of the Britons, the *Roman de Brut*, which seems to have enjoyed great success. Wace's new work, which was no doubt intended to be read out at Henry's court, would provide a eulogy of both Henry and his dynasty whilst at the same time explaining how the Normans came to be in England and justifying their right to the throne. Moreover, it would not only be a history of Henry's ancestors, but also of those of his wife Eleanor. Henry could claim descent from Rollo's son, William Longsword, and Eleanor from Rollo's only daughter, Gerloc, who married William III, Duke of Aquitaine (William I of Poitiers).[3] In turning to Wace, Henry was no doubt looking for a propagandist who could assist in the celebration of both past and present glories of the Norman and Angevin dynasty and confirm him as the rightful king of England. Even in the 1160s, when Wace began his work, some English lords were still refusing to accept the right of William the Conqueror and his successors to the throne of England; in addition, some Norman lords, who had grown accustomed to the freedom afforded them by the lax rule of Henry's predecessor, Stephen of Blois, were reluctant to offer Henry their full allegiance.

---

[1] In place of the traditional title *Roman de Rou* some scholars prefer to use *Geste des Normanz*, advocated, on the basis of *Chronique Ascendante*, v. 43, and Part III, v. 5297, by Gaston Paris in his celebrated review of the Andresen edition (pp. 596–97). For full details of works cited in the Introduction and footnotes to the translation see the Bibliography.

[2] In Part III Wace does allude to events later than 1106. There is a brief mention of the marriage in 1114 of Henry I's daughter Matilda to Henry V, King of Germany (vv. 10143–48), and also an account of the *White Ship* Disaster of 1120, in which Henry I's son, William, was killed (vv. 10149–294). From the way in which the *Chronique Ascendante* is written, it would appear that Wace originally intended to bring his narrative up to the contemporary period.

[3] Gerloc was renamed Adela, as it was common for a spouse to take a name in the language of her husband's country.

Why did Wace abandon his work?

At the close of his narrative Wace tells with obvious resentment of the abandonment of his work because a rival by the name of Maistre Beneeit had, at Henry's behest, undertaken a similar task (III, vv. 11419–24). The writer referred to is probably the same as the Benoît de Sainte-Maure who, in the 1160s, composed the lengthy *Roman de Troie*, and the work in question would become what we now know as the *Chronique des ducs de Normandie*.[4]

Why Henry withdrew his patronage from Wace and commissioned a second work on the same subject remains unclear, but a number of possible reasons have been advanced. Perhaps Wace's general approach to his task was not to Henry's liking, as Wace was more interested in truth than in propaganda. When Wace stopped writing, probably in the mid-1170s, Henry was less secure politically than he had been when he commissioned the work, and by this time any commitment to literature he may once have been willing to make could have given way to concern with his personal prestige and survival. Henry may have thought that Benoît would provide him with a more positive portrait of his ancestors and their deeds than Wace had been willing to do. Benoît's *Chronique* certainly shows that he was keener than Wace to please the king (e.g. vv. 14795–800, 42059–61). Perhaps, however, Henry had a more specific grudge against Wace, thinking that, instead of favouring his grandfather Henry I, he was showing too much support for Robert Curthose and the Norman cause.[5] Another possibility is that Henry was disturbed by the fact that in the investiture crisis Wace took Becket's side.[6] It has also been suggested that Henry was displeased by the fact that Wace's list of the Conqueror's companions reflects the names of those who supported the rebellion of Henry the Young King in 1173–74.[7] A further suggestion has been made that Wace's repeated awowals of ignorance, when he was not certain of his

---

[4] In the 44,542 lines of the *Chronique* the author is named only as Beneit from the Touraine. The references occur, moreover, in passages which may not have been written by Benoît himself. In the *Roman de Troie* he names himself as Beneeit de Sainte-More (v. 132) and as Beneit (vv. 2065, 5093, 19207). It is worth noting that Benoît too failed to finish his chronicle! Rather than continuing where Wace left off, Benoît started with the creation and division of the world and finished with the death of Henry I (1135). Henry no doubt expected both Wace and Benoît to bring the narrative up to his own reign; Benoît may have died before he could do so.

[5] U. T. Holmes, Jr, p. 66. Holmes cites what he sees as an attack on Henry I at the end of Wace's poem: 'He acts very shamefully, no one could do worse, who betrays his liege lord. No man, for any reason, should fail his earthly lord' (III, vv. 11383–85). In her article 'Wace's Craft and his Audience' Jean Blacker reviews three instances in which Wace's departure from his sources may have irritated Henry and she suggests that the depiction of the wars between Henry I and Duke Robert may have been 'particularly repugnant' to him (p. 359). See also her article '"La geste est grande, longue et grieve a translater"', pp. 388–91.

[6] J.-G. Gouttebroze suggests that as a cleric, in spite of his support for the king, Wace would have found it impossible not to be sensitive to the issues raised by Becket and his supporters ('Pourquoi congédier un historiographe', pp. 299–303).

[7] 'Any work that seemed to praise Hugh Bigod, Robert, earl of Leicester, Robert de Ferrers, Hugh (of Cyreiliog), earl of Chester, Roger de Mowbray and William, count of Aumale, to name but a few, was not going to please the king in the immediate aftermath of the revolt of 1173/74' (M. Bennett, 'Poetry as History?', p. 38).

facts, may not have pleased either Henry or other members of his audience.[8] An altogether simpler explanation, however, may be that by the mid-1170s Wace was handicapped by advancing years and the resulting slow progress was proving frustrating for Henry.[9]

Who was Wace?

About half way through Part III of the *Roman de Rou* Wace provides us with a certain amount of information about himself:

> The history of the Normans is a long one and hard to set down in the vernacular. If one asks who said this, who wrote this history in the vernacular, I say and will say that I am Wace from the Isle of Jersey, which is in the sea towards the west and belongs to the territory of Normandy. I was born on the island of Jersey and taken to Caen as a small child; there I went to school and was then educated for a long time in France. When I returned from France, I stayed in Caen for a long time and set about composing works in the vernacular: I wrote and composed a good many. With the help of God and the king – I must serve no one apart from God – a prebend was given to me in Bayeux (may God reward him for this). I can tell you it was by Henry the second, the grandson of Henry and the father of Henry (vv. 5297–318).

Reading between the lines and adding the small amount of extra information we possess, we can tentatively put together the following sketchy picture of Wace's life and career. He does not tell us the year of his birth, but this was almost certainly some time between 1090 and 1110 (Gaston Paris, p. 594, gives his birth as 1100 and Holden, vol. 3, p. 15, as 1110). The later date may be more likely, as Wace seems to have remained active at least until the mid-1170s. In the passage cited above his name occurs in its best known form, Wace, a form found four times in the *Roman de Brut* (vv. 7, 3823, 13282, 14866) and twice elsewhere in the *Rou* (III, vv. 158, 11439). But other forms are also encountered in the *Rou*: Vace (*Chronique Ascendante*, v. 3), Vacce (Part II, v. 443) and Gace (Part II, variant to v. 4569). In the last line of Part II, which in the sole surviving manuscript reads *Volentiers preïst grace* (v. 4425), the form *grace* is certainly an error for Guace (Holden, vol. 3, p. 213).[10] Wace has often been given a forename

---

[8] Jean Blacker, 'Wace's Craft and his Audience', pp. 359–60.

[9] For a general discussion of Henry's patronage of the *Rou* see Broadhurst, pp. 576–58, Damian-Grint, *The New Historians*, pp. 132–40, Schirmer and Broich, pp. 65–77, 86–88, and Tyson, pp. 197–99.

[10] In the *Vie de saint Nicolas* the author's name appears as Guace (vv. 35, variant Gace, and 1546). In the *Vie de sainte Marguerite* the form is Grace (probably an error for Guace, MS M v. 742); in the *Conception Nostre Dame* it is Gace (vv. 2, variant Guaces, and 111, variants Gasce, Guaces, Gaces, Vace and Vuace). The origin of the name Wace is uncertain, but it may stem from the Teutonic Wazo and is perhaps a northern form of the name Eustace. For modern equivalents see H.-E. Keller, 'Le Mirage *Robert Wace*', n. 1. But see n. 21 below.

and called Robert Wace, but this is probably an error, as Wace is more likely to be a personal name than a family name.[11] Wace states that he was born in Jersey. During his boyhood on this island he probably developed the interest in nautical matters which he displays in his writings on a number of occasions; Brian Woledge has pointed out that Wace is skilled at conveying the sense of excitement and adventure which accompany a sea voyage.[12] At some stage, Wace was sent to Caen, perhaps to a relative. There, in his words, he was 'put to letters' (v. 5307). He may have gone to Caen because at that time Jersey, which was in the diocese of Coutances, had no suitable ecclesiastical establishment.[13] Central to 'letters' was the study of Latin, so in this early period of his life Wace could have acquired the interest in translating Latin into French which was to become the cornerstone of his work. Wace was in fact fortunate to be studying in Caen, which was an important educational centre; it had several schools, associated in particular with Lanfranc of Saint-Étienne and Arnulf of Chocques.[14]

Wace informs us that from Caen he went to France, where he stayed for a long time. At that time France was principally the Ile-de-France and Wace presumably went to Paris itself, which, like Caen, was already a flourishing educational centre. Here his studies would have led to his qualifying as *magister* and thereby acquiring the right to teach. Subsequently, he returned to Caen, where he seems to have remained at least until some time in the mid-1160s, when Henry II awarded him a prebend in Bayeux.

Wace does not provide us with any specific dates for the career activities he mentions. But he must have been back in Caen before 1135, the date of the death of King Henry I, for he states that he became a *clerc lisant* in Caen and that he held this office during the reigns of three Henrys, i.e. Henry I, Henry II and Henry the Young King (III, vv. 179–80). The role of *clerc lisant*, literally 'reading or teaching cleric', is not easy to define. Wace may simply have used the phrase to indicate that he was a 'learned cleric', but it is more likely that he had specific duties to perform, such as writing, reading aloud (perhaps at mealtimes),

---

[11] The error may have resulted from a misreading of v. 1549 of the *Vie de saint Nicolas* ('A l'oes Robert le fiz Tiout') or from some confusion with Duke Robert I of Normandy. For further discussion see Keller, *ibid.*

[12] B. Woledge, 'Notes on Wace's Vocabulary', p. 21. Woledge adds that the 'immense number' of technical terms relating to the sea were used by Wace precisely because they were technical terms and were therefore not part of everyday life (*ibid.*). For a list of Wace's nautical vocabulary see H.-E. Keller, *Etude descriptive sur le vocabulaire de Wace*, pp. 221–26; Keller calls Wace an 'excellent connaisseur de la navigation' (p. 14).

[13] The earliest abbey to be established in the Channel Islands was that of St Helier, founded by William FitzHaimo some time between 1125 and 1155. See Raoul Lemprière, *History of the Channel Islands* (London: Robert Hale, 1974), p. 24.

[14] See the chapter 'Caen 1063–1070' in Margaret Gibson, *Lanfranc of Bec* (Oxford: Clarendon Press, 1978), pp. 98–115 (esp. pp. 102–05). Some scholars (e.g. Philpot, pp. 32–33) have suggested that Wace was either influenced by or taught by Arnulf of Chocques (also known as Arnulf of Malcouronne), who seems at some time to have opened a school at Caen dedicated to history and literature, especially profane literature.

composing, acting as notary, studying, teaching and interpreting texts.[15] Early in Part III of the *Rou* he stresses the importance of reading out chronicles and histories when festivals are being held (III, vv. 1–6), and much of the early section of Part III is taken up with the crucial role writing has had throughout history in recording the deeds of kings and heroes and keeping alive the history of famous places. But the function of *clerc lisant* did not necessarily suppose that the incumbent was a priest; indeed, the expression may have been used precisely to indicate that this was not the case (Legge, p. 555). In fact, rather than being a monk or a priest in Caen, Wace may have been involved in particular with the education of young students. Holmes suggests that he 'maintained a psalter school or perhaps a grammar school for the people of Caen who were clerically minded' (p. 57).[16]

Wace was fond of calling himself 'Maistre Wace'. In the *Rou* he does so four times: *Chronique Ascendante*, v. 3, II, v. 443, III, vv. 158, 11439.[17] This may signify either that, from the start of his career, his qualifications allowed him to be both a *clerc lisant* and a *maistre lisant* (an authoritative master in an ecclesiastical school whose teaching was to be respected), or that at some stage he acquired the title *maistre lisant*.[18] What is certain is that Wace was proud of his education; his works demonstrate erudition, an exceptionally enquiring mind and a generally didactic approach to the task of writing.

Wace refers twice to the award of a prebend by Henry II (III, vv. 171–74, 5313–18). A prebend was an endowment funded by the church or by some other body within a diocese. Prebendaries were non-resident canons, who could be in minor orders rather than the higher orders required of a deacon or a priest. They had to live at the church which paid their endowment, perform certain duties and attend the monthly meeting of the bishop's chapter. Prebends at Bayeux were granted in accordance with the will of the patron, who was none other than Henry II himself; the award may have constituted some form of payment by Henry for the *Roman de Rou*, or even, belatedly, as a reward for the success of the

[15] The expression *clerc lisant* had already been used by Gaimar in his *Estoire des Engleis*: 'Si cum distrent les clers lisanz' (v. 2380, see also vv. 3455–56). For Gaimar the duty of the *clerc lisant* was to preserve, transmit and make public documents relating to the past. See J.-G. Gouttebroze, 'Henry II Plantagenêt', p. 96. Gouttebroze also cites a line in *La Chevalerie Vivien* in which an example of the expression *clerc lisant* occurs as a variant for the term *jongleur*: 'Nel savroit dire nul jugleor' (v. 210, MS D)/ 'Ne le savroit dire nuls clers lisant' (MS E, ed. by Duncan McMillan, 2 vols, Aix-en-Provence: CUER MA, 1997). Such an association with *jongleurs* would not have pleased a *clerc lisant*. For further discussion of the expression *clerc lisant* see Holden, vol. 3, p. 215, and the articles by E. A. Francis, M. D. Legge and F. Lyons.

[16] Holmes also points out that Wace's early writings suggest that, initially, his principal patrons were Saint-Étienne in Caen and the nearby Saint-Évroult, where Orderic Vitalis was a monk until his death in 1143; later Wace seems to have discovered that it was more profitable to work for the king and queen (p. 57). Holmes even suggests a precise location for Wace's house and school in Caen, 'in the clerical district not far from the Abbaye aux Hommes or Saint-Estienne' (p. 59).

[17] See also *Conception Nostre Dame* (v. 2), *Vie de saint Nicolas* (v. 1546) and *Roman de Brut* (vv. 7, 3823, 13282, 14866). On what he calls the 'scholarly title of *maistre*' (p. 52) see Damian-Grint, *The New Historians*. The title served to designate the writer as serious and learned.

[18] At the beginning of the *Chronique Ascendante* Wace defines himself as a 'clerc de Caen' (v. 3). He was certainly still a 'clerc lisant' in 1170, the date of the coronation of the Young King.

Roman de Brut. It is not certain, however, that after the award of his prebend Wace moved from Caen to Bayeux; it is possible that he continued to live in Caen and, when necessary, travelled to Bayeux, a distance of under thirty kilometres.[19] Four documents, dated *c.* 1166–74, contain a reference to Wace. The earliest of the documents, of uncertain date but probably around 1166, is a charter of Bishop Henry II of Bayeux (1165–1204) confirming the privileges and possessions of the regular canons of Le Plessis-Grimoult; Wace is one of the witnesses and in this document he is called *Magister Wascius*. But another document, an agreement dating from 1169 between Abbot Gilbert of Troarn and Bishop Henry II, designates Wace as *canonicus* 'canon'. It could therefore be that he was appointed canon between *c.* 1166 and 1169. In a document from 1172 Bishop Henry confirms the privileges and possessions of the abbey of Saint-Étienne in Caen. A charter dating from 1174 cites Wace as a witness, in the presence of Bishop Henry and his clergy, to an agreement between the Bayeux chapter and Richard of Le Hommet, the king's constable.[20]

Was Wace of noble birth?

The question of whether Wace came from a noble or a plebeian family has frequently been asked. If he were of noble birth, it is surprising that there is no clear record of his family.[21] There is, however, a passage in the *Rou* which suggests that he was of fairly humble origin. Here he states that his father witnessed preparations for the Conquest of England: 'But I heard my father say

---

[19] See Holmes, pp. 61–62. Holmes cites Michel Béziers, *Mémoires pour servir à l'état historique et géographique du diocèse de Bayeux*, 2 vols (Rouen and Paris, 1896), who states that at Bayeux there were forty-nine prebends and canonicates; they included three from the local chapters at Caen, Saint-Pierre, Notre Dame de Froide Rue and Saint-Jean (I, pp. 2–3), one of which, Holmes suggests, may have been the prebend awarded to Wace.

[20] The documents are discussed by Du Méril, pp. 6–7 (pp. 220–21 in the reprint). They are found in the *Livre noir* of Bayeux (ed. by V. Bourrienne, *Antiquus cartularius ecclesiae Baiocensis (Livre noir)*, 2 vols (Rouen and Paris, 1902), I, pp. 161–64 (nos 74, 56, 103). The copy of the 1169 document which mentions Wace by name is preserved in the Troarn cartulary: see *L'Abbaye de Saint-Martin de Troarn au diocèse de Bayeux, des origines au seizième siècle* (Caen, 1911), p. 81 n. 2. In the documents dating from *c.* 1166 and 1172 Wace's name is spelt Ac(c)ius, perhaps because he was not known to the scribe, as he still resided in Caen (Holmes, p. 60); but van Houts suggests that Acius here could be interpreted as the *Azo subdecanus* who appears alongside Wace in the 1174 charter ('Wace as Historian', p. xxxvii n. 17).

[21] There was, however, a Wace family which possessed lands in Jersey and Guernsey; one member of this family, Richard Wace, was a canon of Bayeux towards the end of the twelfth century (van Houts, 'Wace as Historian', p. xxxvi). A prebend of the sort enjoyed by Wace at Bayeux could be granted as an hereditary fief (Béziers, I, pp. 2–3), so this Richard Wace could be a relative of the author of the *Roman de Rou*. Holmes even suggests that, if Wace were in lower orders only, he could have been married and Richard Wace could have been his son (pp. 66–67). Indeed, Wace's own prebend could have been a family appointment and it need not have been granted to him exclusively for literary activities (van Houts, *ibid.*). See the *Cartulaire de Jersey, Guernesey, et les autres îles normandes: recueil de documents concernant l'histoire de ces îles conservés aux Archives du Département de la Manche*, 6 fascicles (Jersey: Société Jersiaise, 1918–24), III (1920), pp. 202–03, 220–21, IV (1921), pp. 292–93. But if Wace were a member of this family (the forms of the name are Vac, Wac, Wach and Wake), his name would then have to be regarded as a surname rather than a forename (see above, n. 10).

– I remember it well though I was a young lad – that when they set off from Saint-Valery there were seven hundred ships less four, either ships, boats or skiffs, carrying weapons or equipment' (III, vv. 6423–28). From this allusion to his father's knowledge of William the Conqueror's invasion fleet at Saint-Valery-sur-Somme the conclusion has often been drawn that Wace was the son of a carpenter involved in the building of William's ships, or else of a man who was acquainted with those who were so involved.

But those who think that Wace's education and career suggest that he was of good birth take heart from a passage which, if one accepts a textual emendation, indicates that he had links to an important family. Troubled by a passage in Part III, which reads *Tosteins, ki (ert) ses chamberlencs/De sa chambre maistre gardeins/De par sa mere fu sis aives* ('Turstin [or Thurstan], who was his chamberlain, chief guardian of his chamber, was his grandfather through his mother', vv. 3223–25), Gaston Paris suggested that the phrase *de par sa mere* 'through his mother', which makes no sense, should be emended to *de par ma mere* 'through my mother'. This would make Wace a relative (grandson, or more likely great-grandson) of Turstin, chamberlain to William the Conqueror's father, Robert the Magnificent of Normandy (1027–35). The claim, unique to Wace, that in the time of Duke Robert's father all chamberlains and ushers were noble knights (III, vv. 807–08), would show that, at least on his mother's side, Wace was (or hoped he was?) of noble birth. Although the matter remains unproven, Gaston Paris's suggestion has been widely accepted.[22]

However, those who remain sceptical of Wace's noble birth can point to the fact that at no time in his life does Wace appear to have escaped the fear of poverty. This might indicate that he was a man of peasant or bourgeois stock who sought improvement through education, but it would not rule out the possibility that he came from an impoverished family belonging to the lower nobility. Advocates of non-aristocratic birth are often concerned by Wace's seeming lack of sympathy for the peasants when he describes their revolt (III, vv. 815–958). But this need not be a stumbling-block. Dolores Buttry has shown that, although he had no desire to see the social order overturned, Wace does not condemn the peasants; rather he narrates their grievances and suffering with compassion and understanding. In this Wace resembles Chrétien de Troyes, who, for example, treats with sympathy the plight of maidens forced to serve cruel masters in the *Pesme aventure* episode of his *Chevalier au lion*. Both Chrétien and Wace appear to want justice to be allied to the maintenance of social stability.

[22] For example, van Houts comments that 'most historians, including myself, are in favour of accepting Paris's attractive hypothesis' ('Wace as Historian', p. xxxv n. 3). She adds that a number of charters relating to Duke Robert's attempted invasion of England in 1033 were witnessed by a Tursting[us] or Turstin[us] (*ibid.*). The fleet was diverted from its course and ended up in Jersey. Wace's maternal ancestors may have provided, through family tradition, intimate knowledge of Duke Robert's family, including William the Conqueror, for which Wace offers unique information (*ibid.*, pp. xxxv–vi).

Wace and the Plantagenet court

One is on safer ground in saying that for much of his later life Wace was proud of his association with Henry II (reigned 1154–89), and also with two other Henrys, Henry I (reigned 1100–35) and Henry the Young King; the latter was crowned in 1170, but, as he predeceased his father, he never reigned as king. Both at the beginning and the end of Part III Wace alludes to the fact that he had seen and known the three Henrys (vv. 179, 11431–38); he also concludes the biographical details cited above with a reference to Henry II, whom he defines as the grandson of Henry and the father of Henry (III, vv. 5317–18). When he first mentions the prebend given to him by Henry II, he states that the second Henry was born of the first and was father to the third (III, vv. 171–84).

Wace clearly associates the three Henrys, especially Henry II, with his career as both cleric and writer. He mentions Henry II early in the *Chronique Ascendante* and warns him to remain vigilant where the French are concerned: 'He [Rou] conquered Normandy, like it or not, against the pride of France, which still threatens them – may our King Henry recognise and be aware of this' (vv. 5–8). He goes on to remark that King Henry took as his wife Eleanor, a lady of noble birth, and that they both showed generosity towards him: 'They do not let me waste my time at court; each of them rewards me with gifts and promises' (vv. 20–21).[23] But Wace would also be the first to acknowledge that promises can be broken; in the concluding lines of Part II he presents himself as a victim of poverty and in dire need of a boost to his professional career: 'He who sings must drink or take some reward. He who can should progress in his profession; Wace would gladly accept bounty, for he needs to take something' (vv. 4424–25). It was seemingly because he finally fell out of favour with Henry II that Wace laid down his pen and grudgingly allowed the task of completing his work to pass to Benoît de Sainte-Maure ('Since the king asked him to do it, I must abandon it and fall silent', vv. 11423–24). He makes it clear that he associates this indignity with broken promises: 'The king in the past was very good to me; he gave me a great deal and promised me more, and if he had given me everything he promised me, things would have gone better for me. I could not have it, it did not please the king' (vv. 11425–29).

So it seems that, for much of his later life, the Plantagenet court and its largesse (or occasionally lack of it) were fundamental to Wace's way of life. He expresses dismay in the *Rou* that he could scarcely find anyone who had bestowed anything on him apart from Henry II; in addition to the prebend at Bayeux, Henry II had also given him many other gifts (III, vv. 171–75). His references to the three Henrys show evident affection for them and he wanted his work to bring them honour: 'All three were kings of the English and all three

---

[23] According to the English poet Layamon, Wace presented his *Roman de Brut* to Eleanor (see below, n. 47). Jean Blacker suggests that Wace was using the *Brut* as a means of introducing himself as a writer in order to enter Henry's employ ('Wace's Craft and his Audience', p. 356). D. D. R. Owen sees the dedication of the *Brut* to Eleanor as 'likely' (*Eleanor of Aquitaine: Queen and Legend* (Oxford: Blackwell, 1993), p. 109, see also pp. 38–39, 183, 210).

were dukes and kings; they were kings of England the Rich and dukes of
Normandy. In honour of the second Henry, who was born of the lineage of Rou,
I have spoken at length of Rou and his powerful family and of Normandy which
he conquered and of the acts of prowess which he performed there' (vv. 181–90).
Even if things turned sour in the end and it was not possible for him to complete
his narrative, Wace had, and knew he had, much to be thankful for. But at the
same time he was also convinced that he himself had done nothing wrong and
was not to blame for what happened: 'Mais n'est mie remés en mei'/ 'But it was
not my fault' (v. 11430).

Wace and the theme of largesse

In examining Wace's relationship with Henry II, one cannot, as we have seen,
avoid the question of largesse, which was a recurrent theme of Old French and
Occitan poetry. So the extent to which Wace's use of this theme derives from
personal circumstances or from a topos of contemporary literature remains
unclear (nevertheless, one would not expect so many references to it in a work of
history). Wace was certainly quick to praise those from whose generosity he had
benefited, but also just as quick to criticise any signs of avarice or disrespect on
the part of his aristocratic public. In the early lines of Part III he devotes an entire
passage to the question of reward for literary effort:

> Those who wrote chronicles and composed histories used to be greatly
> honoured and very much praised and loved. They often used to receive
> handsome gifts from barons and noble ladies, for giving an account of
> their lives, so that they would be remembered for all time. But now I can
> put in a great deal of effort, write and translate books, compose vernac-
> ular works and *serventeis*, but I will scarcely find anyone, however
> courtly he might be, who would offer me and place in my hands enough
> to employ a scribe for a month, or who could do me any other favour
> than to remark: 'Master Wace says this very well; you ought to keep on
> writing, you who are skilled in good and elegant speech'. I am content
> with this and put every effort into it; I will never get more than this from
> many people. I speak to rich men, who have money and a good income,
> for through them are books composed and good deeds written down and
> recounted. What used to be nobility is dead and largesse has disappeared
> along with it. However near or far I may travel, I cannot find anyone who
> upholds its customs (vv. 143–69).

At the beginning of the *Chronique Ascendante*, just after he has told Henry II
to be on his guard against the French, Wace also launches into an attack on the
stinginess of his contemporaries: 'Largesse has now succumbed to avarice;
it cannot open its hands, they are more frozen than ice. I do not know where
largesse is hidden, I can find no sign or trace of it . . . It was not at all like this
at the time of Virgil and Horace, nor of Alexander, Caesar or Statius; then
largesse had strength and virtue' (vv. 9–16). This no doubt exaggerated praise
of times gone by may have been a ploy on Wace's part to put pressure on Henry,
who had been generous to Wace and hopefully would continue to be so, but
it also highlights the vulnerability of a writer to poverty if adequate support is

not forthcoming. Artists are seen here as subject to individual whims and contemporary fashion. Wace's frequent references to his poverty may also have annoyed Henry and been yet another contributing factor to his fall from favour.[24]

Editions and translations of the *Roman de Rou*

Three complete editions of the *Roman de Rou* have been published so far, by Frédéric Pluquet (1827–29), Hugo Andresen (1877–79) and Anthony Holden (1970–73).[25] In each case the presentation of the text differs. Holden's text, which is translated here, begins with a 315–line section entitled *Chronique Ascendante des ducs de Normandie*. This section narrates the history of the dukes of Normandy in reverse order, from Henry II back to Rollo, the founder of the lineage. However, certain doubts remain concerning the authenticity of this section, which was given its name by Pluquet.[26] After the *Chronique Ascendante* Holden places what he calls the Deuxième partie (Part II), which consists of 4,425 lines (Holden's line numbering for this section begins again at line 1). This is followed by the Troisième partie (Part III), a section of 11,440 lines, also numbered again from line 1 (vv. 1–3240 appear in volume 1 of his edition and the remaining lines in volume 2). The edition ends with a 750–line Appendix entitled *Le Roumanz de Rou et des dus de Normendie*. The total number of lines in Holden's edition and in the present translation is therefore 16,930.

In Pluquet's edition of the *Rou* the lines are numbered from 1 to 16547 (with lines 1–8398 in volume 1 and the remaining lines in volume 2). His text begins with the material now found in Holden's Appendix (vv. 1–750), followed by a section written in Alexandrines (vv. 751–5164, Holden's Part II) and finally a section which Pluquet calls the 'Seconde partie' (vv. 5165–16547, Holden's Part

---

[24] This suggestion is made by Jean Blacker, '"La geste est grande, longue et grieve a translater"', pp. 388–89.

[25] Before publishing his complete edition of the *Rou*, Pluquet had edited the *Chronique Ascendante* (in 'La *Chronique Ascendante des ducs de Normandie* par Maître Wace'), and in his *Notice sur la vie et les écrits de Robert Wace* (1824) he introduced his readers to the text of the *Rou* by providing some extracts (pp. 23–64). In 1824 P. R. Auguis also printed some extracts of the *Rou* in his *Les Poètes françois, depuis le XIIe siècle jusqu'à Malherbe*, 6 vols (Paris: Crapelet), II, pp. 89–92. In 1828 Sir F. Palgrave published 1,258 lines of the *Rou*, but he abandoned his intention to provide a complete text when he became aware of Pluquet's edition.

[26] R. R. Bezzola advances a number of doubts concerning the *Chronique Ascendante*, which he sees as the work of a reviser: (i) it is unlikely that Wace would call himself 'un clers de Caen, qui out non Mestre Wace' ('A cleric of Caen, whose name was Master Wace'), (ii) the homage to Henry and Eleanor (vv. 17–42) is written with a 'désinvolture' ('off-handedness') uncharacteristic of Wace, (iii) the mention of the siege of Rouen would place the composition of this section after 1174, (iv) the request for recompense is too obvious, etc. Bezzola suggests that the author of the *Chronique Ascendante* was working from a now lost dedication to the royal couple written by Wace around 1160 (p. 178). See also Du Méril, pp. 42–43 (pp. 270–72 in the reprint). These arguments are countered by Holden in 'L'Authenticité des premières parties du *Roman de Rou*'. See also Becker, 'Der gepaarte Achtsilber' and 'Die Normannenchroniken', and Hormel, *Untersuchung über die Chronique Ascendante und ihren Verfasser*.

III). Pluquet did not print the *Chronique Ascendante* in his edition because he considered it to be a separate work by Wace, written after 1173 and not constituting part of the *Roman de Rou* itself.[27] Like Pluquet, Andresen began with the material in Holden's Appendix (vv. 1–751). He followed this with what is Holden's Part II, but, unlike Pluquet, he numbered this section from line 1 to line 4424. Also unlike Pluquet, he printed the text of the *Chronique Ascendante*, placing it at the end of volume 1, after Part II. The whole of Holden's Part III is found in Andresen's second volume, which also contains material on the manuscripts of the *Rou* (pp. 3–28), a lengthy linguistic study (pp. 485–600) and copious notes (pp. 601–781).

In 1835 Pluquet's edition was translated into German by Franz Gaudy (with some abbreviated passages), and in 1837 a partial English translation of it was provided by Edgar Taylor (corresponding principally to Part Three, vv. 3235–9340 of the present volume). In 1860 Sir Alexander Malet published, with a facing English translation, the section of Pluquet's text dealing with the battle of Hastings (corresponding in Holden's edition to Part III, vv. 5543–9340). Leger Brosnahan's translation of the *Rou* (dissertation, Harvard University, 1957) remains unpublished.

Versification

An unusual feature of the *Rou* as we have it, and one which is of significance for its dating, is that it is not composed entirely in the same metre.[28] The *Chronique Ascendante* is written in twelve-syllable lines arranged in stanzas known as *laisses*.[29] The *laisse* form had not been used by Wace in his earlier writings, but it is well known from earlier epic poems such as the *Chanson de Roland*. However, the epics tend to use a line of ten syllables rather than one of twelve, and before Wace's time the use of the twelve-syllable line, known as the Alexandrine, was rare.[30] Wace continued his use of Alexandrines in Part II, but this time employing assonance rather than rhyme.[31] Part III is written in octosyllabic rhyming couplets, the form Wace had used when he composed the

---

[27] Pluquet, *Notice sur la vie et les écrits de Robert Wace*, p. 10.

[28] A change of metre was not, however, unknown in the twelfth century. In his *Bestiaire*, dating from around 1121, Philippe de Thaun changes at v. 2889 from six-syllable to eight-syllable lines in order to improve the arrangement of his material ('Or voil [je] mun metre muër/Pur ma raisun mielz ordener', vv. 2889–90, ed. by E. Walberg, Paris: Weller, 1900). Philippe de Thaun wrote in rhyme, but occasionally he made use of assonance (Walberg, p. xviii).

[29] A *laisse* is a stanza of variable length which groups together lines based on a single assonance. The *Chronique ascendante* has eleven *laisses* with an average length of 28.6 lines.

[30] The term Alexandrine is named after Alexandre de Paris, from Bernay in Normandy, who used it around 1155 in his redaction of the *Roman d'Alexandre*. This dodecasyllabic line was also used in the *Pèlerinage de Charlemagne*, dating perhaps from the middle of the twelfth century. See Knud Togeby, 'L'Histoire de l'alexandrin français', in *Études romanes dédiées à Andreas Blinkenberg* (Copenhagen, 1963), pp. 240–66.

[31] Assonance, also used in the early epics, is the rhyming of words in successive lines using the identity of the accented vowels, but not that of the consonants. In the first 735 lines of Part II the *laisses* are short, often no more than four lines; the remaining lines of this section largely revert to the longer *laisse* form.

Roman de Brut and also when he began the *Roman de Rou* (i.e. in the material which now forms the Appendix to Holden's edition).[32]

The decision made by Wace to move from the octosyllabic line to the Alexandrine and back again cannot easily be explained. Holden makes two suggestions: (i) when embarking on his work, Wace thought that the material merited a more solemn form than the flowing octosyllabic line, but later became frustrated by the slower rhythm of the longer line, (ii) he misinterpreted public taste, which, in spite of its fondness for novelty, was fundamentally hostile to radical change (vol. 3, p. 77). The reason may simply have been, however, that, having experimented with the Alexandrine for a time and then abandoned his work, Wace opted, when he eventually picked up his work again, to use a metre with which he felt more comfortable.[33]

Manuscripts of the *Roman de Rou*
The *Roman de Rou* is preserved in four manuscripts and one fragment:

A   London, British Library, Royal 4.C.XI, ff. 249r–278r. Beginning of the thirteenth century.

B   Paris, Bibliothèque Nationale de France, fr. 375 (formerly 6987), ff. 219r–240v. End of the thirteenth century.

C   Paris, Bibliothèque Nationale de France, nouv. acq. fr. 718, ff. 1a–149a. End of the fourteenth century.

D   Paris, Bibliothèque Nationale de France, Duchesne 79, ff. 1r–83r. A seventeenth-century copy, of which three further copies are also extant (see Holden, vol. 3, p. 24).

A[2]   London, British Library, Royal 13.A.XVIII, f. 115. Fragment. Fourteenth century.[34]

None of the four surviving manuscripts provides a complete text of the original poem. The *Chronique Ascendante* and Part II are preserved only in Duchesne's seventeenth-century copy (D). But, although of late date, this manuscript appears to offer a faithful representation of an older model. Consequently, for the *Chronique Ascendante* and Part II an editor has no choice of manuscript. Part III, however, has been preserved in four manuscripts, including Duchesne

---

[32] The octosyllabic rhyming couplet was first used in the tenth-century *Passion du Christ* and the eleventh-century *Vie de saint Léger*. Used at the beginning of the twelfth century by Benedeit in his hagiographic romance the *Voyage of St Brendan*, it became the standard metre of romance in the second half of the twelfth century, thanks to the three *romans antiques* (*Thèbes*, *Eneas* and *Troie*) and writers such as Chrétien de Troyes, Marie de France and Beroul.

[33] In v. 3 of Part II Wace makes a comment which has proved difficult to interpret: 'Mes por l'euvre esploitier les vers abrigeron' (translated here as 'But, to speed our task, we will reduce the number of lines in each stanza'). Whether Wace is referring to the number of syllables in his lines, to the number of lines in each *laisse* or to a general curtailment in the length of his narrative remains unclear. See Brosnahan, 'A Propos du vers 3', and Holden, 'De Nouveau le vers 3'.

[34] For a description of the manuscripts see Holden, vol. 3, pp. 19–24.

79. Holden bases his edition of this section on MS A (which was originally at Battle Abbey), but he also provides variants from the other three manuscripts. The British Library fragment corresponds to the first 44 lines of Part II; it was probably copied directly from A.[35]

Foremost among those responsible for bringing Wace and the manuscripts of the *Rou* to the attention of the public were André Duchesne, the Abbé Gervais de la Rue and Georges-Louis de Bréquigny. In the early seventeenth century, as already noted, Duchesne rescued the *Chronique Ascendante* and Part II of the *Rou* by copying it in his own hand from a manuscript which is now lost. The Abbé de la Rue was a priest and historian from Wace's city of Caen. Forced to leave France at the time of the Revolution, he came to England and set about investigating Norman and Anglo-Norman manuscripts and authors, starting with Wace. In 1796 he published in the journal *Archaeologia* the first substantial study of Wace. By this time, Bréquigny, working on manuscripts recently deposited in the Bibliothèque Nationale, had discovered and described MS B (he also discusses two of the copies of Duchesne 79); in 1795 he published his findings in *Notices et Extraits des Manuscrits de la Bibliothèque Nationale*. It is interesting to note that, in an early judgement on the quality of Wace's poetry, Bréquigny classified him as a tedious stringer of artless, disorganised and sterile rhymes without warmth or colour.[36]

The dating of the *Roman de Rou*

At the beginning of the *Chronique Ascendante* Wace records that he began working on the story of Rou and his lineage in the year 1160 (vv. 1–4).[37] What he actually wrote at this early stage would appear to be an introductory section, which he was to abandon after 750 lines; this section now forms the Appendix to Holden's edition. It is not known why Wace decided that this early work was unsatisfactory. At some point, he began his work again, this time using the Alexandrine rather than the octosyllabic line. This new introductory section is what is now called the *Chronique Ascendante*.[38] He then proceeded, it seems, to compose what is now Holden's Part II, which advances the story as far as the confirmation of peace between King Lothar of France (954–86) and Count Richard I of Normandy (943–96). At this time, he again for some reason brought his work to a halt, a decision which was based on both professional and financial motives (vv. 4423–25).

[35] See Brosnahan, 'Collation', p. 84 n. 4, Holden, vol. 3, p. 21, and Suchier, 'Zur Handschriftkunde'.

[36] 'La poésie de Wace n'est qu'un amas de rimes accumulées sans art et sans règle; son style dégénère le plus souvent en une battologie fastidieuse, une abondance stérile d'expressions sans chaleur et sans couleur' (p. 78). These views are quoted approvingly by Brial (p. 527) and disapprovingly by Philpot (p. 19).

[37] Wace had concluded his *Roman de Brut* with a precise date of completion: the year 1155 (vv. 14865–66). On the date of the *Rou* see Paradisi, pp. 295–307.

[38] Holmes suggests that the *Chronique Ascendante* was composed by way of a request for money from Henry and Eleanor, as it includes both a eulogy of them and stress on his own dire poverty (p. 65).

The precise date at which Wace stopped work on Part II is not known, but it was probably some time in the early or middle 1160s. It was certainly not until some years later that he began to write once more. It is unlikely that he did so before being awarded his prebend at Bayeux (probably, as we have seen, some time in the mid to late 1160s), and he may not have resumed his work until some time after 1170. This new and lengthy section is Holden's Part III. After writing a further 11,440 lines, Wace stopped work again. On this occasion, as discussed above, he had a more precise reason for abandoning his efforts: Henry had commissioned from a certain Benoît a new history of the Normans. Again we do not know the precise date at which Wace ceased writing. The task of writing over eleven thousand lines would have occupied him for at least two years, probably more.[39] The references to three King Henrys at the beginning and the end of Part III (vv. 179, 11431) must have been incorporated after the coronation of Henry the Young King in 1170. At some time, probably after ceasing work on Part III, he revised the *Chronique Ascendante*; the allusion in v. 62 to the siege of Rouen, which took place in 1174, but not to any later events, suggests that he may have finally stopped writing around the mid-1170s.[40] He does not mention the Young King's death in 1183, so it can be assumed that he did not work on his poem after this date.

Wace's previous works

Wace states twice in the *Roman de Rou* that earlier in his life he had composed what he calls *romanz*: 'De romanz faire m'entremis'/ 'I undertook to compose *romanz*' (III, v. 5311); 'Faire rumanz e serventeis'/ 'Compose *rumanz* and *serventeis*' (III, v. 153). The term *romanz/rumanz* indicates above all that the works in question were written in the vernacular rather than in Latin; they were probably not, however, what we would now term 'romances'.[41] These *romanz* (or works in *romanz*) are likely to have been translations and adaptations from Latin. Wace himself distinguishes between *romanz* and *serventeis* (III, v. 153, cf. also II, v. 4149); the latter were a common type of political poem, sometimes humorous, praising or denouncing an outstanding character or offering an observation on an important event.[42] The works Wace designates as *romanz* may have been longer poems, those which could deal with a wide variety of topics, including subjects of an ecclesiastical nature.

---

[39] Urban T. Holmes points out that a twelfth-century poet's work-rate varied considerably with the individual, but that 'the usual rate was from 3,000 to 5,000 lines a year' (p. 61). He adds that 'Wace was not on the quick side' (*ibid.*).

[40] The date of the siege of Rouen (lifted on 14 August 1174) coincides with that of the latest of the four surviving documents which contain a reference to Wace (14 January 1174).

[41] When the word *romanz* first came into French, at the beginning of the twelfth century, its only meaning was 'the vernacular French language', e.g. 'En letre mis e en romanz'/ 'Put into writing (or into Latin) and into French' (Benedeit, *The Anglo-Norman Voyage of St Brendan*, ed. by I. Short and B. Merrilees (Manchester: Manchester University Press, 1979), v. 11).

[42] Wace is the first person to use the term *serventeis* in French, but the term is known from the Occitan lyric in the form *sirventes* (meaning 'like a servant'), first used by the Gascon troubadour Marcoat.

Three of Wace's religious poems, all written in octosyllabic rhyming couplets, have been preserved. The order of their composition remains uncertain, but the first may well have been the *Vie de sainte Marguerite*, a Life of Saint Margaret of Antioch (around 750 lines). Wace may have been asked to write this work in connection with the chapel dedicated to Saint Margaret at the cathedral of Bayeux. This poem, composed between 1130 and 1140, is one of the oldest surviving saints' lives in French. His second poem was probably the *Conception Nostre Dame* (1810 lines), a work intended as propaganda on behalf of those who favoured the establishment of the feast of the Immaculate Conception of the Blessed Virgin Mary. This feast had been proposed principally by Abbot Anselm of Bury St Edmunds, but it was opposed, amongst others, by Saint Bernard of Clairvaux. Approval of the feast was granted in England by 1129, but in Normandy it was withheld until 1145. The *Conception* is a compilation of three different legends, the first relating to the miracle of Helsin, Abbot of Ramsey, the second to that of Joachim and Anna, the couple to whom the Virgin was born, and the third to that of the Virgin's death and assumption. This poem can also be dated to the period 1130–40.[43] Wace's third work was the *Vie de saint Nicolas* (1563 lines), apparently written for a certain Robert, son of Tiout, a citizen of Caen ('A l'oes Robert le fiz Tiout/ Qui seint Nicholas mult amout'/ 'For the use of Robert, son of Tiout [Theoldus], who loved Saint Nicholas very much', vv. 1549–50). Both Robert and Wace may have been attracted to this subject because of the presence of the church of Saint-Nicholas in the Saint-Étienne quarter of Caen. Einar Ronsjö, the editor of the poem, dates it to around 1150 (p. 26).[44] We can note that Wace claims to have composed 'many' works in *romanz*, so we can assume that other poems written in the period 1130–50 have been lost.

Before he undertook the *Roman de Rou* in 1160, Wace's major work was the *Roman de Brut* (or *Geste des Bretons*), which he probably began some time around 1150. By embarking on a translation of Geoffrey of Monmouth's secular chronicle, the *Historia regum Britanniae*, Wace was progressing from the perhaps rather slight hagiographical pieces to a much more substantial work requiring considerable time and effort. Before writing the *Brut*, he seems to have travelled to England, presumably in order to gather information for his work, and to have visited places in the south-west of England.[45] The *Roman de Brut* is a long work (14,866 lines) and he records that he finished it in 1155

---

[43] Holmes suggests that the *Conception* was written for the church of Notre Dame de Froide Rue in Caen (p. 59).

[44] For further details concerning the content, dating and relative chronology of these three poems, see the respective editions by Ashford (pp. xii–xvi), Keller (pp. 37–40) and Ronsjö (pp. 15–26). It is largely on stylistic grounds (the exploitation of various rhetorical techniques, the number of personal interventions, the use of synonyms, etc.) that the order *Vie de sainte Marguerite*, *Conception Nostre Dame* and *Vie de saint Nicolas* is established.

[45] Philpot suggests that Wace was so conscientious that he visited in person many of the English places mentioned by Geoffrey of Monmouth (p. 52). Wace might also have been encouraged and helped by Geoffrey of Monmouth himself, who did not die until 1155. See also Houck, pp. 219–28, 284–87.

(vv. 14865–66).[46] It was translated into English *c*. 1200–20 by Layamon, a parish priest from Areley Kings in Worcestershire, who, as pointed out above, states that Wace dedicated the work to Eleanor of Aquitaine.[47] It is unlikely that either Eleanor or Henry commissioned the work; if Wace began his *Brut* before 1152, Eleanor was still married to Louis VII of France and Stephen of Blois was still King of England. Holmes (p. 62) suggests a possible connection between the *Brut* and the influential Henry of Blois, who was Abbot of Glastonbury, Bishop of Winchester and uncle of Henry the Liberal of Champagne (patron of Chrétien de Troyes).[48]

Although famous for its biography of King Arthur and its celebration of his court (Wace even introduces the Round Table, which is not mentioned by Geoffrey), the *Roman de Brut* traces the history of the Britons back to the Trojans. Wace was too sober a man to be fooled by Geoffrey's pseudo-history, but he must have found within his source attractive narrative possibilities which he could exploit. Indeed, when he wanted to refer to his work as a whole he called it a *roman* (v. 14866) and on this occasion one has the impression that we are dealing with a new form of literary text, a genuine romance.[49] The fact that the *Brut* survives in thirty-two manuscripts or fragments (see Weiss, pp. xxv–xxix) is testimony to its popularity. No doubt Wace also realised that in the *Brut* he could exploit the interest of the Normans in the history and legends of England, thus following in the footsteps of Geffrei Gaimar, who had composed his *Estoire des Engleis* a few years earlier (between 1135 and 1140).

Sources of the *Roman de Rou*

THE PRINCIPAL WRITTEN SOURCES

When Wace began his *Roman de Rou*, he was to a great extent embarking on yet another work of translation and adaptation, albeit one with more than one major source. But Wace was never a slavish translator and at times he is a historian in his own right, using both oral and written sources and providing a number

---

[46] There are over two hundred surviving manuscripts of the vulgate text of the *Historia regum Britanniae* of Geoffrey of Monmouth, which was begun 'at some date before 1135' and 'completed in 1138' (Wright, I, p. xvi). A shorter, apparently less successful Variant Version, surviving in eight manuscripts, was produced by an unknown author between 1138 and the early 1150s; this version in its turn was revised at least twice. Leckie thinks that Wace's *Brut* was based on the first Variant Version, but on a slightly fuller version than is currently extant (pp. 102–19), whereas Wright is of the opinion that Wace 'combined the First Variant and vulgate texts with other matter found solely in the *Roman de Brut*' (I, p. viii, see also p. lxx).

[47] Ed. by W. R. J. Barron and S. C. Weinberg (London: Longman, 1995), vv. 19–23. See above, n. 23.

[48] For the possibility that Henry of Blois was also a patron of Chrétien de Troyes see G. S. Burgess, *Chrétien de Troyes, Erec et Enide* (London: Grant and Cutler), 1984, p. 97.

[49] A similar example occurs when Chrétien de Troyes writes of his intention to compose a *roman*: 'Puis que ma dame de Chanpaigne/ Vialt que romans a feire anpraigne' ('Since my lady of Champagne wishes me to undertake to compose a romance') (*Chevalier de la Charrete*, ed. by M. Roques (Paris: Champion, 1958, vv. 1–2).

of historical details, names and anecdotes which are not found elsewhere. At times it is easy to discover the main source of his material, whereas at others it is difficult or even impossible. In 1893 J. C. Round went as far as to say that: 'Based on a *congeries* of authorities, on tradition, and occasionally, of course, on the poetic invention of the *trouveur*, it [the *Rou*] presents a whole in which it is almost impossible to disentangle the various sources of the narrative' ('Wace and his Authorities', p. 677). More recently, E. van Houts has observed that the number of Wace's sources is 'astonishing' ('Wace as Historian', p. xxxviii). These sources were wide-ranging, 'historiographical and documentary as well as oral traditions' (*ibid.*). Be that as it may, there can be no doubt that Wace, although he never mentions any specific source, was especially indebted to a relatively small number of historical works, mainly written in prose:

(i) The *De moribus et actis primorum Normanniae ducum* of Dudo of Saint-Quentin

Dudo, a Frank and a canon of Saint-Quentin by 987, wrote his *De moribus* between *c.* 996 and *c.* 1020. It was intended as a work of propaganda to legitimise the Viking settlement. The invitation to compose the work came from Richard I during the years 994–96 and it was renewed by his half-brother, Count Radulf of Ivry, and his son Richard II (duke 996–1026), for whom he acted as chancellor. Much of the material is clearly unreliable.[50]

(ii) The *Gesta Normannorum Ducum* of William of Jumièges.

Probably born *c.* 1000, William of Jumièges took up Dudo's *De moribus* in the early 1050s, revising, abbreviating and updating it. William added to Dudo an account of the reigns of Richard II, Richard III (1026–27), Robert I (1027–35) and William II. He claims to have been an eyewitness to some events in the reign of Richard III. The text as first revised by William of Jumièges (known as Redaction C) initially came to an end shortly before 1060, but around 1067, probably at the request of the new king of England, he later added an account of the Conquest up to *c.* 1070, presumably with the aim of justifying William's right to the throne. William of Jumièges's work is of particular importance for our purpose as it was a fundamental source of information for both Wace and Benoît and the principal influence on the structure of their poems.

A number of authors revised and extended the *Gesta Normannorum Ducum*.[51] The first revisers merely made minor alterations (Redactions alpha and A). More substantial changes were introduced in Redaction B, which contains

---

[50] See Henri Prentout, *Étude critique sur Dudon de Saint-Quentin et son histoire des premiers ducs normands* (Paris, 1916). But see also E. Searle, 'Fact and Pattern in Heroic History: Dudo of Saint-Quentin', *Viator*, 15 (1984), 119–37, who prefers to see Dudo as a writer of heroic or lineage history rather than of objective history (pp. 122–23). Francine Mora-Lebrun describes Dudo as an apologist and a panegyrist (*L'Enéide médiévale et la naissance du roman* (Paris: Presses Universitaires de France, 1994), p. 26).

[51] The following information is based largely on E. van Houts, *The Gesta Normannorum Ducum*, ed. and trans., pp. lx–xc. See also Paradisi, pp. 340–51.

four interpolated anecdotes concerning Duke Richard II and Duke Robert I and the addition of an account of the death of William the Conqueror entitled *De obitu Willelmi*.[52] Redaction D, based directly on William's own text of the *Gesta*, has few innovations.[53] But two further and much more elaborate revisions were undertaken. The first (Redaction E) was by Orderic Vitalis, who began his work between *c.* 1095 and took the material up to *c.* 1113.[54] Orderic not only revised William of Jumièges's style but added lengthy interpolations concerning Robert I and William the Conqueror. This work provided Orderic with an apprenticeship for his more famous *Historia ecclesiastica* (begun around 1114). Orderic's version of the *Gesta Normannorum Ducum* is of great importance because it was principally on his version and that of Redaction B that Wace relied.[55]

The second major revision (Redaction F) was undertaken by Robert of Torigny in the late 1130s.[56] His revision of the *Gesta Normannorum Ducum* began *c.* 1139, but he continued to work on it over a period of at least twenty years. Relying mainly on Orderic's text rather than on William of Jumièges's original, Robert reinstated many of Dudo's passages which William had omitted (books I and II); he also added in book VI a short history of Bec and in book VII made five lengthy interpolations relating to William the Conqueror. In addition, he composed a new book on Henry I. Van Houts expresses the view that, even though Robert wrote in Latin and Wace in French, 'Wace worked as a historian very much in the mould of Robert of Torigni' ('Wace as Historian', p. xl). However, it was Benoît de Sainte-Maure, rather than Wace, who used for his work on the history of the Normans Robert of Torigny's version of the *Gesta Normannorum Ducum* (van Houts, p. xxxvii n. 20).

(iii) The *Gesta Guillelmi* by William of Poitiers
Planned after 1066 to recount William the Conqueror's preparations for the Conquest, to describe the battle and to justify William's right to the throne, William of Poitiers's work, the first extended biography of a Norman duke, remained unfinished.[57] The bulk of the writing seems to have been done after

---

[52] Jean Marx attributed the four anecdotes and the *De obitu Willelmi* to a monk of Saint-Étienne in Caen, but see the discussion in van Houts, *ibid.*, pp. lxi–lxv. Van Houts concludes that the anecdotes, aimed at illustrating the generosity of the dukes, may have been written by the author of Redaction B, but the *De obitu*, a piece of propaganda in favour of William Rufus, was not from the same pen as the anecdotes and it was not written by the redactor of B (p. lxv). Redaction B dates from 1097–1125.

[53] The most important difference between Redactions C and D concerns Robert Curthose as his father's successor in Normandy (van Houts, *ibid.*, p. lxvi). Redaction D was written after 1106.

[54] Orderic was born near Shrewsbury in 1075. His father was a clerk in the household of Roger II of Montgomery and his mother was English. From the age of ten he spent his life in the monastery of Saint-Évroul in Normandy. He died in 1142 or 1143. For further details on Orderic's life and work see Marjorie Chibnall, *The Ecclesiastical History*, I, pp. 1–44.

[55] See van Houts, 'The Adaptation of the *Gesta Normannorum Ducum* by Wace and Benoît', p. 116, and 'Wace as Historian', p. xxxvii n. 20.

[56] Robert, born at Torigni-sur-Vire in Normandy, entered the monastery of Bec in 1128. He became prior in 1149, then abbot of Mont-Saint-Michel in 1154. He died in 1186.

[57] What is known about William of Poitiers derives largely from Orderic Vitalis, who states that he was Norman by birth and came from Préaux. Born *c.* 1020, he was of good family and trained

1071, but before 1077. William of Poitiers was influenced, but not to any great extent, by Dudo of Saint-Quentin and William of Jumièges.

(iv) *Gesta regum Anglorum* by William of Malmesbury

William of Malmesbury first brought his account of the deeds of the kings of England to a conclusion before 1118.[58] But he continued to revise it, and in the final edition of *c.* 1140 the work covers in five books the years 449–1127. Earlier writers on his sources were not convinced that Wace had made use of the *Gesta regum*, but since the article 'Wace and his Authorities' by J. H. Round (1893) Wace's debt to William has been accepted.[59]

(v) *Brevis relatio de Guillelmo nobilissimo comite Normannorum*

The *Brevis relatio* was written by a monk of Battle Abbey and it was in existence by the mid-1120s. It is a brief history of Normandy and England from around the year 1035 up to the battle of Tinchebray in 1106. It was used by Robert of Torigny for his revision of the *Gesta Normannorum Ducum* and it was certainly consulted by Wace.[60] The author of the *Brevis relatio* may well have drawn on the testimony of Abbot Ralph (1107–24), who knew both William the Conqueror and Lanfranc.

A BRIEF REVIEW OF WACE'S USE OF HIS SOURCES

Although the notes to the present translation draw attention to the instances in which Wace provides information not found in his sources, a detailed analysis of the way in which he used these sources, and a specific indication at each point in his work of the precise source involved, are beyond the scope of this volume. Detailed scholarly work on this subject began in the nineteenth century; Gustav Körting's *Über die Quellen des Roman de Rou* (1867) is of particular importance. Hugo Andresen also included a large amount of material in his edition (vol. 2, pp. 601–781). Their conclusions have been re-examined by Holden, who provides both a general account of Wace's sources (vol. 3, pp. 97–117) and a detailed discussion of his text, section by section (pp. 118–68).

In brief, it can be said that for material relating to the period before the time of William the Conqueror, a period covering the lives of the first six dukes of

---

as a knight. He studied for several years in Poitiers and then became one of Duke William's chaplains. At some stage he was archdeacon at Lisieux. He lived until after 1087, but was unable to complete his *Gesta Guillelmi*, which he intended to continue up to the death of William the Conqueror.

[58] William was born *c.* 1080 and he died *c.* 1143. He spent most of his life as a monk and librarian at the monastery of Malmesbury in Wiltshire.

[59] For a full discussion see Holden, vol. 3, pp. 108–10.

[60] For example, Wace used the *Brevis relatio* for his anecdote concerning the generosity of mind shown by Robert the Magnificent (III, vv. 2996–3036), but he altered Robert's answer to his men who wished to avenge the beating he had received, and for the incident of the incorrect way in which Duke William's hauberk was offered to him (III, vv. 7500–30). Also, as in the *Brevis relatio*, Wace describes as an ox-eye the relic on which Harold swore. See Holden, vol. 3, pp. 111–12, and the edition of the *Brevis relatio* by E. van Houts, pp. 23–24.

Normandy, Wace relied fundamentally on Dudo of Saint-Quentin and on William of Jumièges, who were in Wace's day, and indeed remain, the fundamental authorities for the period in question. As he progressed through Part III of his work, from around v. 3560 to v. 5296 (the end of the first major section), there are signs that he was becoming less dependent on William of Jumièges or his continuators and beginning to incorporate some descriptive material of his own. From v. 5297, when he begins the narration of the life of William the Conqueror, Wace was manifestly less influenced by William of Jumièges. Amongst his sources at this stage is the *Gesta Guillelmi* of William of Poitiers (who himself used William of Jumièges). Written by a man who had himself participated in warfare, the *Gesta Guillelmi* clearly assisted Wace with his descriptions of the military operations against Geoffrey of Anjou and with some of the events preceding the battle of Hastings. The *Historia novorum* of Eadmer of Canterbury, who provides an English account of the battle of Hastings, and the work of Simeon of Durham, also provided Wace with an English perspective on the Conquest.[61] The question of Wace's knowledge of, and possible debt to, the Bayeux Tapestry when he composed the section on the Conquest remains unresolved.[62]

When he reached the beginning of the 1070s, Wace had to cope without the *Gesta Normannorum Ducum* and attempt to compile his history using a variety of new materials, the sources of which are often impossible to determine. But there is no doubt that important contributions to this section were made by William of Malmesbury's *Gesta regum* (here Wace may in fact have occasionally been drawing on material from the same source as William, rather than taking his material directly from him), by Orderic Vitalis's *Historia ecclesiastica*[63] and by the *Brevis relatio*. However, in the later stages of his work it is noticeable that oral tradition and his own imagination played a considerable part in the narrative. The final sections of the work, devoted to William Rufus and Henry I, give a clear impression of independence from any particular source, something which adds to the poem's overall importance as a work of history.[64]

---

[61] Wace's account of Edward's comments to Harold before his journey to France (III, vv. 5588–96) and that of the death of William Rufus are similar to those of Eadmer (*Historia novorum*, trans. by G. Bosanquet, pp. 6–9, 120). See Holden, vol. 3, pp. 112–14. With reference to Edward's comment to Harold that William may trick him if he goes to France, David Rollo states that 'the import of Wace's debt to Eadmer can hardly be exaggerated' (p. 160).

[62] See Prentout ('La Source de la conquête de l'Angleterre', pp. 27–28), and Holden (vol. 3, pp. 116–17), who both point to divergences between the Tapestry and the *Roman de Rou*.

[63] Holden emphasises Wace's debt to the *Historia ecclesiastica* for material on the illness, death and burial of William the Conqueror, material which Wace reproduces 'with striking fidelity' (vol. 3, p. 111). After the accession of William Rufus Wace's borrowings from Orderic are of lesser importance. Wace may have known the copy of the *Historia ecclesiastica* copied at Saint-Étienne at Caen; all other surviving manuscripts were copied, probably by Orderic himself, at his own monastery of Saint-Évroul.

[64] Van Houts suggests that both Wace and Benoît brought their narratives to a conclusion where they did because, once the *Gesta Normannorum Ducum* had come to an end, they no longer had a major source of information on which to rely ('The Adaptation of the *Gesta Normannorum Ducum*', p. 116).

Wace as writer and historian

In the title of his book on Wace J. H. Philpot calls him a 'pioneer in two literatures'. Indeed, Wace could be said to be one of the earliest and foremost contributors to three genres: hagiography, romance and the writing of history. All three are linked by the concept of translation from Latin into the vernacular.[65] Two of Wace's hagiographical writings specifically allude to the process of translating from Latin into *romanz* 'French' (*Vie de sainte Marguerite*, v. 739, *Vie de saint Nicolas*, v. 1548). In the *Vie de saint Nicolas* he states that his aim is to make his work comprehensible to those ignorant of Latin: 'I want to tell you in French a little about what the Latin says, so that laymen, who do not understand Latin, can learn it' (vv. 41–44). Although in the *Brut* he graduated from hagiography to what we would call pseudo-history, Wace was undertaking yet another translation ('Maistre Wace l'ad translaté', v. 7) and he also became not only an early vernacular historiographer but a precursor of countless practitioners of courtly romance. 'The *Brut*', writes Holmes, 'was a forerunner of the romance in form and style' (p. 62). In the *Brut* Wace introduced into French literature the court of King Arthur and at the same time helped to develop the concept of courtliness (*cortoisie*).[66] As Margaret Pelan has shown, the influence of the *Brut* on contemporary writers of romance was considerable (especially on Chrétien de Troyes, who made full use of the Arthurian material it contained[67]).

A few years after completing the *Brut*, Wace took a further step and moved with the *Roman de Rou* into the domain of dynastic history; again he tells us that he put the story (*estoire*) into *romanz* (III, v. 5300).[68] Wace's honesty and conscientiousness as a historian have rarely been doubted, but his reliability has been examined with varying results. Taking as a specific example his list of William the Conqueror's companions (III, vv. 8329–705), it can be noted that when scholars first became aware of the list it was regarded as an important source of information. But in 1895 J. H. Round branded it more or less worthless and his view was supported by a number of scholars including D. C. Douglas, who, in his article 'Companions of the Conqueror', stated that Wace was not a 'reliable authority' as his work was of 'untrustworthy character' (p. 131). More recently, Matthew Bennett and Elisabeth van Houts have re-examined the list. Van Houts concludes that Wace's material is not infallible, but neither is it arbitrary or fictitious ('Wace as Historian', pp. xlv–vi). Of particular interest are van Houts' conclusions concerning Wace's historical method, which, she

---

[65] In Wace's time translation usually implied adaptation rather than literal translation.

[66] For a discussion of the terms *corteis* and *corteisie* in the 1150s and 1160s see G. S. Burgess, *Contribution à l'étude du vocabulaire pré-courtois* (Geneva: Droz, 1970), pp. 5–34. For Wace's specific contribution to *corteisie* see R.T. Pickens, '*Vasselage* épique et courtoisie romanesque dans le *Roman de Brut*', in *De l'aventure épique à l'aventure romanesque: Mélanges offerts à André de Mandach*, ed. by J. Chocheyras (Geneva: Droz, 1997), pp. 165–200, and *id.* 'Arthur's Channel Crossing: Courtesy and the Demonic in Geoffrey of Monmouth and Wace's *Brut*', *Arthuriana*, 7 (1997), 3–19. Wace is seen by Pickens as broadening the concept of *corteisie* and preparing the ground for the link between courtliness and *aventure* in Chrétien de Troyes.

[67] With five works amounting to 35,919 lines Wace's surviving output is very similar to that of Chrétien de Troyes.

[68] On the interpretation of the term *estoire* see Damian-Grint, '*Estoire* as Word and Genre'.

emphasises, was based on the use of both written and oral sources. Wace not only 'delved into monastic archives and looked through charters for additional information to supplement the narrative sources he found' (p. xlvi), but he also made especially good use of information available from colleagues at Bayeux, whom he could interview, men such as Richard of Bohun (dean of the cathedral), Philip of Harcourt (the bishop) and Roger of Le Hommet (archdeacon). Bennett concluded that Wace was a serious historian who wanted to 'establish the true course of events' and that his work 'probably conveys genuine traditions not found in other sources' ('Poetry as History', pp. 23, 38).

Such findings are in conformity with the opinions of scholars who over the years have emphasised Wace's desire to present the truth as he saw it. René Stuip examined the battle of Hastings episode in the works of Gaimar, Wace and Benoît and concluded that whereas Gaimar was pro-English and Benoît pro-Norman, Wace was impartial.[69] When Wace had personal knowledge of something, he informed his public of this fact. We have seen that he reports what his father had said about William's ships (III, vv. 6423–28). He also claims to have been present in Fécamp at the reburial of Richard I and Richard II behind the main altar: 'Si que jel vi e joe i ere'/ 'As I saw him and I was there' (III, v. 2242).[70] When personal research was required, he was clearly prepared to do what was necessary. The most famous example of this is his unsuccessful visit to the forest of Brocéliande in search of the marvels associated with the fountain of Barenton; his conclusions were that this was a foolish quest and he had been a fool to pursue it (III, vv. 6393–98).[71] On this occasion his gullibility clearly saddened him, for he had no doubt prided himself on his ability to avoid being taken in by what he heard. He knew, for example, that it was wise to beware of what one heard from *jongleurs*: 'In my youth I heard in the songs of the *jongleurs* that in the olden days William had Osmund blinded, Count Riulf's eyes put out, Anquetil the brave treacherously killed and Balzo from Spain placed in custody; I know nothing of this and can find out nothing about it. When I have no evidence, I do not wish to say anything about it' (II, vv. 1361–67).

Gaston Paris described Wace as an engaging figure who was the 'first true type of the professional writer'.[72] But not only did Wace want to be paid properly for his endeavours, he clearly thought, in his capacity as Maistre Wace, that his narrative should carry authority. Such devices as listening to what people told him, being an eyewitness, doing personal research, whether in archives or in forests, were part of his desire to avoid setting down in writing anything he

---

[69] In 'La Conquête de l'Angleterre dans la littérature française du XIIe siècle', p. 127. Jean Blacker states that 'even though Wace does not articulate the desirability of impartiality, he does make an effort to appear impartial' (*The Faces of Time*, p. 42). But she also points out that running the length of the poem there is a 'tension between monetary self-interest and impartiality' (*ibid.*, p. 40).

[70] 'It would be very surprising to think', writes van Houts, 'that Wace did not take advantage of his visit [to Fécamp] by collecting details for his *Roman de Rou*' ('Wace as Historian', p. xlvi).

[71] See also the note to the translation of these lines.

[72] 'Cette curieuse et attachante figure, qui nous présente pour la première fois le vrai type de l'écrivain de profession' (p. 592).

did not think to be true. The phrase *ne sai* 'I do not know' is one of the refrains of his work (e.g. III, vv. 2340, 5288, 5615, 6293, 8970). His overall justification as a historian, as he states in the famous opening lines of Part III of the *Rou*, was to preserve accurately the memory of famous deeds and famous men: 'To remember the deeds, words and ways of our ancestors, the wicked deeds of wicked men and the brave deeds of brave men, books, chronicles and histories should be read out at festivals. If documents were not composed and then read and recounted by clerics, many things which transpired in times gone by would be forgotten' (vv. 1–10).[73]

Whilst endeavouring to provide a lay audience with an authoritative account of times gone by, Wace at the same time wove into his narratives a strong view of what human beings and human society were like or should be like. He took a firm view of the proper ordering of feudal society: for example, a vassal should give good service and be able to serve a good, strong lord, who in his turn should provide him with proper protection (II, vv. 1460–61); an owner of land should be able to defend it (II, v. 2918); anyone who cannot defend his own lands has very little hope of capturing anyone else's (III, vv. 5007–08); everyone should fight for his natural lord, not against him (III, vv. 3891–96); there could be no more shameful crime than to betray one's liege lord (III, vv. 11383–84); no one can serve two lords and love them equally (III, vv. 10833–36). All in all, Wace's view of human life was that of a churchman and a moralist: things change swiftly; everyone who is born dies (III, vv. 1851–52); everything declines and turns to dust; joy can lead to sorrow (II, v. 2866); success can quickly be followed by failure (III, v. 11154); pride and boasting can be a prelude to one's downfall (II, vv. 111, 932–37); those in high places can soon come down to earth (II, v. 2866), but a man who is down can come up just as swiftly (III, v. 11157); one day a man wins and another day he loses (II, v. 3214), but the man who loses things can soon get them back (III, v. 9054); sorrows do not come alone (II, v. 4109); expectations can falter (III, vv. 1109–10); something which has to happen cannot fail to do so (III, vv. 5609–10); in all things prudence and intelligence are to be cultivated, folly and shameful behaviour to be avoided (III, vv. 2634–35, 3431).[74]

Wace's later work is characterised by his use of literary techniques to further his aims as both a historian and a commentator on human affairs. In 1834 his ability to provide animated descriptions which paint a picture was praised by the Abbé de la Rue.[75] Wace liked to make events arise from the interplay of human beings and thus render his narrative more dramatic. To this end, he made full use in the *Rou* of the rhetorical opportunities afforded him by direct speech. More often than not the speeches he presented were his own invention, for

---

[73] On this passage see Damian-Grint, '*Estoire* as Word and Deed', p. 191.

[74] As can be seen from these formulations, Wace often uses proverbs to express his views of the world. See Brosnahan, 'Wace's Use of Proverbs', Holden, 'L'Authenticité des premières parties', pp. 35–37, and Schultze-Busacker, pp. 87–93.

[75] *Essai historique sur les bardes*, p. 182. It is interesting to note that a few years earlier B. Capefigue had said that Wace's poetry did not deserve the attention of enlightened readers (*Essai sur les invasions maritimes*, p. 422).

honesty and the love of truth did not prevent him from inventing verbal battles of wits, such as the discussions between Harold and his brother Gyrth before the battle of Hastings. The long stretches of dialogue help to move the story line along and hold the attention of his public. In this, Wace is reminiscent of other twelfth-century vernacular writers, who often show great skill in the handling of dialogue.

In addition to being a historian and a moralist, Wace was a good poet and an excellent storyteller. He loved a good yarn, particularly one which could illustrate an important characteristic of one of his personages, and he seems to have been especially fond of a story based around or including some form of joke, for example his anecdote concerning Rou, who turned King Charles the Simple over instead of kissing his foot (II, vv. 1153–56), that of the monk whose behaviour led to the joke 'Lord monk, go quietly and mind how you cross the plank' (III, vv. 509–10) and of King Rufus, whose joke about filling a ditch with any sort of debris to hand was misunderstood and taken to include peasants and horses (III, vv. 9927–42). Nevertheless, Wace was above all a serious man who could hold together a complex historical narrative based on wide-ranging sources. Although a cleric, he had a profound knowledge of both nautical and military matters; indeed, he seemed to revel in the description of a good battle and the planning which led up to it.[76] He was also confident enough in himself to think that he was working to a high standard and deserved support and a good reward (something which, to his chagrin, he did not always receive). When the end came and the completion of his task passed to Maistre Beneeit, he clearly thought that once again he was being unjustly treated and that he still had plenty to offer. But, however bitter he may have felt at that late stage in his life, he must have realised that by then he had made an outstanding contribution to the vernacular culture of his day.

---

[76] 'Wace is very knowledgeable about many aspects of warfare' (Matthew Bennett, 'Wace and Warfare', p. 37).

WACE AS HISTORIAN

Elisabeth van Houts

The purpose of this paper is to assess Wace's reliability as an historian in his *Roman de Rou*, and more in particular the historical basis for his list of the Conqueror's companions drawn up in Part Three, lines 8329 to 8705.[1]

Wace was born around 1110 at Jersey.[2] His maternal ancestor (grandfather or, more likely, great-grandfather) was almost certainly Turstin, chamberlain of Duke Robert the Magnificent.[3] He occurs as witness to a number of charters issued in connection with the attempted invasion of England by Duke Robert in 1033.[4] The fleet was diverted from its course and ended in Jersey.[5] Turstin's position in the ducal household made him a colleague of Fulbert, father of Herleva, Duke Robert's concubine, and may therefore account for Wace's unique information on the reigns of Robert the Magnificent and William the Conqueror, for example concerning Herleva herself and her children by Herluin of Conteville, who were half-siblings of the Conqueror, Bishop Odo of Bayeux, Count Robert of Mortain and the often forgotten Muriel. She married Eudo 'au chapel', vicomte of the Cotentin, whom Wace lists as one of the Conqueror's advisers in 1066.[6] Other information provided exclusively in the *Roman de*

[1] I am very grateful for the comments, additions and corrections provided by David Bates, Matthew Bennett, Michael Jones, Katherine Keats-Rohan, Daniel Power and Ann Williams.

[2] Most of what follows is based on E. du Meril, 'La Vie et les ouvrages de Wace', *Jahrbuch für romanische und englische Literatur*, 1 (1859), 1–8; C. H. Haskins, *Norman Institutions* (New York, 1918), pp. 267–72; A. J. Holden, *Le Roman de Rou de Wace*, 3 vols (Paris, 1970–73), vol. 3, pp. 15–18.

[3] The identification of Turstin the chamberlain (*Tosteins* in III, v. 3225 as Wace's maternal ancestor was first suggested by Gaston Paris (*Romania*, 9, 1880, 526–27; Holden, vol. 3, pp. 140, 225)) on the basis of an emendation of an otherwise incomprehensible passage. Although the point cannot be proven, most historians, including myself, are in favour of accepting Paris's attractive hypothesis.

[4] Fauroux, nos 69 and 76, which were both re-edited by S. Keynes, 'The Aethelings in Normandy', *Anglo-Norman Studies*, 13 (1990), 173–205 (pp. 202 and 204); J. Adigard des Gautries, *Les Noms de personnes scandinaves en Normandie de 911 à 1066* (Lund, 1954), pp. 332 (no. 21) and 333 (no. 26).

[5] Jumièges, ed. van Houts, II, pp. 76–78.

[6] *Roman de Rou*, III, vv. 6003–09: 'E Yon manda al Chapel,/ qui a feme aveit Muriel,/ seror le duc par sa mere,/ e Herluin aveit a pere;/ ne sai se enfes d'els nasqui,/ mais onques parler n'en oi'. Cf. E. M. C. van Houts, 'The Ship List of William the Conqueror', *Anglo-Norman Studies*, 10 (1987), p.161, n. 15.

Rou concerns the history of the abbey of Cerisy-la-Forêt and its early grants, which Wace traced in charters still available today.[7] Details of Duke Robert's pilgrimage to Jerusalem cannot easily be corroborated in a similar way and the most likely source of his knowledge would have been family tradition.[8]

While Wace's maternal ancestors help to explain some of his intimate knowledge of the ducal family, we do not, unfortunately, know anything about Wace's paternal family. All we know is that his father told him the number of ships of the 1066 invasion fleet stationed at Saint-Valéry-en-Caux, but whether this is based on his father's eyewitness account or someone else's remains unclear.[9] Perhaps Wace was a member of the Wace family whose members held extensive possessions in the Channel islands of Guernsey and Jersey. If so, it is puzzling that, unlike the poet Wace, they all are listed with first names and the surname Wace.[10] One of them, Richard Wace, was a canon of Bayeux in the last quarter of the twelfth century. This appointment suggests that now and then a prebend was set aside for the Waces and, if indeed there is a relationship with our Wace, that he did not receive his canonry exclusively for services rendered as a court poet and historian.[11]

Wace himself had first been destined for a military career, for he refers to himself as having been a *vaslet* (a boy before he was knighted).[12] As a still young boy, he was sent to Caen for some elementary education, presumably at Saint-Étienne, after which he went to the Ile-de-France for further studies.[13] He returned to Normandy to work again, as 'clerc lisant', at Caen, until in the 1160s he moved to Bayeux after King Henry II had given him a prebend.[14] While at

---

[7] Fauroux, nos 99, 167, 195; Haskins, p. 271.

[8] A variety of pilgrimage stories circulated in eleventh-century Normandy, e.g. in the *Brevis relatio*, ed. J. Giles (London, 1845), pp. 1–3; Jumièges, ed. van Houts, II, pp. 82–84; E. M. C. van Houts, 'Normandy and Byzantium in the Eleventh-Century', *Byzantion*, 15 (1985), 544–59. The loss of the first part of William of Poitiers's biography of William the Conqueror is particularly sad for our assessment of the veracity of this group of narratives.

[9] *Rou*, III, vv. 6417–32 (translation Van Houts, 'The Ship List', p. 163, n. 22).

[10] *Cartulaire des îles normandes: recueil de documents concernant l'histoire de ces îles* (Jersey, 1924), pp. 202–03, 220–21, 292–93; *Antiquus cartularius ecclesiae Baiocensis (Livre noir)*, ed. V. Bourrienne (Rouen and Paris, 1902), I, pp. 50–51 (no. xlii). Geoffrey Wac acts as witness in a charter of Herbert Poisson of 1135x47.

[11] *Antiquus cartularius*, I, pp. 73–75 (no. lvi): Richardum Wacii canonicum nostrum (24 June 1200), and I, pp. 102–03 (no. lxxx): Ricardo Wasce (listed with other canons as witness in 1182x1205).

[12] *Rou*, III, v. 6424: 'Bien m'en sovient, mais vaslet ere' ('I remember it well although it was before I was armed as a knight'); van Houts, 'The Ship List, p. 163, n. 22, and M. Bennett, 'Wace and Warfare', *Anglo-Norman Studies*, 11 (1988), 37–57.

[13] *Rou*, III, vv. 5305–08: 'En l'isle de Gersui fui nez,/ a Chaem fui petiz portez,/ illoques fui a letres mis,/ pois fui longues en France apris'. For the school of Caen, see R. Foreville, 'L'École de Caen au XIe siècle et les origines normandes de l'Université d'Oxford', in *Études médiévales offertes à M. le doyen Augustin Fliche* (Paris, 1952), pp. 81–100; D.M. Nicholl, *Thurstan of York (1114–1140)* (York, 1964), pp. 3–7; M. Gibson, *Lanfranc of Bec* (Oxford, 1978), pp. 102–05.

[14] *Rou*, III, vv. 5309–18: 'Quant jo de France repairai/ a Chaem longues conversai,/ de romanz faire m'entremis,/ mult en escris e mult en fis./ Par Deu aie e par le rei/ – altre fors Deu servir ne dei – / m'en fu donee, Deus li rende,/ a Baieues une provende./ Del rei Henri segont vos di,/ nevo

Bayeux, he appeared in at least three documents. The earliest dates from 1169 and is an agreement between Bishop Henry II of Bayeux (1165–1204) and Abbot Gilbert of Troarn. The document as printed in the *Livre Noir* of Bayeux does not give any witnesses, but the copy preserved in the Troarn cartulary mentions *Wacius canonicus*.[15] The second charter is from 1174 and lists *Wascius* among the witnesses of an agreement between Richard of Le Hommet and the Bayeux chapter in the presence of Bishop Henry II.[16] The third one is undated and refers to Wace as *Magister Wascius*. Since there is no reference to his status as canon the document probably predates Wace's appointment as canon. It is, however, interesting to point out here that the charter in question concerns the regular canons of Le Plessis-Grimoult, a house founded on the forfeited estates of Grimoult of Le Plessis, one of the rebels of the Val-ès-Dunes uprising in 1047 about whom Wace, as we will see, is so knowledgeable.[17] We do not know when he died.

The connections with the ducal house assured him of a request to write his *opus magnum*, the *Roman de Rou*, after 1155 when he had finished the *Roman de Brut*, his adaptation of Geoffrey of Monmouth's *Historia*, possibly dedicated to Eleanor of Aquitaine.[18] Writing the *Roman the Rou* took several years. He put down his pen after 1173/4 when he was forced, so he tells us, by Henry II to hand over his work to his colleague Benoît de Saint-Maure.[19] Why this happened is still something of a mystery, although recently Professor Gouttebroze has argued that Wace took Becket's side in the investiture conflict and was therefore sacked from his job as court historian.[20] Whatever the reason for falling out with the king it is important to understand that he began writing the *Roman de Rou* while favoured by Henry II and his wife Eleanor and that he received his canonry, as he confesses himself, as a reward for his labour.

Henri, pere Henri'; see also III, vv. 172–76: 'Fors li reis Henris li secunt;/ cil me fist duner, Deus lui rende,/ a Baieues une provende,/ e meint autre dun me ad duné;/ de tut lui sace Deus bon gré!' For the term 'clerc lisant', see *Rou*, III, v. 180: 'E clerc lisant en lur tens fui'.

[15] The documents were first discussed by Du Meril, 'La Vie', pp. 6–7. See *Antiquus cartularius*, I, pp. 161–64; R. N. Sauvage, *L'Abbaye de Saint-Martin de Troarn au diocèse de Bayeux des origines au seizième siècle* (Caen, 1911), p. 81, n. 2 which refers to Paris, BNF, lat. 10086, fol. 13r–v.

[16] The 1174 charter is printed in *Antiquus cartularius*, I, pp. 54–56 (no. xlv).

[17] The charter is unpublished, but quoted by Du Meril, 'La vie', pp. 6–7. A fourth charter from 1172 (Migne, *PL*, cl, c. 77), cited by Du Meril, should be dismissed, for it refers to a *Magister Acio canonicus*, who is probably the same as the *Azo subdecanus* who appears alongside Wace in the 1174 charter.

[18] Ed. I. Arnold, 2 vols, SATF (Paris, 1938–40).

[19] *Rou*, III, vv. 11419–40.

[20] J.-G. Gouttebroze, 'Pourquoi congédier un historiographe, Henri II Plantagenêt et Wace (1155–1174)', *Romania*, 112 (1991), 289–311; see also E. M. C. van Houts, 'The Adaptation of the 'Gesta Normannorum Ducum' by Wace and Benoît', in *Non nova, sed nove: mélanges de civilisation médiévale dédiés à Willem Noomen*, ed. M. Gosman and J. van Os (Groningen, 1984), pp. 115–25. Both Professor Gouttebroze and I stress the importance of the fact that Wace relied on the *Gesta Normannorum Ducum* (*GND*) as edited by Orderic Vitalis, in contrast to Benoît who used the *GND* in the version of Robert of Torigni, who inserted many passages from Dudo of Saint-Quentin's chronicle on the dukes of Normandy.

The *Roman de Rou* can be divided into three sections, of which we are concerned with the third part. This comprises the history of the dukes of Normandy from Duke Richard I (943–996) to the battle of Tinchebray in 1106. It is an adaptation of the *Gesta Normannorum Ducum* in the version of Orderic Vitalis with some material deriving from the anonymous B-redaction. Besides the *GND*, Wace used an astonishing number of other sources, both historiographical and documentary, as well as oral traditions. The most striking examples of his unique information, which can be verified by documentary sources, relate to the early part of William the Conqueror's reign and to the post-Conquest history of the Cotentin and the Bessin up to the years 1106. With regard to the pre-Conquest period, the most important example of Wace's original historical work is his account of the 1047 rebellion culminating in the battle of Val-ès-Dunes. While he may have used a lost *chanson de geste* for this episode, it is much more likely that he tapped local sources, both narrative and oral. One line of investigation represents Wace's interest in Grimoult of Le Plessis, who was, it seems, the main Norman protagonist besides Duke William's cousin Guy of Burgundy.[21] After his defeat, Guy was sent back home; the other rebels were punished, but eventually all were pardoned, except for Grimoult. He was thrown into prison at Rouen where he remained chained in fetters for just under thirty years, until his death in 1074. The harsh justice exercised by William the Conqueror was obviously meant to deter any other people from committing treason.[22] Not only did Grimoult lose his freedom, he also lost his estate. After his death in 1074, it was granted in its entirety to Odo of Bayeux, who used the fief to create seven prebends for the canons of Bayeux, while he himself held on to the manor of Le Plessis and the nearby forest of Montpinchon.[23]

The charter confirming the grant, as well as several documents describing the Le Plessis fief, like the 1133 inquest and Geoffrey of Anjou's charters, were readily available to Wace at Bayeux cathedral where he consulted them. He also

---

[21] Neither William of Jumièges nor William of Poitiers mention Grimoult of Le Plessis (Jumièges, ed. van Houts, II, pp. 120–22; Foreville, p. 16).

[22] It is perhaps significant that Grimoult was not killed straightaway. For a stimulating discussion of the gradually changing attitudes to punishment for treason, see J. Gillingham, '1066 and the Introduction of Chivalry into England', in *Law and Government in Medieval England and Normandy: Essays in Honour of Sir James Holt*, ed. G. Garnett and J. Hudson (Cambridge, 1994), pp. 31–55.

[23] *Antiquus cartularius*, I, pp. 4–6 (no. iii), at p. 5: [after a detailed list of Grimoult's estates William explains that treason is the reason for the forfeit and grant to Odo]: 'Nunc vero quum ipse [Grimoult] perfidus, pro reatu infidelitatis suae et crimine insidiarum suarum quibus adversum me perjuraverat, ea jure justiciae sibi et heredibus suis perdidit . . .'. That Bishop Odo created seven, and later an eighth, prebend, is explained in the 1133 Bayeux Inquest (H. Navel, 'L'Enquête de 1133 sur les fiefs de l'évêché de Bayeux', *Bulletin de la Société des antiquaires de Normandie*, 42 (1934), 5–80 (pp. 15–16): 'Dixerunt etiam praedicti juratores quod rex Willelmus dedit Odoni, fratri suo, Baiocensi episcopo, feodum Grimoudi de Plesseyo in incrementum ecclesiae Baiocensis totum integrum, post mortem Grimoudi, qui in carcere regis apud Rothomagum mortuus est et sepultus in cimeterio Sancti Gervasii extra villam, habens adhuc tibias in compedibus ferreis, in signum proditionis de qua erat ab ipso rege acussatus. Episcopus vero de eodem feodo fecit septem praebendas, et retinuit in dominium suum manerium de Plesseyo, cum foresta de Montpinchon.'

combined them with oral information given to him presumably by the descendants of those involved. For example, Wace tells us about one of Grimoult's men, Serlo of Lingèvres, father of Hugh.[24] This Serlo lived on and became a benefactor of Saint-Étienne at Caen, where he intended to become a monk. Of his sons, only Ranulf can be found in charters.[25] Serlo died after 1082, but another Serlo of Lingèvres, who was presumably his grandson, still had business contacts with Bayeux, for he shared the rights of crop at Carcagny most of which was held by the bishop of Bayeux, as we know from the 1174 charter, which I mentioned earlier, as one of the ones witnessed by Wace. This evidence confirms the view that Wace consulted documentary, narrative and oral material for the compilation of his *Roman de Rou*, describing events which took place about one hundred years before his own time.

For the post-Conquest history of Normandy, Wace's editor A. Holden and Marjorie Chibnall agree that Wace used Orderic Vitalis's *Ecclesiastical History*.[26] However, they also agree that Wace supplemented details not found in Orderic's story. In particular, his detailed account of the final days of Robert Curthose's reign in Normandy: the fighting in the Bessin, the fall of Bayeux and the treason of the inhabitants of Caen form stories which are virtually unequalled by other sources.[27] Without the *Roman de Rou* we would not be aware that before the fall of Bayeux a tournament took place just outside its walls between Robert of Arques, for Robert Curthose, and a soldier called Bruno who fought for Henry I. Henry's champion Bruno was killed and after Duke Robert's defeat Robert of Arques found it safer to leave the country and seek a new career in Apulia.[28] The treacherous behaviour of the citizens of Caen meant that that city escaped the fire and destruction that had befallen Bayeux earlier on. A prominent role, according to Wace, was played by Thierry, son of Ralph FitzOgier, who was one of the wealthiest burghers of Caen. The charters of both Saint-Étienne and Sainte-Trinité confirm Wace's story. On several occasions at the end of the eleventh century Ralph FitzOgier acted as witness for Saint-Étienne benefactors and for the abbot and monks. His son's support for Henry, as related by Wace, reflects his own support for Henry against Duke Robert, which went back to at least the

---

[24] For Serlo of Lingèvres, see Fauroux, no. 169, a charter for Cerisy-la-Forêt from 1035x66. I have been unable to trace his son Hugh.

[25] *Les Actes de Guillaume le conquérant et la reine Matilde pour les abbayes caennaises*, ed. L. Musset (Caen, 1967), nos 7 and 18. Serlo's son Ranulf received a horse from Abbot Gilbert as payment for his father's gift. Ranulf also was a tenant of the nuns of Sainte-Trinité, see *Charters and Custumals of the Abbey of Holy Trinity, Caen, Part 2: The French Estates*, ed. J. Walmsley (Oxford, 1994), p. 110.

[26] *Rou*, III, 111, *Orderic Vitalis, Ecclesiastical History*, ed. M. Chibnall, 6 vols (Oxford, 1969–80), IV, pp. xxi–xxii.

[27] The siege and fall of Bayeux has also been movingly described in a contemporary Latin poem by Serlo, canon of Bayeux , see E. M. C. van Houts, 'Latin Poetry and the Anglo-Norman Court: the *Carmen de Hastingae proelio*', *Journal of Medieval History*, 15 (1989), 44–55.

[28] *Rou*, III, vv. 10945–1060. David rejects as wishful thinking Wace's picture of fierce resistance of the inhabitants of Bayeux by pointing out that Canon Serlo describes the fall as quick and due to weak and incompetent resistance (*Robert Curthose, Duke of Normandy* (Cambridge, Mass., 1920), pp. 165–66).

period 1087 to 1094, when he was present at an agreement between the royal brothers arranged by the nuns of Sainte-Trinité. He acted on Henry's side, not Robert's.[29] It is interesting that Wace is not too shy to hide his own feelings about the treason of the Caen burghers and frankly expresses his horror of the way in which Duke Robert Curthose lost Caen.[30]

These examples concerning Wace's conscientiousness as an historian of Normandy in the eleventh and early twelfth century can easily be multiplied. I will not do so here, but instead I would like to stress the point that, writing in the 1150s, 1160s and 1170s, Wace worked as a historian very much in the same mould as his colleague and contemporary Robert of Torigni, abbot of Mont-Saint-Michel, despite the fact that Wace wrote verse and used the vernacular. Although we can prove his authority for some of his pre- and post-Conquest Norman information, there still exists a huge historiographical question mark over Wace's authority for the history of the Norman conquest of England. Like the passages I have discussed above, this subject deserves fresh investigation. The list of the Conqueror's companions has proven to be the most controversial aspect, and it is time to open the discussion from a new point of view.

I hardly need to remind readers of the roller-coaster fate of this list. Up to the time of Edward Freeman, historians and genealogists happily quoted it as an important source, but John Horace Round's vitriolic assault on Freeman's use of the *Roman de Rou* dealt the study of this topic a blow from which it has hardly recovered.[31] Round's influence even permeated the minds of independent scholars who, it seems, wished to accept Wace's testimony, for example, L. C. Loyd, who included Wace's testimony on Hugh Bigot as the only reliable section of the list: 'Speaking generally this catalogue of Wace's seems historically worthless, but he was a canon of Bayeux cathedral and his statements as to persons and still more to places cannot be entirely neglected.'[32] Similarly, the anonymous editors of the *Cartulaire des îles normandes* inserted in their discussion of the Carteret family, without disclosing their source, Wace's information on the earliest known members of the family: the 'novel chevalier' Humphrey and Malger. Wace and these editors were right, for the two new knights did exist and received land in south-west England, as we can read in Domesday Book.[33] As if it were not enough that hardly any *bona fide* historian dared to mention Wace, in 1943 David Douglas in his article on the companions of the Conqueror expressed his scepticism of the value of this section of the *Roman de Rou* in strong language.[34] It took another forty years for counter arguments to surface. In 1981 Matthew Bennett returned to the problem of the list and proposed an intriguing hypothesis. He argued that the list contained some real historical

[29] *Les Actes*, ed. Musset, nos 7, 14, 18, 25, 27; *Charters and Custumals*, ed. Walmsley, pp. 123–24.

[30] *Rou*, III, vv. 11285–96.

[31] J. H. Round, *Feudal England: Historical Studies on the Eleventh and Twelfth Centuries* (London, 1895, new ed. 1964), pp. 258–321.

[32] L. C. Loyd, *The Origins of some Anglo-Norman Families*, ed. C. T. Clay and D. C. Douglas (Leeds, 1951), p. 15; see below, Appendix, no. 54.

[33] See p. lii.

[34] D. C. Douglas, 'Companions of the Conqueror', *History*, 27 (1943), 129–47.

names, but that the names did not reflect historical persons participating in the conquest of 1066, but rather reflected names of those Anglo-Normans who in 1173–74 supported the rebellion of the young Henry against his father, King Henry II. Bennett concluded that perhaps Wace's roll-call of Young Henry's partisans contributed to Wace's fall from royal grace shortly after the rebellion. Bennett's suggestion is particularly interesting because it draws attention to Wace's attempt to redress the balance between the Norman contribution and that of other 'nations' within the Plantagenet realm.[35] His conclusions, however, like those of Round and Douglas were based only on a study of a sample of names. No one has yet, as far as I am aware, tried to identify and list all the names. This I have now done, but before we can embark on a thorough assessment of the list's historical value, we must first look closely at the lay-out of the list.

The list appears as lines 8329 to 8705 of Part Three of the *Roman de Rou* and it forms the end of the account of the battle of Hastings. Wace's editor, A. Holden, used the early thirteenth-century manuscript of Battle, London, BL, MS Royal 4 C XI, ff. 249rb–278rb, as his base text and therefore the spellings of the names are those of the Battle copy.[36] All other copies, judging by the critical apparatus of Holden's edition, present many variations, which only in a few cases where the Battle scribe went astray help to restore the correct name. The narrative of the main account of the battle is mostly based on the well-known Latin chroniclers like William of Jumièges, William of Poitiers, Orderic Vitalis, William of Malmesbury and the anonymous author of the *Brevis relatio*. While they mostly agree about the main stages of the battle, they give very few details on the individual fighters concerned. The few who are mentioned in Wace's account based on earlier sources have been omitted from my discussion on the grounds that their presence in 1066 is undisputed and has been surveyed satisfactorily elsewhere. Thus here I will concentrate on the 116 names of the list itself.

There are, roughly speaking, three types of references to people. Firstly, there are participants mentioned by first name and surname with a short or long account of their actions. They form the smallest group of seventeen names.[37] Secondly, there are the participants mentioned by first name and surname without any information on their deeds; they amount to twenty-two.[38] These two categories do not present any serious problems, for most of the persons can be identified and the likelihood of them having taken part in the battle of Hastings is very great indeed. The third category, however, contains the names of participants who are indicated merely as the lord of such and such a place. Douglas called them 'territorial designations' which formed 'the most damning argument against [Wace] being regarded as a reliable authority'.[39] They amount

---

[35] M. Bennett, 'Poetry as History? The 'Roman de Rou' of Wace as a Source for the Norman Conquest', *Anglo-Norman Studies*, 5 (1982), 19–39.

[36] For the manuscript, see Holden, vol. 3, pp. 19–21, and above p. xxii.

[37] Appendix, nos 1a, 10, 11, 13, 24, 32a, 40, 42, 50, 51, 53a, 54, 65, 89, 95a, 97, 110.

[38] Appendix, nos 1, 2, 8, 9, 12, 14, 15, 16, 26, 35, 56a, 57, 63, 64, 66, 67, 68, 69, 72, 82, 98, 108.

[39] Douglas, 'Companions of the Conqueror', 131; Appendix, nos 3, 4, 5, 6, 7, 17, 17a, 18, 19, 20, 21, 22, 23, 25, 27, 28, 29, 30, 31, 32, 33, 34, 36, 37, 38, 39, 41, 43, 44, 45, 46, 47, 48, 49, 52, 53, 55, 56, 58, 59, 60, 61, 62, 70, 71, 73, 74, 75, 76, 77, 78, 79, 80, 81, 83, 84, 85, 86, 87, 88, 90, 91, 92, 93, 94, 95, 96, 99, 100, 101, 102, 103, 104, 105, 106, 107, 109.

to seventy-seven names, and as such form the largest number. I have arranged Wace's list of names alphabetically in an appendix, which is printed at the end of this article. Each name carries a number which corresponds with the one on the map (p. xlviii below) and shows the locality. If a second number follows the name, this means that Wace links the two names in one or two sentences. I also give the precise quotation of Wace followed by my notes, which help to identify the individual of 1066 or give more information about his family. For the identification I have used charter collections, Domesday Book and the Linacre Unit for Prosopographical Research. Whereas most of the names can be identified, there remain a few problem cases. There is only one name, 'Victrie' (Appendix, no. 107), which I cannot identify. Then there are several names for which there is more than one possible identification: Ferté, La Mare, Sassy and Tracy (Appendix, nos 36, 56, 92 and 101).[40] Also, there are three names which I have identified with place names, but for which I cannot find families: Cintheaux, Lithaire and Rubercy (Appendix, nos 25, 53 and 83).

The most encouraging result of this exercise is the sheer number of names which can be identified. They belong to men who witnessed charters for the monasteries of Saint-Étienne and Sainte-Trinité at Caen, the cathedral of Bayeux, and other churches in Normandy in the second half of the eleventh century or the first half of the twelfth century. Very often, they are the grandfathers or indeed great-grandfathers of Wace's contemporaries, and in that respect Bennett's work has been confirmed; for example, we find the old Gilbert of Asnières (no. 2), Robert of Beaufour (no. 12), Robert Bertram (no. 13), the old Humphrey of Bohon (no. 15) the old Hugh of Bolbec (no. 16) or, when we jump to the end of the list, William of Roumare (no. 82), William of Sémilly (no. 93), William of Vieuxpont (no. 108) and William of Warenne (no. 110).

Interesting supplementary information about some of the people can be found in the cases of Thurstin, son of Rollo, who carried the Conqueror's banner and whom Wace identifies as originating from Bec near Fécamp (Appendix, no. 11). He might have got Thurstin's name from Orderic's *Ecclesiastical History,* but if he did, he supplemented it with extra details.[41] Another very important story is that of William Patrick of La Lande (Appendix, no. 51). With his wife Gisela he was a benefactor of Saint-Étienne at Caen and also held land of the bishop of Bayeux both in Normandy and Kent. Lucien Musset, the editor of the Caen charters, not having used Wace's information, failed to identify his place of origin. According to Wace, William, when he was a small boy, saw William the Conqueror and Earl Harold passing through La Lande on their way to Brittany in 1064. On that occasion William Patrick witnessed Duke William giving arms to Earl Harold. What is so extraordinary about this story is that it occurs as testimony of William Patrick in the list of companions and not, as one might have expected, in the chronologically more correct place, his brief account of the

---

[40] Appendix, no. 62 is Montfort. In theory, this could be a reference to the lord of Montfort-l'Amauri in France.

[41] Even Douglas seems prepared to accept Wace's information here ('Companions of the Conqueror', p. 140).

Breton expedition, which Wace relates in Part three, lines 5665–72. That story is the standard Norman story as given by William of Poitiers and therefore represents the written tradition, whereas in the list Wace relates the oral tradition handed down, as I will suggest below, by William Patrick's namesake and grandson. Other stories provide snippets of information highlighting aspects of the fighting at Hastings. William of Vieuxpont, the lord of Montfort, who probably is Hugh II of Montfort, and William Malet were helping each other against the English (Appendix, nos 108, 62, 53a). Nigel of the Cotentin, undoubtedly a son of Nigel II, who himself did not take part in the Conquest, is described as having been in the company of Ralph of Gael and Breton soldiers, a combination which, judging by the fact that they were neighbours, is very likely indeed (Appendix, nos 40 and 89). Henry of Ferrières is said to have fought at one stage alongside the castellan of Tillières, presumably Gilbert Crispin (Appendix, nos 35 and 98). The archers of Vaudreuil and Breteuil are singled out for their courage, as is a vassal of Grentemesnil who at one point helped the duke (Appendix, nos 19, 105 and 44). Then there are also the sad stories of Engenulf of L'Aigle and Robert FitzErneis, who were both killed during the battle (Appendix, nos. 32a and 50).

With regard to the third category of names Douglas's territorial designations, I have been able in most cases to show that persons carrying these names lived in 1066 and that cirumstantial if not more positive evidence shows that that are very likely to have taken part in the events of 1066. Often Wace links two names together, no doubt in order to save space and prevent the list from being unnecessarily long. Douglas's argument that these names don't count because if Wace couldn't find a person's first name that must mean that he never existed is flawed.[42] He is scathing about Wace's alleged ignorance of Hugh of Bigot's ancestor.[43] However, Wace does not refer to Hugh Bigot's ancestor, but to Hugh Bigot the ancestor in a similar way as he refers to the old 'so and so'. Another good example illustrating Douglas's ultra critical attitude can be found by applying his own method of the use of charters. Douglas cites several cases of individuals witnessing 1066 charters and concedes that these people were very likely companions of Duke William's English expedition.[44] However, he did not use the charter issued at Bonneville in the summer of 1066 while preparations for the invasion were well under way. It lists as witnesses amongst others, but grouped together, Geoffrey of Sai, Turgis of Tracy and Ralph of Saint-Jean-le-Thomas, three of the people who almost certainly crossed with the Conqueror to England and yet are listed only by their place of origin in the *Roman de Rou*.[45]

The Appendix also shows that many of the names listed by Wace can be found in Domesday Book. In cases where we have the first name and the surname there is usually no doubt that it concerns the same person. A good example is the old

[42] Douglas, 'Companions of the Conqueror', pp. 131–32.
[43] Douglas, 'Companions of the Conqueror', p. 132.
[44] Douglas, 'Companions of the Conqueror', pp. 141–42.
[45] Fauroux, no. 232, dated to the period between 27 May and 16 July 1066. Appendix, nos 84, 86 and 101.

William of Moyon mentioned by Wace (Appendix, no. 67) who can be identified with William of Mohun the tenant-in-chief in Somerset, whose grandson William of Moyon was a contemporary of Wace in Normandy. More problematic are the names belonging to the third category of 'territorial designations'. The lord of Saint-Clair-sur-Elle is listed by Wace as having taken part in the battle of Hastings (Appendix, no. 85). Whether he was one of the two Domesday land-holders, Haimo and Hubert, we do not know. And whether these two men were related to the William of Saint-Clair who was a tenant of the bishop of Bayeux from 1120 onwards is also unclear. Despite these uncertainties the evidence suggest that men from Saint-Clair, including the lord of the manor, took part in the Norman conquest and that Wace knew this. Another objection raised by Douglas in the context of the debate on the Conqueror's companions is the fact that Domesday landholders did not necessarily take part in the conquest and that therefore identifying names from Wace's list with names in Domesday Book distorts our image of the historical reality.[46] In the two decades following the conquest of England there are indeed many cases in which land changed hands once, or twice, from English owners to newcomers, but also between new settlers.[47] While I accept these facts, I am inclined to follow my common sense, which suggests that William the Conqueror handed out land to those who had supported him in 1066. This does not exclude the possibility of the arrival of newcomers in the wake of the conquest. As far as Wace is concerned, he probably listed all names of those whom he thought had at the time of the Conquest fought for Duke William.

A different aspect of Wace's list is the order in which the names are listed and the possibility that the list reflects the organisation of fighting in *conrois*. Military historians agree, mostly on the basis of *chanson de geste* material, that fighting in *conrois* was the norm. A *conroi* would consist of about twenty men who knew each other well, trusted each other and had had experience of fighting together. Contamine suggests that they were units which were 'usually recruited through a family lineage or feudal relationship and were supposed to stay grouped together around a flag or a leader or were united by a common war cry'.[48] Wace does not give any evidence for war cries in his account of the battle of Hastings, but in his story on Val-ès-Dunes he gives four examples: the French cried 'Monjoie', Duke William cried 'God help', Nigel of the Cotentin and Ranulf of Bessin used variations of 'Saint Sauveur', while Haimo del Denz cried 'Saint Amant'.[49] Presumably similar cries were used at Hastings. There is only one occasion in the list where Wace specifically refers to the fighting in one *conroi*. In lines 8471–72, he says that the lords of 'Victrié', Lassy, Vaudry and Tracy fought in one *conroi*.[50] Apart from the first name we can identify all other places as being in the neighbourhood of Vire. Vaudry lies just to the east, Lassy lies about 10 km to

---

[46] Douglas, 'Companions of the Conqueror', pp. 132–33.
[47] R. Fleming, *Kings and Lords in Conquest England* (Cambridge, 1991), chapter 5, pp. 144–82.
[48] P. Contamine, *War in the Middle Ages*, trans. M. Jones (London, 1984), pp. 229–30 and references given there.
[49] *Rou*, III, vv. 3935–44.
[50] Appendix, nos 52, 101, 106, 107.

the north-east while Tracy-le-Bocage is another 10km further north. Lassy and Tracy-le-Bocage were both fiefs of the bishop, while Alice of Vaudry was a benefactor of Bayeux and contemporary of Wace. As a canon of Bayeux, Wace was in an excellent position to know whether and how men were recruited to collaborate in tactical units. Of course one can raise the objection that Wace might have projected knowledge of military logistics in his own time back to a previous century. But even if one could prove that this is the case, there still is a fair chance that the formation of tactical units or *conrois* in 1066 followed similar patterns as in the mid-twelfth century. Other places in the 1066 list linked by Wace may also reflect groups of soldiers fighting together, for most of them originated from places not too far from each other to make a joint effort impracticable. But how precisely the logistics of recruitment and action in battle worked we do not know. Much more research into patterns of landholding and military service is needed before we can draw any definite conclusions.[51]

The evidence suggests very strongly that the list is neither arbitrarily put together nor fictitious. If, then, it reflects the historical reality as Wace and his contemporaries, on whose testimonies he based his account, saw it about one hundred years after the events took place, how did Wace collect the stories? One glance at the map makes it plain that the majority of names occur in the modern departments of Manche and Calvados, which cover precisely the area with which Wace was most familiar as we have already seen from the examples taken from the pre-and post-Conquest history of Normandy. Fortunately, we can be much more specific about his sources of information, for just under half the names belong to tenants, sub-tenants and benefactors of Bayeux cathedral and the ducal monasteries at Caen, the very places where Wace worked and lived. In other words the names belong to the members of the churches' *familia*, the patrons and servants who were daily commemorated by the monks and clercs, including Wace, who prayed for the well being of their souls. Wace's likely informants from Bayeux were his colleagues. Richard of Bohun, grandson of Humphrey of Bohun (Appendix, no. 15), was dean of the cathedral. Philip Harcourt was its bishop, while his nephew William was the cathedral's treasurer; both were descendants of the lord of Harcourt, who at some stage during the battle gave his horse to Duke William (Appendix, no. 45). Radulf and Robert Gouvix were both canons (Appendix, no. 43), Roger of Le Hommet was archdeacon till 1161 (Appendix, no. 47) and William of Tournebu was dean from 1151 until 1182 (Appendix, no. 100). They would have told Wace about their grandfathers' exploits in William the Conqueror's army, even though we can only find documentary trace of William Tournebu's grandfather shortly after 1066. Amongst the Bayeux tenants was William Patrick, grandson of the eye-witness of the 1064 Breton campaign. At least two occasions are known when William Patrick the younger attended Bayeux meetings, where he might have met Wace, eager to collect more

---

[51] Michael Jones suggested the possibility that Wace's linking of names in pairs of two may reflect the formation of brothers-in-arms as we know the system from the late Middle Ages. This is an exciting proposition which, on the basis of today's knowledge, unfortunately cannot be assessed.

information about 1066.[52] Not only men, but women connected with Bayeux also passed on family traditions relating to the Norman conquest. The information about the participation of the lord of Sémilly probably came through Cecily, sole heiress of Sémilly and benefactor of Bayeux cathedral. She married Enguerrand of Le Hommet, who took her name and passed it on to their son William of Sémilly who became dean of Bayeux in the early thirteenth century (Appendix, no. 93). And there was Alice of Vaudry, who told Wace about her own, or her husband's, ancestors from Vaudry near Vire (Appendix, no. 106). A similar list can be composed for families connected with the Caen monasteries.

Whereas the links between Wace and the Norman peninsula are obvious, those between him and the Pays-de-Caux in the north are less self-explanatory. Some stories may have reached him through descendants of the contemporaries of 1066. For others the monks of Fécamp were responsible. In 1162 Wace was present at the *translatio* ceremony in the monastery of Fécamp, when King Henry II had the bodies of Dukes Richard I and II reburied behind the main altar.[53] The role of this monastery in the logistical organisation of the Norman conquest is well known. The *Ship List*, which I discussed several years ago, was compiled by its monks.[54] It would be very surprising to think that Wace did not take advantage of his visit by collecting details for his *Roman de Rou*. I have already referred to Thurstin of Bec's origins from Fécamp's neighbourhood (Appendix, no. 11). Other interesting evidence concerns Wace's identification of Duke Williams's messenger to Earl Harold on the eve of the battle with Hugh Margot, a monk of Fécamp. Hugh's name was obviously preserved at that monastery.[55]

Having stressed the importance of oral witnesses in the transmission of information bridging two or three generations after the events of 1066, one should not forget the importance of the written sources. We have already seen that Wace delved into monastic archives and looked through charters for additional information he could add to the narrative sources he used. In this process he may have used charter material for the names of those he listed. That he did not chose arbitrarily from the documents is clear, for they contain many more names he could have cited than he actually did. For the main narrative of the conquest he used the Latin sources I have listed before. Many must have been available at Bayeux as part of the cathedral library or as part of individual bishop's collections, the most important of which was that of Bishop Philip of Harcourt which after his death went to Le Bec.[56] Wace probably read Orderic's work at

---

[52] *Antiquus cartularius*, I, 15 and *Recueil des actes de Henri II,* ed. L. Delisle and E. Berger, 4 vols (Paris, 1909–27), I, pp. 480–81, no. 335 dated to 1156 and 1172–73. *Regesta*, III, no. 810 shows that he was in Bayeux in 1151.

[53] *Rou*, III, vv. 2241–46.

[54] Van Houts, 'The Ship List', pp. 167–68.

[55] Wace, III, vv. 6757–58.

[56] For the cathedral library of Bayeux, see E. Coyecque, in *Catalogue général des manuscrits*, X (1889), pp. 205–06; *Catalogue des manuscrits en écriture latine portant des indications de date, de lieu ou de copiste*, VII, ed. M. C. Garand, G. Grand and D. Muzerelle (Paris, 1984), p. ix. An inventory of Bishop Philip of Harcourt's library is printed in *Catalogi bibliothecarum antiqui*, ed. G. Becker (Bonn, 1885), no. 86, pp. 199–202.

Saint-Étienne at Caen, whose mid-twelfth-century copy has survived as Rome, Vatican, MS Reg. Lat. 703b.[57] The *Brevis relatio*, also in a mid-twelfth-century copy (London, BL, MS Sloane 3103), was available at Saint-Sauveur-le-Vicomte.[58]

By way of conclusion, I should like to argue that Wace interviewed his contemporaries in western Normandy, and in particular at Bayeux and Caen, about their knowledge of their ancestors' past. This information concerned not only the pre- and post-Conquest history of the duchy, but also the Norman conquest period itself. The testimonies about the involvement of his contemporaries' grandfathers and great-grandfathers in 1066 formed an important addition to the Latin chronicles, which barely relate the names of individual soldiers of the Conqueror's army. In order to preserve their memory Wace included them in the *Roman de Rou*. His information is not infallible. It should be used in conjunction with other material. But where charter material clearly supports the list of Wace we cannot ignore this evidence. Surely the third and fourth generation living in Normandy in the mid-twelfth century knew more of the history of the Norman conquest of England than we do. The stories of the descendants of the Conqueror's companions might be piecemeal, slightly distorted or incomplete, but Wace nevertheless recognised their importance and included them in his history. Where he could, he put them alongside written traditions as found in the Latin narratives or charters. This combination, then, of oral and written family history is perhaps Wace's most important contribution to the historiography of the Norman conquest of England.

APPENDIX

Names mentioned by Wace in the *Roman de Rou*, Part III, vv. 8329–705

Abbreviations used:

Ant. cart., ed. Bourrienne: *Antiquus cartularius ecclesiae Baiocensis (Livre noir)*, ed. V. Bourrienne, 2 vols (Rouen and Paris, 1902–03).

Barlow, *Rufus*: F. Barlow, *William Rufus* (London, 1983).

Battle: *Anglo-Norman Studies. Proceedings of the Batttle Conference.*

Cartulaire des îles normandes: *Cartulaire des îles normandes. Recueil de documents concernant l'histoire de ces îles* (Jersey, 1924).

Crouch, *The Beaumont Twins*: D. Crouch, *The Beaumont Twins: The Roots and Branches of Power in the Twelfth Century* (Cambridge, 1986).

DB: Domesday Book

Delisle, *Saint-Sauveur-le-Vicomte*: L. Delisle, *Histoire du château et des sires de Saint-Sauveur-le-Vicomte* (Valognes, 1867).

---

[57] *Orderic Vitalis, Ecclesiastical History,* ed. Chibnall, I, p. 121. It is one of the very few manuscripts from this monastery which survived the plundering of 1562 (*Catalogue des manuscrits en écriture latine*, VII, p. ix, n. 10; Gibson, *Lanfranc of Bec*, p. 104, n. 1).

[58] Van Houts, 'Ship List', p. 180, n. 4.

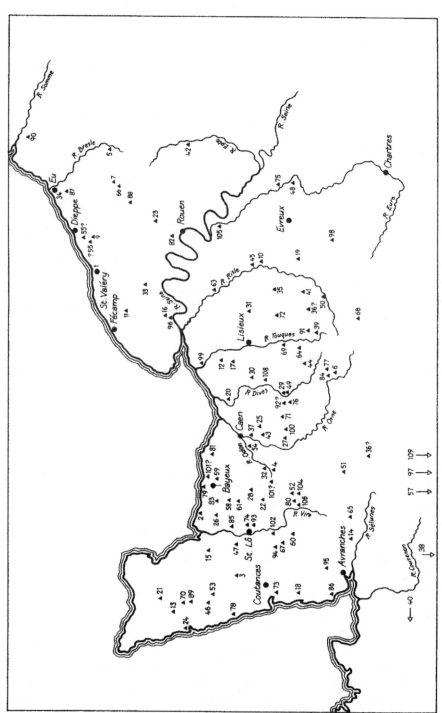

Names mentioned in Wace's *Roman de Rou*, III, vv. 8329–705. The numbers correspond with those in the Appendix to this article.

Douglas, 'Companions': D. C. Douglas, 'Companions of the Conqueror', *History*, 27 (1943), 129–47.

Douglas, *DM*: D. C. Douglas, *Domesday Monachorum of Christ Church Canterbury* (London, 1944).

EYC: *Early Yorkshire Charters*, ed. C. T. Clay, 10 vols (Edinburgh, 1935–65).

Farrer: W. Farrer, *Honors and Knights' Fees . . .*, 3 vols (Manchester, 1923–25).

Fauroux: *Recueil des actes des ducs de Normandie de 911 à 1066*, ed. M. Fauroux (Caen, 1961).

Green, *Government*: J. Green, *The Government of England under Henry I* (Cambridge, 1986).

Green, 'Lords of the Vexin': J. Green, 'Lords of the Norman Vexin', in *War and Government in the Middle Ages: Essays in Honour of J. O. Prestwich*, ed. J. Gillingham and J. C. Holt (Woodbridge, 1984), pp. 47–65.

Haskins: C. H. Haskins, *Norman Institutions* (New York, 1918).

IEAL: *Inquisitio Eliensis*, in *Inquisitio Comitatus Cantabrigiensis*, ed. N. E. S. A. Hamilton (London, 1876).

Keats-Rohan, 'Aspects of Robert of Torigny': K. S. B. Keats-Rohan, 'Aspects of Robert of Torigny's Genealogies Revisited', *Nottingham Medieval Studies*, 37 (1993), 21–27.

Keats-Rohan, 'Le Problème': K. S. B. Keats-Rohan, 'Le Problème de la suzeraineté et la lutte pour le pouvoir: la rivalité bretonne et l'état anglo-normand 1066–1154', *Mémoires de Bretagne*, 58 (1991), 45–69.

Keats-Rohan, 'The Prosopography': K. S. B. Keats-Rohan, 'The Prosopography of Post-Conquest England: Four Case Studies', *Medieval Prosopography*, 14 (1993), 1–52.

Loyd, *Origins*: L. C. Loyd, *The Origins of Some Anglo-Norman Families*, ed. C. T. Clay and D. C. Douglas (Leeds, 1951).

Musset, *AC*: *Les Actes de Guillaume le Conquérant et la reine Mathilde pour les abbayes caennaises*, ed. L. Musset (Caen, 1967).

Navel: H. Navel, 'L'Enquête de 1133 sur les fiefs de l' évêché de Bayeux', *Bulletin de la Société des antiquaires de Normandie*, 42 (1934), 5–80.

OV: *Orderic Vitalis, Ecclesiastical History*, ed. M. Chibnall, 6 vols (Oxford, 1969–80).

Porée: A. A. Porée, *Histoire de l'abbaye du Bec*, 2 vols (Évreux, 1901).

Recueil des actes de Henri II: *Recueil des actes de Henri II*, ed. L. Delisle and E. Berger, 4 vols (Paris, 1909–27).

Reg.: *Regesta Regum Anglo-Normannorum*, 3 vols (Oxford, 1913–68).

Rotuli, ed. Round: *Rotuli de dominabus et pueri . . .*, ed. J. H. Round (London, 1913).

Sanders, *English Baronies*: I. J. Sanders, *English Baronies, a Study of their Origin and Descent: 1086–1327* (Oxford, 1960).

Sauvage: R. N. Sauvage, *L'Abbaye de Saint-Martin de Troarn au diocèse de Bayeux des origines au seizième siècle* (Caen, 1911).

van Houts, 'Robert of Torigni as Genealogist': E. M. C. van Houts, 'Robert of Torigni as Genealogist', in *Studies in Medieval History Presented to R. Allen Brown*, ed. C. Harper-Bill, C. Holdsworth and J. L. Nelson (Woodbridge, 1989), pp. 215–34.

van Houts, 'Ship List': E. M. C. van Houts, 'The Ship List of William the Conqueror', *Anglo-Norman Studies X, Proceedings of the Battle Conference 1987* (Woodbridge, 1988), 159–83.

Walmsley: *Charters and Custumals of the Abbey of Holy Trinity, Caen, Part 2: The French Estates*, ed. J. Walmsley (Oxford, 1994).

1. Abbeville (Somme)
'Wiestace d'Abevile', III, v. 8429.
Eustace, count of Boulogne, an important Domesday Book landholder.

1a. Alan Fergent, error for Alan Rufus
'Alains Fergent, quens de Bretaigne', III, vv. 8689–98; also vv. 6367–68.
Alan Fergent, duke of Brittany, did not take part in the conquest. Wace confuses him with
Alan Rufus, son of Eudo, count in Brittany and brother of Count Brian, a tenant-in-chief
in England (Keats-Rohan, *Battle*, 13 (1990), pp. 160–61, n. 15).

2. Asnières (Calvados, c. Isigny)
'Gilebert li viel d'Asnieres', III, v. 8533.
Musset, *AC*, nos 8, 22. Radulphus de Asnières occurs in connection with William of
Colombières [qv] and William of Sémilly [qv]; Walmsley, pp. 56 and 127: Sainte-Trinité
had thirty acres at A. The bishop of Bayeux held land there as well (*Ant. cart.*, ed.
Bourrienne, I, 22, 49; Navel, p. 18).

3. Aubigni (Manche, a. Coutances)
'e li boteilliers d'Aubinié', III, v. 8470.
There is no contemporary evidence that Roger d'Aubigni, father of William I d'Aubigni,
was a *pincerna* (Loyd, *Origins*, p. 7). Before 1047 a William d'Aubigni (Roger's
brother?) had married a sister of Grimoult of Le Plessis. Bougy and Danvou (Calvados)
held by this couple of Grimoult passed to the bishop of Bayeux (Navel, pp. 16, 27, nn.
20–22, Green, *Government*, pp. 229–30); in the twelfth century these lands were held of
Bayeux by William II d'Aubigni (d. 1176), who married Queen Adela of Louvain, widow
of King Henry I (Navel, p. 36, n. 144).

4. Aulnay-sur-Odon (Calvados) **+ 27**
'cil de Combrai e cil d'Alnei', III, v. 8645 (cf. Gohier de l'Aunei, vv. 10935, 10939,
11065–68).
Ingelran, son of Ilbert, gives the church to Saint-Etienne at Caen (Musset, *AC*, nos. 7,
18–19). For Gunther of Aulnay as castellan of Bayeux, see OV, VI, pp. 60, 78.

5. Aumale (Seine Mar., a. Neufchatel)
'sire d'Aubemare', III, v. 8419.
Adelaide, half-sister of William the Conqueror, married (1) Enguerrand of Ponthieu, lord
of Aumale, (2) Lambert of Lens, (3) Odo of Champagne. Odo's son Stephen succeeded
to Aumale. Loyd, *Origins*, p. 9. It is possible that this Aumale represents an unidentified
place in the Cotentin from which Robert 'de Albemarle', tenant-in-chief in Devon
originated (DB 113a).

6. Aunou-le-Faucon (Orne, a. Argentan)
'e cil qui ert sire d'Alnou', III, v. 8426.
Fulk I d'Aunou, benefactor of Saint-Etienne and Sainte-Trinité at Caen (Musset, *AC*,
nos 2, 8, 10, 22; van Houts, 'Ship List', p. 169).

7. Auvilliers (Seine Mar., c. Neufchâtel)
'od lui li sire d'Auviler', III, v. 8618.
Hugh of Auvilliers, tenant of Robert Malet (Loyd, *Origins,* p. 9).

Avenel, *see* Biards les

8. Avranches (Manche)
'D'Avrancein i fu Richarz', III, v. 8467.
Richard Goz, vicomte of Avranches, was still alive in 1068 (van Houts, 'Ship List',
p. 169); also Loyd, *Origins*, p. 9.

9. Bacqueville-en-Caux (Seine Mar., a. Dieppe)
'de Basquervile i fu Martels', III, v. 8521.
Geoffrey Martel, father of William Martel, steward of King Henry I (van Houts, 'Robert
of Torigni as Genealogist', p. 228).

10. Beaumont-le-Roger (Eure, a. Bernay)
'Roger [var. Robert] le viel, cil de Belmont', III, vv. 8329–38.
Robert, not his father Roger, took part in the conquest of England. He was a large tenant-in-chief in England. Loyd, *Origins*, p.13.

11. Bec-aux-Cauchois (Seine Mar., c. Valmont)
'E cil qui tient son gonfanon/ – Tostein, filz Rou le blanc out non,/ del Bec, joste Fescamp, fu nez', III, vv. 8673–75; also vv. 7633–46.
Thurstin, son of Rollo, benefactor of the abbey of Boscherville (*Reg.*, II, no. 1012). Tenant-in-chief and tenant of Walter Giffard (DB, 147r, 151b; OV, II, p. 172; Douglas, 'Companions', pp. 140–41).

12. Beaufour (Calvados, c. Cambremer)
'Robert, li sire de Belfou', III, v. 8425.
Robert of Beaufour and his brother William were witnesses to a charter of Humphrey of Bohun (Fauroux, no. 185 (c. 1042–66)); Robert is probably the father of Richard de Beaufour (Fauroux, nos. 141, 183), who with his brother Humphrey witnesses gifts of Hugh of Montfort for Saint-Etienne (Musset, *AC*, nos., 2, 56). Richard's daughter married Hugh II of Montfort.

13. Bertram, Robert [Bricquebec (Manche, a. Valognes)]
'Robert Bertram, qui esteit torz,/ mais a cheval esteit mult forz,/ cil aveit od lui grant efforz,/ mult i out homes par lui morz', III, vv. 8501–04.
Robert Bertram, son of William Bertram, who was a son of Thurstan of Bastembourg, was vicomte of the Cotentin. On his deathbed (?), Robert donated land to Sainte-Trinité and Saint-Etienne at Caen (Musset, *AC*, nos. 2, 7, 8, 14; also Fauroux, nos. 147, 148, 151, 156, 205, 224; *Reg.*, I, no.168); for his son William, see Walmsley, pp. 126–27.

14. Biards, Les (Manche, c. Isigny-le-Buat)
'ensenble od lui cil de Biarz /. . . Des Biarz i fu Avenals', III, vv. 8468, 8499.
Rannulf Avenel, tenant of Robert, count of Mortain, c. 1082 (*Reg.*, I, no. 146; Keats-Rohan, 'The Prosopography', p. 32).

Bigot, see **Maltôt**

15. Saint-André-de-Bohon (Manche, a. Saint-Lô, c. Carantan)
'e de Bohon li viel Onfrei', III, v. 8450.
Humphrey de Bohun (Fauroux, nos. 151, 185; *Reg.*, I, nos. 121, 125, 133, 165). Landholder in England (DB, 262b). Father of Humphrey II (d. 1129). Humphrey III (d. 1166); Geoffrey of Bohun, witness for Bishop Odo in 1093 (*Ant. cart.*, ed. Bourrienne, I, 32); Richard I of Bohun, dean of Bayeux (?–1151) and bishop of Coutances. Loyd, *Origins*, p. 16; Green, *Government*, p. 236.

16. Bolbec (Seine Mar., a. Le Havre)
'li vielz Hue de Bolebec', III, v. 8535.
Hugh of Bolbec, tenant of Walter Giffard; *Rotuli de dominabus et pueris . . .*, ed. J. H. Round (London, 1913), pp. xxxix–xli; Loyd, *Origins*, p. 17; Porée, I, 329–30; Landholder in England (DB, 150d).

17. Bonnebosq (Calvados, a. Pont-l'évêque)
'e li sires de Bonesboz', III, v. 8537.
The earliest attested member is Robert of Bonnebosq, despoiler of lands of Sainte-Trinité at Caen (Walmsley, p. 126) and King Henry I's only (?) casualty at Tinchebray (letter of the priest of Fécamp, *EHR*, 25 (1910), p. 296); Robert of Bonnebosc left a widow, Avicia of Crèvequeur in 1185 (*Rotuli*, ed. Round, p. 16).

17a Botevilain, probably a toponym, but Holden, vol. 3, p. 263, suggests a first name +
103

'Botevilain e Trosebot,/ cist ne dotent ne colp ne bot,/ mult s'i firent le jor hair/ as cols receivre e al ferir', III, vv. 8581–84.

Robert, son of William, Botevilain held the honour of Wahull according to the Northamptonshire Survey (Farrer, I, pp. 80–81).

18. Bréhal (Manche, a. Coutances) **+ 86**
'de Saint Johan e de Brehal', III, v. 8512.
Ilger 'de Brehelo' attested a charter for Mont-Saint-Michel 1066x86 by John of Dol (Avranches BM, MS 210, f. 66v).

19. Breteuil (Eure, a. Evreux)
'ensenble od els cil de Bretoil,/ a maint Engleis creverent l'oil/ od les saetes acerees/ qu'il aveient od els portees', III, vv. 8507–10.
The honour of Breteuil belonged to William FitzOsbern, a large landholder in England.

20. Brucourt (Calvados, c. Dives-sur-Mer) **+ 30, 31**
'de Crievecoer e de Drincort/ e li sire de Briencort/ *sivent* le duc quel part qu'il tort', III, vv. 8642–44.
Robert, son of Ralph 'de Brucourt', and his brother Gilbert occur in the time of William I (Cartulary of Saint-Pierre at Préaux, nos. 454–56 (Arch Eure H 711, f. 141v–143r); in no. 458 William 'de Brucourt' makes a grant before the count of Evreux and Hugh of Montfort; at the foundation of Saint-Evroult of Mortain in 1082, Gilbert 'de Brucourt' gave a moiety of the church of Roncey (Manche, c. Cerisy-la-Salle). Geoffrey and Gilbert 'de Brucourt' occur in 1154x64 (Haskins, p. 325). Robert, 'de Brucourt', was a witness for bishop of Bayeux in 1179x89 (*Ant. cart.*, ed. Bourrienne, I, 18); he was lord of Maizy, which Walter Giffard held of Bayeux (*ibid.*, index s. Maizy).

21. Brix (Manche, a. Valognes) **+ 47**
'cil de Brius e cels de Homez', III, v. 8513.
Robert de Brus was tenant-in-chief in Yorkshire (DB, 332c–333a).

22. Cahagnes (Calvados, a. Vire) **+ 28**
'de Chaaignes e de Coisnieres', III, v. 8534.
William of Cahagnes, sheriff of Northampton (*Reg.*, I, nos 288b, 383, 476); J. Green, in *Battle*, 5 (1982), p. 141; Barlow, *Rufus*, p. 188); major tenant of Robert of Mortain, and perhaps of Odo. In 1133 Cahagnes was fief of bishop of Bayeux (Navel, p. 16; B. Golding, *Battle*, 13 (1990), pp. 137–38); Loyd, *Origins*, p. 52; Green, *Government*, p. 239. William was a tenant-in-chief in England (*DB*, 225c).

23. Cailly (Seine Mar., c. Clères) **+ 88**
'Cil de Saint Segus e de Quaillié', III, v. 8519.
Osbern of Cailly, brother of Roger of Clère, benefactor of Saint-Ouen at Rouen (Fauroux, no. 191 c. 1050x66); William of Cailly was a tenant of Warenne in Cambridgeshire and Norfolk (Loyd, *Origins,* p. 22; *EYC*, VII, no. 109; *DB* 160a; C. Lewis, *The Haskins Society Journal*, 5 (1993), p. 40). Another William of Cailly was tenant-in-chief in Berkshire (*DB* 61b).

24. Carteret (Manche, a. Valognes)
'de Cartrai Onfrei e Maugier,/ qui esteit novel chevalier', III, v. 8451.
Humphrey and Malger of Carteret; Humphrey, Mauger and Mauger's son Drogo are mentioned as tenants in England (DB, 102b, 103a, 105b); Renaldus (d. c. 1125) and his wife Lucy are mentioned in charters. One of their sons was called Humphrey (*Cartulaire des îles normandes*, pp. 50–62; Loyd, *Origins*, p. 25).

25. Cintheaux (Calvados, a. Falaise) **+43**
'Cil de Goinz e de Sainteals', III, v. 8523.
???

26. Colombières (Calvados, c. Trévières)
'e Guillame de Columbieres', III, v. 8532.
William of Colombières had interest in lands at Asnières given by Radulf of Asnières [q.v.] to Sainte-Trinité at Caen (Musset, *AC*, nos 8, 22); also link with William of Sémilly [q.v.]. William of C. gave land to abbey of Troarn in 1068 (Sauvage, no. ii, pp. 348–51). In c. 1149x51 Philip de C. excommunicated by bishop of Bayeux (*Ant. cart.*, ed. Bourrienne, I, 235–63) and in 1153x63 benefactor of Bayeux to attone for his nephew Robert's murder of Beatrice of Harcourt, niece of Bishop Philip of Harcourt (*ibid.*, I, 39–40; *Recueil des actes de Henri II*, I, no. cxciv (1156x61); Loyd, *Origins*, p. 30).

27. Combray (Calvados, a. Thury-Harcourt) + 4
'Cil de Combrai e cil d'Alnei', III, v. 8645.
The earliest attested member is Alfred of Combray, nephew of Ranulf of Presles (*Reg.* II, nos 1023 (1113?) and 1088a (1115).

28. Cornieres [now Actoville] Calvados, a. Caumont) + 22
'de Chaaignes e de Coisnieres', III, v. 8534.
Church of Cornières granted to Lessay by Turstin Haldup and his son Eudo (*Reg.*, II, no. 1441).

29. Courcy-sur-Dives (Calvados, a. Falaise, c. Morteaux-Couliboeuf) + 49
'Cil de Corcié et cil de Jort/ i ont le jor maint home mort/ . . . e li seneschals de Corcié', III, vv. 8481–82, 8526.
Richard of Courcy, witness in the time of William I and tenant-in-chief in England (*Reg.*, I, many attestations; *DB*, 159a; Loyd, *Origins*, p. 36; Green, *Government*, pp. 242–43).

30. Crèvecoeur (Calvados, a. Lisieux) + **31, 20**
'de Crievecoer et de Drincort/ e li sire de Briencort/ *sivent* le duc quel part qu'il tort', III, vv. 8642–44.
Earliest attested members: Hugh, jurer of Bayeux inquest of 1133, who had a son called William. And Robert, possibly Hugh's brother, who held land of Haimo III in 1130 (Douglas, *DM*, p. 55, n. 16); Bayeux held mill at C. in 1149 (*Ant. cart.*, ed. Bourrienne, I, 49; for Hugh and William of C. encroaching on Bayeux's right of holding a fair at Crèvecoeur (*ibid.*, I, 223).

Crispin, see **Tillières**

31. Drucourt (Eure, c. Thiberville) + **30, 20**
'de Crievecoer et de Drincort/ e li sire de Briencort/ *sivent* le duc quel part qu'il tort', III, vv. 8642–44.
The church of Drucourt was given by William Crispin II to Le Bec (Porée, I, 331, 656).

32. Epinay-sur-Odon (Calvados, c. Villers-Bocage) +**79**
'cil d'Espinei e cil de Port', III, v. 8480.
Herbert, son of Geoffrey, d'Epinay and his sister Matilda were benefactors of Troarn in 1068 (Sauvage, no. ii, p. 350 and pp. 302–03).

32a Erneis, fitz de
'Robert, qui fu filz Herneis' [died during battle], III, vv. 8621–34.
Robert, son of Erneis and nephew of Rodulf I of Taisson, died at Hastings (Douglas, 'Companions', pp. 142–43; Douglas, *DM*, p. 35); grandfather of Robert who in 1151x2 encroached on Bayeux land (*Ant. cart.*, ed. Bourrienne, I, pp. 33–34).

33. Etouteville (Seine Mar., a. Yvetot)
'e li sire de Stotevile', III, v. 8428; see also III, v. 5033 [siege of Ambrières]; soldiers of 'Stutevile' guarded the castle.
Robert I of Stuteville attested a charter of Saint-Évroult before 1089; he fought on Robert Curthose's side at Tinchebray in 1106 (OV, VI, p. 84; *EYC*, IX, 1–14).

34. Eu (Seine Mar.) **+ 90**
'Li sire de Saint Galeri/ li quens d'Ou bien i feri', III, vv. 8699–700.
Robert, count of Eu (d. c. 1090); tenant-in-chief in many counties in England.

35. Ferrières-Saint-Hilaire (Eure, a. Bernay, c. Broglie)
'Henri, li sires de Ferrieres', III, v. 8365.
Henry of Ferrières (many attestations in *Reg.*, I) and tenant-in-chief in many counties in England.

36. Ferté-Frénel (Orne) or **Ferté Macé** (Orne)
'e li sire de la Ferté/ maint Engleis a acraventé;/ grant mal i firent li plusor/ e mult i perdirent des lor', III, 8577–80.
If Ferté-Frénel, see the honour of Breteuil and their tenants, the Frenels (OV, II, p. 36, III, p. 332, VI, p. 218; Crouch, *The Beaumont Twins*, p. 106); if Ferté-Macé, William, nephew of Bishop Odo of Bayeux, was its lord (Douglas, *DM*, p. 35; Fauroux, no. 131).

37. Saint-André-de-Fontenay (Calvados, a. Caen)
'e li sire de Fontenei', III, v. 8646.
Godfrey or his son Peter, according to the charter of Peter's son Roger for Saint-Etienne at Caen (*Reg.*, II, no. 1352).

38. Fougères (Ille-et-Vilaine)
'Grant priés en out cil de Felgieres,/ qui de Bretaigne out genz mult fieres', III, vv. 8363–64.
Maino of Fougères (Fauroux, no. 160, c. 1050x64) died c. 1066 when his son Ralph was not of full age. By 1086 Ralph was married to a daughter of Richard of Clare and a tenant in Buckinghamshire (DB, 151c); Keats-Rohan, *Battle*, 13 (1990), pp. 162, 167; Loyd, *Origins*, pp. 142–43.

39. Gacé (Orne, a. Argentan)
'ensenble od els cil de Gacié', III, v. 8528.
Tithe of church at Gacé given by William the Conqueror to Sainte-Trinité at Caen (Musset, *AC*, nos 8, 11, 12; Walmsley, pp. 6, 11).

40. Gael, Ralph de (Ille-et-Vilaine, a. Rennes)
'Joste la compaigne Neel/ chevalcha Raol de Gael,/ Bret esteit e Bretons menout,/ por terre serveit que il out,/ mais il la tint assez petit/ ker il la forfist, ço fu dit', III, vv. 8493–98; also vv. 6371–72.
Ralph of Gael, son-in-law of William FitzOsbern; exiled after the 1075 rebellion (Keats-Rohan, *Battle*, 13 (1990), p. 167).

41. Glos-la-Ferrières (Orne, a. Argentan, c. Ferté-Frenel) **+ 91**
'e cil del Sap e cil de Gloz', III, v. 8538.
For Glos family, tenants of honour of Breteuil, see Crouch, *The Beaumont Twins*, pp. 104–06.

42. Gournay-en-Bray (Seine Mar., a. Neufchâtel)
'e li viel Hue de Gornai,/ ensenble od lui sa gent de Brai;/ od la gent que cist menerent/ mult en ocistrent e tuerent', III, vv. 8455–58; see also III, v. 4818 [battle of Mortemer].
Hugh of Gournay (Fauroux, nos 190, 219; *Reg.*, I, nos 6a, 69, 105, 125, 170–71). His daughter (?) Matilda was a nun of Sainte-Trinité at Caen (Musset, *AC*, no. 25). He held land in Essex (DB, 89b); Loyd, *Origins*, p. 47.

43. Gouvix (Calvados, a. Falaise, c. Bretteville-sur-Laize) **+ 25**
'cil de Goinz e de Sainteals', III, v. 8523.
Roger of Gouvix held Bayeux land in 1144 (*Ant. cart*, ed. Bourrienne, I, pp. 46, 52–53) and witnessed for Bayeux in 1151 (*Recueil des actes de Henri II*, I, no. xx); Radulf and

Robert of Gouvix were canons of Bayeux in 1185 and 1165x1205 (*ibid.,* I, 122–23, 101, 148–49).

44. Grentemesnil (Calvados, c. Saint-Pierre-sur-Dives)
'un vassal de Grenstemaisnil . . . ', III, vv. 8437–48.
Hugh of Grentemesnil? (William of Poitiers, p. 197; Douglas, *DM*, p. 56), Loyd, *Origins*, p. 47.

45. Harcourt (Eure, c. Brionne)
'li sire poinst de Herecort/ sor un cheval qui mult tost cort,/ de quantqu'il poet le duc secort', III, vv. 8639–41.
For the Harcourt family, tenants of the Beaumonts, see Crouch, *The Beaumont Twins*, Loyd, *Origins*, p. 51. Philip of Harcourt was bishop of Bayeux (1142–63); William of Harcourt was treasurer of Bayeux in 1152x3. Albereda of Harcourt was widow of William Trussebut in 1185 (*Rotuli*, ed. Round, pp. 27–28).

46. Haye-du-Puits, La (Manche, a. Coutances)
'Donc point li sire de la Haie/ nul n'esparne ne ne manaie/ ne nul n'en fiert qu'a mort ne traie,/ ne poet garir qui il fait plaie', III, vv. 8571–74.
Earliest attested members of the La Haye family are Robert, grandson of Turstin Haldub, and his wife Muriel (charter for Lessay = 1126 *Reg.*, II, no. 1576; also Loyd, *Origins*, p. 51). According to the Spalding Register (f. 413r), Robert's wife Muriel was the daughter of Picot, son of Colswain of Lincoln. Thus she was the granddaughter and not the daughter of Colswain, cf. Green, *Government*, p. 258.

47. Hommet, Le (Manche, a. Saint-Lô) **+ 21**
'cil de Brius e cels de Homez', III, v. 8513.
Belonged to the honour of Reviers; Loyd, *Origins*, p. 52; Keats-Rohan, 'Aspects of Robert of Torigni', pp. 24–27; in 1161 Roger of Le Hommet, archdeacon of Bayeux, became archbishop of Dol (*Chronique de Robert de Torigni*, ed. L. Delisle (Rouen and Paris, 1872), I, pp. 332–33); Enguerrand of Le Hommet married Cecilia of Sémilly [q.v.] (*Ant. cart.*, ed. Bourrienne, I, pp. 110–12).

48. Ivry-la-Bataille (Eure, a. Evreux) **+ 109**
'Cil de Vitrié e d'Urinié', III, v. 8575 [var. Ivrié B; Lirié C].
Hugh of Ivry was butler to William the Conqueror in 1067 (*Reg.*, I, no. 55; Loyd, *Origins*, p. 52). Roger was a benefactor of Saint-Etienne at Caen (Douglas, *DM*, p. 56) and held land in many counties in England.

49. Jort (Calvados, a. Falaise, c. Morteaux-Couliboeuf) **+ 29**
'cil de Corcié et cil de Jort/ i ont le jor maint home mort', III, vv. 8481–82.
Robert, son of Nigel, gave the church at Jort to Saint-Désir at Lisieux in 1049x58 (Fauroux, no. 140). Is he the same person as the Robert of Jort, who held Hoton (Leics.) from the king (DB, 236d)?

50. Laigle (Orne, a. Mortagne)
'E Engerout de Laigle i vint. . .', III, vv. 8459–64.
Engenulf of Laigle died at Hastings (OV, II, p. 176; Loyd, *Origins*, p. 52).

51. La Lande-Patry (Orne, c. Flers)
'Guillame Patric de la Lande. . .' [saw Harold being given arms on way to Brittany], III, vv. 8585–600.
William Patrick of La Lande and his wife Gisela were benefactors of Saint-Étienne at Caen (Musset, *AC*, no. 14, cf. nos 8, 11). After Odo of Bayeux lost his lands in Kent, William held Patricksbourne (Sanders, *English Baronies*, pp. 135–36). He was a tenant of the bishop of Bayeux in Normandy (*Ant. cart.*, ed. Bourrienne, I, 15; Loyd, *Origins*, p. 76).

52. Lassy (Calvados, a. Vire) + **107**
'cil de Victrié e de Lacié /. . . e uns chevaliers de Lacié', III, vv. 8471, 8527.
Ilbert I of Lassy (d. c. 1093), tenant of the bishop of Bayeux in Normandy and England
(W. E. Wightman, *The Lacy Family* (Oxford, 1966), pp. 215–26; Loyd, *Origins*, p. 53).

53. Lithaire (Manche, c. La Haye-du-Puits)
'e li sire de Lutehare', III, v. 8421.
???

53a. Malet, Guillaume
'Guillame que l'en dit Malet. . .' [receives support from the lord of Montfort and William
of Vieuxpont [q.v.]], III, vv. 8339–52.
William Malet was at Hastings (William of Poitiers, p. 204; *Carmen*, vv. 587–92; Loyd,
Origins, p. 56).

54. Maltôt (Calvados, c. Evrecy)
'l'ancestre Hue le Bigot/ qui aveit terre a Maletot/ e as Loges e a Chanon', III, vv.
8547–49.
Hugh Bigot was the brother of Roger Bigot (d. 1107); they were tenants of the bishop of
Bayeux. Their tenants were Ansketil of Maltôt and his son Roger (Musset, *AC*, nos 7, 18);
Loyd, *Origins*, pp.14–15; for Loges and Savenaye as Bayeux fiefs, see Navel, p. 18.

55. Manneville (Seine Mar., either c. Bacqueville or c. Offranville)
'e li sire de Magnevile', III, v. 8430.
Geoffrey of Mandeville, tenant-in-chief in many counties in England (Keats-Rohan, 'The
Prosopography', pp. 8–12).

56. Mare, La, unidentified + **99**
'e cil de Touke e de la Mare', III, v. 8422.
???

56a. Marmion, Roger
'de Cinqueleis Raol Taisson/ e li viel Roger Marmion/ s'i contindrent comme baron,/
pois en orent grant guerredon', III, vv. 8489–92.
Roger Marmion, father of Robert Marmion (d. 1106) and brother of William Marmion,
who agreed that in 1106 Robert's widow Hadvisa would become a nun at Sainte-Trinité
(Musset, *AC*, no. 27; Walmsley, no. 9, pp.119–20); Loyd, *Origins*, p. 60.

57. Mayenne (Mayenne)
'De Meaine li viel Gisfrei', III, v. 8449 [Holden identifies him erroneously with Geoffrey
de Mortagne, William of Poitiers, p. 196].
Geoffrey of Mayenne, although his participation is very unlikely (Keats-Rohan, 'Le
Problème de la suzeraineté', pp. 66–67).

58. Molay, Le (Calvados, c. Le Molay-Littry) + **58** + **83**
'del Viez Molei e de Monceals/ . . . de Reberchil e del Molei', III, vv. 8524, 8647.
The forest of Le Molay was granted to Cérisy in 1032 (Fauroux, no. 64); Le Molay was
the home of William Bacon, benefactor of Sainte-Trinité where his sister became a nun.
The Bacon family were tenants *de vetere* of William Montfiquet in 1166 (Loyd, *Origins,*
pp. 10–11).

59. Monceaux (Calvados, a. Bayeux) + **58**
'del Viez Molei e de Monceals', III, v. 8524.
William of Monceaux was tenant of the bishop of Coutances (DB, 87d, 88c–d, 89a; Loyd,
Origins, p. 67).

60. Montbray (Manche, a. Saint-Lo, c. Percy) + **84**
'cil de Monbrai e de Saié', III, v. 8576.

Robert of Mowbray, earl of Northumbria, benefactor of Saint-Etienne; Roger of Mowbray gave daughter as a nun to Sainte-Trinité (Musset, *AC*, nos 2, 7, 8, 22; Loyd, *Origins*, p. 71).

61. Montfiquet (Calvados, c. Balleroy)
'E li sire de Monfichet,/ qui de bois garder s'entremet', III, vv. 8545–46.
Loyd, *Origins*, p. 68: William of Montfiquet held fief of Robert of Gernon in 1087; father of ? William of Montfiquet (*Reg.*, II, nos 1283, 1400–2, 1518, 1609, 1645, 1719).

62. Montfort, probably the same as **63**
'quant vint li sire de Monfort', III, v. 8346.

63. Montfort-sur-Risle (Eure, a. Pont-Audemer)
'Hue, li sires de Montfort', III, v. 8479.
Hugh II of Montfort; see Douglas, *DM*, pp. 65–70; van Houts, 'Ship List', p. 169. Loyd, *Origins*, p. 68. He was a tenant of the bishop of Bayeux (Navel, p. 16).

64. Montgommery (Calvados, c. Livarot)
'e Roger de Mongomeri', III, v. 8701.
Roger of Montgomery, large landholder in Normandy and England (K. Thompson, *Historical Research*, 60 (1987), 251–63; Lloyd, *Origins*, pp. 68–69).

65. Mortain (Manche)
'Li quens Robert de Moretoig. . .', III, vv. 8635–38.
Robert of Mortain, half-brother of William the Conqueror, d. 1095. Large landholder in Normandy and England (B. Golding, *Battle*, 13 (1990), 119–44).

66. Mortemer (Seine Mar., c. Neufchatel-en-Bray)
'Donc poinst Hue de Mortemer', III, v. 8617.
Hugh of Mortemer (d. 1148/50) in error for his father, Ralph, who was a large landholder in England (Loyd, *Origins*, p. 70; Keats-Rohan, 'Aspects of Robert of Torigny', pp. 23–24).

67. Moyon (Manche, a. Saint-Lô, c. Tessy-sur-Vire)
'Li viel Willame de Moion/ out ovoc lui maint compaignon', III, vv. 8487–88.
William of Mohun, tenant-in-chief in Somerset (DB, 95c–96b); is probably related to Alfred of Moyon, whose sister and niece were nuns at Saint-Trinité (Musset, *AC*, no. 8) and to William of Moyon, tenant of bishop of Bayeux in 1154 (*Ant. cart.*, ed. Bourrienne, I, 32–33).

68. Moulins-la-Marche (Orne, a. Mortagne)
'e dam Willame de Molins', III, v. 8433.
William of Moulins-la-Marche, son of Walter of Falaise, who married Albereda, daughter of Guidmund of Moulins-la-Marche (OV, III, p.132; Fauroux, no. 225; *Reg.*, I, nos 140, 310; *Reg.*, II, no. 1594). He died in 1100.

69. Moustiers-Hubert (Calvados, a. Lisieux)
'des Mostiers Hubert Paienals', III, v. 8500.
William Paynel, who also held land at Bricqueville and Hambye, died in 1087; he was the father of Ralph Paynel (OV, IV, p. 113; *Reg.*, I, nos 228, 269, 299, 319, 412, 446, 477), who was sheriff of Yorkshire, where he held much land (Loyd, *Origins*, p. 77; *EYC*, VI, 1–10).

70. Néhou (Manche, a. Valognes)
'e li sire de Neauhou', III, v. 8423.
For the Reviers family, see Keats-Rohan, 'Aspects of Robert of Torigny', 26–27.

71. Ouilli (Calvados, c. Bretteville-sur-Laize) + **92**
'e cil d'Oillié e de Sacié', III, v. 8529.

Robert I d'Oilli held land in many counties in England (*Reg.*, I, *passim*; Sanders, *English Baronies*, p. 54; Green, *Government*, pp. 264–65).

72. Orbec (Calvados, a. Lisieux)
'e dam Richart, qui tint Orbec', III, v. 8536.
Richard of Clare, see R. Mortimer, *Battle*, 3 (1980), pp. 119–41.

73. Orval (Manche, a. Coutances, c. Montmartin-sur-Mer) + **94**
'Cels de Sole e cels d'Oireval', III, v. 8511.
Renaldus of Orval (Musset, *AC*, no. 19) held one half of the church at Baupte; benefactor of Lessay (*Reg.*, II, nos 621, 1442); Richard of Orval was chaplain of King Henry I (*Reg.*, II, nos 544, 572, 1431).

74. Oubeaux, Les (Manche, c. Isigny) + **85**
'cil d'Onebac e de Saint Cler', III, v. 8619.
The cantor of Bayeux was financed by income from Les Oubeaux in 1271 (*Ant. cart.*, ed. Bourrienne, II, 163–64).

75. Pacy (Eure, a. Evreux)
'cil qui ert sire de Pacié', III, v. 8525.
FitzOsbern family (Loyd, *Origins*, pp. 75–76).

76. Perrières (Calvados, c. Morteaux)
'de Torneor e de Praeres', III, v. 8531.
Robert of Perrières, tenant of bishop of Bayeux (*Ant. cart.*, ed. Bourrienne, I, 97); Radulfus of Perrières was canon of Bayeux and witnessed charters together with Wace (*ibid.*, I, 56, 142–46).

77. Pin-au-Haras, Le (Orne, c. Exmes)
'e cil qui iert sire des Pins/ tuit cil furent en la bataille,/ n'i a cil d'els qui mult n'i vaille', III, vv. 8434–36.
For the Le Pin family, tenants of Beaumont, see Crouch, *The Beaumont Twins*, pp. 5, 23.

78. Pirou (Manche, c. Lessay)
'e un chevalier de *Pirou*' (MS Peitou), III, v. 8424.
The church of Pirou was given to Lessay by Turstin Haldup (*Reg.*, II, no. 1441). William of Pirou was butler in 1115, 1123 (*Reg.*, II, p. xii).

79. Port-en-Bessin (Calvados, c. Ryes) +**32**
'cil d'Espine*i* e cil de Port', III, v. 8480.
Hugh, son of Hubert of Port, sheriff of Hampshire; retires c. 1096 as monk of St Peter at Gloucester (*Reg.*, I). He was tenant of Bishop Odo (Douglas, *DM*, p. 54; Navel, p. 30, n. 66) and held land in many counties in England.

80. Prêsles (Calvados, a. Vire, c. Vassy)
'dejoste lui cil de Praels', III, v. 8522.
Roger of Prêsles, tenant of Earl Hugh of Chester. His widow Ada gave the tithe of Colomby-sur-Thaon to Sainte-Trinité at Caen (Musset, *AC*, no. 27); Ranulf, son of Turstin of Prêsles, had as his heir Alfred of Combrai [q.v.] (*Reg.*, II, no. 329; Keats-Rohan, 'The Prosopography', pp. 27–28; Sauvage, p. 155).

81. Reviers (Calvados, c. Creully)
'cil ki fu sire de Re*v*iers/ out grant plenté de chevaliers,/ cil i ferirent as premiers,/ Engleis folent od les destriers', III, vv. 8483–86. See Néhou.

82. Roumare (Seine Mar., c. Maromme)
'e dam Guillame de Romare', III, v. 8420.
William of Roumare, son of Gerold of Neufmarché; see the latter's charter of c. 1070, *ex inf.* D. Bates.

83. Rubercy (Calvados, c. Trévières) **+ 58**
'de Reberchil e del Molei', III, v. 8647.
???

84. Sai (Orne, a. Argentan) **+ 60**
'cil de Monbrai e de Saié', III, v. 8576.
Geoffrey of Sai, present at Bonneville in 1066 (Fauroux, no. 232); died after 1084 (*Reg.*,
I, no. 199). Loyd, *Origins*, p. 96; Powicke, *The Loss of Normandy*, 2nd ed., p. 351.

85. Saint-Clair-sur-Elle (Manche, a. Saint-Lô) **+ 74**
'cil d'Onebac e de Saint Cler', III, v. 8619.
Haimo of Saint-Clair held land from Eudo 'au Chapel' and Roger Bigot shortly after
1086; much of the land had been taken from Ely (*IEAL*, 182–83); Hubert of Saint-Clair
was a tenant of the count of Mortain in Somerset and Dorset (DB, 79c, 92a); William
of Saint-Clair was a tenant of the bishop of Bayeux and the honour of Gloucester, from
1120 onwards (*Reg.*, II, nos 1231, 1512–13, 1719, 1821–22, 1824, 1363); Loyd, *Origins*,
p. 88); for suggestions concerning the family connections, see Green, *Government*,
pp. 272–73.

86. Saint-Jehan le Thomas (Manche, c. Sartilly) **+ 18**
'de Saint Johan e de Brehal', III, v. 8512.
Ralph of Saint-Jean-le-Thomas was present at Bonneville in 1066 (Fauroux, no. 232);
Thomas of Saint-Jean was sheriff of Oxfordshire (*Reg.*, II, nos 885, 897, 958, etc.). With
his brothers John and Roger he witnessed for Mont-Saint-Michel (*Reg.*, II, nos 1422,
1459; Loyd, *Origins*, pp. 88–89).

87. Saint-Martin-le-Gaillard (Seine Mar.)
'e li sires de Saint Martin', III, v. 8432.
Reinald of Saint-Martin (Fauroux, no. 123; van Houts, 'Robert of Torigni', p. 228; Loyd,
Origins, pp. 90–91).

88. Saint-Saens (Seine Mar., a. Neufchatel-en-Bray) **+ 23**
'Cil de Saint Segus e de Quaillié' (var. D, S.: Saint Sen or Seu; B: Sere; C: Sanc Sen), III,
v. 8519.
Lambert of Saint-Saens (d. c. 1089x93), father of Helias. J. de Bouvris, in *Autour du
pouvoir ducal Xe–XIIe siècles*, ed. L. Musset (Caen, 1985), pp. 155–57.

89. Saint-Sauveur-le-Vicomte (Manche, a. Valognes)
'Bien firent cil de Beeissin/ e li baron de Costentin,/ e Neel de Saint Salveor', III, vv.
8353–62; 8493 'Joste la compaigne Neel'.
If Nigel II of Saint-Sauveur (d. 1092), vicomte of the Cotentin, Delisle (*Saint-Sauveur-
le-Vicomte*, I, 21) doubts whether he took part in the conquest of England. It is much
more likely that it was Nigel, son of Nigel II, who was alive in 1073, 1076 and
predeceased his father (*ibid.*, pp. 26–27). Liesse, daughter of Nigel II, in due course
inherited the honour of Saint-Sauveur. She married c. 1145 Jordan Taisson (d. 1178), son
of Radulf Taisson and Adeliza (*ibid.*, pp. 31–34), whom she survived.

90 Saint-Valéry-en-Caux (Seine Mar., c. Yvetot) **+ 34**
'Li sire de Saint Galeri/ e li quens d'Ou bien i feri', III, vv. 8699–700.
Ranulf of Saint-Valéry was tenant-in-chief in Lincolnshire in 1086 (DB, 364d), probably
enfeoffed by Bishop Remigius, who had been the aulmoner of Fécamp (Loyd, *Origins*,
p. 92, and van Houts, 'Ship List', pp. 167–68).

91. Le Sap-André (Orne, a. Argentan) **+ 41**
'e cil del Sap e cil de Gloz', III, v. 8538.
The family were tenants of the honour of Breteuil. OV mentions Robert, son of Heugon
c. 1050 (II, 32, 36); Crouch, *The Beaumont Twins,* pp. 104–05.

92. Sassy ? (Calvados, c. Morteaux) + **71** (other possible identifications are Sacey (Manche, c. Pontorson); La Saussaye (Eure, c. Amfreville-la-Campagne); Saussay-la-Campagne (Eure, c. Etrepagny); Le Saussey (Calvados, c. Villers-Bocage) or Sassey (Eure, c. Evreux).
'e cil d'Oillié e de Sacié', III, v. 8529.
Osbern 'de Salceid/t, Saceio' was a tenant-in-chief in Devon (DB, 116d), while Ralph 'de Salceit' was a tenant of the Lacy family in Herefordshire (DB, 181b).

93. Sémilly (Manche, a. Saint-Lô, c. Saint Clair-sur-Elle)
'e li sire de Semillié', III, v. 8520.
William of Sémilly sold land at Asnières to Radulf of Asnières [q.v.] with the consent of William of Colombières [q.v.]. This land was given to Sainte-Trinité (Musset, *AC*, no. 8; cf. nos 7, 22). He was still alive in 1080x2. His great-granddaughter Cecily married Enguerrand of Le Hommet (*Ant. cart.*, ed. Bourrienne, I, 110–12). Cecily's son William of S. was a canon of Bayeux 1213–26 (*ibid.*, II, *passim*).

94. Soules (Manche, c. Canisy) + **73**
'cels de Sole e cels d'Oireval', III, v. 8511.
The church and forest of Soules were given to the bishop of Coutances (Fauroux no. 214: 1056x66). For the family of Soules, tenants of earls of Huntingdon and kings of Scotland, see Barrow, *Anglo-Norman Era*, p. 98.

95. Subligni (Manche, a. Avranches, c. la Haye-Pesnel)
'e li sires de Sollignié', III, v. 8469.
Tenants of the earl of Chester (Loyd, *Origins*, p. 98; Keats-Rohan, 'The Prosopography', p. 11).

95a. Taisson, Raoul
'de Cinqueleis Raol Taisson/ e li viel Roger Marmion/ s'i contindrent comme baron/ pois en orent grant guerredon', III, vv. 8489–92, also the section on the battle of Val-ès-Dunes, vv. 4830ff.
Rodulf II Taisson was at Caen in June 1066. He was a benefactor of Sainte-Trinité, where his sister became a nun (Musset, *AC*, nos 8, 11). See also his cousin Robert FitzErneis [q.v.]; Jordan Taisson witnesses for bishop of Bayeux in 1169 and frequently occurs with King Henry II (*Ant. cart.*, I, 62; *Recueil des actes de Henri II, passim*). His wife was Liesse of Saint-Sauveur (q.v.).

96. Tancarville (Seine Mar., c. Saint-Romain)
'li chanberlenc de Tancharvile', III, v. 8427.
Probably Ralph, father of William of Tancarville, chamberlain of King Henry I; Loyd, *Origins*, p. 101.

97. Thouars (Deux Sèvres, a. Bressuire)
'e li visquens, cil de Toarz/ n'i fu mie le jor coarz/ . . . e de Toarz dan Nameri', III, vv. 8465–66, 8702; also vv. 6364–66.
Aimeri, vicomte of Thouars, see J. Martindale, in *Battle*, 7 (1984), pp. 224–45.

98. Tillières (Eure)
'e cil qui donc gardout Tillieres, . . . Guillame que l'en dit Crespin', III, vv. 8366, 8431.
Gilbert II Crispin and his brother William of Neaufles, or his nephew William II Crispin; Green, 'Lords of the Vexin', pp. 55–56; Porée, I, 179.

99. Touques (Calvados, a. Pont-l'évêque, c. Trouville-sur-Mer) + **56**
'e cil de Touke e de la Mare', III, v. 8422.
Land held by Robert and Croc, sons of Roger, given to Saint-Martin-du-Bosc, priory of Fécamp (Fauroux, no. 218 (1059x66)).

100. Tournebu (Calvados, c. Thury-Harcourt) + **76**
'del Torneor e de Praeres', III, v. 8531.
William of Tournebu witnessed a charter for Sainte-Trinité at Caen in 1080/1–83
(Musset, *AC*, no. 15); Simon of Tournebu was steward of Bishop Philip of Harcourt
at Neuilly and William of Tournebu was dean of Bayeux, 1151–82 (*Ant. cart.*, ed.
Bourrienne, I, 90); Simon of Tournebu frequently witnesses charters of King Henry II
(*Recueil des actes de Henri II, passim*).

101. Tracy (Calvados, c. Villers-Bocage or Calvados, c. Ryes) + **106**
'cil de Victrié e de Lacié,/ de *Valdairié* e de Tracié,/ icil furent en un conrei', III, v. 8472.
Turgis of Tracy was at Bonneville in 1066, cf. Geoffrey of Sai [q.v.] and Ralph of Saint-
Jean-le-Thomas [q.v.]. In 1133 William Picot held land of the bishop of Bayeux at Tracy,
identified by Navel, pp. 17, 30 n. 62 as Tracy-sur-Mer. Loyd, *Origins*, p. 104; Sanders,
English Baronies, p. 104.

102. Troisgots (Manche, a. Saint-Lô)
'e cil qui donc teneit Tresgoz', III, vv. 8539–44.
Humphrey, son of Alberic, was a tenant in Norfolk and Essex (DB, 262a–b, 417b), where
he also held land in exchange for possessions in Normandy (DB, 436a; Loyd, *Origins*,
pp. 106–07). Identification *ex inf.* K. Keats-Rohan.

103. Trossebot unidentified toponym + **17a**
'Botevilain e Trosebot,/ cist ne dotent ne colp ne bot,/ mult s'i firent le jor hair /as cols
receivre e al ferir', III, vv. 8581–84.
Earliest attested members: Roger of Trussebut (*Reg.*, II, no. 1749) as witness with Ingran
of Sai; William of Trussebut, mentioned by OV as having been raised from low origins
(OV, VI, pp. 16–17; *EYC*, X, 5–22); at an unspecified date Robert of Trussebut
encroached on land of Bayeux (*Ant. cart.*, ed. Bourrienne, I, 315).

104. Vassy (Calvados, a. Vire)
'e li sire de Vaacié', III, v. 8530.
Enguerrand of Vassy was tenant of bishop of Bayeux in 1133 (Navel, p. 18). Alfred of
Vassy witnessed for the bishop of Bayeux in an undated charter of the third quarter
of 12th c. (*Ant. cart.*, ed. Bourrienne, I, 287); cf. Robert 'de Veci', who held land in
Lincolnshire and Northamptonshire (DB, 363b, 225b).

105. Vaudreuil (Eure, c. Pont de l'Arche)
'Li archier de Val de Rooil/ qui esteient de grant orgoil', III, vv. 8505–06.
Belongs to the ducal demesne.

106. Vaudry (Calvados, c. Vire) + **101**
'de *Valdairié* e de Tracié' (var. nal daiaire MS, Du Vaudari D, Del Val dairi B), III,
v. 8472 [with Lassy, 'Victrie' and Tracy in one *conroi*].
During King Henry II's reign Alice of Vaudry ('de Waldari') gave her land at Rucqueville
(Calvados, c. Creully) to the bishop of Bayeux (*Ant. cart.*, ed. Bourrienne, I, 37; *Recueil
des actes de Henri II*, I, no. ccclxvi, p. 503 for correct identification). Sainte-Trinité had
been given land there by Adelaide, sister of Eudo 'au Chapel' (Walmsley, 4, 6).

107. 'Victrié' unidentified + **52**
'cil de Victrié e de Lacié', III, v. 8471 [with Lassy, Vaudry and Tracy in one *conroi*].
???

108. Vieux Pont (Calvados, 4km north-east of Saint-Pierre-sur-Dives)
'e dam Guillame de Vez Pont', III, v. 8347 [mentioned with William Malet and the lord
of Montfort].
Robert of Vieuxpont was juror in 1076 (Delisle, *Saint-Sauveur-le-Vicomte*, pp. 26–27,

no. 36) and William of Vieuxpont was listed as one of the despoilers of the lands of Sainte-Trinité (Walmsley, p 127) in the reign of Robert Curthose.

109. Vitré (Ille-et-Vilaine) + 48

'Cil de Vitrié e d'Urinié', III, v. 8575.

Andrew of Vitré, son-in-law of Count Robert of Mortain, held land in Cornwall (DB, 120a, 125a); Keats-Rohan, *Battle*, 13 (1990), p. 170 and 'Le Problème de la suzeraineté', p. 56 (n. 24).

110. Warenne (Seine Mar.)

'e de Garene i vint Willemes/ – mult li sist bien el chief li helmes –', III, vv. 8453–54.

William of Warenne; see van Houts, 'Ship List', p. 169; *EYC*, VIII, 1–9.

NOTE ON THE TRANSLATION

This translation is based on the edition of the *Roman de Rou* by Anthony J. Holden (Paris, 1970–73). Wace's twelfth-century French verse has been rendered in English prose as faithfully as possible. No attempt has been made to maintain Holden's punctuation in cases where alternative punctuation seems preferable in order to satisfy the rhythms of English. Occasionally, awkward repetition has been suppressed and the link between sentences made clearer by the addition of a conjunction not found in the text. This has been done sparingly, however, as matters such as repetition and the relationship between sentences or clauses can have an important stylistic function. Like his contemporaries, Wace moves back and forth repeatedly between present and past tenses, but the text has been translated here using the English past tense.

From time to time, when the text is unclear and evidently corrupt, Holden makes a suggestion in his notes aimed at elucidating the meaning of the word or passage concerned. When these suggestions have been adopted in the translation, which consequently does not render precisely the wording of the text, this is brought to the reader's attention by means of an asterisk.

Wherever practicable, the divisions in Holden's text between stanzas or episodes have been maintained in the present translation. However, at the beginning of Part II the breaks in the text are so numerous that stanzas have been linked together in the translation to form more substantial paragraphs. Further divisions, especially in Part III, have been made in order to produce a translation which conforms to the normal paragraph divisions of modern English.

Notes in this volume have been kept to a minimum; readers are encouraged to consult the extensive notes in Holden's edition (vol. 3, pp. 169–253). The present notes have three main functions: (i) to clarify the meaning of a particular passage, (ii) to provide useful background information or, (iii) to draw attention to historical detail in the *Roman de Rou* which is unique to Wace. The notes in this latter category have been provided by Elisabeth van Houts, whose article 'Wace as Historian' is reprinted above.

THE *ROMAN DE ROU*

PART ONE

CHRONIQUE ASCENDANTE DES DUCS DE NORMANDIE

One thousand, one hundred and sixty years in time and space had elapsed since God in His grace came down in the Virgin, when a cleric from Caen by the name of Master Wace undertook the story of Rou and his race; he conquered Normandy, like it or not, against the arrogance of France which still threatens them – may our King Henry recognise and be aware of this.[1] He who has very little income has very little benefit from it. But largesse has now succumbed to avarice; it cannot open its hands, they are more frozen than ice. I do not know where largesse is hidden, I can find no sign or trace of it. He who does not know how to flatter has no opportunity or place in court;* many people are forced to await their turn.[2] It was not at all like this at the time of Virgil and Horace, nor of Alexander, Caesar or Statius; then largesse had strength and virtue. (1–16)

I want the subject of this first page to be King Henry, who took as his wife Eleanor, a lady of noble birth; may God inspire both of them to good works! They do not let me waste my time at court; each of them rewards me with gifts and promises. But need, which sails and rows swiftly, often presents itself and often forces me to make pledges in order to obtain money.* Eleanor is noble and both kind and wise; she was Queen of France at a young age. Louis took her as his wife in a marriage of great power; they went on a lengthy crusade to Jerusalem and each suffered great hardship and pain there. On their return, the queen, on the advice of the barons, was parted from him on grounds of consanguinity.* But this separation did her no harm; she went to Poitiers, her native home, to which she was the sole family heir. King Henry, who held England and all the coastal land between Spain and Scotland, from shore to shore, took her as his wife and made a rich marriage. People often talk of him and his courage, and of the evil-doers he destroys, like birds trapped in a cage. No baron in his land owns so much property that, if he dares infringe the peace, whether in open country or in woodland,[3] he is not shamed through mutilation if he can be caught, or who does not leave his body or soul behind as hostage. (17–42)

---

[1] For further comments on the hostility between the Normans and the French see the passage below, vv. 43ff, where Wace stresses the deceit of the French and their constant desire to dispossess the Normans. This hostility was clearly still very real at the time Wace was writing. See Anderson, 'Wace's *Roman de Rou* and Henry II's Court', pp. 67–69, and Ferdinand Lot, *Fidèles ou vassaux? Essai sur la nature juridique du lien qui unissait les grands vassaux à la royauté depuis le milieu du IXe jusqu'à la fin du XIIe siècle* (Paris: Emile Bouillon, 1904), pp. 177–235.

[2] The meaning of the expression *faire la cue lovinace* is not certain. It could indicate that many people at court are 'subject to mockery'.

[3] The phrase *en plein ne en boscage* 'in open spaces or in woodlands' occurs a number of times in the *Rou*. On some occasions (especially the present example and III, vv. 820, 4800), it may refer to different agricultural systems in Normandy, with *plein* referring to the cultivation of open fields and *boscage* to that of enclosed fields. The normal meaning of *bosc(h)age* is 'wood, woodland' and *plein/plain* normally corresponds to the English term *plain*. See Holden's note to III, v. 820 (vol. 3, p. 217).

I want to relate the history of Rou and the Normans; I must give a proper record of their deeds and their prowess. The treacherous acts of the French cannot be concealed; they are always determined to disinherit the Normans and have always taken pains to vanquish and harm them. When the French could not overcome the Normans by force, they used to employ many a trick to harm them. They are a far cry from the heroes of songs;* they are treacherous and disloyal, no one should trust them. They are greedy for possessions and cannot be satisfied; when it comes to giving, they are niggardly and mean with the necessities of life.[4] In stories and books one discovers that the French were never willing to keep faith with the Normans, either with regard to promises made or oaths sworn on holy relics; nevertheless, the Normans used to hold them in check successfully, not by treachery but by dealing great blows. If the French could realise their ambitions, the King of England would own nothing on this side of the Channel; if they could do so, they would send him back across it in disgrace. At the siege of Rouen they thought they could mock him; if they could have captured Rouen or entered it forcibly, they would have treated him with scorn for ever more. But, when Henry arrived, they did not dare remain and could not stay there in safety any longer.[5] Through our new king [Henry the Younger], who cannot rule as king,[6] they thought they could capture or lay waste the whole of Normandy; in order to do harm to the father, they gave the sons bad advice. (43–69)

Then you would have seen Henry racing through the border country, dashing from one area to another and doing three days' journey or more in a single day; his men thought he must be flying. I cannot count the number of knights he took prisoner; he put them in chains and fetters, but, being such a noble man, he did not want to hang them or tear them limb from limb. The barons in the land – I do not wish to enumerate them – who caused a son to abandon his natural feelings for his father and set father against son, wanted to dishonour the father in favour of the son. They could not boast of the gains they made; if they wanted to consider and estimate their losses, they would never in their lifetime be able to put things to right, nor could their sons or daughters do so. The king had their vineyards and their woods destroyed, their houses burnt and their castles laid waste. The only thing they had to show for their efforts was their shame;

---

[4] This reading is based on Andresen's suggestion, *et de viande aver*.

[5] As pointed out in the Introduction, this reference to the Siege of Rouen in 1174 helps to date the *Chronique Ascendante*, as Wace seems to have revised his text to incorporate this event. When Henry II arrived in Normandy on 8 August 1174, King Louis and his allies had been besieging Rouen for some time and making little progress. Attempting to take possession of the city before Henry reached it, the French broke a truce agreed on 10 August to celebrate the feast of Saint Lawrence, but the garrison just managed to prevent the French from scaling the walls. Henry arrived next day and the French were soon defeated. Louis fled and sued for peace before the end of September. See W. L. Warren, *Henry II* (London: Methuen, 1973), pp. 135–36.

[6] On Henry the Younger (or Henry the Young King) see Warren, *Henry II*, esp. pp. 580–93. Also known as Henri au Cort Mantel, he was crowned in 1171 but never possessed any real power. He revolted against his father in 1173 and did not live to inherit the throne of England (he predeceased his father in 1183). He had many positive characteristics and Warren describes him as 'everyone's ideal of a fairy-tale prince' (p. 583).

nevertheless, they were lucky to escape as lightly as they did. May Henry put a stop to the comings and goings of the French. Let him speak to them through messengers and keep them at a distance. They are determined to deceive him, may God protect him from them; they are so envious of him that they have no love for him and would gladly change the way things are. But Henry is so wise, so powerful and so brave; he has so much land and so many towns, and he is able to call upon so many men that he can make Louis and his men tremble. (70–96)

Henry, who held Tours and the Touraine, had many lands; from his father he had inherited Anjou and Maine and from his mother he had the Normans and the English, and with the queen he took the whole of Poitou and Gascony. The king I am telling you about has a fine reputation; he is not loathe to go about his business, to hang his shield around his neck and to don his byrnie. He loves hunting and hawking when there are no other urgent matters; he punishes and pursues the arrogance of evil-doers and spares from justice neither priest nor canon. Everyone is as peaceful in his land as monks in a cloister. (97–107)

Henry was young at the outbreak of the war, which King Stephen launched against him most wrongfully. The Empress Matilda, Henry's mother, endured much hardship from this and suffered constant grief. At the siege of Winchester her fine qualities were manifested; she was there for forty days, may the Lord God help her! At no time could she eat or drink in safety; she had taken a thousand armed men there. O God, how many lances were broken there!* There was no vassal, however good, who did not sweat from his toil; no man could attack another without capturing or killing him. Count Robert, who helped Matilda, was captured; the battle to rescue his sister never ceased and Matilda departed as far as her horse could run.[7] She remained inside Oxford for three months and three days, besieged in a castle with no opportunity to get out. She escaped at night, unbeknown to anyone, apart from those who took her away for she needed an escort; as she left, she did not even say farewell to her closest friends. There was deep snow, but the freezing of the water beneath the snow helped her;[8] she dressed herself in a bed-sheet and deceived her enemies. She came to Wallingford, where Brian received her. The king was very upset since he could not catch up with her. Stephen never had peace and never deserved to have any, for he accepted bad advice and bad advice harmed him. The king so harried her* that she recognised his right and gave him the kingdom as an inheritance; this was greatly to the advantage of both those whom the war pleased and those whom the peace pleased;[9] he was king for nineteen years, after which time he died.[10] (108–35)

---

[7] Count Robert is Robert of Gloucester, eldest illegitimate son of King Henry I and thus a half brother of Empress Matilda and was one of her principal supporters in her attempt to oust King Stephen. He died in 1148.

[8] The notion that ice beneath the snow assisted Matilda's escape is confirmed by Henry of Huntingdon (pp. 742–43), who states that the Thames, which she was forced to cross, was iced over at the time. See Holden's note to v. 126 (vol. 3, p. 171).

[9] As Holden points out (vol. 3, p. 171), at the end of v. 333 one can read either *moult acrut* 'was very favourable to' or *moult encrut* 'caused great difficulty for'.

[10] On this passage see Anderson, 'Narrating Matilda', pp. 56–61. Anderson thinks that Wace virtually removed Matilda from the line of descent and that he saw her as a threat to a symbolic order of identification, which moved from Henry I directly to Henry II (pp. 56–57).

Henry was the grandson* of Henry and son of his daughter Matilda, Empress of Rome; he could not have been of more noble birth. His grandfather was a very powerful king and had no neighbour, however high born, whom he could not topple if he wished; he spared from justice neither high born nor low. Because of his love of women he had many ups and downs. He built many a good castle and captured many by assault; in Reading he built a very worthy abbey. At his death there was great sorrow, but the evil-doers did not mind, for to them it scarcely matters who comes or goes. He was king for thirty-seven years, less about half a year. (136–46)

Henry, as* many people have heard, was the son of William [the Conqueror], who loved the Holy Church and paid a great deal of attention to it. He was a courageous and bold knight, but when he first held the land – he was ten years old, I do not think he was any older* – many of the barons in the country failed him; they failed to keep and were untrue to their oaths and promises. William was small and a young boy, yet they showed no love for him; he was unable to protect either the rich or the poor. In the twelfth year in which he held and governed the land, he launched a battle on the plains of Val-ès-Dunes, defending the land against Nigel and Ranulf,[11] two arrogant vicomtes who had conceived a hatred for him.* He had begged the King of France so much and given him such service that he came to his aid and dealt many a blow there. One of the men from the Cotentin struck him on the shield; people still talk about this, saying that from the Cotentin came the lance which felled the king who ruled France. Nigel was defeated and Ranulf fled, and with his men the duke pursued those who were fleeing; he despatched many of them into the Orne, forcing them into it. Then he took Domfront by force; he besieged it for fifteen months. He built three castles outside it, and Martel, the Count of Anjou, who lost the castle, considered himself greatly shamed; he had ruled the region and afterwards never enjoyed possession of it. (147–70)

William, about whom I am telling you, was very valiant and brave. He took Maine and Le Mans away from their inhabitants and built a stone tower there which he held and equipped for a long time. On many an occasion he destroyed the arrogance of the Bretons and he conquered England and the English; it was in the month of October, on Saint Calixtus's day, that the battle, in which many men perished, took place. Then William was made king and he received great honour; one thousand and sixty-six years had elapsed since God was born from the Virgin in Bethlehem when the duke became king and received the honour; he built an abbey where the battle had taken place. He built two other abbeys in Caen; in one of them he buried his wife, the queen, and in the other his own body lies, just as he chose. He was duke for thirty-two years and things went well for him; then he was king and duke for twenty-one and a half years. Throughout the whole of Normandy he proclaimed peace and a suspension of hostilities from daytime on Wednesday until Monday morning. Anyone who captured or attacked another man during this period

---

[11] The form *Ernouf* in the manuscript, here and in v. 164, is an error.

incurred a sentence of excommunication and owed the bishop a fine of nine pounds.[12] (171–92)

When he died, the king divided up his lands; to Robert his eldest son he left Normandy, and William was put in possession of the throne of England;[13] England was his own conquest and he could act in this way. He gave the contents of his treasury to his youngest son Henry, and this Henry, who lived for a long time, later had everything. William lay ill in Rouen and died in Rouen; his men and his friends took him to Caen and buried him in the church of Saint-Étienne before the main altar, may God have mercy on him! (193–202)

King William was the son of Robert, a baron from the fief of Normandy and a very noble man. He was, it is said, the most generous of all the Normans; he gave rewards to each man who served him and gave provisions and clothing to lepers. He was noble, courtly and of noble demeanour. From his noble actions, as we read about them, and from his way of life at home – the candles, the wine and other provisions – a wise cleric could create an inspiring story. He built Cerisy and placed monks in it; barefoot and in rags, he made a pilgrimage to Jerusalem with great devotion. Throughout this great journey his aim was to seek pardon; he kissed the Holy Sepulchre and prayed there. Then he was killed by poisoning in Nicaea; a young boy poisoned him on the advice of a wicked relative; this was an act of great treachery. He held Normandy in his power for seven years, and Lord Richard, his brother, did so before him, as we know. (203–22)

Robert was the son of Richard, who loved monks; he helped the poor and the needy with tenderness, giving food and clothing to beggars. He never started a war against lord or vassal; if anyone did wrong by him, he sought what was rightfully his, and if any harm was done to his vassals he avenged them fiercely. He maintained and provided for monks; Fécamp, an abbey which his father Richard had originally founded, was considerably expanded and much enhanced. Richard had installed canons in it, but Robert replaced them with monks he brought from Dijon. He held the land for twenty-nine years and died in the thirtieth. Richard was the son of Richard, about whom I will soon be telling you; anyone who reads the story will get to know him well. He is Richard the First, who married Gunnor and was the son of Sprota, about whom many people spoke. He never displayed any fear or hesitation. He saw many marvels and came across many apparitions; his heart never took fright at anything. He travelled by night just as easily as by day; he loved woodlands and rivers and derived a great deal of pleasure from them. As long as he remained in the country, the Normans remained proud. With great splendour he established Saint-Ouen at Rouen, to which he frequently went, and the abbey of Mont-Saint-Michel. He also endowed

---

[12] The Truce and Peace of God movement was begun in the south in the 1020s, but it found favour with a number of rulers in western Europe and was first proclaimed in Normandy in 1048. The reference here to a specific fine of nine pounds is not found in Wace's sources. See Michel de Boüard, 'Sur les origines de la Trève de Dieu en Normandie', *Annales de Normandie*, 9 (1959), 169–89, and *The Peace of God: Social Violence and Religious Response in France around the year 1000*, ed. by T. Head and R. Landes (Ithaca and London: Cornell University Press, 1992). See also note 224 below.

[13] For *Guillaume le roiz* in v. 195 Andresen reads *Guillaume le rous* 'William Rufus'.

Saint-Wandrille in the Pays de Caux with some of his lands and had the church
of Fécamp built and constructed, placing clerics there to serve in it and establishing for it sources of revenue, which the monks later enjoyed when things
changed. He ordered a watch to be kept on all the dead bodies in Normandy;
this was not the custom, but he began it, doing so because of one corpse which
he discovered in a church. He came to the church at night, intending to pray, and
went in; the corpse was on the bier and the count walked past it and came before
the altar. While he was praying, the body stretched out its arms and stood up.
When the duke had prayed, he looked around and saw the big, tall body looking
like the Devil. Richard drew his sword and tried to speak to him. He dealt the
body a blow, knocking it to the ground, then left the church and mounted his
palfrey. He gathered his people together and explained his adventure to them;
then he had the body taken care of, proclaiming and demanding that a body
should not remain alone at night with no one present. Richard had blond hair
tinged with red;[14] he governed the land for fifty years and three more after the
death of his father, who departed from him when he was a young boy. (223–68)

The duke was considered a very good and loyal man; he had a great love
for his barons and his own people. The French caused him much pain and much
hardship; they betrayed him on many occasions out of mortal hatred. Richard
was brave on foot and brave on horseback. He fought many a fight and many a
pitched battle; in a mêlée he was fierce and bold, like a hunted boar when it has
turned at bay. His enemies in high places were brought low; in his whole family
there was no better vassal. He was the first to set up an order of canons in
Fécamp, where his son later installed an order of monks. Richard held the land
equitably for fifty years and three more; he feared and loved God, the Spiritual
Father. (269–82)

Richard the Old was the son of William Longsword, whom the Flemish
betrayed (that is a proven fact); they killed him treacherously, the truth of this
cannot be concealed. The deed was carried out on the advice of the French, but
no individual will subsequently be blamed for this by me;* this treachery became
very famous. In William's time Normandy was feared; there was joy there in
abundance and peace was assured, once Count Riulf, who had upset both the
inhabitants and the peace for a long time,* had left the region.[15] William was a
fierce and strong man of considerable power; he had a large body and long arms,
broad hips and rather curly blond hair. From his own lands, revenues and money
he rebuilt Jumièges, the abbey which Hasting had laid waste. The monks he
brought to it came from Poitou, because of his sister Gerloc, who was married
there. William's mother, Popa, was born in Bayeux. He was duke for twenty-five
years; he had a very short life. Afterwards, Normandy lived in terror for a long
time; the French gave the Normans many a bad day. (283–303)

---

[14] The reference to Richard I's blond and red hair is unique to Wace, as is the story of the body
watch.
[15] Count Riulf is probably Riulf of Évreux (see Orderic, I, p. 154). He is presumably a Frank, as his
name is Frankish, but little is known about him.

William was the son of Rou, the good conqueror, the brave, bold, good warrior, who waged many battles and withstood many combats; the Normans call him the head and the flower of the family. He waged war so much against the French and instilled so much fear in them that they became reconciled with him and agreed to peace and love. The king who loved him dearly showed him great honour,* giving him his daughter Gisla as his wife and also the whole of Normandy, both what was in it and what surrounded it. Rou was a man of great nobility and great valour; many of his neighbours regarded him as their lord; he ruled Normandy for thirty years with full power. (304–15)

PART TWO

We have reached the figure of Rou and we will speak to you about Rou; the tale we have to tell begins at this point, but, to speed our task, we will reduce the number of lines in each stanza;* the road is long and hard and we fear the toil. Hasting, who never did anything but harm, was in France; his heart was never other than arrogant and treacherous. He brought much destruction to the Holy Church and much violence to Christians, having no fear of God or of His curse. His soul should be destined for great tribulation, since that is what he has deserved and what we ask from God. (1–11)

Rou and Hasting were both Danes, but very different men; Rou acted in accordance with justice, whereas Hasting did the opposite.[16] Rou was friendly, Hasting arrogant and fickle, displaying no mercy to nobleman or serf and never showing any love for cleric or non-cleric, monk or lay brother. The people of Denmark were always arrogant, always overweening and very covetous; they were cruel, proud, unruly and lustful. None of them was content with just one wife; from several wives they had a remarkable number of children, many little ones and many older ones. They had so many sons, daughters, wives and servants that even the richest man could not feed everyone. (12–24)

No matter what they acquired, it was not enough to feed their children who were becoming very numerous. So it often happened that, by casting lots, they rid the land of its strong and finest men, driving them out of the country either by land or by sea; wherever they went, these men did a great deal of harm. On one occasion, it is said, this caused violent disagreement in Denmark. The sons started a great war and a great dispute with their fathers, who wanted to drive them away, whether they liked it or not. They were ordering them to get out of the land and make their home in other regions; they were to capture other lands peacefully or forcibly and leave their inheritances to their little brothers. (25–38)

The sons told their fathers that they would certainly not leave or take anyone else's inheritances by force; not wanting to be in exile throughout the world, they would share the land with their little brothers. The old and most senior barons in the country conferred about this and explained matters to the king,

---

16 Note also the positive comment on Rou with which Wace ends the *Chronique Ascendante*. On the figure of Rou/Rollo see D. C. Douglas, 'Rollo of Normandy', *English Historical Review*, 57 (1942), 417–36, repr. in *id.*, *Time and the Hour* (London: Eyre Methuen, 1977), pp. 121–40. On Hasting see Frederic Amory, 'The Viking Hasting in Franco-Scandinavian Legend', in *Saints, Scholars and Heroes: Studies in Medieval Culture in Honour of Charles W. Jones*, ed. by M. H. King and W. M. Stevens (Collegeville, Minn.: Hill Monastic Manuscript Library, Saint John's Abbey and University, 1979), pp. 269–88. For Wace's portrait of Rou and Hasting see J.-G. Gouttebroze, 'Exclusion et intégration'. Rou and Hasting are presented here as a pair of antithetical heroes. Both are pagans and both receive baptism, but Wace stresses Rou's positive qualities and it is he who becomes the founder of a dynasty, representing future Norman values and legitimising the activities of Henry II. See also Anderson, 'Narrating Matilda', pp. 305, 309.

telling him the whole truth about their sons, that they wanted to remain in the land against the barons' wishes. The king ordered them to be thrown out and they almost went mad with rage. They did not know what to do or where to take refuge; they were unable to hold out against the king. They had no fortress to protect them, yet they did not dare invade anyone else's land. (39–52)

They spoke to the two brothers who were in that land. They dwelt on the border of Denmark and were strong and powerful, strong in castles and also in friends; they asked for their advice and their help. The brothers replied that they would never let them down; they all swore together not to fail each other and not to fear the king, their fathers or anyone else. They discussed the matter and acted in such a way that they became allies, swearing oaths to join forces against kings and others when they saw the need to do so. The brothers swore to them and pledged their faith that they would never let them down and the others did the same. What more could I say about this? In this way they parted; their fathers were distressed when they heard what had happened. (53–66)

The elder of the two brothers was called Rou and the other, who was born later, was called Gurim; each of them was intelligent and wise in counsel and each was experienced and well tested in battle. The father who had these two children was very powerful; he came from a noble family and was a wealthy man. There was never a king, however strong and powerful, to whom he was willing to do homage, so courageous and valiant was he.* Neither he nor his ancestors wanted to serve any king; they did not deign to accept the authority of any king or count, nor did they deign to obey any king or count or to become anyone else's vassal. (67–78)

They had conquered by great force the lands which they held, subduing all their neighbours and capturing their lands; if any of them owned a castle, they besieged them vigorously and their owners never had any peace until they gave them up. The King of Denmark was unable to impose justice on them; they had even taken a great deal of his own lands. He often waged war on them, but won no victories; since he could do no more, he remained alert and bided his time. Between two other lands, Alania and Denmark, there was an area of borderland which they had conquered and held on to firmly; they put their trust in their castles, their great family and their numerous knights and barons. (79–90)

It is true that no one is born who does not have to die and he who comes from the earth has to return to the earth; no one can escape or avoid death, no matter how much wealth he has acquired or gives up. The man with the two sons died when his time came; the fact that he was fierce and strong could not protect him. This made the king very happy; he summoned his warriors and spoke to his barons, explaining to them the wrongs, the losses, the damage and the great and dreadful harm which this man and his ancestors had done to him on many occasions. His sons would never have any truce or peace with him and he would recover from them the losses and damages sustained. (91–102)

'My lords', said the king, 'if you are willing to help me, we can avenge ourselves on the father through the sons; the man who used to do much harm to you and me is dead. For what the father has done we must avenge ourselves on the sons; if we allow them to increase their power in the land, they will not be easy to destroy later on. Your sons, whom I wanted to drive out of this country, are joining forces against me in order to oppose you.' A man who thinks he can avenge himself can cause his own downfall and some people put forward their opinions when they should have kept quiet. The barons set a date for carrying out their plans, but the brothers discovered this and acted without delay. (103–14)

Rou summoned the young men in his household, whom he had earlier protected from the king and their fathers; he asked earnestly for their help, for they would lose their land if the barons succeeded. Then Rou asked them all to get ready at once and ride with him into the king's territory; they should burn the houses and carry off booty before the king or his army entered their land. They all replied that they would serve him well. Wherever he wished to go, they would follow him; whatever he wished to do, they would do whatever he did. If he wanted to fight, they would fight for him. (115–26)

They all made due and swift preparations and went through Denmark, causing a good deal of damage; the king and the barons rode out to oppose them and they did battle with each other ferociously. Rou and his brother Gurim attacked them violently and all their companions struck boldly. On this side and that they fought for a long time, but the king was defeated and the Danes fled. Many men were wounded there and many captured; on both sides many men, young and old, were killed there. Many were dead there and many still alive; that day each man lost a number of his friends. (127–38)

Rou had his men sought and he buried them all; the other corpses he left to the dogs and the birds. Thus the war continued relentlessly;[17] each man gained from it and each man lost. The king was harmed and damaged by the war; he was often harmed and often suffered losses. He reflected, as a man does when distressed, that he would never avenge himself on the two brothers through the use of force. With great cunning he made peace with the two brothers, who agreed to it with good intentions. But the peace brought them great tribulation; they had not suspected that the king would act treacherously. (139–50)

The peace was concluded, but it did not last long; for without their knowledge the king assembled his army. One night he rode into the land belonging to the two brothers; they were not expecting this and he had issued no challenge. He placed a force in ambush close to the city, then rode on until Rou emerged, followed by his brother Gurim and his men; they did not have many men with them and were badly betrayed. Their men were dispersed throughout the region and they attacked the king with as many men as they had. The king withdrew when he knew Rou was coming; he placed his men in front of him and made it look as if he were taking flight. Rou's men came spurring after him, intending to strike, but the king was able to get well away and depart. (151–64)

Rou and his men rode together towards the king, who moved farther and farther away with his men. The king's men fled and the brothers pursued them until the men emerged noisily from the ambush. When Rou had pursued him until he had gone past the waiting enemy,* the latter darted forward and the king turned round; Rou was terrified when he looked around and he did not know

---

[17] For *ainz dura la guerre* in v. 141 ('thus the war lasted'), Andresen suggests the reading *cinq anz dura la guerre* ('the war lasted for five years').

which way to turn, for each direction frightened him. Rou saw his enemies in front of him and behind; there was no one who did not hate him and seek his death. The king threatened him severely and glared angrily at him; Rou did not know which men to turn towards or which to strike first. (165–76)

The king was in front of him, with the men from the ambush on his tail; the brothers were caught between their enemies. Many blows were dealt there and many men died there; the king had the upper hand, because he had the larger forces. Many of the king's men were killed or wounded and a large number of the brothers' men were killed there. Gurim was killed and Rou escaped; he fled to a sea port. The king feared that Rou would try to return once more; he had his castles destroyed and his walls pulled down, his dwellings, towns and woods set on fire, leaving nothing which could be razed to the ground. (177–88)

Rou was at the port with only a few of his men. With just six ships he crossed over to Scanza;[18] this is an island and he remained there for a long time. He was grief-stricken, troubled and anxious about how he could avenge himself on the king and his men and how he could recover his land. One night, as he was lying asleep in his bed, he had the impression that a voice was telling him, as he slept, that he should go over to the English, for there he would learn how to get back safely and joyfully to his own country. Then he would be at rest and have great peace; no one, strong or weak, would wage war against him. (189–200)

He related the dream to a Christian, who replied to him:

'Have confidence. You have been a pagan and you are a pagan's son, but through Christianity there are many good things in store for you.'

'Rou', he said, 'you will cross over the sea, that is the world, and become a Christian by holy baptism. By dint of the labours of this world you will reach the English, that is the angels in Heaven, where you will reign with God.' Rou believed the words the Christian spoke to him. He gathered together many young men and took ships and boats, promising the youths part of whatever he conquered. When he was ready and the wind favourable, he set out and reached England; he intended to remain there if the people in that land would accept this willingly. (201–14)

The English refused to let him into the country. They gathered their neighbours together and attempted to harm Rou; I do not know whether they intended to capture booty or plunder.[19] The Danes, who had no wish to flee, defended themselves. The English joined battle with them, but they were defeated; later they sought more men and came back. The first time they were discomfited and next time they suffered even worse; the Danes captured the best of their men. Many barons and vavassors were captured there; the Danes bound them and threw them on to their ships. They terrified the inhabitants of the country and many people cursed the ships which had brought them. (215–26)

---

[18] Scanza or Scania is the southern part of Sweden. See Christiansen, trans. of Dudo of Saint-Quentin, p. 182 n. 63. The text here actually reads *Escosce* 'Scotland', clearly a mistake for *Escance*.

[19] To improve the sense of this passage, the order of vv. 216 and 217 has been reversed in this translation. It is possible that there is a lacuna in the text after v. 215.

Rou thought very deeply and was very doubtful about whether he should return to Denmark to seek vengeance on the king, whether he should cross over to France in search of land or whether he should remain where he was with the English. He was very upset that he had quarrelled with the English and would have gladly sought reconciliation with them. One night, when he was thinking of many things, he saw a vision which terrified him. He had the impression of sitting on a mountain, so high that there was none as high in the whole of France. On the top, in its own channel, was a spring from which water flowed which was fine and clear, pure and healthful. Rou was completely discoloured and blackened with leprosy; he was bathing in the water and was cured at once. The mountain Rou dreamed of was teeming with so many birds, small and large, that they completely covered it. (227–42)

All the birds went and bathed in the spring on the mountain; they flapped their wings and went gathering, carrying straw and branches and making hiding-places for themselves. Many birds were there, taking up the entire mountain and seeking a number of places in which to make their nests and homes. Wherever they went, they obeyed Rou, and their left wings were completely red. When Rou got up next morning, he called his prisoners to him and summoned his companions from all his ships. When they had gathered, he related his dream to them, telling them in the correct order just how he had dreamed it. There was a Christian amongst the prisoners and he explained the dream as Rou had recounted it: the mountain in France, he said, on which Rou was sitting, was the Holy Church which he would be embracing. The spring on the mountain was holy baptism, the leprosy was sin, than which no evil is greater; no medicine or doctor is of any use against leprosy, nor is any king or emperor, however great his empire. (243–61)

'In baptism', he said, 'you will be reborn and the sins you have committed will be pardoned, and by holy baptism you will be saved; you cannot be blessed in any other way than this. The birds, who bathed in the water after you, are your companions who will be baptized; then they will lodge with you in that land, up there with the angels in very great harmony. They will make their homes and their nests on the ground, that is dwellings and towns which they will build. They will receive together the body of our Lord and the holy, blessed blood through which they will have salvation. By the red wings which are on the left you can understand the shields they will carry round their necks. Men from many lands will obey you, as did the birds which were on the mountain.' (262–77)

When Rou heard the interpretation of the dream, he gave a great reward to the man who explained it to him and released him from prison a free man, and because of him his companions were also freed. Then Rou took his messengers and sent them to the king, who was called Æthelstan, duly informing him that no blame was attached to the harm which had been done; his own men, who initiated it, were in the wrong. If anyone took a different view,* he should make it known to him, and if he was in the wrong he would make amends out loud in his court, just as he wished. Rou recognised Æthelstan as a powerful and strong man; he would do right by him, he said, if he had done wrong. Henceforth, they should have an agreement such that neither would let the other down, whether they lived or died. (278–92)

The good Æthelstan listened to the messengers, honouring them greatly and cherishing them dearly; he gladly granted the peace which Rou was seeking and discussed it with his friends and counsellors. The king accepted Rou's friendship and arranged a day with the messengers for it to be confirmed. Rou came to the king at the appointed time and the peace was sworn; then he came to his ships and looked at the sea.[20] The Danes sailed until they reached Walcheren; the inhabitants came to meet them and refused to let them land. They did battle with them, expecting to be victorious, but they were defeated and turned and fled. The Danes destroyed their houses and their towns. Whether they liked it or not, the Danes remained there for a long time. (293–306)

Because of the havoc they wrought and the length of their stay, and because they robbed the peasants of their ploughed land, their seed, their goods and all their other equipment, and because the peasants were dying of fear – they were not safe by day or by night – famine came to the land; there had never been greater. Æthelstan heard of this and gave Rou a fine present, ten ships all laden with meat and wheat, and he promised him ten ships full of good men, fine warriors filled with great daring. The inhabitants of Walcheren saw that Rou had laid waste their lands and intended to settle there by force; he was robbing them of their goods and refusing to spare them. They gathered together their neighbours with the intention of driving them away. Radbod, the Duke of Frisia, was the first to bring help, and the Count of Hainault, a valiant knight called Rainer (his sobriquet was Long Neck). They did battle with Rou, but were all defeated. All the bravest and strongest men took flight; their lands were destroyed, as were all their men. The peasants fled and no ox or cow made a sound. Radbod, Duke of Frisia, took no pleasure in this; the man who had caused him to fight had deceived him greatly. (307–29)

Radbod was grief-stricken that Rou had defeated him; he had threatened him greatly and harmed him greatly. He had no wish to rest there or to lie in his bed; gathering his men and an army together, he attacked Rou without delay. If he could not avenge himself, he would never again have any pleasure; he preferred to die a violent death or drown than to give in to Rou or ask him for peace. Beside a large river called the Almere [Zuyderzee], Rou did battle with Radbod the Frisian; he defeated the inhabitants of Walcheren and took many prisoners. He had them bound and placed in his ships and obtained a large ransom for them. He took all the foodstuff from the region and was determined to bring destruction to Rainer's land. (330–42)

From there he went by land to Rainer Long Neck, who was on the side of the inhabitants of Walcheren, but he had cause to regret it. The ground was marshy and the land soft; the Danes did not travel easily through the region:

'I will have no more respect for myself than for a cabbage-leaf', said Rou, 'if I can get my hands on Rainer and do not strip him of his arrogance.' Rou entered the Scheldt, a river in that land, doing harm in many places, plundering and waging war; he seized the towns and conquered the lands. Rainer summoned his men and did battle with Rou, attacking him many times and fighting him many

---

[20] There may be a lacuna in the manuscript at this point. See Holden, note to v. 300 (vol. 3, p. 176).

times. Without a word of a lie, Rou defeated him many times and Rainer Long Neck was unhorsed many times. (343–55)

Finally, Rou captured Rainer and put him in chains, but Rainer's men captured in battle twelve of Rou's most powerful companions, amongst those whom Rou considered to be his closest friends. When Rainer's wife discovered for certain and heard that Rou held her husband, she was very distressed. She was grief-stricken and frightened that she would lose her husband and that Rou might behead him, for he had a great hatred for him and each regarded the other as his mortal enemy; but Rou did not treat Rainer badly or hate him. The countess feared Rou and his men a great deal; she dressed the twelve prisoners in new clothes and did not harm them or treat them cruelly. She sent them back and restored them to Rou as free men. (356–69)

She gathered together all the gold and silver in the land, and whatever she could find of the churches' possessions, and sent it all to Rou as a present, asking him humbly for the return of her husband. When Rou saw the present the lady offered him, he was delighted to have his men back and he took the gold and the silver; he had Rainer brought forth and released him from his chains. He spoke to him very politely, asking him about his intentions. Rou asked him if he would go on fighting and Rainer said he would not, for things were going very badly for him; he would never bear lance or shield against him. If he freed him, he would be grateful to him and become his liegeman and serve him well, and if he ordered it he would go with him, for he considered him a wise, noble and worthy man. Rou replied to him that great profit would accrue to him from this. (370–85)

Rou was a very noble man and he took pity on Rainer; he gave him leave to return to his wife as a free man. He had half the money taken and sent to Rainer's wife through her husband, and he also entrusted Rainer with many possessions of his own to present to the lady as a mark of friendship. When she had her husband back, her heart was filled with joy. Eight hundred and sixty-six years had passed since God was born of the Virgin in Bethlehem when Rou was reconciled with Rainer Long Neck. Then he left the Scheldt and departed from Flanders. Rou left the Scheldt behind, followed the coast until he came to Normandy and sailed up the Seine, making his way up the river until he came to Jumièges. He came to Jumièges and arrived before the Pays de Caux. On the altar of the church of Saint-Vaast he humbly presented the body of Saint Ameltrudis,[21] which he had brought in his ship. (386–402)

Rou came straight to Jumièges in Normandy. He was not a Christian and had not been baptized, yet in his heart he loved and feared God; he often recalled the dreams he had had and earnestly hoped that things would go well for him. Franco, an archbishop in Rouen, heard that foreigners were seizing the land; hearing it said that Rou was coming from Walcheren, he thought hard about how he could save the city. Hasting had destroyed it and Rou would destroy it; the town would be destroyed if he did not take things in hand, for the King of France would never intervene, as he lacked the strength and the courage to do so.

---

[21] Saint Ameltrudis (Wace uses the form *Ernouftrute*) has not been identified.

Archbishop Franco went to Jumièges and spoke to Rou and his men through an interpreter. He said so much to them, did so much, promised so much and gave so much that he obtained a truce in respect of Rouen, that no harm would be done to it. When he wished, Rou could go to the town in safety and he would not seek to harm the inhabitants of the town. Then Rou came to Rouen, sailing up the Seine and anchoring his ships near the church of Saint-Martin. (403–23)

Rou had brought with him a very large number of barons; many noblemen were there and many proven vassals. They decided to make Rou their lord, as he was a brave and wise man of good family; they entrusted their support and their affairs to him. They were all of one mind and one will. Because they came from the north they were called Normans. Norman means 'man of the north', that is the truth; they were all called Normans at that time, all those who were born in the north. The north is a wind which comes from the septentrion; it is that which one calls the Great Bear in the starry sky.* The ancients found this in writing. The country which the Normans captured and peopled received the name Normandy from the Normans. In ancient times it was called Neustria, but its name was changed because of the new inhabitants. The ancients' name for it persists amongst their heirs; they are Normans, they were Normans and have been Normans.[22] I, Master Wace, who am telling this, found it in writing. (424–43)

It was a fine day and there was a great company of men; you could scarcely have found one stronger or more daring. They all put their ships in the harbour of Saint-Martin. Rou surveyed the scene and went round the town; he looked at it frequently, inside and out. It seemed fine and beautiful to him and it pleased and satisfied him greatly; all his companions praised it to Rou. They told him and advised him to remain in the town; he should come and go from there, leave from there and return there. The river which ran in the city was fine and deep and the spring waters in the city were good and sweet. He did not need to seek a better place; let him remain there.* So the region was good and the city good; nowhere had they ever seen such a plentiful supply of things to live on. They asked to remain there and Rou agreed to this; they spent I do not know how many joyful days there. (444–59)

Rou wanted to see Hasdans [the Damps], which is now called Arche [Pont-de-l'Arche]; he saw that the land was fertile and the region beautiful. News about Rou quickly spread throughout France, that he showed no mercy either to maidens or to the unfortunate. Rou left Rouen,* taking all his Normans with him, and sailed up the Seine to reconnoitre the land. On a slope they discovered a fortified castle with a single gate, which was not large. Rainald, a French count, who at that time held the land,[23] that is Paris, the region round it, and everything which belonged to it, heard that foreigners were coming to his land and was concerned about how he should defend the country. He summoned Hasting, for he wished to speak to him; this was Hasting the Dane who made frequent

---

[22] Cf. vv. 45–80 in Part III.

[23] The manuscript indicates here that Reginald held Lucenee, but no territory of that name has been identified. The form *lucenee* is possibly an error for *la terre* 'the land' or *le renne* 'the kingdom'.

voyages by sea, a man who reduced so many unfortunate men and women to tears and completely destroyed the city of Luna. Rainald spoke to Hasting below the river Eure; as he knew their language, he sent him to the Normans, along with two of his barons who knew of his hereditary possessions.[24] He sent them to the Normans, as he did not care for their presence.* (460–79)

Hasting came to the Normans and asked them who they were, what region they came from, what they wanted and where they were going; if they had plunder in mind, the French would defend themselves, and if it were land they were after they would not even obtain a foothold. Rou replied first, because he was a skilful talker:

'We are from Denmark and have come from the direction of Walcheren. It is our intention to take plunder and hold the land; if the French challenge us, we will do battle with them.'

'Upon my word', said Hasting, 'these are outrageous words.'

'And who are you', said Rou, 'who know our language? Are you, who bear this message, one of the Danes or one of the French? In countenance and bravery you seem like a very worthy man.' Hasting replied:

'My name is Hasting. The land of which you speak nourished me in its bosom. I have tamed many evil-doers, as one tames a horse with a bridle. I coveted this land, as I saw it was filled with good things. I have Chartres from the King of France and do my best to serve him; I have never feared a castle any more than a haystack.' (480–97)

'Upon my word', said Rou, 'I have no knowledge of you, but I do know that Hasting did a lot of harm to people. Whatever he wanted to do started well and whatever he started finished very badly.' Then Hasting spoke to them and related his deeds, the strange and the dreadful, the fair and the ugly, and also his great deeds of prowess and the tasks he had accomplished.

'From now on', said Rou, 'you should remain at peace.' Then the Normans said:

'You have told us a great deal about your great deeds and your great valour. Go back and take care of your city. You can tell the French how you have fared.' The messengers could not learn any more. They went to Duke Rainald and put it to him that he had lost his land unless he could defend it; the Normans had already besieged it and intended to capture all of it. (498–513)

Rainald spoke to Hasting on another occasion and Hasting discouraged him from fighting. The Normans, he said, were strong and there were many of them. Without many more men, he would never defeat them. Then a knight named Roland spoke, saying:

'Why do you ask for advice from such a tyrant? A lamb does not take a wolf or a fox as his counsel;[25] he has brought the people of his land here to attack us.' Hasting became angry and replied:

[24] The reading *teneüre*, translated here as 'hereditary possessions', is not certain.
[25] The manuscript reading, which translates literally as 'One does not take a wolf or a fox under one's bench', is unsatisfactory and the present translation is an attempt to convey the meaning intended. See Holden's note to v. 520 (vol. 3, p. 178).

'From now on, I will say nothing.' Meanwhile, the Normans had fortified the castle; they had reconnoitred the land and become acquainted with the area. Theobald tricked Hasting out of Chartres; he bought the city outright by bargaining. Theobald was born in France and was one of its noblest barons; he had many castles and fortified dwellings throughout the land and he was skilled in speech and the art of manipulation.

'Hasting', said Theobald, 'the king is looking for a chance to destroy you, for you have done him a great deal of harm. You have, he says,* brought some unknown people upon us, who are laying waste the land and leaving nothing behind.' (514–34)

Theobald handled Hasting so cunningly and did so much to him one way or another, telling him both truth and lies, that he sold Chartres to him and took some of his money; because of the money he received for it, he made Theobald his heir. Theobald bought Chartres and Hasting sold it to him; having done so and received the money, Hasting went away one night, abandoning the city. I do not know what became of him, nor have I heard of him since.[26] (535–42)

Rainald gathered his army together and summoned his neighbours. He handed his banner to a vassal named Roland and set off to attack the Normans. But he came upon them too soon; he did battle with them, but gained nothing by it. Roland, who carried the banner and was in charge of the troops and commanded all the other men, was killed in this battle; Rainald, who was very frightened, took flight, leaving behind him many of the men he trusted most. Then Rou said to his men:

'The war has started. The French have begun it, now let it be returned to them. We have won the first battle against them and will do the same with the rest, if each man fights hard.' They sought their horses and arms in the French manner, which seemed to them to be the most splendid and most appropriate.[27] The great booty they had acquired filled them with pride and joy; if it distressed the French, this scarcely worried them at all. Then they captured Meulan and the whole region, killing the barons and laying waste the land. Rainald had gathered a larger force of men in Paris; he fought against Rou and there was a very great battle. But Rainald took flight and, as on so doing, was killed. Then the Normans went and besieged Paris. They plundered the towns and seized everything in them; you would have seen many tears shed by the wretched inhabitants. (543–66)

Meanwhile, Rou had spies sent to Bayeux, which is situated more than fifty leagues from Paris,[28] and also to Évreux and Lisieux, for he had not agreed peace or a truce with any of them. On their return, the spies said the land was beautiful and the region fertile. He could capture Bayeux, which would be easy, as the people were not accustomed to battle. When they had laid everything waste and there was no more booty to be had, they made their way straight to Bayeux. A spy

---

[26] The *Gesta Normannorum Ducum* (*GND*) states that Charles of France gave Chartres to Hasting as tribute (I, pp. 26–27) and that Count Theobald bought Chartres from Hasting, who 'having collected all his possessions, wandered off and disappeared' (I, pp. 56–57).

[27] This comment on the 'French manner' is unique to Wace.

[28] This information concerning the distance from Bayeux to Paris is not given in Wace's sources.

came out to meet them and give advice; they could easily capture it, as it lacked fortifications. At that time Berengar was lord of Bayeux; he was recognised as count of the Bessin as far as the Vire.[29] He heard through messengers and spies that the Normans were coming towards Bayeux without delay.* His men were outside and they threw themselves into the battle, attacking the Normans and causing them great anguish. They captured Rotim, the noblest of all the Norman princes.[30] Because they handed him back, they obtained a year's peace. The truce lasted a year, but the following year the Normans returned. They attacked Bayeux and damaged it greatly, destroying the farmsteads and the people; all the barons in the land went over to their side. (567–90)

Count Berengar had a very beautiful daughter; she was called Popa and was a very noble girl. She did not yet have a woman's breasts on her bosom; no more noble a lady or maiden was known. Rou, who desired her greatly, made her his beloved; from her was born William, called Longsword, whom the Flemish killed in proven treachery. The Normans all went together to Paris and everyone in France trembled for fear of Rou; they did not know where to seek protection and it seemed to them that God hated them. Those who could flee caused no disturbance; they merely left. Rou left there and came to Évreux, a good city, but he spent scarcely any time there. Ysembard, the bishop – I do not know how this happened – fled to Paris until peace returned.[31] (591–605)

When Rou had captured Évreux, he came to Paris. He was greatly feared everywhere on account of the harm he was doing; he had destroyed and defeated all the barons to such an extent that they gave him a great tribute as a means of protecting their land. Rou was strong and daring. He laid siege to Paris and would have captured those inside, just as one captures a hind in a trap, had it not been for the width of the Seine at the point which had to be crossed; it was impossible to take it by assault unless he employed some trick. Meanwhile, a messenger came to Rou from beyond the sea in England, telling him that Æthelstan was at war. His family and his men were taking away his land; he had sent word to Rou in order to obtain help and assistance. Then Rou told those in Paris that they should hand the city over to him; they should hand it over to him or hold it from him as a fief. If they wanted anything from him, they could have a large sum of money; they replied that they would not do so any day of their lives. (606–21)

Then Rou attacked them and they had no way of protecting themselves; no one was so idle that he did not perspire in anguish. The more they were attacked the more the losses grew; men on both sides fell and died in large numbers. Rou withdrew when he realised this; unable to force an entry, he had to depart. Rou withdrew since he could achieve no more; I do not know if they sought a truce or if he granted one. He went straight to the sea and made ready his ships. When there was a wind and he was able to depart, he arrived at Southampton.[32]

---

[29] This information concerning Berengar as Count of the Bessin is not given elsewhere.
[30] Rotim is not mentioned by Dudo or the *GND*. Perhaps Wace encountered a scribal error for Rotomagim [Rouen] and interpreted it as a man called Rotim.
[31] This information concerning Ysembard is unique to Wace.
[32] This information that Rou landed in Southampton is new.

The king came to meet him and greeted him joyfully; he was delighted that he had come and took him in his arms. Then Rou thanked him for the ships he had sent him. The king told him of his urgent need, relating his complaints against his English subjects and asking for Rou's help; if he wanted any part of his kingdom, he could take half of it. (622–37)

The king entreated Rou and begged him humbly to avenge him against the English, who had harmed him greatly; he would give him half of his entire kingdom. Rou granted him whatever he asked. Then they assembled their men and did battle with the English, taking their cities and destroying their castles. If the English had gained any advantage, they bought it at twice the price; those who set the war in motion were contorted with anger and tore at their skin. They had shown great scorn for the king and his men, but it was Rou's men who had defeated all of them; from many he cut off the ears and feet.[33] They could not rest securely in their beds and were finally all destroyed; no one had any respite.* (638–50)

The English saw that Rou had defeated them many times and discomfited and destroyed them so many times. Begging for mercy, they spoke to him and pledged their faith; if he could reconcile them with the king, they would all do right by him. He did so and then took leave of the king, who wanted to give him half of the kingdom. Rou refused to take it and in fact left it all to him:

'I will not have', he said, 'a single foot or inch of it.' As soon as Rou had brought about peace between the king and his people and freed the land of its enemies, he gave the king back his kingdom, not wanting to have as much as could be ploughed in a single day. He proudly put him in possession of it with one of his own swords. (651–62)

In the pommel of his sword he had ten pounds weight in gold:[34]

'I give you back your land', he said, 'by this glove of mine. I ask for no part of your land and for none of your wealth, except for this. If there is in your land any warrior who is willing to come with me in search of something better than he has, allow him to come.' The king said:

'I agree to this.'

'Noble baron', said the king, 'if God blesses me, I am ready, if you wish, to come to your aid with all my men and all my ships.'

'You will not', said Rou. 'I do not ask this of you. Look after your kingdom and your lordship, and your men and all your barons as well.' Then Rou sailed back to Normandy. He made his way to Rouen, going up the Seine.[35] (663–77)

---

[33] The term *oreilles* in v. 648 has been translated here as 'ears', but Holden prefers to read *curailles* 'entrails' (vol. 3, p. 179). See also v. 990. Whatever the correct reading, the information concerning the savage punishments meted out to the rebels by Rou is unique to Wace.

[34] The information concerning the ten pounds of gold is unique to Wace.

[35] Wace's account of Rou's support for King Æthelstan is much shorter than that of Dudo (trans. Christiansen, pp. 39–40). But Anderson points out that Wace has added details to the episode which stress Rou's 'loyalty, his virtue in refusing to take what he might, and his love of ornamental ceremony' ('Wace's *Roman de Rou* and Henry II's Court', p. 72). Rou is 'plainly a model for successful kingship' (*ibid.*).

The King of France heard that Rou had come to Rouen and that he had helped King Æthelstan, giving him back his cities and his castles, which against his will he had lost in war; those he had been fighting had all been destroyed. The king was very fearful of being defeated, for no one would be able to vanquish Rou. From Rouen he summoned Franco, the archbishop, and gathered all the barons of France together. He was afraid of the pagans and wanted to seek advice about how he could reach an honourable peace with Rou. (678–88)

'Advise me', he said. 'I do not know what I should do. Rou has done us much harm and he continues to threaten us. He is destroying our land and driving away our men; neither the strong nor the weak can withstand him. The people in this country are very disconsolate. Some of them have fled and some have been killed; there is no ox at* the plough nor peasant at his furrow, no vineyard pruned nor fields sown. Many churches have already been destroyed and laid waste; if this war continues, the land will be ravaged. Ask Rou for a truce lasting just three months and have it confirmed between us and his men. Meanwhile, we will discuss peace, and if he is willing to make peace I will gladly do so. I will give him so much of my gold and silver that he will have to keep the peace if his men agree to it. If Rou were willing to become a Christian for us, to receive baptism and to abandon paganism, and if he wished to keep peace and friendship with us, I would give him so much that he ought to serve me; he would have no more need to rob and plunder. Lord Franco, on our behalf you must agree to do this; go and seek the truce and find out what he wants.' (689–711)

Franco went in search of the truce* and Rou agreed to it; but before doing so he took advice from his companions. The peace lasted for three months and each of them kept it; the peasants were upset that it did not last longer. Anyone wanting to go from one land to another did so; those who wished to plough ploughed and those who wished to sow sowed. Ebles, Count of Poitiers, who was lord of the Gascons,[36] and Richard, who was lord and duke of the Burgundians, heard the news of the king and the barons who asked Rou and his companions for peace and promised great gifts in order to achieve it. They reviled and cursed the king greatly. Later they sent word to them that they were acting outrageously in tolerating the presence of Rou and his pagans; it was very wrong of them not to do battle. If they required it, they would come to their aid, and if the French could not destroy them before their arrival they should remain at peace and they would avenge them. (712–29)

Because these men spoke ill of the truce when it came to an end, the king did not prolong it and Rou refused to wait any longer. The French summoned up their courage to fight Rou and threatened him severely, for they had a great hatred for him. Rou considered himself dishonoured by the truce he had given; they had mocked and insulted him greatly, he said. Rou was furious and his heart inflamed with anger; the French, he said, who had scorned him so much, had reviled and mocked him a great deal because of the truce. He called for and summoned as many men as he could; they entered France and performed many acts of great cruelty, destroying lands and killing people. They burnt and laid waste everything

---

[36] This reference to the Gascons is new information.

as far as Sens below the Yonne. Rou made for Saint-Benoît and in honour of the good saint he saved the church, not allowing anything the monks claimed as their own to be removed or taken from it; he kept their town and their church safe. In the Gâtinais he destroyed and plundered a great deal, destroying Étampes, laying waste the burg and reducing the entire land to misery; no king or baron there was able to thwart him. (730–51)

From Étampes Rou went straight towards Villemeux; wherever he went, he did great harm. He besieged the towns,* capturing and plundering their possessions. Then he set out towards Paris, and he was intending to attack it when someone or other told him that a large number of men were following him; a huge cloud of dust was visible from a distance. The knights in the towns and the good peasants, vavassors, magistrates, villeins and men-at-arms had seen that there would be no protection for them from the king, nor from duke, count or any of their leaders. One day they all assembled; there was a huge crowd, carrying old shields, old spears and old lances. They had not seen their weapons for a long time. They rode after Rou, following him closely; when Rou saw them, he did not take flight. (752–66)

Rou looked back and could see the dust rising; it was so dense that he could not estimate the numbers.[37] He did not know if they were men-at-arms and could not distinguish them. He called his barons and brought them all to a halt:

'Behind us I can see I do not know how many men riding fast. I cannot tell whether they intend to join battle with us. Send our infantrymen and our men ahead and let them drive the booty and the packhorses ahead of them. Let those who are on horse mount at once. When battle begins, we will know who the brave men are.' At once they had their men equip themselves swiftly, knights and men-at-arms to protect the others. Rou saw the French arriving and, standing firm on the plain, waited for them; he arranged his battalion and divided up his squadrons, placing his troops to the right and the the left. The French charged at them all together with one cry and the Normans stood fast, with no one yielding or breaking away because of any blows from the French or from others. The French found them to be strong, and they pulled away, dispersing throughout the battlefield and abandoning it. Some thought they could strike who failed to do so; others who fell at the first attempt thought they could knock down their opponent. There were those who thought they could pursue their opponents who very soon fled, those who thought they could make gains who lost what they had. Others who thought they could fell their opponent died in the battle. (767–91)

The weather was fair and the countryside fertile. Many Frenchmen were there; the company was huge. But they had no lord, duke or captain who could send one man forward and have another remain behind; they were not accustomed to such procedures. They found their adversaries to be very cruel and very savage in the way they defeated, felled, killed and maimed them. Whoever lost that day, Rou's men were victorious and the French fell in large numbers on the plain; one fell down, one lay there, another died, another was bleeding. There was not a single

---

[37] The reference to the dust is not found in other sources.

Frenchman, whoever he might be, who did not have cause to lament; Rou stained and bathed in their blood the sword he carried. Hardly any of the French left there without injury and many of them remained there who never again entered a bath; the French suffered great losses and the Normans enjoyed great gains; I do not praise the gains or mourn the losses.* (792–807)

That day the Normans had the French under their control; from there to Châteaudun they did not leave behind them in open countryside the dwelling of a vavassor or peasant whose bread and wine they had not consumed. They plundered and pillaged and were never thwarted; the peasants fled, both the sick and the healthy. Anyone who could flee in the evening did not wait for the morning. When they had laid waste the Chartrain and the Dunois, pillaged, plundered, burnt and laid everything waste, they made their way to Chartres and besieged the city; the town was very fine and very old. There were wealthy burgesses there with plenty of money and a beautiful and venerable church; the shift worn by the Virgin Mary, the mother of God, was held there in great reverence. (808–22)

The Normans besieged Chartres, wishing to get hold of the property which made the burgesses wealthy and affluent; they would not leave,* they said, without stealing all of it. The burgesses in the town went to the gates with Count Theobald, who led a large number of people. They hurled objects at the Normans and often skirmished with them; a number of mêlées took place there and many men were killed. Bishop Antelmus[38] exhorted everyone repeatedly, pardoning the sins of each brave man so that the town and Christianity would be defended. The burgesses ran to the gates without any delay; the clerics and canons sang psalms and litanies. They fasted and the priests and monks said Mass. Bishop Antelmus was a man of good faith. At this time of crisis he summoned the barons in the land; he summoned Duke Richard, who was lord of Burgundy, and Ebles of Poitiers, who was lord of Gascony. They came gladly and there was no one who did not arrive with all speed; no one sought respite, a fixed time or any delay. (823–41)

The barons came from France and Burgundy. Early next day they left Chartres and launched a great attack on Rou and the Normans. Many lances were broken there and many shields shattered; many horses were won and many men received blows. At first, things went badly for the French; they were forced back against the gates because Rou and the Normans had greater strength. Bishop Goucelme was very distressed; he gathered together the clergy and the ordinary citizens and from the reliquary in which it was kept he drew forth the shift belonging to the Virgin who was mother of God. You would have seen many people throughout Chartres yelling and shouting; there was no one whose face was not damp with tears. They called upon Him who makes thunder and lightning, asking Him to defend them against Rou, their terrible enemy, and against the other Normans, who were very evil men; they were afraid that their war would turn out badly for them. The bishop was a fine and learned cleric; he very quickly took out all the

---

[38] For the name Antelmus, found in the *GND* (I, p. 62 and p. 63 n. 3), Wace uses the form Goucelmes. He was Gualtelmus or Waltelinus, Bishop of Chartres from *c.* 898 to *c.* 911.

sacred relics and holy objects, phylacteries, holy gospels[39] and other sacred things. They left no cross, reliquary or chalice in the repository. He had the clerics and the weakest inhabitants join in a procession; many were dressed in sackcloth or hair shirts.[40] (842–65)

The bishop was a very devout man; he did not speak at length or utter great exhortations. He pardoned the warriors for their sins and gave them full absolution for the evil they had done; they prostrated themselves with great earnestness and he raised his hand and blessed them. He took the relics with great devotion, and as they left the church there was great contrition; as a banner, the bishop himself carried the most precious relics throughout the procession. They sang litanies and the *kyrie eleyson*; the senior clerics and their young pupils sang.[41] Along with the procession came the barons, knights, burgesses, archers and infantry, everyone who could strike with stone or staff; those who could not walk prayed God to take care of their deliverance. (866–82)

Rou was so terrified and astonished by the procession which left Chartres, the relics they carried, the singing he heard and the holy shift worn by the lady who was mother and virgin when God was born of her that he dare not remain any longer and fled towards his ships.[42] As many people have reported, he lost his sight, but soon recovered it and was quickly cured.[43] Most of the Normans followed Rou as he fled; the others abandoned the siege, but remained together without dispersing. The French pursued them with hue and cry, showing no mercy towards those they caught, rebuking them severely for the harm they had done there. They fled until they caught sight of a hill; going over to it, they took up their position on it. (883–99)

The French harmed and assaulted the Normans, driving them a good distance away from Chartres; they returned to Chartres, leaving the Normans in the hills. When that very day was only half over, Count Ebles of Poitiers, a man of great reputation, arrived; he had very brave and well-equipped knights, some recently dubbed and others with greater experience. When he discovered that the French had crushed the Normans and that he had arrived late, he was very angry:

'My lords', he said, 'vassals, why, having summoned me, did you not wait for my arrival? If I had come in time, not a single man would have got away.'

'My lord', they said, 'do not be upset. We could not wait, for you were taking too long. You can still catch up with them if you hurry. There they are on that hill; go and avenge yourself.' (900–15)

Count Ebles of Poitiers had a large number of knights. When he heard what they had said, he set out in pursuit of the Normans; those in the region joined forces with him, including the Duke of Burgundy, who led a large company of men. They spurred on keenly towards the hill and attacked the Normans without sparing any of them; the Normans defended themselves like very brave men.

---

[39] In addition to conveying the notion of 'holy gospels', the term *teste* (Modern French *texte*) indicates the metal ornamentation serving as covering for the gospels.

[40] Much of this story concerning the relics is new information.

[41] This information concerning singing is unique to Wace.

[42] As suggested by Holden (vol. 3, p. 181), v. 883 has been omitted.

[43] This story of Rou's blindness is unique to Wace.

Count Ebles of Poitiers insulted and threatened them repeatedly and shouted at them; he proudly swore by the arms of his beloved that there was no one brave enough to escape death by his sword. The Duke of Burgundy insulted them arrogantly; he had no interest in a threat which was not carried out. He who finds his enemy in open conflict, armed on his horse, does not challenge him for nothing; let him not boast or utter threats, but do the best he can until the task is accomplished. A soul can come to its end with but little misfortune and a soul can perish for almost no reason at all. A man can think he can kill another who loses his life before him; boasting and lying, both are folly. (916–37)

The French and the Poitevins attacked fiercely and the Normans and the Danes defended themselves stoutly; they sustained great losses on both sides. The French captured Normans and dragged them down the hill; Normans killed and slaughtered them with their axes. The more they lost there, the more they redoubled their efforts. The French destroyed one thousand eight hundred Normans between morning and evening, for as they left Chartres they struck them well and cut them down from the hill where they were. The battle went on and they continued to fight until darkness fell, at which time they broke up. The French spread out through the fields hither and thither, setting up their quarters in huts and tents. They had bread and wine and provisions brought from the towns; when they had had enough to eat, they were glad to get some sleep. (938–52)

The French were asleep, dozing in their shelters, as men do who are weary after bearing arms all day. They felt very safe, for if they had feared the Normans would descend from the hill that night and make for Rouen so boldly they would have watched over them very anxiously all night, guarding* the paths, the battle-fields and the roads; they would not have got out of their clutches without great discomfiture. Who would have thought that so many men would have passed by so many others or that men who were defeated would have dared to undertake such a thing?* But those who think they are about to die are glad to escape.* The Normans would happily have rested that night if they had had something to eat or drink, but they were not certain they would ever get away from there. (953–66)

The Normans were on the hill, afraid and fearful; there was no one who was not concerned for his life. Many of them were severely wounded and weary. They expected to die in the morning and saw no other outcome. There was a knight of great valour there. He was brave, highly esteemed* and on good terms with his lord; there was no stronger warrior in the company. He had come from Frisia in search of fame and honour; he expended a great deal of sweat in order to share in the spoils and Rou cherished him greatly because of his very great valour.[44]

'If the French find you here at daybreak', he said, 'you can only die and come to grief, for against one of your men there are a good three of theirs. We have no Rou, our protector, nor any of those who left this battle with him.' (967–81)

'My lords', said the vassal, 'if we wait until daybreak, until day has dawned, we will never escape. The French will kill us or we will die of hunger, because there are so few of us in comparison with their men. But take my advice and let us depart, going down the hill silently and stealthily. The French are asleep. Let

---

[44] This story of the Frisian knight is not found in Wace's sources.

us go between them, opening up a passage with iron and steel and cutting off heads, fists, feet and ears. Since they are going to kill us, let us make them pay for it;* once they have done so, we will receive death with tranquillity. There is risk in everything, so let us take a risk; let us all stick together and die together. We are dead and dishonoured if we become separated from each other; let us get as far away from here as possible, I do not know of any other advice which could save us. Perhaps* we will survive if we do this well. We want to conquer land and we are seeking battle; since we are looking for it, we must find it.' (982–1000)

They accepted his plan, just as he had outlined it. They all went down the hill into the valley in close formation; there was no one who did not carry a naked sword of steel or a pike, an axe or a sharp spear. They passed amongst the sleepers, making their way where the great throng had lain down that night. They did not do so willingly, but it was a risk they took; they slaughtered many men who lay in their path, severing the heads of many a man as he slept and sparing no one, bald or hairy; the grass was stained red, so much blood did they spill. Those who lay asleep had no strength; the others who were awake were all overcome.[45] Ebles fled in terror. (1001–14)

Count Ebles of Poitiers was very frightened. The uproar caused by the lamentations over the dead and the wounded led him to think and fear that Rou had returned and joined battle against the Poitevins and the French. On foot and unarmed, he went into a fuller's cottage and hid inside, remaining concealed there until it was broad daylight. The Normans passed amongst the Poitevins and the French, leaving behind a large number of dead and wounded; as they went, they killed and trampled over many men. They got a good distance away, showing no fatigue and travelling swiftly through pastureland and cornfields; in the morning, they went into a meadow in order to rest. They had brought with them horses and animals, which they had discovered in the nearby towns. They killed them and placed them all round them in a circle, skinning them down the middle and reversing their hides, which they covered in the animals' blood.* They surrounded themselves with their equipment and their men, having no other enclosure of walls or ditches. (1015–34)

In the morning, when the French barons realised that the Normans had left and escaped them and that they had experienced such a loss of their men that night, they set out and rode off in great anger, pursuing the Normans until they caught up with them. When they first drew near* them and were about to attack them, they were astonished. The horses came to a standstill; they moved back and the men diminished in number. The French threatened the Normans greatly and swore by the power of God that they would be dead and destroyed if they were to settle in that region. The Normans listened quietly and tolerated this; they sought food and ate and drank; when they had eaten, they rested and lay down. (1035–47)

The French turned away and left the Normans; they dispersed their men throughout the regions and were delighted that they had defeated the Normans. But the Normans did not remain in their beds. As soon as Rou had assembled all

---

[45] This story of the attack while the French were asleep is unique to Wace.

his men and cured the sick and the wounded, he launched a violent attack against the French, along with the Normans who had a great hatred of the French. They laid waste the entire country from Blois to Senlis, destroying the inhabitants and plundering their possessions. No burg remained to be knocked down, however well fortified, unless it was fully enclosed by walls and palisades. You would have seen a terrible slaughter of men; they had no more pity than a wolf for sheep, killing young and old, great and small. They turned wives into widows and sons into orphans and violated women in front of their husbands; no freeborn man would willingly put up with such shame. (1048–65)

The bishops of France and the good priests, the barons and the counts, the older and the younger men, saw the noble kingdom reduced to great shame; they begged for mercy from King Charles the Simple, asking him to give some thought to Christianity. They saw the burnt-out churches and the dead bodies, caused by the king's absence and his weakness; they saw the treachery and the cruelty of the Normans and of Rou, who had laid waste the kingdom. From Blois to Senlis there was not an acre of corn; merchants did not dare go to castle or city, peasants did not dare work the vineyards or the meadows. If this went on, they would have a terrible famine. As long as the war continued, they would never know plenty; let him make peace with the Normans, this evil had gone on too long. (1066–80)

The king saw the dismay of the barons and the people; he had grief in his heart and felt nothing but grief; he would gladly have made peace between them if he could:

'You must advise me loyally', he said, 'and you must help me when I need it most. I cannot bring justice to the kingdom by myself and cannot drive out Rou or the Normans by myself. I am a mere man of flesh and blood, I cannot struggle against everyone on my own. What can just one man do, and what can he accomplish if the men who should be helping him let him down? Good men make a king strong and fierce. I want to have peace with the Normans and I seek your advice about this; I do not want to let the people or the kingdom be destroyed. Listen to how I want to bring about reconciliation between myself and Rou. If Rou is willing to renounce and abandon paganism and be baptized as a Christian, and if he is willing to accept peace and cherish me, I will give him Gisla, one of my daughters, as his wife, and the land along the coast if he wishes to accept it. From where the Epte* flows, as far as Mont-Saint-Michel, there is scarcely any better land beneath the vault of heaven. From there we are accustomed to obtain honey in abundance; so let us be friends without arrogance and without gall.' (1081–1104)

'My lords', said King Charles, 'let Rou become my vassal and become a Christian, changing his faith and his name; let him not allow robbers or thieves in the land. I will give him a noble and comely wife and the land along the coast, as far as the Couesnon. At that point the land belonging to Berengar the Breton begins; he will have meat and fish in abundance, and boars, stags and other animals.'

'My lord', said the French, 'that is a noble gift. If he refuses this, he has a very cruel heart. Archbishop Franco, who is a gifted speaker, can take this message to him and we entrust it to him.' (1105–16)

Archbishop Franco was highly regarded for his wisdom. He was sent to Rou to carry the message and was well able to do so, as he knew many languages:

'Rou', he said, 'God wishes to increase your honour and your prowess. You have spent your life in hardship and wickedness and lived off plunder and the tears of others. You have destroyed and reduced many men to serfdom. You have caused many women to turn to prostitution out of poverty and you have stolen their castles and their rightful inheritances. You are not taking care of your soul, any more than a wild beast would, and you will go to Hell as your painful abode and be in permanent pain which is never alleviated. You have no pledge or guarantee of living a long life. Change your evil life and change your way of thinking: receive Christianity and do homage to the king. Learn to live in peace and abandon your anger. Do not destroy his land, for you are committing a great outrage. He has a very noble daughter, who is of high lineage, and he wishes to give her to you with a rich dowry, all the land along the coast from the Epte to the sea. You will be able to live off your revenues without plunder or theft and will have many good fortresses and many fine dwellings. Things can be better for your entire family. Give him a truce for three months without harming or damaging him. You will not have any need of sail or oar. To confirm this agreement I will give you good hostages. You will have no shame in taking a king's daughter as your wife.' (1117–43)

Rou heard what he said and it pleased him greatly; on the advice of his men he confirmed the truce. The agreement was good and each of them accepted it. At the agreed date, Rou gathered his men together and the king summoned all his barons to Saint-Clair. Rou was on this side of the Epte and the king on the other. Duke Robert, who wanted the peace, was with him. The matter was discussed until agreement was reached; Rou became the king's vassal and put his hands in his. When he was to kiss the king's foot, he did not deign to bend down. He put his hand down and raised the king's foot, bringing it up towards his mouth and thus turning the king over; everyone laughed a lot and the king picked himself up.[46] In everyone's presence he gave his daughter and Normandy to him; he wanted to add Flanders to it, but Rou refused; the land was poor, he said, and would never yield much.[47] He asked for Brittany and the king gave it to him, ordering Berengar and Alan to serve him; each of them swore fealty to him mendaciously. Then the king left and Rou went back home; Duke Robert, who took the lady, went with him. Franco, the archbishop, baptized Duke Rou; Duke Robert was his godfather and he named him Robert; when he was baptized, Rou married his wife, daughter of the King of France, who confirmed the peace. Duke Robert, who took the lady, went with him.[48] The joy was very great and it lasted for a long time. (1144–70)

---

[46] The story Wace tells about the kissing of the king's foot is different from that in both Dudo (p. 49) and the *GND*, where Rou has a knight do this for him because he never bows his knees before another man and never kisses the foot of a Frank (I, pp. 66–67). Such foot-kissing was normal practice at Caroliginan courts (see Christiansen, p. 196 n. 207).

[47] In Dudo (p. 49) Flanders is offered first and then rejected in favour of Normandy.

[48] The statement in v. 1186 is redundant in view of the identical statement in v. 1188.

Nine hundred and twelve years were completed and over since God was born of the Virgin in Bethlehem when Rou was reborn at the font in Rouen and reconciled with the King of France at Saint-Clair. When the marriage took place, the celebrations were splendid, as were the provisions which had been prepared; anyone who wanted to come to the wedding was very well looked after. Rou had begged and exhorted all his men so earnestly that he had them all baptized and honoured them greatly, giving many of them towns, castles and cities; to others he gave fields, revenues, mills and meadows, woodlands, estates and great inheritances.[49] In accordance with the quality of their service and their worthiness, and according to their nobility and their age, he retained and enfeoffed everyone in Normandy. He paid them all according to their wishes; he honoured and loved them very much and paid them all well, as they wished, because he had taken them away from their lands. (1171–89)

Rou had himself served honourably and richly; in his dwelling he lived a life of luxury and accepted gifts from others* whenever he was able to repay them. He loved peace and sought peace and had peace established: throughout Normandy he had it proclaimed and announced that no one should be bold enough to attack anyone else, burn houses or towns or rob or steal, nor should he wound, kill or put anyone else to death, nor beat or strike anyone, whether he be standing or on the ground, erect any ambush or betray anyone else. No one should dare to steal or allow anyone else to do so, for those who permit it must share the punishment of the thief;* the punishment of the one must affect the other. Anyone who commits an act of treachery will not, if he can be caught, avoid dishonour, however noble he may be; he will expiate his crime either by fire or by the gallows.[50] (1190–1205)

Rou imposed stern justice and was much talked of. Two knights from France, I do not know their names, went to Rouen for their pleasure and sport. I do not know who they were looking for, but I dare not blame them. The duchess* had them lodge with her. The duke came to see how things were; they were being very well looked after in the lodgings. The duke's knights heard about this and told their lord about it, not daring to conceal it; the duke had the French knights taken and brought to the market. In the presence of everyone at the market he had their heads chopped off. The duchess almost went out of her mind with grief and sorrow and for three or four days she would take no nourishment. King Charles himself wanted to quarrel with Rou over it, but the barons on both sides brought about peace between them. In this way the duke inspired fear in many; he had thieves and robbers torn limb from limb, or else he had their eyes put out, or he had them burnt to a cinder and their feet and hands cut off; he had each one punished according to his crime. In the burgs, the towns and the markets he had it proclaimed that anyone who wanted to plough or till the land would be at peace, come in peace and work the land in peace; he did not need to bother uncoupling the shares from his plough or hiding them beneath the furrow or taking them home for fear of thieves or robbery; he need not bother removing

---

[49] These rewards are more those of a twelfth-century than a tenth-century lord.
[50] The details of Rou's laws are unique to Wace.

ploughshare, blade or harness, for he would never find anyone who dared to touch them; if they were stolen from him and could not be found, the duke would give him the equivalent from his own money and the peasant would easily be able to buy a ploughshare and a blade. (1206–35)

In Longueville[51] there was a peasant who had his fine oxen and his ploughing team; he had a wife – I do not know whether he had any children – but the wife was somewhat light-fingered; she would take other people's property if the coast was clear. She went on foolishly practising this trade until she came to a bad and appropriate end. One day the peasant went out as he always did and came back home at meal time, leaving the harness, ploughshare and coulter on the plough; he did not want to remove anything, trusting to the peace and to the fact that, if he lost them, the duke would give them back to him. The peasant's wife, while he was eating, came to the plough, took the shares and hid them. When the peasant returned to the field and could not find the shares, he looked high and low for them; his wife waited patiently. He had his wife come to him and begged her earnestly, if she did not have his shares, to tell him who had them. The wife was greedy and she denied the charge; the peasant came to Rou and put in a claim for his ploughshares. Rou took pity on him and gave him five sous; he returned home with the money.

'May the person who got us this money be praised', said the wife. 'Now you have five sous and here are your ploughshares.' Then she leaned over towards him and pointed beneath the bench; she was a fool to steal and a fool to hide them. (1236–60)

It is true, God said so, and the matter is proven, that nothing is so well hidden that it will not eventually be revealed, and no act is so obscure that it will not be made known; each act of goodness must be rewarded and all crime must be paid for. The matter was so carefully investigated, so many questions were asked and the men in the region so badly tortured, either by fire or water, that the matter was uncovered; the crime could not be concealed for long. The peasant's wife was seized and taken to Duke Rou; captured and proven guilty, she confessed everything. Then Rou had the peasant seized and brought before him. When he was before him, he said:

'Do you know, tell me, whether your wife stole anything after she came to you,* and whether she is wont to be of bad faith?'

'Yes, my lord', he said, 'I must not lie to you.'

'By my faith', said Rou, 'I do not disbelieve you. With your own mouth you have decreed your own fate. You will be hanged with her; you have clearly explained why.' (1261–80)

'You yourself', said Rou, 'have pronounced sentence on yourself; the same law, the same punishment, the same suffering awaits you. Those who steal and who consent to it have the same sentence.' The wife was hanged and the husband as well. As a result of this affair and others, Rou was greatly feared. He lived for a very long time in honour and joy; he had no child by Gisla, who was his first

---

[51] In place of Longueville, Dudo (p. 52) and the *GND* (I, pp. 68–69) have Longpaon (now Darnétal, Seine-Maritime).

wife, and the lady died childless. Then Rou married Popa, whom he held thereafter for a long time. Longsword, her son, was a fine young man; he was tall and of high intelligence and could bear arms and had no fear them. On the advice of his men Rou made him his heir. He quickly summoned Berengar and Alan, to whom Brittany belonged, and the powerful Normans, giving so much to each of them and promising so much more that they became his son's vassal in true friendship; each man swore an oath of homage to William. (1281–98)

After Duke William had received the land and had the homage of the barons I have mentioned, Rou held the land for five years, keeping and establishing peace. He had the men in his land who had served him convert and devote themselves to doing God's service. Thus he came to his end, as a man who had grown old and was weakened by the toil and the hardships he had experienced; but his memory and his wits never left him. He lay sick in Rouen and ended his days in Rouen, leaving this mortal world like a good Christian; he had confessed properly and avowed his sins. In the church of Our Lady, on the southern side, the clerics and laymen buried his body; the tomb is there and the epitaph as well, which recounts his deeds and how he lived.[52] (1299–1313)

Here ends the story of Rou's exploits
and that of William Longsword, Duke of Normandy, begins

William Longsword was very tall; he was noble, handsome, very well formed and broad-shouldered with a slim waist, long, straight legs and broad hips. He had straightforward, open eyes and an amiable expression; but to his enemies he appeared very fierce and harsh. He had a fine nose, a fine mouth and fine speech; his face was not downcast or gloomy and he held his head high and had long hair.[53] He was as strong as a giant and exceptionally bold; anyone who waited for a blow from him had no chance of living. Lord Herbert of Senlis was a wealthy landowner; William took his daughter in rightful marriage. (1314–26)

For a long time the duke ruled Brittany and Normandy in peace; he conducted himself splendidly and led a very good life. Berengar and Alan were envious of him and had no interest in him or his companionship, not deigning to serve him or be in his power. Each of them openly broke faith with him and the duke took possession of their land in Brittany, destroying their castles and impoverishing the land. Poverty forced everyone to flee. Alain, who first embarked on this treachery, was driven out of Brittany, abandoning it to the duke completely. Showing sense and sagacity, Berengar made peace; never again did he commit an act of treachery towards William or his heir. Thereafter, he went to William's aid wherever he wanted it; anyone who chastises his friend must indeed use the rod. (1327–41)

The Duke of Normandy disinherited Alain because he had started the war against him and Alan crossed the sea when the duke pursued him. He remained in England until Æthelstan brought about a reconciliation; then they were good friends and loved each other. There was great peace throughout the land and no

---

[52] The reference to Rou's tomb and epitaph in the church of Our Lady is new information.
[53] The physical description of William Longsword is more detailed than in the *GND* (see I, pp. 76–77).

one waged war. But there was one man in the country who disturbed the peace; it distressed him that William had risen so high and that, through having taken a wife, he had made peace with the French. From this a war arose which brought about great misfortune; he who had everything lost and abandoned everything. (1342–53)

May anyone who can hear me pay attention and listen to me; I am not telling tales and do not intend to tell tales. Those in Fécamp are my witnesses. This story is a great one, long and difficult to translate, but my skill could be given encouragement; work is very sweet to me when I expect to profit from it. I must continue with the Normans and their history. In my youth I heard in the songs of the *jongleurs* that in the olden days William had Osmund blinded, Count Riulf's eyes put out, Anquetil the brave treacherously killed and Balzo from Spain placed in custody;[54] I know nothing of this and can find out nothing about it. When I have no evidence, I do not wish to say anything about it. I have heard of the death of Anquetil, who was killed, as we know; I do not want to exonerate* anyone, but I do not know how he was killed, nor who should be blamed. I do not wish to assert lies instead of the truth, nor do I wish to conceal the truth if I know it. Riulf was a Norman who was very much feared; he was a wise and courageous count[55] who was good at doing harm and skilled at starting a war and at disturbing the peace. He was Count of the Cotentin between the Vire and the sea, and he envied William, whom he saw to be so successful; he was upset to see him gaining power over his neighbours and he wanted to see the French shamed.[56] He was afraid that he would cease loving the Normans in favour of the French; it upset him that William was unwilling to follow his advice. On other pretexts he was able to cite, he caused all the barons in his land to quarrel with the duke. He made everyone hate him and renounce their allegiance to him and he caused everyone to break their homage and their fealty.[57] (1354–85)

Riulf was old and cunning and of good family. He had an abundance of wealth, relatives and vassals; he envied William who had risen so high. It upset him that William was not afraid of him and had no affection for him; he thought that William had contempt for him because of the French. If there was any other reason for it, I do not know the truth of it. For one reason or another he conceived a great hatred for William; things would never go right for him, he said, until he had killed him, driven him from the land or disinherited him completely. Riulf was arrogant and displayed enormous pride; he was absolutely brimming with

---

[54] V. 1365 is clearly corrupt and the meaning of the phrase 'o un escu garder' is uncertain.

[55] The term *quens* 'count' in v. 1373 is perhaps an error for *cointe* 'clever, elegant'.

[56] Holden (vol. 3, p. 187) suggests that the meaning of this line is diametrically opposed to what is required. He cites possible alternatives and suggests that *Franceis* should be replaced by *Normanz*, so that the line would indicate that Riulf was upset when he saw the Normans being shamed. However, Riulf may be seen as concerned that William was competing too much with other Normans rather than devoting time to shaming the French.

[57] The information given in this passage concerning witnesses and *jongleurs* is new. The identity of Ormont, Anquetil and Balzo remains unkown. Riulf is said to be a Norman, i.e. a Viking, but Dudo (pp. 64–68) and the *GND* (I, pp. 78–79, 92–93) do not give his ethnicity. His name would suggest that he was French. There is no reference in Dudo or the *GND* to his being Count of the Cotentin between the Vire and the sea.

evil and cruelty; he hated William bitterly and made his hatred clear to him. Through his devilish deceit and his falsehood he made all William's barons quarrel with him, and he destroyed, seized and laid waste the country. I do not know how he became so powerful, but he went in search of William until he found him in Rouen. He crossed the Seine and besieged the city. He was there I do not know how many days with a large number of his men. He thought he could do whatever he liked with William and that he could rule Normandy during his lifetime. William saw that the people had gone over to Riulf's side completely and he saw himself surrounded by his own men. On Riulf's advice they had broken faith with him; he was not even sure of his beloved daughter.[58] William, Rou's son, was very fearful; he had only three hundred armed men, some Norman, some French, apart from the squires and the burgesses. Anslech was on William's side and also Bernard the Dane and Botho of Bayeux, Count of the Bessin; of the barons in his land the duke had only these three. Botho was his tutor, a very brave and courtly man. They would not have failed the duke whether it meant loss or gain; in order to protect their lord, they would without hesitation let themselves suffer blows to the body or burn in Greek fire.[59] (1386–1420)

William Longsword was very saddened by this; his men had not kept their oath or their fealty and had made an alliance with Riulf against him. He was distressed that he lacked the strength and the power to take vengeance on any of them. He was afraid of Riulf because of their great treachery and said he intended to take flight and go to France.

'William', said Botho, 'these are very shameful words. You have not yet struck a blow with sword or lance, yet you wish to flee. What you have said is very foolish. Fight with your men, be confident. They have perjured themselves against you and you will win the day without fail.'

'Botho', said William, 'I do not dare fight, for against one of my men Riulf has four. I am finished if he can capture me or strike me down.'

'You are a coward', said Botho, 'by Saint Fiacre![60] By the faith I owe to the Holy Father's son, if anyone could do so, someone should certainly give you a beating. You do not dare arm yourself or don your armour.'

'Have mercy', said William, 'Riulf has besieged me. With him are those who have betrayed me, against whom I have committed no crime. They all have a mortal hatred for me and have caught me here unawares. I cannot maintain this land on my own; I could not survive, they are too numerous. I want to go to France and am putting the land at their disposal.' (1421–45)

Then Bernard replied:

'We will never come with you. We have wronged them too much and will soon pay for it. Since we have no lord, we will go to Denmark. If we lose this land, we

---

[58] The meaning of v. 1410 is uncertain. There is no reference to Riulf's daughter in other sources.

[59] On Greek fire see J. R. Partington, *A History of Greek Fire and Gunpowder* (Baltimore: Johns Hopkins Press, 1998).

[60] Fiacre (d. *c.* 670) was an Irish hermit whose cult is associated with France rather than Ireland. He came to Meaux, was given land in Breuil by the bishop, and settled there. He is a patron of horticulturists and sufferers from venereal disease. He has given his name to the *fiacre*, because these four-wheeled cabs plied their trade from the hotel Saint-Fiacre in Paris.

will not seek another. If you do not dare fight and engage in battle, go to France where you will live a worthless life. There is no timorous woman who is not better than you. You wretch, are you afraid that the Lord God is failing you? Rou conquered this land as a brave and bold man; you do not give the impression that you are his son. So far you have not been touched or attacked, yet you wish to flee like someone who is overwhelmed. You can see your enemies who have frightened you; they have not yet touched you and already you are dying of fright. A brave man will be greatly shamed by serving a bad lord; one will never gain honour from serving a weakling.'

'Bernard', said William, 'I have listened to you carefully. You have reproached and insulted me a great deal. You will soon see me strike like a madman. I will be very grateful to anyone who helps me now.'

'Friend Botho, and you, my friend Bernard', he said, 'do not think I am weak or cowardly. I wanted to test you and was speaking cunningly, for I intend to fight and I am keen to strike.' (1446–69)

Then they all ran to arm themselves. When they had done so, there were three hundred of them. They attacked Riulf and his knights fiercely; William struck fine blows, and so did Bernard. William was armed and he attacked his enemies, shouting 'God help!'. He attacked them violently. You could never have seen a man who struck greater blows; nothing could protect anyone he attacked with his sword. William went about striking like an enraged ox; anyone he struck with his sword never knew joy again. The three hundred struck good blows with their lances and spears, pushing back and harming the enemy greatly; they all struck well and with goodwill. Riulf saw many of his men lying in the fields and he saw William's men displaying great ferocity. He took hold of his reins, turned his horse and, spurring it, rode until he was hidden in a wood; he threw off his hauberk, his shield and his lance. Riulf was followed by I do not know how many of the duke's knights; they thought they could capture Riulf, but the wood robbed them of him. Who cares if they did not capture him, for Riulf had fled; he was not seen again and never came back. (1470–91)

Many men men died on the battlefield in sorrow and shame. So many drowned in the Seine that they could not be counted; the water carried the bodies away on the rising tide. Then everyone talked a great deal about Count William. Of the three hundred knights William led, not a single one was left there dead, thanks to God's power; he brought them all back alive when he returned. When he got back, he met a messenger who told him news which caused him to speed up his journey; the victory had filled him with joy, but his joy was doubled. The messenger came straight towards William and said in everyone's hearing that he had come from Fécamp; with his beloved Sprota* he had a new son. The duke replied: 'May God be thanked.' The duke asked for the Bishop of Bayeux, whose name was Henry, and Boton, a baron who was a friend of his, and spoke to them. He sent these two men to Fécamp together, the bishop to baptize the child and Lord Boton to see the child and watch over him. The duke, who was much loved, was in Rouen, causing his enemies to fear him greatly. There was great joy in Rouen when Riulf was defeated and great joy at the birth of the child. The place was given the name Pré de Bataille and the name still survives; it has not been changed since. (1492–1517)

The duke ruled Normandy and had Brittany in his power; peace was properly maintained everywhere and anyone who wanted to do so could cultivate his land. No one, however rich or poor, who destroyed anyone else's dwelling, remained safe and sound if he could be caught. Because of Riulf, over whom he scored such a fine victory with three hundred armed men, William acquired great fame. His reputation was greatly enhanced and the memory of it survived; he was praised and feared, as history tells us. (1518–25)

Æthelstan of England became aware of the duke's acts of valour. He had a nephew, his sister's son, whom many people called Louis Outremer because he was brought up overseas for a long time. He was the son of Charles, King of France, but because of hatred neither the dukes nor the nobles were willing to accept him. The king sent word to the duke that for love of him he should persuade the French that his nephew should have the domain and that they should recognise him as lord and heir. The duke spoke about this to Hugh of Paris and to Lord Herbert, who was his close friend; he secretly sought the views of the counts, abbots and bishops of the land and of the other barons. He begged some and made promises to others until they retained Louis as their lord; but they later regretted it, for he treated them very cruelly. (1526–41)

All those in the marches were subject to the duke; his aims were peace and the end of warfare. No one was bold enough to destroy even a path; everyone, near and far, feared him greatly. There was no need to seek safe-conduct through the land, for many people feared him and everyone loved him. In Lyons [Lyons-la-Forêt], one year in September, he held during the rutting season a great festival and a great court with much celebration. Many foreigners were there and many who had been raised there. William of Poitiers, who was brave and bold, Hugh, a duke from France, and Herbert of Senlis, came to this celebration and each was well served. Hugh was Duke of Paris and had great power and Herbert of France was the prince of chivalry; both were very noble men of great wealth. They came to William in good spirits. Joyfully and merrily and to witness the hunting, they came to Duke William to enjoy themselves and also to talk to the Normans, advise them, make peace with the duke and become their allies. William was delighted by their arrival; he received them joyfully and honourably. They remained together for I do not know how long, greatly honoured and richly served. (1542–65)

The Duke of Normandy had a sister who was a fully-grown girl but without a husband. William of Poitiers fell in love with her and her brother gave her to him; he made her his wife. William of Poitiers spoke to the Norman duke:

'We will be friends', he said, 'from this time onwards. You have a sister and I am asking for her as my wife.' The duke replied and said with a smile:

'My lord Count of Poitiers, would it be fitting for me to give my sister, who is so beautiful and so worthy, to a Poitevin? People tell me that they are mean and cowardly and not true warriors.[61] No one of them can lose any blood and remain

---

[61] It seems that in the Middle Ages Poitevins had a poor reputation. See P. Meyvaert, ' "Rainaldus est malus scriptor Francigenus": Voicing National Antipathy in the Middle Ages', *Speculum*, 66 (1991), 743–63 (p. 748).

on his feet; either the fever takes him or he takes to his heels.' The count blushed and apparently felt ashamed. The duke addressed him, saying:

'I will gladly do whatever you wish. I was just testing you and making a joke.' The lady who was Rou's daughter was called Gerloc;[62] there was scarcely a more beautiful maiden in Poitou or in the whole of Normandy from Mont-Saint-Michel to Eu; the man who was Count of Anjou willingly took her as his wife. (1566–87)

In France there was a king by the name of Louis; he was the son of the King of France and a very noble man. But neither counts nor barons had much respect for him; everyone with a fortress waged war against him. To a man the barons in the land hated him. They had no respect or love for him; they laid waste his lands and destroyed his towns, wanting to disinherit him completely and drive him out. They all opposed him and did not love him; they wanted to drive him out of the kingdom and out of the country. He found no one in the land who could help him; if he wished to remain there, he was obliged to find a means of doing so. (1588–99)

The King of France sent a letter and a messenger to Henry the German,[63] a king of great power, asking him to come and enter into friendship and alliance with him; a friendship without deceit, which would never be severed, would be assured between them by means of an agreement, so that neither of them need have any fear or suspicion of the other. King Henry sent back word that he would not do anything of the sort and would never trust him, whatever oath he might make, unless William, Duke of the Normans, was present as well; through him, however, he would do whatever he required. When King Louis heard what the king was saying to him, he went to Rouen and visited William; he asked him humbly to undertake this for him and do what was required in respect of King Henry, so that he would not lose Henry's aid because of his refusal. The duke promised him his help to the best of his ability. (1600–15)

Then Louis was in Rouen for I do not know how many days and he was, I believe, richly served; William looked after him like someone who had never known a care in the world. He summoned the finest men from all Normandy and also the finest from Brittany. Henry sent Cono,[64] a man of very good family, to the Duke of Normandy, to ensure that he would have a good hostage and have nothing to fear on his journey, and so that he would suffer no harm either on his way to his court or leaving it. Cono came to William, who was in the prime of life, spoke to him and relayed his message well; he saw the duke, the court and the great barons and thought him to be very courtly, noble and wise. Cono could speak German and Norman, and from his appearance and his words he seemed to be a man of worth. The duke had him served and honoured greatly; he did not have him held in Rouen as a hostage, rather he had him taken to many places in

---

[62] The form in the manuscript here is Elborc; in the *Chronique Ascendante*, v. 299, the form Gerbout is used.

[63] Henry I, known as the Fowler.

[64] Cono remains unidentified; he is mentioned by Dudo (pp. 71–74), but omitted by the *GND*. Clearly Wace consulted Dudo independently of his material in the *GND*, as the basis of the discussion between Cono and Henry is found in Dudo.

his land and shown his woods, rivers and castles; when it was time for him to depart, he gave him a large number of trinkets and fine gifts. (1616–37)

The Duke of Normandy left his land with five hundred men in helmets in his company, all esteemed knights and all well equipped; on his part King Louis had a large number of knights. They both set out along the Meuse, where King Henry had taken up quarters.[65] He had not come with just a few men; he was a very powerful man and had many barons with him. The French told our men not to join them; during the day they should remain on their own and ride on their own; they should remain on their own at night and camp on their own, so that no strife or quarrels would ensue. You would have seen a great throng rushing to their lodgings, men-at-arms and squires seizing and occupying lodgings and driving the horses out of the stables.* Neither stocks nor halters could hold them; with pickaxes and pieces of wood they made them take flight. When the duke heard the noise, he felt nothing but anger; he sent his sword there and made them disperse. (1638–56)

A quarrel had broken out amongst the squires. The duke sent his sword there through one of his barons; as soon as the man carrying it had brandished it above the Normans, there was no one who dared to strike or deal blows. Cono spoke to Henry, King of Germany; he was full of praise for William whom he had served:

'My lord', said Cono, 'upon my word, I have never seen such a worthy man. He has honoured and cherished me greatly for love of you.' The king said to him:

'May he be warmly thanked. He should indeed act honourably, as he was raised by a worthy man.' Then the king took the duke, kissed him and made him very welcome; he offered him jewels, trinkets and gifts.

'Upon my word, my lord', said Cono, 'I have never seen a household like Duke William's, nor one so well equipped, with such delightful land or such well-bred people. His men are always ready to ride out and fight.' (1657–72)

The Duke of Normandy was wise and courtly; all the Germans[66] honoured him greatly. They made him spokesman between the kings and he made them come to an agreement; this upset the French. He carried the terms of the agreement between the kings and they accepted it as he dictated it, that neither would fail the other as long as they lived. None of the rich barons wanted this peace, yet they all guaranteed it with hostages and committed themselves to it on oath. Duke Hugh the Great, who was lord of Paris, and Herbert of Senlis were very distressed by this. You would have seen many people grumbling and contorted with anger; they could not and dared not disturb or oppose the agreement. (1673–85)

Louis returned home with all his barons; he had accomplished his business as he had set out to do. When he entered his land, he met a man-at-arms who told him that the queen had had a child. The king praised God, then spoke to the Norman:

---

[65] In v. 1642 the term *amedeuls*, translated here as 'both', must represent in the original a place name, which remains unidentified. See Holden's note to v. 1642 (vol. 3, p. 189).

[66] The text refers to 'Alemanz et Tyois'; both these terms are used to designate Germanic peoples.

'Lord duke', said the king, 'you will come to Laon. The queen has a son and you will raise him at the font and be his god-parent, giving him the name Lothar.'

'My lord', said the duke, 'let it be just as you wish.' The duke raised the child at the font and gave him the name Lothar. The king wanted to give him and offer him many rich gifts, but the duke refused to take the slightest thing. He went back to his own home in Rouen and was joyfully welcomed with a procession; the vavassors and barons returned to their lands. (1686–1700)

The duke came with his household to Jumièges to see the abbey which he had built and which Hasting, the scoundrel, had destroyed and laid waste. Lord Martin, the good abbot, told him everything; the duke saw the abbey and was very pleased and happy with it. Then he told the abbot that he had come to enter orders; he wanted to become a monk and change his life in order to punish his flesh and save his soul. He had done a great deal of harm in the world and had much to make amends for.

'My lord duke', said Martin, 'why have you said this? You are a very powerful man, may God and faith help me; I would not advise you to take on any other habit than that of your father, whoever might contradict me. Do what is right by great and small, do not allow the strong to disinherit the weak or the poor to spend a long time appealing to you about their rights. Mind you do no wrong and in this way you will avoid getting caught up in sin; this is what religion is, as we discover in scripture. Behave better than a monk who lives in this cloister.' (1701–19)

'My lord abbot', said the duke, 'I want to become a monk. I wish to abandon completely the futility of this world. I would like to expiate the sins I have committed, for a man who lives in the world cannot abstain from sin, swearing, trickery, lying, drinking, eating, repudiation[67] and falsehood, and a large number of other evils which make me afraid of dying.'

'My lord duke', said the abbot, 'if you please, you are wrong. May you never become a monk who has entered or taken orders; you are a young man and can live for a long time. We will be monks on your behalf and you will support us. Maintain rightful justice, look after the Holy Church, love the poor and defend the country.'

'I would rather be a monk', he said, 'if you advise it.'

'Mind you say nothing more about it', said Martin, 'for I can see and am well aware that great harm would come from it. Who would have your land and who would defend it?'

'Richard, my son', he said, 'if God allows it.'

'He is too young', said Martin, 'he would not be competent to do so. Those who now serve and fear you would wage war on you.' (1720–40)

Martin told the duke clearly that he should not think of becoming a monk or of entering the cloister, rather he should support his men and look after his land, until his son Richard was grown up and was better placed. Then he begged him

---

[67] The interpretation 'repudiation' for *neer* in v. 1725 is by no means certain.

earnestly to take a little food, to accept their charity[68] and dine with them for a short while. But the duke refused to take dinner or other refreshment. He refused to stay and dine with the abbot, even though the whole assembly begged him to do so. Before he reached Rouen, he became so ill that he never tasted any other food that day; he was sick for a long time before regaining health. He was ill, it is said, because he had refused the entreaties of the monks to accept their charity. He summoned the finest of his barons to come before him. (1741–54)

He disclosed his thoughts to a number of his men, saying that he wanted to take holy orders at Jumièges; they all thought this was folly and madness.

'Richard, my son', he said, 'who belongs to my lineage, is my heir, whatever happens to me;* you will become his vassals and be acting very wisely, because Richard is very brave and has great courage.' Richard could speak Danish and Norman. He had reddish hair and a bright, open face; he knew how to take his own and other people's property and give them away. He could read a charter and distinguish its sections; his father had had him well educated and trained.[69] He could defeat an opponent at chess and backgammon, and he knew how to feed a bird, how to let it go and how to carry it. He was skilled in woodland pursuits, shooting and hunting; he knew how to cover and protect himself with a shield, how to advance his right foot and double his blows when fencing. He could turn on his heels, withdraw and strike,[70] jump to the left and thrust[71] quickly; this is a harmful blow if not parried. But one should not linger over this for long. (1755–75)

Between King Svein and his father Harold there was a great quarrel over the possession of Denmark. Harold* should have been king, but Svein would not permit this. So his father, who was unable to remain, went away; he had to go, for his son was driving him away. Harold came to Normandy; he did not know where else to go. He had left Denmark because of his son and came to William with sixty ships. Harold had a large number of men, lances and shields and William received them all with honour. He equipped and clothed them well, honouring and feeding them properly. William was a noble man of very great valour; he retained Harold and his household with great honour, giving them the Cotentin as a place to live and stay until he had peace and his own domain from his son. (1776–91)

Arnulf, a very powerful count of Flanders at that time, captured Herluin's castle at Montreuil; he had not issued a challenge and found the castle unprepared. Herluin could not recapture it, neither did Arnulf surrender it. Count Arnulf was widely known as a traitor because of this, but he never abandoned the castle because of any censure. Herluin was distressed at the prospect of losing the castle and he went to Duke Hugh, who lived in Paris; he held this castle from

---

[68] The term *charité*, translated here simply as 'charity', would imply the taking of a light meal offered to visitors to a monastery.

[69] Rather than his ability to read charters, clearly anachronistic, Dudo stresses Richard's religious education (p. 105). But like Wace, Dudo does mention his hawking ability (p. 104).

[70] The verb *noxer* in v. 1772 seems to be an error.

[71] *Treget* in v. 1773 is a fencing term indicating a certain type of thrust.

him as his vassal. He complained that Arnulf was taking Montreuil from him and, unless it were with his aid, he would never get it back. Duke Hugh told him he would not get involved in this matter; Arnulf was one of his friends and he would not quarrel with him. But if he found help elsewhere, this would not upset him. (1792–1805)

Herluin departed and went to the King of France, begging him humbly and explaining the urgent matter to him. The king replied that he would do nothing, for Arnulf was a vassal of his in respect of all his lands; he was strong and powerful and he would never quarrel with him over this.

'If you find help elsewhere, that will not upset me.' Herluin was upset that he was losing Montreuil, which he had inherited from his father and grandfather; he would rather have fallen into the depths of the abyss, and if he could not recover the castle he would be very distressed. When he had completely failed in France as far as his lords were concerned, Herluin went to the Duke of Normandy for help and support; he did not know where else to go. He begged the duke for mercy and help against his persecutors, against Arnulf of Flanders, who had been the source of this misfortune. He fell at the duke's feet with great entreaties and tears, as if he had witnessed there the death of all his ancestors. The complaint he made brought tears to the eyes of many people. (1806–23)

Herluin made his complaint and, in tears, asked for mercy. The duke, who listened to his pleading, took pity on him:

'Herluin', said the duke, 'you have come here for aid. What is Hugh the Great doing? Has he abandoned you? You are his vassal, has he conceived some hatred for you? What does Louis say, whom you have served so much? Have you asked them?' He replied:

'Yes, my lord, upon my word, but they have failed me. They do not wish to quarrel with him, for they are his friends.'

'Would it upset them if I helped you?'

'No, my lord, upon my word, I heard them say so.'

With great humility Herluin entreated the duke. The duke was noble and took pity on Herluin. He sent at once for Normans and Bretons, telling them all to come to* him on horse or on foot. They came as soon as they could, without any attempt at delay; they were all equipped to undertake this task. Duke William rode hard with his men and besieged Montreuil in the Ponthieu. (1824–42)

The Flemish who were inside refused to come out. They kept the gates closed, not deigning to open them; they thought they could defend themselves and hold on by force. The duke attacked them violently; weapons were hurled and thrown and arrows shot with great ferocity. Then the duke had the men from the Cotentin come forward; they were to strike blows before all the others.

'Men of the Cotentin', said the duke, 'you have a fine reputation. I have no men in my land valiant and daring enough to stand up to you or to turn their backs on you. Bring me the stake with which the castle is closed. The sooner you have attacked it, the sooner you will have rest.' They darted forward to the ditch with pickaxes and crooks,* knocking down the palisade as if it were mere reeds; anyone caught beneath it had his bones badly crushed. The duke took Montreuil very quickly; he had his men take quarters in the town and the burg.[72] He himself took up residence in the highest hall. One day he was sitting eating with great honour and Herluin was on his feet, serving him joyfully, when the duke looked at him and said amiably:

'Have your castle, Herluin, I give it back to you. But mind you look after it more diligently.'

'My lord', said Herluin, 'I will take nothing. Let the castle be yours, and whatever belongs to it.' (1843–67)

'My lord', said Herluin, 'I owe you a great reward. You have suffered great hardship for God and for me. Keep the castle, I give it and grant it to you. I could not hold it, for I do not have the wherewithal to do so. The Flemish are my neighbours and they maintain faith with me no better than faithless Saracens would do. The more the Flemish swear oaths to me, the more I mistrust them.'

'Do not be afraid', said the duke, 'I will give some thought to it. I will make the castle such, and place such equipment in it, that you will easily be able to defend it from both count and king, and I will not be so far away that, if I heard from you, I could not help you or send you help.' The duke gave Herluin assurances. He enclosed Montreuil properly, fortified it and strengthened it with iron-tipped beams, walls and a ditch; then he provided it with men, arms and wheat. He spent a long time there in joy and delight, then returned to his city of Rouen; those in his borderlands feared and respected him greatly. (1868–86)

The Duke of Normandy was a very noble man; he conducted himself splendidly and lived a very good life. He would have remained as a monk in the abbey of Jumièges if his companions had advised it. Arnulf, Count of Flanders, was very envious of him. Since he could not avenge himself with his own knights, having lost Montreuil thanks to him and his aid, he would commit some act of treason, no matter who rebuked him later. Arnulf hated the duke, which does not surprise me, but I am surprised that he committed such a crime. He preferred to be dishonoured rather than fail to kill him and he committed a wretched act of treason which caused him much shame. (1887–98)

Arnulf sent word to the duke that he wished to be reconciled with him; he had gout in his feet and could not wage war. If he rode far, it would cause him great pain, so he would go as far as Amiens and wait for him there. If either of them had wronged the other, he would gladly do right by him; let them have such peace between them that it would remain secure for all time, for neither would wage war on the other for any reason. Herluin, who would also be there when peace was agreed,[73] came and told the duke that he would not advise him to go to the Flemish, for he would never trust any of them. The duke replied that he feared no harm; he would go to the count, speak with him and hear what he had to say. He could well be planning something he would be unable to carry out, and he would be so well guarded on his journey that he would have absolutely no fear of them.

---

[72] To *eu boiz* 'in woodland' Holden prefers the reading *eu borc* 'in the burg'. The term *borc* was used in Old French either to designate a town or that part of a town which lies outside the castle walls and is inhabited by the *borgois*. See G.S. Burgess and G. Gaughan, 'The Role of the *borgois* in Old French Literature', *Zeitschrift für romanische Philologie*, 108 (1991), 103–20.

[73] As it stands, v. 1906 seems to represent two lines in the original. See Holden's note, vol. 3, p. 79.

The Duke of Normandy was on his way to Amiens when Arnulf sent him word that he was in Corbie, but would come to him on the Somme at Picquigny; the region was beautiful and this was a good place to meet. On the Somme there was an island, for it was surrounded by water; anyone wishing to reach it had to have a boat. The man who was bent on treason gave much thought as to how and where he would deceive him as soon as possible. The duke went there; I very much fear that he was acting foolishly. (1899–1921)

Count Arnulf was very concerned and worried about how to kill William without killing any of his companions. He landed on the island with four of his friends; Balzo, the foolish and cruel traitor, was there, the evil Riulf, and also Robert and Henry; they were aware of the decision Arnulf had taken.[74] Balzo was the nephew of Riulf, a man of great age whom William had defeated when he besieged Rouen. O God, why did William come amongst his enemies? They will be very reluctant to let him leave. (1922–31)

Duke William entered a boat with twelve of his closest companions; he crossed over to the island on the other side of the river. The others rose to meet him and he greeted them. Arnulf came to meet him, limping, disfigured; two of his knights supported him.* What you hear me describe to you was nothing other than deceit. They took each other by the hand and sat side by side. O God! How ignorant the duke was of their intentions and their thoughts! The parley was paid for very dearly; if the duke had left at the earliest opportunity, he would have been saved.

'My lord duke', said Arnulf, a man of very arrogant disposition, 'if God allows me to take either wine or bread, I am very anxious both morning and night to have your love until the Day of Judgement. I shall not live long and my heart is not strong. I pardon you for the earlier crime, that of Herluin, my close neighbour; from now on, if you please, I want to be at your service. Let there not be a long discussion of this and let us not behave badly. Let us be loyal to each other, secure and steadfast.' (1932–52)

Peace was concluded between Arnulf and the duke. On both sides their companions agreed to it; each one pledged and swore it by his hand. If any crime were to occur, which caused the one to hate the other, the matter would be recounted before the judges and properly set to right by their judgement. The good love should be firmly maintained and protected so that at no time would there be any quarrel between them.* O God, what a wretched peace! How briefly it lasted. Through this peace William Longsword was murdered; it did not survive intact for a day or an hour. Arnulf was deceitful and very treacherous. He granted William a tribute for his land in order to gain his peace and friendship securely; if he survived him, he would be heir to his fief. When it was time to depart and the duke took his leave, he came to the boat. Hear what crime was committed! The boat was already fully loaded with himself and his companions when Balzo came running after him with three companions. (1953–71)

---

[74] The names of the four assassins, Balzo, Riulf, Robert and Henry, are mentioned by Dudo (p. 83) and in the *GND* (I, pp. 92–93).

'My lord duke', said Balzo, 'come back here to us and let your men cross. The boat will come back. My lord wants to tell you something very urgent, but he forgot all about it because of the other things being discussed. It is the main reason why he made the peace. Come and speak with him; you will soon be able to go back.' The duke jumped out and the boat made the crossing; the peace had been sworn and he was not afraid. Alas, what treachery! O God, why did he go back? Balzo raised his sword, which he was carrying beneath the skins he was wearing, and gave him such a blow on the head that it brained him completely; the other three struck him and the duke staggered. When they had killed him and he was still and silent, they went back and Arnulf got ready quickly; they got on board their boat and crossed to the other side. If you had seen how the Normans yelled and shouted, looking at the traitors who had killed their lord. They almost went out of their minds* since they could not help him. The Flemish on the other side, who were laughing and joking, were rebuking them because of Montreuil and insulting Herluin; the Normans threatened them and made a mortal challenge to them. They called them traitors and cursed them in God's name. They did not dare enter the water, not trusting the boat, but they challenged them to join battle immediately.* (1972–95)

The Normans and Bretons, who were on the bank, were yelling; they could see the traitors – may God curse them – who had killed their lord and were getting away in safety; they could not get near them and were beside themselves with grief. They could not cross the Somme; there was no path or bridge. They found the way closed and the channel deep; there was only one channel[75] and no boat or lighter. They were almost demented with grief that they were not on the other side of the river; they would gladly have joined battle. O God, alas, what grief they displayed! Filled with anguish, each man tore and pulled at his hair. As soon as the Normans could get over to the island, they brought William, their lord, back to Rouen. From the end of his belt they detached a key . . . ,[76] and they removed from him his monk's hood, shirt and habit, an entire monk's outfit which they gave to a poor man; there was no other treasure and they found nothing else. Nine hundred and sixty-six years had elapsed since the birth of Jesus, as the clerics measured it, when the duke was killed and the Normans buried him. They took their lord to the Church of Our Lady; the body still lies there and his deeds are still visible.[77] (1996–2016)

Here ends the story of William Longsword, and that of his son, Richard of Normandy, begins

The Bretons displayed great sorrow, as did the Normans, but whoever displayed sorrow or shed tears, whoever mourned the duke and whoever felt distraught, Richard, William's son, displayed the greatest sorrow, and it was right that he

---

[75] Rather than *chanel* 'channel' the correct reading here may be *chaland* 'a flat boat used for transporting goods'.

[76] There seems to be a lacuna in the text here, which would convey the discovery of a chest containing the objects later mentioned.

[77] William's burial at Saint Mary's church in Rouen is new information.

should do so because no one lost as much as he did. The great service which the
duke had performed for the king on many occasions in his lifetime was of no
use to him; the great service rendered by the father did not benefit the child.
The Normans and the Bretons buried the duke. The strongest men in Brittany,
whose names I do not know, did not act like traitors. They saw Richard and his
companions weeping and called to the Normans, summoning them all:

'Since we have lost this man, we will remedy the situation through Richard.
Richard is William's son, we should not doubt it for a moment; he very much
resembles his father in his ways and his appearance. We were his father's vassals,
let us be his son's vassals. We supported the father, so let us support the son; as
long as we can put on our spurs, he will not lose any land, even the distance one
can throw a stick, providing he defends us and we are able to do so.' Then Richard
received the barons' fealty.[78] (2017–38)

Richard had in his power Normandy and Brittany, which his father, the
duke, had ruled with great joy during his lifetime. He did not break up his father's
followers; anyone his father had cherished he cherished even more. Lord Bernard
the Dane had the stewardship, the lands, the revenues and the other possessions.
Richard sent him away accompanied by many barons and provided him with
a very fine body of knights. In Richard's hands justice was not weakened. He kept
control over the barons and punished wrongdoers; no one dared steal or rob. No
one attacked or opposed others without losing, if he could be caught, a limb or
his life. (2039–51)

When King Louis, who was in France, heard that Arnulf the Fleming had
betrayed the duke and that on his advice Balzo had murdered him, he was
dismayed, he said, and felt great shame; but later he acted in such a way that no
one believed this. With the large army he had raised he came to Normandy and
was gladly received in Rouen by the Normans. They thought he was mourning
the death of his friend, who had supported him and served him with a large
number of men. The king came to Rouen, entered the city and took up splendid
quarters; he asked for Richard, and Osmund brought him; the child came to the
king and the king kissed him. O God, why did he kiss him when he did not keep
faith with him? He greeted him with his mouth, but there were different thoughts
in his heart. He said how grateful he was to his father and how much he missed
him. That night he retained Richard, refusing to let him leave, and he did the
same the next day and kept him for a third day. When Osmund realised this, he
was very alarmed and told Bernard the Dane everything in secret; Bernard told
the burgesses and all the knights he could find in the town what he wanted. Then
he came to the king and spoke of one thing and another; their thoughts differed,
but each of them kept them to himself. (2052–75)

---

[78] This passage presents a positive view of the Bretons, something which is by no means unusual
throughout the *Rou*. Wace was clearly a little supicious of the Bretons' liking for gain (e.g. III,
vv. 2703, 10876–78), and on one occasion he describes them as 'fiere e grifaigne' ('arrogant and
violent', III, v. 8691). But, overall, perhaps mindful of the sympathy shown towards them by
Henry II, he admired their sense of independence and displayed gratitude towards them for
supporting the Normans on a number of occasions. See H.-E. Keller, 'Wace et les Bretons'.

The news spread all over the town that the king was holding Richard prisoner and keeping him hidden. All the Bretons and the Normans, knights and burgesses, villeins and peasants, were very upset; they ran to their arms and seized them at once, some an axe, some a pike, some a sharp sword. You would have seen new weapons and old being drawn, whatever they could get their hands on; they did not spend long searching. They threatened Louis and his men repeatedly and there was such noise in the streets that you would not have heard God's thunder. Suddenly the town was in an uproar, with everyone yelling loudly that if the king did not give the child back to them quickly he would never again betray a lord or a servant. The burgesses and other common people made a tremendous noise, even women of slight build, the old women and the white-haired crones, with sticks, stakes, bars and clubs; all of them in their dishevelled state went searching around the streets and they were all running straight to the king's quarters. They were not silent when it came to threatening the king and asked insistently where he was; if their advice had been followed, the dwellings where he was would soon have been demolished. They quickly reached the doors of the dwellings and would have stormed in without asking permission.* But when those within became aware of them, they barred the doors and remained inside. (2076–2100)

The king heard the commotion in the city.[79] He summoned his men-at-arms and asked them:

'What is the matter with these people who are shouting? Who has frightened them so? Is there a fire or an affray? Has someone been killed?' Those who knew the answer said:

'Their thoughts are entirely different. If they can get their hands on you, they will soon have killed you.'

'Why?' said Louis. 'Have they gone out of their minds?'

'You have imprisoned Richard, our overlord.'

'I was keeping him here', he said, 'out of loyalty, and cherishing him in order to teach him courtliness.'

'Upon my word', they said,* 'we are not grateful to you.' (2101–11)

'Bernard', said Louis, 'there is no need to be afraid.'

'Yes', said Bernard, 'I am very much afraid they might kill or dishonour you. Out there are many burgesses and many good vavassors. If they begin a skirmish, you will see great sorrow. If they do harm to you, they will not mourn the day. If you want to survive, give them back their lord at once.'

'I was keeping him here out of goodness and honour.'

'Upon my word', said Bernard, 'this does not look like love. You are holding on to him too tightly, since he has had no freedom since yesterday.' The King of France saw that Richard had to be given back. He did not dare hold on to him unless he wanted to meet his death. He was in a very sorry plight because he did not dare defend himself. He gave Richard back to them, making them understand that he had held on to him in order to give him training in courtliness and bring him up in his court until he saw him possessed of some refinement.*

---

[79] This story of the noise created by the people in the town is new information. See Dudo, p. 105.

'You want to sell him his upbringing at a high price', they said. 'If anyone else had done it, his actions would have been severely rebuked.' (2112–29)

The Normans and the Bretons pressed the king until he brought Richard out to them in his arms. They were able to plead their cause to Richard according to their wishes. The king took his homage and his fealty and in the sight of all the barons gave him back his rightful inheritance, Normandy and Brittany and everything he had claimed from him. Then Louis swore on the holy relics, and after their lord the barons and bishops whom the king had brought from France swore the same thing on the relics, that they would maintain life, limbs, honour, peace and loyalty in respect of Richard, each one in his lifetime.[80] In this way they gave each other assurance on both sides. (2130–41)

The Normans and the Bretons had harried the king until he handed Richard over to them and gave him everything which was his right, Normandy and Brittany and everything belonging to them. Then he swore to him on the holy relics that he would keep faith with him and support him everywhere in life, limb and honour; the bishops and barons of France who were present swore that the king would keep this oath. O God, why did he swear it when he had no intention of keeping it? Because of what he did he was afterwards considered an outright traitor; anyone reading the story would be able to understand this clearly. (2142–51)

When the king departed, he called to Bernard, Anslech and Ralph and drew them to one side; they were Norman noblemen and getting on in years.

'I will be leaving', he said, 'and taking Richard with me. I will get my men together. I am very anxious to do this. If God and faith protect me, I will never rest until I have taken revenge for you on Arnulf, the wretched coward. If I could capture him by force or by cunning, I would send him to the gallows with a rope around his neck.' The king told the Normans he was going to Laon; he would gather his men together from all over his land. He intended to besiege Arras; he would take it by force. Then he would seek out Arnulf until he had found him; if he could capture him, he would avenge the duke. He would take Richard, their overlord, with him and in his court give him training in courtliness with his son, far better than he would get in Rouen, of which he would become lord. He told them so many lies that he deceived them and took Richard, the young duke, to Laon; with him was Osmund a knight who took care of him. If Osmund had not gone, Richard would never have come back. Arnulf, the Count of Flanders, was not unmindful of his interests. He was told that the king was threatening him greatly and he wisely appeased the king's anger and wrath with just ten pounds of gold which he sent to him[81] and by other gifts which he gave to the barons. (2152–77)

The messengers from Flanders came to Louis and found him in Laon, sitting at dinner. When he had got up, they asked to speak to him in private and presented him with the gold, promising him more.

'The Count of Flanders', they said, 'has sent us to you. He is your vassal and he sends you word that from now on he is also your friend. You intend, people tell

---

[80] The story of Louis swearing on holy relics is not in Dudo or in the *GND*.

[81] Arnulf's gift of ten pounds of gold to Louis is not mentioned in Dudo or in the *GND*.

us, to destroy his country. There is no need to do so; it is already entirely yours. Everywhere you can dispatch your stewards and bailiffs. All you need to do is to issue your orders and state your commands; you can always have tribute from Flanders from now on. The count would come to you, but he has been taken ill; he has gout in his feet and is in a very bad state.* He has been rebuked for the death of the duke and is ready to defend himself in court; let the surety be given, according to whatever legal system he is to be subjected to, and he will give as a hostage a vassal or one of his friends. He has no fear of any law, providing justice is recognised. (2178–95)

He is ready to argue in court that he did not kill the duke; he did not know of it, desire it or have a hand in it. He had nothing to do with it and was not involved in it; neither by himself nor through anyone else did he seek mortal harm to him, nor did the man who perpetrated the act do so on his advice. If he had known about it, he would have protected the duke from it; he did not later make common cause with those who killed him. If he had known them to be, or seen them, in his court and could have captured them, he would gladly have hanged them or kept them in prison until he had handed them over to you. In spite of the dreadful crimes the duke committed against him, he was never heard to seek a truce with him.' (2196–2207)

'My lords', said Louis, 'I do not know what to say. The duke was my vassal and many a time he came to my aid. This matter is very serious and it would be wrong to ignore it; if I do not punish him, I will be reproached and be said to share the blame for the crime.' The barons and knights, who had received a large reward from the Count of Flanders, spoke after the king:

'You must not', they said, 'exaggerate this matter. Arnulf is your liegeman and he can bring you aid; if it pleases you, you can adjourn this trial. Make some enquiries about it and you will be in a better position to judge. Since the count offers to defend himself fully in court, you can no doubt postpone and delay things. When you want to harm and damage the count, it will be as easy for you to punish Flanders as it would be to shatter a glass vessel. Remember what the Normans did to you the other day; they made you swear under duress and confirm with hostages that you would hand over to them whatever they wished to ask for and lay claim to. If you leave Richard until he becomes a knight, he will bring repeated distress to your children. You can clearly see how proudly he behaves already; he already acts arrogantly and does a great deal of harm. You will never see anything worth a single penny from the Normans,* either land or revenues, without his selling it to you dearly. The duke was your friend and he performed many praiseworthy deeds. But now he is dead, you cannot bring him back; you cannot avenge all those who have been killed.' (2208–35)

'My lord', said the messengers, 'just listen to us. This is what the count says to you, give it a little credence. You should put Richard, William's son, in prison and never let him go as long as he lives. You would have the land he holds as your own property; the land is very fine and you would be the stronger for it. If you let him go, with eyes, hands or feet and without having his hamstrings burnt through and his two feet cut off, in due course he will make the French angry and distressed. Rou, William's father, held Normandy wrongfully. He was driven out of his land, by the drawing of lots in some way or other, and travelled by sea, going from port to port and conquering Normandy through the strength of his men; many of your ancestors were killed trying to defend it. There is now no hope of this, but your ancestor used to find great assistance there in the form of men and great wealth. He used to take pleasure there from hunting and hawking. If Richard escapes, you will regret it; because of all his ancestors, let him bear harsh penance.' (2236–54)

When the king had received the money from the Flemish, and each of his dukes had had his reward, and he had heard the advice given by each one of them, he broke his word completely and believed this evil; he never kept his promise or his oath. Calling to Richard, he forbade him from leaving the town for any reason at all. He swore to the Lord God and His power that if he were to leave it would cost him dear; it would not bring him any profit or advantage. Osmund heard what was said and was very displeased by it; he would like to have been in Rouen with Bernard the white-haired, together with Richard whom he thought was lost. (2255–67)

Richard was in Laon, lying in his quarters. By day he was at the court and at night he returned to his own quarters. He used to serve the king and queen as they ate. The Queen of France hated Richard because of her sons, because he was more handsome than they were and more noble in appearance. She would have preferred her sons, rather than Richard, to have Rouen and Normandy and everything he held.[82] Richard was handsome and good and he conducted himself properly; he spoke to people well and behaved well. He spent all his time training birds and dogs. One day he went out with the dogs as usual; the king was away, seeing to some legal matter or other. (2268–79)

The king was away, but when he returned the queen told him how Richard had behaved, how he went out with the dogs and carried his bird:

'He never asked my permission or told me about it.' The king was wicked and cruel and became very angry. If Richard went out again, he would have his eyes put out and the hamstrings cut from his tutor's legs. He summoned two men-at-arms and told them to take charge of him. Richard was in front of him, listening to what he said. He went pale, his face became gloomy and he sighed deeply; his whole face was wet with tears. Osmund said to the king:

'Everything will be as you wish. Richard will never, God willing, be harmed by you; he is your liegeman and will serve you well. He will never leave your court without permission.[83] If he ever did leave, he would come back here; he has never done any wrong and will never do so.' (2280–96)

'Osmund', said Louis, 'I swear by God and his saints that if I ever find out that Richard has left these walls none of your limbs, by Jesus Christ, will be safe. He will not escape me before the fruit ripens on the trees; I will make him suffer and what he eats will be bitter and sour.' Osmund knew the king to be cruel and harsh;

---

[82] The story concerning the queen's hatred for Richard, and also that of the time he spends training birds and dogs, is new information.

[83] On the question of *congié* 'permission', here and on other occasions in Wace's text, see S. D. B. Brown, 'Leavetaking: Lordship and Mobility in England and Normandy in the Twelfth Century', *History*, 79 (1994), 199–217 (p. 208 *et passim*).

as far as Richard was concerned, his heart was not pure or honourable. He did not dare leave the town in daylight or at night. The king would have liked to hold Richard beyond the river, in Saumur;[84] he would never be able to leave, unless he were to sneak away like a thief.* (2297–2306)

'In Rouen', said the king, 'I was among your people. All my men and I considered ourselves fools. We could not go farther than birds shut up in pots, so many magistrates, beadles and stewards were there. I did not dare speak there or even utter two words. I would rather have been with the Scots in London and could not be sure of protection for all my great forces. I could not wait to leave at the double or to take to my heels. Anyone who could have kept up with me would have been a worthy man indeed. Richard, you are here now; you will speak to us. If you escape from me safe and sound, you will be right to praise God. But I think your eyes will first be put out with hooks.'*[85] (2307–18)

Richard was handsome, wise and of fair appearance; he was well educated and eloquent. He heard the words spoken by the king and he turned as black as a piece of coal. 'My lord', he said to the king, 'you are a very noble man. If it pleases God, you will never commit treason against me which would bring great disgrace to your heir. You will never do me any wrong or harm without due cause. For this reason I came here to your dwelling; I sought safe-conduct from you alone and it is only from you that I have one. If my men acted wrongly towards you in Rouen, it was not because of me and I should be forgiven for this. I have no defence against you and will have to suffer everything with resignation. My father served you loyally, as is known, and I, my lord, will act according to my own purpose. I expect to be rewarded for my father's service.' The discussion came to an end; there was no further dispute. Richard was kept under guard for a long time. Osmund was very worried and very fearful; he sent a servant to the Normans in Rouen, telling them that the king was holding Richard prisoner. He would be maimed and destroyed unless he could sneak away like a thief, without taking leave. (2319–41)

The bishops were summoned and so were the barons; processions were held everywhere and people were made to give alms, to fast and to exercise great abstinence. The great and the small devoted themselves to prayer, each urging the other to pray and act virtuously. Old men and women were on their knees, asking God to protect Richard through His holy names. Throughout the land there were many tears and lamentations. There were no fiddles or rotes and no songs[86] sung or tunes played; in many households even the children wept.[87] (2342–51)

Richard was in Laon, fearing for his life; yet he still behaved well. He was amazed that the King of France and his barons were not willing to keep their

---

[84] This reference to Saumur is new.

[85] The speeches of Osmund and Louis are an embellishment of material Wace would have found in his sources.

[86] A *rotuenge* (more frequently *rotrouenge*), translated here simply as 'song', was a song with an indeterminate number of stanzas, each with two to eight lines, and a post-strophic refrain of one or two lines.

[87] The behaviour of the Normans in Normandy and the fact that they pray for Richard's release are embellishments of material in Wace's sources.

oath or their fealty to him. He repeatedly swore to God and His holy power –
but he told only Osmund about this, not sharing it with anyone else* – that if
God allowed him to live long enough to get out of France so that he could hold
his sword and carry his shield and lance, he would yet avenge himself, if he
could, on the most powerful men. Osmund, who was very upset, comforted him
greatly:

'My lord', he said, 'put your trust in God. You have to continue to conduct
yourself well until God has delivered you. We are here together and from now
on our lives are in danger; but I have firm faith in God that because of what is
done to us someone will yet have to undergo harsh penance for us. The king
is committing treason and acting most wretchedly. He has captured us in this
way and is holding us here permanently, but not repenting in the least for his
treacherous thoughts.[88] He will never again be trusted in respect of fealty or any
other commitment.' (2352–71)

'Fair master', said Richard, 'I am very much at a loss. Louis our king has
broken faith with me. Arnulf, the evil traitor, has become reconciled with him
and sent him great presents of gold and silver, praising and entreating the barons
in his court. The king has me guarded and frightens me greatly, for apparently he
is very angry with me. I am very fearful of being put to death or maimed. I need
advice; if you can give me some, I would do whatever you wished.'

'Fair lord', said Osmund, 'pretend to be ill. Lie in your bed, not eating
or drinking. Moan a great deal, sigh and complain as if you were dying, and
lament loudly. Ask for the priest as if you were dying. With God's help you will
escape.'

'I will do what you tell me', said Richard. Richard and his tutor Osmund were
no fools.[89] (2372–89)

Richard and his tutor Osmund were not distraught.[90] Richard lay in bed and
went without food until he became very weak. He complained about his feet
and his heart, uttering great laments and great cries; he abstained from eating
until he became very weak, his skin wasted away and his face turned pale;
he gave every sign of being on the point of death. When the king heard this, he
was not upset; he thought his son would be able to inherit Richard's domains.
Osmund displayed much grief and wept profusely:

'Lord Richard', he said, 'you were so noble. It was a waste of time hating you
because of your fief; very soon you will be handing it back to Louis. It is not right
that you are hated so much.[91] I had often said to your* friend Bernard that you
would never be a robust man. If you had died in Rouen, where you were raised,
it would not have meant so much to me; I leave you very unwillingly. Everyone
thought they would be loved and cherished because of you and that you would
be honoured and cherished by them. The great hopes invested in you are now

---

[88] The second half of v. 2369 is corrupt and its meaning is therefore difficult to determine.

[89] The story of the feigned illness and the discussions between Richard and Osmund are new
     information.

[90] The repetition of the phrase 'Richard and his tutor' suggests that these lines do not reflect the
     original reading for vv. 2389–90.

[91] The expression *contre bien* in v. 2402 is an error and thus the meaning of this line is uncertain.

dashed.'[92] Those who heard Osmund, his lamentations and his cries, thought that Richard would soon be dead and that he was mourning him as if he had been buried and as if his spirit had already left his body. (2390–2413)

One night the king was sitting at dinner. The men responsible for guarding Richard left him; they had no hope of his recovering, for he was not eating and could not speak, and they saw all Osmund's lamentations and tears. When Osmund saw the guards leaving the house, he had the horses saddled at once. Then he came to Richard's bed and made him get up straightaway. He had him wrapped in a bundle of grass,[93] well bound and trussed, then he ran to his horse and had his men lay him crosswise in front of him; he put a cloak over him and set off. It was a dark night and there was no light. When he was outside the town, he gave Richard a horse which he had led behind him; then each of them spurred on as hard as they could. There is no need to ask whether they went fast; they had no intention of stopping until they reached Coucy. Those inside the castle let them in and were all delighted to give lodging to Richard; he was the nephew of their lord and they loved him greatly. (2414–34)

Osmund, who was anxious to escape, came to Coucy, bringing Richard with him; he no longer had any need to fear the king. Now, whoever was upset by it, he was in his own domain and they gave thanks to God and to Saint Leonard.[94] The king was grief-stricken and thought he had been greatly deceived by Richard, who had escaped so cunningly. He put the guards, Roscelin and Girart, in prison; it did not matter to Osmund whether he hanged or burned them. The castle of Coucy belonged to Count Bernard of Senlis, Richard's uncle. (2435–44)

Richard was in Coucy, and Osmund, who stayed just long enough to have something to eat, left there and rode all night until he came to Senlis. Lord Bernard was asleep, but Osmund woke him up to tell him the news of his nephew Richard; he had got him out of the king's hands and left him in Coucy. He told him in the correct order everything that had happened. Bernard, who was highly delighted, jumped out of bed, embracing Osmund and kissing him many times. He demanded horses and mounted at once, going straight to Paris and speaking to Duke Hugh. Bernard spoke so earnestly to the duke that he promised never on any occasion to fail Richard; where he could not help him, at least he would not harm him. When Bernard had done this, he returned to Senlis, gathered his men together and went to Coucy. He took Richard, his dear nephew, to Senlis. (2445–61)

The king, who was very upset at having lost Richard through such a trick,* was in Laon; there was no one in his household whom he did not make unhappy.

---

[92] Holden suggests that v. 2407 should be placed v. 2409 and this order has been adopted in the translation.

[93] Dudo says 'in a cloak' (p. 106), whereas the *GND* has 'in hay' (I, pp. 104–05).

[94] Saint Leonard was thought to free prisoners who prayed to him. This was largely based on the story that Bohemond, prince of Antioch, released from a Moslem prison in 1103, visited the monastery of Noblac (now Saint-Léonard, near Limoges), which was founded by Leonard, in order to express gratitude for his release. In the later Middle Ages he was one of the most popular saints in western Europe.

He put to death those who were responsible for guarding Richard and threatened Osmund greatly; he would be dead if he caught him. He summoned Arnulf to a parley in the Vermandois and Arnulf came to him with very few companions. They discussed this matter together for a long time and tried to find a way of disinheriting* Richard. Arnulf told the king it should be done swiftly, before Richard had acquired reinforcements; he should make peace with Duke Hugh the Great and they should swear an oath of fealty to each other. As an inheritance, he should give him the whole of Normandy, whatever land lay beyond the Seine; he and his men should conquer it. The king would have Rouen and everything belonging to it; whatever was on this side of the Seine he should hold as his own property. (2462–78)

'My lord', said Arnulf, 'speak to Duke Hugh. Take counsel together and swear amongst yourselves that you will not fail each other as long as you live. Grant him the whole of Normandy the other side of the Seine, Lisieux and Bayeux and the other cities, and let him conquer them with his men and be called their lord; you take the Pays de Caux and Rouen on this side of the Seine. The castles and the revenues you will hold as your own; you will sever the Normans on this side of the Seine from those on the other side. Otherwise you will not be able to conquer or destroy them.'

'Arnulf', said Louis, 'you give me good advice.' (2479–89)

The king left Arnulf and summoned the duke. They spoke together at the cross of Compiègne. The king explained his intentions to Hugh and gave him the greater part of Normandy as a fief, whatever it possessed in cities and towns the other side of the Seine; he should conquer this land by force and have it as his by right. The duke pledged and swore to the king that if he held the gift the king had given him he would serve him willingly. They fixed the date on which they would enter Normandy; each man at his appointed time had gathered together as many men as he could. May God help Richard in His holy goodness, for the duke and the king have conceived a great hatred for him. They did not conceal from Bernard of Senlis that the king and the duke had been together and agreed to capture Normandy. Bernard got news of this and reproached the duke greatly. He went to speak to the duke, finding him in Paris. They greeted each other in friendly fashion. After they had spoken of a number of things, in private Bernard rebuked the duke severely:

'You have behaved wretchedly towards me', said Bernard. 'No man of your standing or your worth ought to have acted disloyally for money. You had given assurances to my nephew Richard and were entirely willing to pledge your faith to me. It is wrong of you to have broken your agreement with me so soon; the king's promises have deceived you. But I believe one thing and hold it as a truth: if you had now disinherited Richard, conquered Normandy and captured or killed Richard, I know so much about the king's great iniquity that he would have taken it all away from you within a year. He would not leave you a few inches of ground which you had not bought dearly.'

'Lord Bernard', said the duke, 'this is the way things have turned out. I cannot withdraw now, as I have sworn it to him, but if the king had infringed the agreement I have with him, you would soon see me transfer my allegiance.'* (2490–2528)

'Bernard', said the duke, 'this is how things stand. As long as the king keeps his agreement with me, I will not betray him in any way, great or small, by failing to do what he has said or commanded. But if the king attempted to deceive me in any way and tried to reduce the gift he has given me, and I were to discover this in word or appearance, I would return and go no farther. Go and see if you can devise some trickery with respect to the king so that I can withdraw without appearing to be a perjurer; I would never, as long as I lived, undertake any agreement with him.'

'You have spoken sensibly', said Hugh, 'and I ask no more.' Bernard departed without delay. In Rouen he sent for Bernard the Norman[95] and told him in private what Hugh was seeking; if the king displayed any sort of trickery, he would never serve him in any way whatsoever. (2529–45)

Bernard of Senlis said:

'We* must apply ourselves so that we can catch the king out by the use of trickery. You cannot defend yourself against him and Hugh; they have joined forces like brother-in-law and son-in-law. Do not let your dwellings be burnt and reduced to ashes and do not let your men be destroyed or the towns in your land, which he wants to give away and sell off, be captured. Try to get him to inform the duke that he no longer intends to capture the land, that he wants to make peace with Richard and give him back the land. If you can start a quarrel between them, they will become less powerful; to this end you will have to await your opportunity.' (2546–56)

When Bernard the Dane had received this advice, he went to Rouen, where his friends were. At the appointed time Hugh, Duke of Paris, and King Louis entered Normandy. The duke made his way towards Bayeux, laying waste the countryside; the king came to the Vexin and then went on to Saint-Denis, which is called Saint-Denis-en-Lions,[96] and acquired a great deal of land. His troops reduced many men and women to wretchedness, burnt many towns and captured much booty. Throughout the whole of Normandy many people were in a state of agitation; I am not at all surprised they were afraid, for they had no lord, master or equivalent who was making preparations to protect them. Bernard was in Rouen and not getting much sleep; repeatedly he prayed God, who created the moon and the sun, that the situation with the French could yet be reversed. He told many barons about his intentions and they all thought him good and loyal. (2557–74)

On Bernard's advice they summoned the king to come to Rouen and receive the land. There was no need for him to use such force to conquer it; it all belonged to him and he was waging war for it to no purpose. On Bernard's advice the messengers said that the king should come and take lodgings in Rouen. The whole of the land was secure and he should not allow it to deteriorate; he would never find anyone to cause him any harm. Let him have peace proclaimed and not allow the land to be damaged. Let the peasants do their ploughing and cultivate

---

[95] Bernard the Norman is Bernard the Dane (also called Bernard the white-haired, v. 2266).

[96] Saint-Denis-en-Lions is the former name for Lyons-la-Forêt (Eure). See II, vv. 1548, 2563, and III, v. 512.

the land; from this he would have some profit and could send all the revenues to Laon. William's son would never get a penny from it. They have no interest in an incompetent lord;* a foolish child must be changed for a wise king. The king had no wish to delay or tarry; he forbade and put an end to the burning and the looting and came straight to Rouen with the intention of putting the people to the test. Bernard had processions made ready; there was no chapel in the town with a bell-tower in which the bell did not toll in honour of the king and they led him in procession into the great church. Those who had no love for him were very kind to him; they would gladly have pushed him into the Seine and would hardly have wept if they had seen him drown. (2575–99)

In Rouen the king was received with joy. The king dismounted that day in the count's hall, accompanied by croziers, censers and clerics in their finery. Many Normans bowed to him and greeted him, and many presents were given to him by people of all ranks.* He was certain that he had defeated and overcome the Normans and that he had conquered them all without a battle; he and his companions rejoiced and joked about this a great deal. Now let the king beware of being deceived; a man can soon rise high only to fall back down very quickly. Bernard the Norman will yet show what he can do. The people in the land were all in a state of agitation; they were astonished at Bernard who had so lost his mind.

'O God', said some people, 'what has become of his wits? This land was handed over to Bernard and placed at his disposal. Why has it not been protected and defended by him? Now the little child has lost all his friends; his rightful lands will never be given back to him.' In private the burgesses held lengthy discussions, but Bernard's plan was not known to everyone. The next day he came to the king after Mass. When he saw it was time to talk, he was not silent or dumb. (2600–21)

'My lord', said Bernard, 'we have had a great desire to be assured of a lasting peace. Now we have reached this point, if it is God's destiny. If we lost a good lord, we have acquired a good one; we are better off because of the change. Now, whoever we have been, we are the king's men. We loved William, our good lord, and would have loved his son if he had turned out well. It is not at our instigation that Osmund took him away; I do not know what has become of him nor where Osmund took him. They both rejected the Normans' advice and it is very wrong of them to have criticised and blamed you for it when you had no intention of harming him.'

'I did not', said the king, 'by my Christianity! Those who blamed me did so wrongly.' 'I know the whole truth about this', said Bernard. 'Throughout this land people are saying, I was informed of this last night, that you have given the flower and the goodness of all Normandy to Duke Hugh as a fief, and whatever is on the other side of the Seine, the length and breadth of it. It is from there that we acquire a plentiful amount of wheat; without the produce of that region we will never have sufficient. Do you know Hugh? Have you forgotten that he has always despised you greatly and caused as many quarrels with your barons as he could? He has waged war and done harm to the very best of his ability. You have provided your enemy with a very rich fief.' (2622–48)

'My lord', said Bernard to him, 'Normandy is very large. You have abandoned nearly all of it to Duke Hugh, leaving only one sixth* of it for your own use, and that the poorest part, no matter what anyone says to you. The duke has the greater part of knights, the greater part of the arable land and the greater part of the good, well-equipped fighting men; if, with God's help, he can join the forces of Normandy with those Paris, who were raised in France, you will not have, this side of Laon, anywhere to lodge over which he will not want complete control, unless it is a strong castle or some abbey. This city will be destroyed or reduced to begging, and the impoverished inhabitants will take flight, for everything we have comes from there.'

'Bernard', said the king, 'I did not know that he would have such great power in Normandy. Hugh must not remain there,* if I have God's blessing!'

'Upon my word', said Bernard, 'that would indeed be folly.' (2649–67)

'I cannot give it any credence, but people here are saying that you have given a great deal of land to the duke, whatever lies on the other side of the Seine, from here onwards. Whoever advised you to make such a promise to the duke was more interested in his own advantage than in yours. Over there are good land and brave men, ten thousand knights who will all mount their horses and leave there if the duke summons them; they are the first to strike in our battles. We hold our lands because of them; they are our protection. The land is fertile and the inhabitants wealthy; there are good villeins there and good peasants. Why take the land away from a small child to give it to Hugh, a traitor and a tyrant, who will always cause you hardship and harm?'

'Bernard', said Louis, 'if the duke has so much of it, I would have little regard for whatever I had left.'

'Indeed', said Bernard, 'you should have no doubt of that at all.' (2668–85)

'My lord', said Bernard, 'Hugh will have the Évrecin, Évreux, Lisieux and the whole of the Auge and the Liesvin.[97] He will have Sées and the Hiémois* and the people of the Avranchin, as far as the point where the sea and the land come to an end, the Cinglais and Bayeux and the plain of the Bessin. There is no better land, say the neighbours; one finds everything in plenty, with the sole exception of vines. Great riches arrive there from the kingdom overseas. Compared with these men ours are inadequate. Along with all this, Hugh will have the people from the Cotentin, Mortain and the Passais and the whole of the Avranchin. By the faith I owe my lord Saint Martin! If* all the men I am mentioning are subject to the duke, your cannot set much store by the Pays de Caux and the Vexin.'

'Bernard', said Louis, 'you are a good prophet, but I say and swear, and in truth I foretell it, that he will never set foot there, nor will any man of his lineage, for I will send him word tonight or in the morning that he should leave my land alone and go on his way.' (2686–704)

'Lord king', said Bernard, 'you were given very bad advice by the man who advised you to give Hugh what lies on the other side of the Seine;* without the goods which come to us from over there, there will never be plenty on our side. As soon as that region fails our own, no burgess will ever remain in this town.'

---

[97] The reading *Evrechin* 'the region around Évreux' is more likely than the manuscript reading *Avrenchin* 'the region around Avranches', and *Lusvin* is presumably *Liesvin* 'the region around Lisieux'.

'Bernard', said the king, 'things will turn out quite differently.' Bernard said so much to the king and deceived him so much, praising Normandy so much and blaming Hugh so much that in the morning the king sent to Hugh a knight who gave him the king's message, that he should leave Normandy alone and never take anything from it; he had made peace with the Normans and would be giving Normandy back to Richard. If he remained there for three days, he would drive him out. Hugh heard the message and was very fearful; he knew how this had come about, but said nothing. (2705–19)

The messenger who came from the king spoke to the duke in a low voice. Because of the foreign barons he gave him good advice, that he should not take from the land ox, pig or ewe; if he waited there for three days, his head would be red with blood. The duke marvelled at the king's instructions; he rolled his eyes a lot and stretched himself. He swelled up like a bottle with anger and spite. May he be cursed by Him who brings sunshine to the world if he ever stirred himself for any emergency affecting the king; very swiftly he made preparations to go to Paris. (2720–29)

The duke came to Paris; he was furious, enraged and filled with wrath at what King Louis had done. He was distressed that he had toiled in vain for so long and distressed that the gift had been snatched from him so soon. Bernard of Senlis was delighted at what had happened to the duke, who had gone back home so soon at the king's bidding. He quickly came to Paris and approached the duke, saying to him with a laugh:

'So you are not happy then? Have you destroyêd and routed the Normans? How many* great castles have you captured? To whom have you given them? You have been badly paid by the king, I think.'

'Bernard', said the duke, 'you were right in what you said.'

'Indeed', said Bernard, 'but you did not believe me.' (2730–42)

'My lord duke', said Bernard, 'tell me what you intend to do with my nephew Richard, whether or not you will help him. You have broken away from the king without committing a single act of perjury. He has failed you completely, you will never trust him again. You pledged your faith to me, I do not know whether you will keep it. How will you go about supporting Richard?'

'Upon my word', said the duke, 'it would be reasonable and right, but I do not see the way to help him, I do not know whether you do, for he has fallen very low. The king has punished and destroyed his Normans; they are hiding like birds caught in a net.'

'By my head', said Bernard, 'you would see something quite different.' (2743–54)

Bernard of Senlis said:

'It is of scant importance if the king has the revenues and the lesser income. I know this much about the matter and tell you in truth that the Normans will never fail their natural heir. They willingly made the king remain in Rouen, not wanting to let him – in this they acted very wisely – destroy the towns and burn the dwellings, for they had no certainty or expectation of receiving assistance. Let the Normans hear what is happening now and make their arrangements; if they saw Richard with a degree of hope and saw the king's strength diminishing, they would soon have turned things round and altered things radically.

Something which is useful in the morning is no longer so at night. If they could become aware of his treachery, he could not stay long in Rouen. He will be forced to leave Rouen and Normandy and will never set foot in them in order to lay siege to a castle.' (2755–71)

The king had a large number of fine young men with him in Rouen; he did exactly as he pleased and had no complaints about anything. Not even the meanest man-at-arms found anyone brave enough to oppose his wishes.* Bernard the Dane had a beautiful and noble wife; she was a cousin or relative of a number of the barons. A Frenchman saw her and she pleased him greatly. He begged the king to let him take her, but the king agreed to this only if it were delayed until he had returned from Laon;* then he would have her together with her wealth. The lady heard this and was sad and grief-stricken. If she did not flee before this happened, she would consider herself very laggardly. When Lord Bernard heard this, he was very frightened by it and swore earnestly to God, who makes it rain and thunder, the Sovereign Power and Almighty Father, that if he lost his wife in this way there would be a great outcry about it; he would make every effort to protect himself from shame and be upset if he did not destroy Louis's arrogance.[98] (2772–88)

When the king had granted the Frenchman the lady he was asked for, together with Bernard's land, all the other men asked for some other woman; they spied on the beautiful women throughout the whole region. The king permitted this, never refusing them any woman, except that the matter should be subject to delay, until he had been to Laon and come back again; then the matter could be completed, each man receiving the woman he desired. A great rumour went through the whole of Normandy that there was no woman in the land who was praised or lauded who had not been granted and given to the Frenchmen. There was no woman in the land who hated her husband so much that she was not frightened by this news. The Normans discussed this matter with one another and conferred about it in private without making any great outcry about it; such news could not and cannot be concealed. The man who sees his spouse married to another man before his very eyes will regard it as shameful; he would rather have her drowned or strangled. Bernard's wife was from a very good family; she was the most prized and the most honoured. She wanted to take flight at once over the salt sea, or she would rather take the veil in an abbey than be given to someone else with her husband still alive. Lord Bernard swore by his pommel and his sword that she would not be kept out of sight because of fear; if he lost his wife, she would be bought dearly. Before it happened, he would have caused many a skirmish on land and separated many a soul from its body in great pain; all Normandy would be troubled and disturbed, the entire situation would be completely overturned and Richard would by then have recovered his land. (2789–2820)

Richard was being guarded in Senlis with great honour; he was served and honoured in his uncle's house. For his age he was tall, strong and wise and he made every effort to act as well and honourably and as possible. He was distressed at having been taken away from his land and distressed for his vassals

---

[98] This story concerning the wife of Bernard the Dane is new information.

whom he had not forgotten;* they had not been aided by him nor given their inheritances by him. He put his hope in God that he would yet be proclaimed duke, trusting greatly in the barons who had been born in Normandy. For, come the right time and place, he would not be forgotten by them; if it pleased God, the king would yet be held in check and not want to have entered his land at any price. Throughout Normandy the king did exactly what he wished, and when he wished and it pleased him he went back to France. Lord Ralph, a vassal, who was called Torta [the Twisted One], was wealthy, powerful and well educated; he had more property than all his relatives and his son was ordained Bishop of Paris.[99] Torta was on good terms with the king* and was his close confidant, for everything he had was at his disposal. The king gave him all the provostships in the Pays de Caux, in Rouen and all other cities. He treated everyone very badly and caused them damage and loss in respect of litigation and court actions, treating them just as if he were an enfeoffed count. If the peasants had dared, he would have been killed on a hundred occasions, but the barons said to them:

'You sons of whores, be patient! This will not last long and the time will soon pass.' (2821–48)

Ralph Torta was treacherous and caused grief to many a man, taking away what they had and behaving in a base fashion. He spared no one at all from litigation and court actions; the barons in the land repeatedly heard complaints and laments about this from the common people, but none of the barons protected them and no one defended them. On a number of occasions they spoke of it amongst themselves in private; they could not tolerate such a thing for long. They saw Torta's overweening behaviour and saw how badly the French behaved, being niggardly with regard to both food and general expenditure;[100] they had taken away Richard's inheritance. They saw the king enjoying himself in a most arrogant fashion and on his return giving away their lands. They were brought to shame and ruin and there was no salvation for them unless God took pity on them. They will soon have attempted to alter things. A man thinks he can know joy when he soon knows sorrow and a man in a high position very soon comes down to earth. Bernard was brave, wise and of great intelligence; from the Cotentin he sent word secretly to Harold, who had been in Cherbourg for a long time, informing him that Richard was losing his lands, Normandy and Brittany and whatever pertained to them, and he no longer had anyone he could trust, friend or relative. Friendship with the father should cause one to love the child. There would be advantage and honour for him if he restored his inheritance to him; he should come to the duke by sea as soon as the wind permitted, bringing his entire navy without delay and they should inflict some harm on the king. Bernard made so many promises, in addition to the message, that Harold hastened to make his preparations; he arrived below Varaville with just six[101] ships, where the Dive enters the sea, very close to Bavent. (2849–82)

---

[99] Neither Ralph Torta (in his translation of Dudo, Christiansen calls him Rolf Twist, p. 123), nor his son the Bishop of Paris, has been identified.

[100] The meaning of v. 2879 remains unclear.

[101] As the number of ships is not specified in the source, Andresen interprets as 'with just *his* ships'.

The Normans were delighted by the arrival of the king and the Danes. All the inhabitants of the Bessin joined forces with him, as did those in the Avranchin and the Cotentin, the valley of Mortain and those from the Cinglais. Peasants and burgesses came in great throngs, rich knights and poor, commoners and noblemen, bringing bread and meat, salted and fresh fish, by land on carts and by sea on ships; the king was received with joy and honour. The Danes and the Normans threatened the French; they would capture Normandy and rule it against their will, and between them they would like to have part of France as well.* They would fight either at once on a battlefield or within a month Richard would have full possession of everything. (2883–96)

When Bernard in Rouen heard of Harold's arrival, that he had come to the Dive, bringing such large forces, and that the people in the land were all joining forces with him, on the surface he appeared upset, but in his heart it pleased him. He informed the king in France of what he had discovered about the King of Denmark,[102] who was laying waste the land, capturing the country and destroying the towns; he would lose Normandy if he did not put his mind to it very soon; he would never set foot in it again if he did not make haste. (2897–2905)

King Louis called and summoned his army; in his entire land there was no baron or steward, no count, vicomte or burgess, however far away, no knight or peasant who dared stay away. They very soon assembled where the king had indicated and no old sword or old shield was left on its hook. Never, said the king, would he eat roast meat if he did not confine Harold in his land like a fool.[103] (2906–13)

When the king had gathered his men together, there was a huge assembly; he came straight to Rouen in Normandy. Then, fully equipped, he crossed the Seine in order to do battle with Harold, who was taking his land; he should not enjoy its service if he could not defend it. On Bernard's advice they held a parley in order to seek some agreement* about Richard, to ensure that in this way he would not lose everything. They all went to the parley together, the French, the Danes and the Normans. When Herluin, who was Count of Ponthieu and everything belonging to it,[104] came nobly with the others, he found a Norman whom he had often seen; he was one of the knights belonging to the duke, who had raised him. He and his people were from the Cotentin. Herluin asked him what he thought about the matter and he made a good reply, saying that he had disinherited Richard wrongly:

'His father gave you back Montreuil as an outright gift, then he was killed because of you, you know how. Since then we have never had any support from you, rather you have done us constant harm. May God, who never fails or lies, bring us justice.' (2914–36)

Beside him was a Dane who had listened to the way the knight had reproached Herluin. He went up to the Norman and asked him who the rich man was to

---

[102] Harold was not, as Dudo and William of Jumièges thought, King of Denmark. He was probably a Viking leader and King of Bayeux.

[103] The meaning of *ne l'enclost* in the manuscript (v. 2913) is unclear.

[104] This is an anachronistic statement, as Herluin of Montreuil was not Count of Ponthieu.

whom he had spoken. Telling the truth, he replied, 'Herluin', the man who had been responsible for the death of William; because of him the Flemish had killed him treacherously. The Dane went forward and dealt him a blow, cutting off his head with some weapon or other. What commotion was created and how the parley was disturbed! They were all frightened by Herluin's death. (2937–47)

You would have seen a great many people swiftly reduced to a state of agitation, a skirmish begun and the parley disbanded. Lambert, Herluin's brother, was the first to jump up. The French were flabbergasted at the death of Herluin and with a yell they all demanded arms; those with the opportunity to do so gladly used them to strike. The brave and the bold struck with great vigour and the cowards fled, for their hearts failed them. The king was very distressed and considered himself greatly dishonoured; much harm had come to him and befallen him. He lost eighteen of the counts from his land there, in addition to the other deaths, of which I did not hear the number.[105] The king withdrew to one side on his horse; the horse was restive and, breaking both its reins, it darted straight into the Norman squadron. Recognising the king, the Normans grabbed hold of him on all sides and handed him over to the guards, for they had a great hatred for him. (2948–64)

The king had sustained great shame and great losses, losing the finest of the French barons, both captured and wounded, of which there were many. His horse was restive and it broke its reins; he came* amidst the Normans, where there was a great throng, and they seized him, captured and retained him. They handed him over to the guards, for they had feared him very much. Those responsible for guarding him had seen the booty acquired by the others who were victorious in the battle. They left the king alone and darted off in pursuit of it; they were more interested in booty than in the king and the king departed without his lance or shield. A Norman, who had seen him, held on to him and the king said to him:

'Have you recognised me? If you can free me, things will turn out very well for you. I will make you a rich man if you take me to safety. I will have no more land and money than you.' The man heard what the king promised and believed him; he placed him quickly on an island in the Seine. But Bernard the Dane saw the whole thing and forced the Norman to give back the king, who lay in prison in Rouen for a long time. Harold and the Dane distributed the booty and as much of the other possessions as they had wanted. (2965–88)

Queen Gerberga was waiting in Laon for the time when her husband Louis would return from the fighting.[106] When she discovered that he had been captured and thrown into prison, she felt and displayed great grief, for she was afraid of losing him as the Normans all had a mortal hatred for him. She sent for help from King Henry, her father, who lived on the Rhine, for she was losing her husband; he would never get out of prison except with his help. Henry replied that he would have nothing to do with the matter and never take up arms to free him. If Louis had been captured, it was rightfully so, for he did not keep faith or maintain

---

[105] The figure of eighteen is also mentioned by Dudo (p. 116).
[106] Gerberga was Queen of France, wife of Louis Outremer and daughter of King Henry I of Germany.

his oaths. He was disinheriting Richard and acting basely, in spite of the excellence of the boy's father, whom he had known. Now everyone was saying he
had been killed by him. He had been faithless with regard to the son and was
taking his land away from him. Louis had believed the traitors Arnulf and Herluin
and it was through the advice of these two that he was betraying a child; so,
if the king suffered shame because of this, he would not be upset by it. When
the queen heard that she would gain nothing more from this and that her father
Henry would do nothing more for him, she made other plans, for she had to do
so. Since she could not free her husband by cunning or by force, unless she
ransomed him, she consulted the barons about providing hostages on his behalf.
(2989–3013)

The queen did so much and achieved so much, saying so much to the barons
and conferring so much that she gave hostages as replacements for her husband
the king; on his behalf she sent the barons of France, the finest members of the
clergy and also one of the king's sons.[107] When the king was free and on his way,
with permission to leave, you would have seen him rejoicing. He would not have
gone back even if it meant losing his entire fief, not even if someone had given
him half the world, for he feared the Normans who had threatened him. He came
to the queen and to his seat in Laon; the lady came to meet him and kissed him
tenderly. Many Frenchmen came on horse and on foot and a great many tears of
joy and pity were shed. (3014–28)

Peace was discussed between Richard and the king, who would give him back
his fief, not retaining even the tiniest part of it; then he would swear to bear him
true faith and not seek to do him any more harm or shame than he would to
himself. The parley took place near Gerberoy; I do not think there has ever been
such an assembly, before or since. There were many rich men there with splendid
equipment, but I cannot name them nor must I name them for you. The King of
Denmark, superbly arrayed on a fine palfrey, brought a large number of noble
warriors with him; if he had been of our faith, he would have been a man of great
repute. He took up his position to one side, at the edge of a heath, accompanied
by a large number of men, old and young; but he gave them all orders not to cause
any disruption. The French hated him greatly and made it clear in what respect;
because of him the whole of France was in fear and terror. (3029–44)

The number of barons on both sides was very large. Suddenly Richard arrived,
having been brought by Bernard, his uncle from Senlis, who loved him dearly. He
was very beautiful and handsome and looked like a true nobleman; his body was
beautiful, his face handsome and he spoke wisely. He was not too arrogant or too
self-effacing. He stood before the king and the king addressed him, giving back
and restoring to him Normandy and Brittany, and freeing him completely from
any homage or service. In this way agreement was reached, and the king accepted
that Richard would not offer service to the king or his heir, nor would the king or
his heir seek service, and, if anyone challenged Richard, he would protect him,
and the king and his heirs would keep any agreement.[108] The king swore what he

---

[107] The son mentioned here would Charles, second son of Louis and Gerberga.
[108] The terms of the treaty between Richard and Louis are drawn from the *Brevis relatio*.

had stated on holy relics, and the barons swore what the king swore, to maintain his power as long as each might live. When the king had sworn, he asked for the Normans and handed the Normans and the Bretons over to Richard; in front of the king Richard took their homage, just as the king himself dictated and demanded. Thus they broke up and the king departed; Harold made his way to his land with a great deal of wealth* and Richard made his way to Rouen as soon as he could. A great procession of people came out to meet him and there was great joy in Rouen when Richard entered it. (3045–70)

The bishop and the clergy, the counts and the barons received Richard in a great procession; he began by praying at the church of Our Lady and performing many acts of contrition before the main altar. The provisions in his house that day were splendid; you would have seen a great throng of barons around him. He was not yet a knight, being still a young boy; on his face he had not yet grown a beard or moustache, yet he was already of very great purpose, understanding what was said to him and recognising reason. He refused to allow any robber or thief in his land to be ransomed if he was caught; he was sent to the gallows or put to death. Richard could fence with rods or staffs and was skilled at training a sparrowhawk, a goshawk and a falcon; he knew how to capture stags and hinds and other venison and to capture wild boar on his own, without any companion. Each day he prayed most earnestly to God; he loved* the saints and gave them many fine gifts. The man who was his steward, Ralph Torta by name, was widely regarded as an out-and-out criminal. He arranged the rations for Richard's house, at eighteen pence per day; later he was regarded as robber, as the money was light and had very little value. In the court he did not permit any minstrel or serving-boy and the court was set on a path of destruction; Ralph earned many a curse.[109] (3071–97)

Ralph Torta was treacherous and considered to be avaricious; he knew just how to litigate and accuse a man, to thwart reason and amass wealth. For eighteen pence he wanted to provision the count's household each day and was greatly blamed for this; he refused to pay the knights their wages and they went and appealed to their lord, telling him about the life they were forced to lead. The duke had Ralph expelled from Rouen and Ralph sent him word that he wished to speak with him; if he had done any wrong, he was ready to make amends for it. The duke swore to God, who saves the world, that, if he encountered him in his path that night, he would put out both his eyes, and if he escaped from this alive he could give thanks to God. When Torta heard what he said, he dared not remain there any longer. He asked for his horses and had his equipment loaded up, not daring to remain anywhere in Normandy; he went to Paris where he used to live. The Bishop of Paris was subsequently unable to effect a reconciliation; Ralph was his son by his wife, but I do not know her name. Hugh, Duke of Paris, heard Richard praised for his conduct as a noble and brave man and one who knew how to protect his men and his land. He summoned to Paris Lord Bernard of Senlis and Bernard of Rouen and began to explain to them that he wanted to give

---

[109] This story of Torta's paltry allowance to Richard is also found in the *GND*, but not the information about the minstrels or serving-boys.

Richard a daughter he had. He would dub Richard a knight, he could bear arms well; while still a child, he could not marry.

'If he wished to join my forces with his, then neither king nor count nor anyone else could do him* any harm.' (3098–3128)

The two Bernards concluded the discussions in such a way that Duke Hugh's daughter was affianced to Richard.[110] The duke had two children by an honoured lady, a son and a daughter, but the daughter was the elder; because of her age she could not yet be married and the duke agreed that she would be given to him as soon as it was reasonable for her to marry. Hugh Capet, his son, acted as surety for her. He was a young man, yet the matter was expedited; Richard became a knight and the duke girded on his sword. The fame of Richard and the duke soon spread throughout France and many regions; there was no king or count who did not fear and hate the love and the agreement between the two such powerful dukes. Richard bore arms well and loved his household greatly. The peace and the agreement, which the king had sworn, would last only a short time if Arnulf the Fleming could do anything about it;* it had lasted three years and in the fourth it was violated. (3129–46)

Arnulf hated Richard, whose father he had killed; he was upset and distressed by the agreement and King Louis was of the same mind. They both had a parley in the Vermandois, where they exchanged opinions on this matter. Then King Louis sent him as a messenger* to Otto the German, for his father Henry, who was Gerberga's father, had abdicated.

'My lord Otto', said Arnulf, 'my lord is greatly afflicted. He is waging a great war in his land against his mortal enemies. The Duke of Normandy has besieged his castles, and through me he has sought succour and help from you. The queen, your sister with the lovely countenance, begs you; help her lord and do not show him any ill will. If you do not bring help within the next two weeks, you will see him leaving France like a beggar. In order to secure your help, this I pledge this you truly, he gives you Lorraine and I put you in possession of it.' Arnulf the traitor begged him so much and promised him so much that Otto summoned his vassals and his allies. With the large number of men he had he came to Saint-Denis, where the King of France had the men from his own country and Arnulf the most powerful of the Flemish. (3147–69)

The armies in which so many men joined forces were very great; they laid waste all Duke Hugh's land around Paris;* the city was strong and they did not dare besiege it. On Arnulf's advice they turned towards Pontoise and camped for a night on the banks of the Andelle. Early next morning, when the barons rose, they entered Normandy on Arnulf's advice. They sent a troop of Germans, the best there were, to Rouen, expecting to take the enemy unawares; but the first group of men achieved very little and many regretted having gone there so soon. The Normans, who had very little fear of them, opposed them; they defended themselves vigorously and protected the town. (3170–82)

It was one morning, when dawn broke and the birds were singing and the roses were in bloom, that King Otto took part of the Germans; he sent a company

---

[110] Duke Hugh's daughter was called Emma.

of them to Rouen in order to take the city unawares before the alarm was raised. One of King Otto's nephews was constable; they had to take orders from him and he led them and guided them.[111] Richard was in Rouen and had fortified his city; he was on his way back from church, having heard Mass, when a spy came running through the Porte Belvoisine. He shouted to Richard, not keeping it a secret, that he would soon see a fierce body of knights.

'Germans', he said, 'are coming in force and with violence.* They think they can have Rouen and all Normandy; they will soon enter here, unless someone opposes them.' The duke heard the news and prostrated himself before God, humbly begging Christ, the Virgin Mary's son, to protect his person, his honour and his life; with his own money he would build a rich abbey. The knights went for their arms, shouting 'God help!'. (3183–3202)

The duke had knights from among the best in Brittany and a good number of men from Paris belonging to Hugh the Great; he ordered them to leave the town and oppose the men from Germany. He placed over them as captain one of his most valued barons; he carried a banner of red Spanish cloth.[112] They remained seated on their horses at the foot of a mountain. Suddenly the Germans arrived, dismounting on the plain. If the Germans had their wish, I do not think anything could prevent shields being smashed and lances shattered. There were those who entered the mêlée in good health and left it bleeding; it is quite normal in war and many other matters for one to lose on one occasion and win on another. (3203–14)

The Germans were very arrogant and fierce, quick to issue threats and prone to boasting; seeing how beautiful the city was and how fertile the countryside, they thought they could take up quarters in the town by force. But the Normans, if it pleased God, intended to challenge them and defend the country with iron and steel. The Normans who came forth from the town were strong knights, each well armed and seated on a good horse; some of them went forward to meet the king's men, for they wanted to start a battle with them. But the others did not dare joust with the Normans; they were not used to or trained in such matters. They kept in close formation, not daring to break ranks, in order to avoid suffering embarrassment on account of some ruse. They wanted to ride towards the gates all together, and the Normans in front of them began to use their cunning, pretending to take flight in order to get them to pursue them. (3215–31)

The Normans took flight cunningly in order to split up the men approaching them, and the Germans broke ranks and came spurring after them. They came galloping up to the gates of Rouen and the Normans rode out into the open,* shouting 'God help!'. Those in Rouen jumped up, calling to one another; they did not display their banners there, but those capable of doing the most were not faint-hearted. You could have seen a great and harsh battle there, many a lance shattered and many a shining sword drawn, many a dark red shield, many a gleaming helmet, many a horse running loose* and dragging its reins and many

---

[111] King Otto's nephews have not been identified.
[112] This information about the red Spanish cloth is unique to Wace.

a knight lying in the streets and the fields. The villeins and the peasants struck with their great axes and the squires followed their lords with pikes. Richard emerged from the town on an iron-grey horse, fully armed and brandishing his sword; after him rode Bretons and Normans. Otto's nephew came, leading many noble warriors; the king had him with him and loved no man so much. He inflicted many great losses on the Normans and mocked them repeatedly. This distressed Richard and his distress showed; he drew his shield in front of him and lowered his lance. Spurring his horse and letting go the reins, he struck the German, causing the sharp iron to pass right through his body, so that neither his shield nor his byrnie were worth one iota to him. He threw him down dead on the ground with no chance of recovery. Richard yelled at him:

'I commend you to the Devil! I will not lose my kingdom during my lifetime because of you.' (3232–61)

A great uproar ensued as a result of this cry. Richard executed a turn and put his hand on his sword, which on many occasions that day was covered in blood. Many people looked at his skilful display, saying that in his hands the land was well placed. When the dead man's body was carried away, the numbers increased, for Germans spurred their horses like madmen and Richard's knights continued to fight furiously. You could have seen many saddles emptied there and many noble Germans lying with mouths wide open, many shields broken in pieces and many others with holes in them; many souls were separated from bodies in great pain, many meshes torn from hauberks and byrnies, and many blows were struck with great Danish axes and many heads knocked senseless with great cudgels. The Germans had a very bad morning there; if they went in search of it,* they found it. Yet they did display their great valour very well; they took away the baron, but his soul had been separated from his body. O God, how the Germans regretted his valour! They cursed Normandy and the people born there, for they had suffered there a loss such as would never be recouped. With his whole body they withdrew to the top of a valley, placing him on a shield, his head bare; they opened the great wound and removed his armour.[113] The Normans had captured alive twelve of the most highly esteemed Germans in the land; they had a very successful day. The ransom given for them was huge, but the man who died there received poor payment. The Normans were in the fields, with their banners displayed; in the press of battle they had captured twelve barons and killed three of the attacking knights. They had acquired horses, white, piebald and sorrel. They took booty from the corpses which lay on the ground like swine. They had no greater pity than they would have had for their bodies,[114] which were stained with blood and entangled in straw. The booty they took was worth as much as the gold which two very rich kings would have in their treasure-houses. (3262–99)

The Normans did not deign to enter the city; they set up their tents outside the walls. They had acquired horses and a good many prisoners. The prisons were

---

[113] This information concerning the removal of the body from the battlefield on a shield is new and probably anachronistic.

[114] The meaning of v. 3296 remains unclear.

full of them, so many men had they thrown into them; they chained many of them together in twos. The inhabitants of the town displayed great pride. When King Otto found his nephew dead, he lamented and wept profusely out of grief and sorrow; in his whole family he loved no one so much. He repeatedly mourned his fame and his valour; he knew no one as good as he, young or old.

'Now I will see', said King Otto, 'who holds me dear. I intend to avenge my friend, whom the Normans have killed. O Arnulf of Flanders, how you have deceived me! Through your false words you have treated me badly; I have lost the flower and the goodness of my men.' Then they ran to arms, remaining there no longer. They attacked the outer edge of Rouen and one side of it; they did not approach the other side, which is enclosed by the Seine. The city was surrounded by a wall and a ditch. French and Germans, when they were armed, launched a violent assault on the inhabitants of Rouen and the Normans defended themselves like proven vassals. They climbed on to the brattices and the crenellated wall; the enemy outside achieved nothing by their attack. (3300–24)

The Normans saw the fields quivering with the enemy, who were coming to attack the city with great anger. They did not want to be harmed outside the gates or risk losses or death, nor did they wish to show or expose themselves at the crenelations. They remained inside the city and strengthened the walls, letting the Germans come right up to the walls. When they arrived to demolish and undermine the walls, those up above hurled large stones and great beams at them with remarkable violence, flattening* many of the men.[115] You would have seen a large number of men kicking their legs and dying, forgetting to confess their sins, to say their *mea culpa* or to distribute their possessions, being unable to stir and flee from where they were. Those outside could not withstand the blows from above; they had to leave the walls and the embankment. The Normans had a postern gate opened beside the Seine and repeatedly let knights out that way in order to cause frequent disturbance and confusion to the enemy; they caused their assailants to abandon the field. When the kings saw this, they felt nothing but distress. (3325–45)

French and Germans strove to attack and the Normans set about striking well; they seized quivers and sheaths and stretched their hand-bows, shooting arrows and quarrels at them cleverly. Those outside did the purchasing and those inside did the selling; they knocked down many men who surrendered their arms, and the Normans made effective progress with their striking, breaking and piercing helmets and splitting shields and heads. They caused their assailants to cease the assault and spread out over the land, abandoning the city and pitching their pavilions and tents; they hung their shields and helmets on the forked part of their lodgings. (3346–56)

You would have seen many armed Normans emerging to look for battles and seeking jousts, jousting and striking with lances and swords and acquiring warhorses, white, speckled and iron-grey in colour, and losing some of theirs; custom has it that booty is not always what it seems. You would often have seen the men-at-arms skirmishing outside with slings, bows and sharp axes. They

---

[115] This story about the fighting near town walls is new information.

dashed out from all parts, and if the numbers had been equal on each side you would have seen the strongest and the best fighters. (3357–66)

In the fields you could have found a remarkable number of dead bodies and seen a great deal of grievous lamentation, with wounded and maimed men being carried away by others.[116] King Otto rose next day in daylight and went to stand with his barons in front of his tent. He could see the comings and goings across the bridge over the Seine, people crossing back and forth over from the direction of Émendreville, leading carts and packhorses into the town, and fully-loaded ships and boats coming from the direction of the sea. He called to the barons and began to say to them:

'This city', he said, 'is very much to be feared. The walls are not easy to knock down, and the knights there are good and skilful jousters, fearing nothing* in hand-to-hand combat. If we cannot deprive them of their access to water, besiege the town and have control over it on all sides, taking away its supply of food and bringing famine to those inside,* we are toiling in vain and will never be able to do them harm.' (3367–84)

'My lords', said King Otto, 'those inside appear to be defending themselves against us. They will never be harmed or destroyed by us if we do not deprive them of the Seine, below the bridge by which those in the country come and go repeatedly.'

'My lord', said a vassal, 'they will never lose it because of us, for they are good knights with a good leader. The town on that side is enclosed by a deep river on which sea-going vessels travel up and down.[117] Unless they are besieged on that side, they will never know fear. But I tell you truly, if God shows me any bounty, if you divide your forces, those who go over there way will not be helped by those who remain here; they will never be able to help each other.' (3385–98)

'My lord', said the vassal, 'those on this side will never cross over to the other side, however much they need to do so. The river is broad and the town strong, with good men in it. You have already lost a number of your barons there; remaining there any longer will lead to further losses. The man who advised you to come here gave you very bad advice. He has betrayed many men and will betray more; there will not be any other way to acquire the castle.' The king knew he was telling the truth; he was very upset, but did not show it and spoke of something else. He sent some monk or prisoner to Richard, asking for and seeking a truce in order to go to the abbey of Saint-Ouen; he wanted to worship at the holy relic and Richard agreed to this. The king came to Rouen and worshipped the holy relic, taking with him I do not know how many bishops and barons. When the king had prayed, he called to the barons, drawing them to one side and looking at the church. (3399–3415)

'Barons', said King Otto, 'tell me what you advise. What advice do you give me in order to give up this siege? Because, as you know, nothing can be done to

[116] For *font as autres porter* Andresen reads *font as tres emporter* 'carried away to the tents'.

[117] Wace's comment that sea-going vessels could reach Rouen because of the deep water in one quarter of the city is not without interest.

capture the city; it is fortified and enclosed by walls and ditches, and it is fortified by rivers which run alongside it and fortified by towers, by other strongholds and by good knights in large numbers. I have lost many of my closest friends there.'

'You will lose more', they said, 'if you stay here any longer, and if you suffer any losses it will be rightly so, as you are the one waging war against Richard and laying waste his lands. But you do not know why, for you hate him wrongly. What harm has he done you and what are you asking of him?'

'Arnulf', said King Otto, 'has deceived us, bringing us here because of his fear of Richard. All day long, he said to us: "Come, my lords, come! Destroy the Normans and take their cities. Without firing arrows or hurling weapons, you can conquer them." In this way Arnulf has deceived and mocked us. His shield will never be pierced or staved in; no one can guard against his iniquities. By the faith I owe you and you owe me, seize the traitor and hand him over to Richard. He will avenge his father, who was killed by him. I intend to hand him over to Richard, if you advise me to do so.' (3416–40)

'My lord', said the barons, 'we will never contemplate taking Arnulf and handing him over to Richard, for that would be considered dreadful treachery on our part; you would be reproached for it and regarded as a criminal. One should never hand over a hostage or a prisoner to someone who will kill him, especially when they are companions.* Arnulf came here with us and we came with him; he is a proven traitor, but we will not betray him. We will not be traitors in order to betray Arnulf. You ask for our advice and we give it you. Make preparations for your journey; tomorrow morning we will depart. Let us leave anyone who wishes to remain behind. Louis would gladly depart, we know, if he knew how and with what excuse.'

'Upon my word', said the king, 'we will leave here.' (3441–55)

'My lord', said a vicomte, 'I will tell you the truth. This town is not easy to besiege; you can often see knights and men-at-arms being welcomed inside it by means of the river and the bridge. They are very worthy men and men of valour; we will not take the smallest part of their possessions when we leave. A man can be happy now who will have a heart filled with sorrow. Even the best have to follow the dictates of necessity. Any who thinks he knows a great deal will end up thinking himself a fool.'

'We can easily discover their situation', said King Otto. 'They are men of worth, wise and very powerful. In the morning I will leave. I have no wish to remain any longer.' (3456–67)

When the king had prayed and conferred a great deal, he knelt in the direction of the altar and took leave of the saint. He saw a large number of men, a large town and a fine burg with many dwellings; he saw clergy and burgesses and rich markets and numerous well-equipped barons; whatever the king saw there, he prized highly. The Normans led and escorted him through the gates. They did not use humble words in his presence, but did say that he was acting harmfully and sinfully in waging war wrongfully against their lord Richard because of what Arnulf had said, a proven felon who never kept faith or friendship with anyone. The Normans returned and left the king, and he and his men made their way back to their tents. Thus they were on horse and on foot that day, because there was no shooting of arrows or hurling of weapons on either side. Everyone was at peace until night fell. (3468–84)

I do not know who informed Count Arnulf that night that the King of Germany intended to capture him that night and hand him over to Richard and the Normans to be hanged or burnt on a pyre and then have his ashes scattered. There is no need to tell you that Arnulf was afraid, for if Richard got his hands on him no one could protect him; he set off on his way, not daring to wait for daylight. However much he may need to do so, he had no intention of* getting off his horse that night. (3485–92)

Count Arnulf was afraid the king would capture him and hand him over to the Normans out of spite. He had his men mount their horses and set off on their way; he did not speak to Otto or tell Louis about it, nor did he seek leave to depart from either of them. Because of the noise and the disruption which Arnulf's men made, there was agitation in the army and great fear gripped them all. They thought that Richard was attacking them in their tents and that he would kill them all one after the other. There was no one bold enough to sleep in his bed; those close to the woods hid there all night. If anyone had seen them and the way they behaved and acted, and heard their sobbing, their lamentations and their sighs, and how they groaned, he would gladly have laughed at them. (3493–3506)

You could easily have seen them trembling one and all, and chamberlains, men-at-arms and squires making haste, servants saddling horses and arming knights; some fought against one of their own vassals without recognising him, and some could not and dared not call out to him, so much had their fear gripped them. You would have seen many thieves and rascals moving about, stealing sacks, cloaks, garments and other bundles and hiding warhorses, palfreys and packhorses. Some hid things they were never to enjoy;[118] crime has always been concealed with difficulty. Those in Rouen heard the commotion the army was making while putting on saddles and bridles and demanding arms; they made all the knights and burgesses get up at once to fortify the brattices and man the loop-holes. The sound of weapons they could hear frightened them and they kept watch all night until dawn, for the besiegers set fire to their huts; they departed, not wishing to remain there any longer. (3507–25)

It was one morning, at daybreak, that the enemy set off, all fleeing together. Those behind put great pressure on those in front; godson did not wait for godfather, son left his father and father his child. Those who could move quickest did not hold back and anyone who looked round was considered a fool. The Normans and the Bretons spurred after them, pursuing them on horse and foot, catching up with them in the forest of Maupertuis.[119] Then the French and the Germans were very afraid. The peasants arrived with great yells and shouts; over hedges and along paths they came before them, carrying poles or bows or heavy clubs. They struck their opponents at once with spades and forks; those who could reach an opponent did not waste time threatening him. Those who were

---

[118] The idea here seems to be that they would not live long enough to take advantage of their ill-gotten gains, or that they would be captured before returning for them.

[119] Maupertuis is a hamlet in Lilly, seven kilometres west of Lyons-la-Forêt.

fleeing defended themselves in a cowardly manner, throwing their arms into ditches and valleys; some made for the woods and the undergrowth. The villeins and the peasants hauled them out roughly, killing many of them as they tried to defend themselves. They pursued them as they fled as far as Amiens, capturing so many of them that they all became wealthy. (3526–48)

The duke acquired considerable fame and reputation from discomfiting two kings by his power, King Otto of Germany and Louis of France. Because of grief and sorrow, Louis could not from that day forward Louis carry sword, shield, hauberk or lance. He became ill and died; his arrogance came to an end. Lothar, his son, became king without delay;* there was no one to cause him any disturbance or harm in this. Richard thanked God, in whom he had placed his trust, for giving him such vengeance over Louis. Hugh did not forget Richard; he wanted him, he said, to keep his promise in every respect, as he had given his word that he would take his daughter in marriage. (3549–61)

Duke Hugh the Great saw his end approaching. Through old age and sickness he began to get very much worse and his money could not prolong his life. He had his daughter given and married to Richard; she was now old enough to experience pleasure with a man. He had affianced her and did not wish to be disloyal to her; he could not have found a better match for her. He handed his son and his wife over to Richard's protection and gave him jurisdiction over his vassals and all his lands, until his son was old enough to be dubbed a knight. Richard protected everything well and held the son very dear. Then Hugh Capet behaved with great disdain when he became King of France on Lothar's death. Theobald, Count of Chartres, who* had a very high opinion of himself, envied Richard, whom he heard praised so much. Along with other reasons, which I do not wish to state, he made war on Richard with the men from his borderlands, ransoming the peasants and seeking booty; he would gladly have devoted his energy to harming Richard. A man can instigate a war and begin one who cannot bring about peace when he wishes to do so; people think they can enhance their reputation who seek their own misfortune, and someone who thinks he can destroy someone else is the first to stumble. (3562–84)

Theobald hated Richard and did not conceal this in any way. He was happy to seek to harm and damage him, ransoming his men and laying waste his lands; he set fire to his towns and plundered them, supporting and protecting those who hated Richard. Richard summoned Bretons and assembled Normans, doing harm on many occasions to the Chartrain and the Dunois. The war, which lasted a long time, was very fierce; each man was strong and fierce and waged war powerfully. Theobald beseeched the king and came to an agreement with him; they gave each other assurances concerning their war with Richard. On Theobald's advice and according to the plot he devised, the queen sent a messenger to her brother in Cologne, to Bruno, the archbishop, in whom she had great trust; he was both count and archbishop and had jurisdiction over many men. She sent him word that there would never be peace in France, and his nephew Lothar would never hold the land in peace, as long as Count Richard was alive in Normandy. He should summon him to a parley and Lothar would then capture him, keep him in prison, or* put him to death at once; he believed the queen, but acted foolishly. Bruno, the archbishop, sent a bishop to Richard who told him that Bruno would come to Beauvais;[120] he should come and speak with him, for he would await him there. He would bring about such harmony between him and the king that it would bring him honour and great advantage; the king and his kingdom would be grateful to him. Richard believed the bishop, suspecting no treason, and gladly agreed to the parley he was seeking. At the appointed time he made preparations for his journey, left Normandy and entered the Beauvaisis; from a path he was on he looked to the right. (3585–3616)

The count looked to the right from a path he was on and saw two knights who had emerged from a copse; they were spurring towards him over the fields, wrapped in cloaks. He did not recognise either of them; they were bathed in perspiration as they had ridden so hard. They were Theobald's men and had found out about his plans. Richard saw them coming and held on to his reins. The first man to speak said to the duke:

'Where are you going? You do not know where it is that you are going and have trusted bad advice. It is better for you to be safe and sound in full vigour than to become a humble shepherd, poor, miserable and naked.'

'Who are you?' he said. They replied:

'We are your vassals and seek your salvation.' The count listened intently to what they said. He gave his sword to one of them, which was worth five marks, and the other knight received a good gift; in addition to this, the count gave him a good shield.[121] (3617–33)

When the two knights had left him, the duke was concerned by what he had heard. He made his men go back and returned to Rouen, giving thanks to the Lord God.

'God', he said, 'Lord Father, I glorify your holy name, I adore you, I beseech you and prostrate myself before you, who have saved me from treachery so many times.' Richard prostrated himself before God and served him gladly, honouring the Holy Church and giving gifts of clothing to the poor. Bruno, the archbishop, waited in Beauvais; because Richard failed to come he considered himself deceived. Suddenly a messenger arrived who explained everything to him:

'Richard', he said, 'sends you word that you have let him down. You will not set eyes on him this year, I think. It is not your fault that you did not betray him; through you his mortal enemies would have killed him, but he has escaped from you, thanks to the Lord God. He did not come here because he found out about your plans.' Bruno, the archbishop, thought himself greatly dishonoured; for this act of treason he received great blame and great reproach. The king was blamed for it and Gerberga as well, and Theobald, who hatched this plot, was blamed. (3634–55)

The archbishop was blamed for this treason, and the king and those in his household likewise, and the queen was severely cursed for it. The pope himself heard about it and almost deposed Archbishop Bruno. Theobald was regarded as an outright felon, but he was scarcely concerned about who blamed him and who

---

[120] The text has *Bernei* 'Bernay' (Eure) here, but this is an error.

[121] Dudo states that the sword had four pounds worth of gold in its hilt and that the further gift to the knight was an arm-ring (p. 141, cf. the *GND*, I, pp. 122–23).

did not. He would never at any time love Richard and did his very best to seek his disinheritance, his death, his loss and his destruction. May he be prevented from doing so by the Lord God, who underwent suffering to save sinners and bring them to salvation. (3656–67)

Theobald, the Count of Chartres, was treacherous and deceitful. He had many castles and towns and was very greedy. He was a very brave knight and very chivalrous, but he was very cruel and very envious. He envied Richard, who had escaped danger so successfully, and, cunning man as he was, attempted to get the king to harm him.

'My lord king', said Theobald, 'we are all shamed by Richard, this Norman, this foreigner, this traitor[122] who has held out against you for such a long time. He did harm to your father and will do harm to you. He is too close a neighbour and is causing you great harm.' (3368–78)

'My lord king', said Theobald, 'Richard, who behaves in such an arrogant and proud manner, can cause you great distress. All his ancestors have been accustomed to harm and damage your family. Louis, your father, who always strove to wage war against the Normans, was unable to avenge himself; he never managed to put an end to things or to destroy them. Richard shows no concern for your entire jurisdiction and does not deign to humble himself towards you in respect of his fief; because of him you cannot rule your men. The French have never succeeded in getting the upper hand over the Normans. They do not have the slightest regard for the French or for their pride. Unless you can outwit him,* he will have no trouble there can be no question of them deceiving you. It is astonishing that you cannot trick Richard; he cleverly manages to be on his guard against your wiles.[123] Arrange to speak to him with the apparent intention of reaching a reconciliation and have him killed and cut to pieces at the parley.' Theobald spoke so cunningly and said so much to Lothar that they made preparations for another act of treachery. (3679–97)

Theobald was full of cunning and full of deceit. He had no love for man or woman and showed no mercy or pity to freeman or captive; he never showed any fear of committing wrong or sinful acts. He spoke at length with Lothar and gave him a great deal of advice, encouraging him to commit treason. Lothar sent a messenger at once to Richard, a very shrewd and amiable baron from his land. He went in search of Richard and rode until he found him in Rouen in his own fief. With him he found many barons and clergy; Richard's court always seemed like a fair or a market. The messenger told him what the king had entrusted to him, just as Theobald had indicated to him. (3698–3711)

'Richard', said the messenger, 'listen to what I have to say. The king has been very tolerant of you and does not intend to go on being so. You are constantly attempting to do wrong by him, to harm him and to damage him. You wish to

---

[122] The term translated as 'traitor' is *roux*, literally 'red-haired'. Red hair was often associated with deceit, cunning and treachery.

[123] As Holden points out (vol. 3, p. 207), the order of vv. 3689–93 is unsatisfactory. Vv. 3692–93 have been translated here before vv. 3690–91. In v. 3693, Holden's suggested reading *se vous nel decevez* has been accepted here; the meaning of *neent est de vous boissier* is uncertain.

disinherit him, to take away his land and to destroy and disgrace him treacherously. You consider him cowardly enough to have to take flight and wretched
enough to be willing to hand over to you his land which you hold, for which you
are not willing to give him service, and you do not deign to do or offer to do right
by him. If he has accepted this, he does not intend to do so any more. If he were
willing to believe those who wish to hate you, who killed your father and wish
to betray you, nothing apart from God could protect you, and neither castle nor
city could defend you. You would have to go back where your ancestor came
from. Do you realise that he is king and you should hold your land from him?'
(3712–27)

   'You must honour your lord', said the messenger. 'You are his vassal and
must bear him faith and love, protecting his honour, his life and his limbs.
You must not fail him or let him down at a time of need. You are his liegeman, yet
you are not willing to admit it, and you should not despise him because he is
young. If the king wanted to gather together all the men he could muster, there
would be no one left to kill in your land, strong or weak, and no castle or city
could protect you. If he were willing to believe and listen to your enemies, and
you were willing to make peace with those who have broken faith with him, there
could never be any love between the two of you. He would rather quarrel with
Theobald and the Flemish than with you, he said, if he could feel secure about
this. In order to make peace and to seal love between you, come to the king, this
he says to you, at the crossing near the Eaulne. He was your father's godson and
this should not be forgotten. Through the king you can do harm to Theobald
and the Flemish, destroying their towns and laying waste their lands, and through
you he can damage those who have broken faith with him. If the two of you are
willing to help and love each other, no one will be bold enough to raise his head.
In bringing about this parley, you will have to conceal a great deal, for they are
doing their best to destroy the peace. Have peace made and sworn* between
you and you will be able to bring despair to the evil-doers. You will be able to
go in safety throughout the whole of France.' (3728–54)

   Count Richard thought the messenger* was telling the truth. He did not
suspect that he was betraying him, and I do not know in truth if he did so know-
ingly, but he spoke the words which the king had indicated to him. Richard was
deceived by his promises. This was no surprise. Who would have thought he
could be lying? The parley, which the messenger arranged, was at hand and the
day and the place as the king fixed them. Richard did not suspect that the king
would betray him, but, if God does not protect him from it, he has betrayed him
and brought about his death. (3755–64)

   Count Richard went to the parley on the Eaulne, but not without many of his
companions; he had some suspicions about the French and their treachery. He
had his men dismount beside a wood next to the river, asked for his dinner and
ate superbly; he had as much to eat as was appropriate for such a place. More
than a hundred squires and pages served him. Secretly,* he sent out three spies
to discover the whereabouts of the king, who had not appeared. He had his
movements and his actions watched, to find out what men he had with him and
see where he came from and in what way. They found the king speaking in private
to Richard's enemies, all together, Baldwin the Fleming and also Theobald and

Geoffrey of Anjou, who hated Richard very much. Suddenly a spy came running to Richard: 'How are things going?' said Richard.

'Badly. Your enemies are advising the king intently.'

'This', said Richard, 'is a very bad sign. But I have complete trust in the Almighty King, who judges truly the good and the bad. Woe betide a treacherous king who lies for no purpose and a lord who does not keep an oath to a vassal. If God now keeps me from prison or harm, I will make the most arrogant of them know sorrow and do the same to the others, if God permits. Companions, noble men, now eat happily! Today I want to see each man's courage.' As the count was speaking, the other spy dismounted. (3765–93)

The spy dismounted and came running to Richard. He found the duke still sitting at dinner and did not conceal from him the news which he knew:

'The French', he said, 'are arming themselves and asking for horses. They do not seem to be seeking peace or reconciliation. Withdraw beyond the Dieppe,[124] for they have a large number of men.'

'I entrust myself', said the duke, 'to the Lord God in Heaven. Companions, now to arms! Do not delay! Today we will see who will strike with lance and sword. All stick together, do not take flight. Today I will see who is the most courageous and the best fighter. If we cannot withstand them, because there are so many of them, we will get as far away from here as the river Dieppe; but before we cross this river, I will strike blows. Gather all the equipment together and send it on ahead. Let the cry be raised as the men pass through the region, and the villeins and good peasants will then come; with picks and clubs they will strike hand-to-hand and kill their horses with their bows. If the French pursue us that far, they will not, if it pleases God, make fun of us as they leave. King Lothar keeps his promises very badly. May he not be spared by anyone who is able to harm him; he has wronged me greatly, I call upon God as my witness.' (3794–3818)

Then the other spy arrived, like a frightened man; he had run so hard that he was exhausted.

'What are you doing?' he said. 'Look over there, look! Head for the Dieppe and wait for the French there, for compared to you the king has a large number of men.'

'Do not worry', said the count, 'we have enough men. God had delivered us from many a peril.' Suddenly the French were there, eager to fight;* they wanted to cross the fords. The Duke of Normandy went to meet them with his very noble company of close companions. He spurred his good horse, which was well tested. He struck on the shield a knight who had strayed from the ranks, unhorsing him; his shield was broken in pieces and his hauberk shattered. The iron passed right through his body and he was knocked down dead on the bank of the Eaulne.* Then there were many jousts, up hill and down dale. The battle remained where it was for a very long time; if the king had not arrived, it would not have moved. The Normans did as they pleased with the first comers. When the king appeared with his armed barons, Richard withdrew and turned towards

---

[124] The river Dieppe is now the Béthune (Seine-Maritime).

the ford;* he safely entered the river Dieppe, where he found vavassors and villeins gathered together and archers and men-at-arms ready to fight. The king went lower down the Eaulne with his forces; he was upset that he had not joined battle with the Normans. He pursued them until he found them, but they had guarded the crossing-points over the Dieppe so that they could not cross and he became all the more enraged. (3819–47)

When the king appeared, Richard withdrew towards the Dieppe; having crossed it, he stopped on the bank and the king rode until he caught up with him. When they drew nearer, the battle became fiercer.* Richard was first to reach the point where the king intended to cross, and many a joust took place there and many lances were broken;* many men fell into the river and drank their fill and many who could not manage to get out drowned. Many men were wounded there and many died, many lost consciousness and lay there all day; there was not a single Norman, however brave, who was not sweating. Richard showed great valour, over and above that of all his companions; if any Norman fell, Richard helped him. He felt the need to do this and everyone noticed it; he delivered many blows that day and received many. He soon forced his way to the spot where he knew the king would be; he struck no knight without knocking him down or killing him, bringing great harm to the king, as he intended to do. The king saw his great blows and his heart sank; he could not cross the Dieppe and this caused him terrible grief. (3848–68)

When the fords were being crossed at the Dieppe, you would have seen a great battle; never would you have seen a greater one with so many men. The king had his finest men and the flower of his land and many of the barons in his kingdom were there. As they crossed, they knocked down Walter the hunter; there was no better warrior in the company. Walter knew a great deal about falcons and goshawks, about dogs and forests and whatever appertained to hunting.* The Duke of Normandy loved him greatly and each day derived pleasure from his companionship. He saw him captured by the French and was filled with sorrow; if they killed him in front of him, he would never again know honour. He took his shield, drew his sword and spurred his horse in great anger, going in amongst the enemy where he saw Walter. Then you would have seen a remarkable sword battle; barons and vavassors ran after him. The Normans were afraid that in rescuing Walter they would lose Richard, their natural lord. Each man was soaked in sweat; it was around midday and very hot. Walter got on to his feet again and regained his strength; he would have been killed if he had not had such a good rescuer. He lost his horse, which was of great value, but Richard gave him one which was better and more handsome. He often called the king a scoundrel and a criminal and Count Theobald a felon and a traitor. (3869–93)

When Walter was rescued, the throng was very great.[125] You would have seen many barons pressing* on all sides. On both sides there were valiant knights, on this side very brave and on the other very fierce. The squires dealt blows with

---

[125] Walter the hunter has not been identified. Dudo refers to him as *venator*, translated by Christiansen as 'henchman' (p. 146). See the *GND*, I, p. 124, n. 2. The entire account of the battle near the river Dieppe is much more elaborate than in Dudo or the *GND*.

stakes and bits of lances.* You would have seen many blows with iron and steel, many lances of fir and ash broken, many shields shattered and many hauberks broken, many helmets flying off and many a cuirass torn off,* people slaughtering each other with good swords, many knights wounded and many wounded men bleeding. You would have seen the French striving and toiling; they wanted to drag Walter away, but they paid dearly for this,* for Richard and his men did not intend to leave him there. Walter was in a great throng and could not get back on his feet. You would have seen many Normans striving to rescue him; he did not have the impression he had gone out hunting, or was waiting at a tryst[126] with a limer or a greyhound. (3894–3911)

When Richard had dragged Walter back to his company, he said:

'Friend Walter, may God bless me. Chivalry is a stern and harsh profession; hawking and hunting are a lot more comfortable. I would rather lose part of my land than let the French have you in their power for long. You took too much of a risk and acted foolishly.'

'It was because I hate to be cowardly', said Walter. 'I saw knights jousting and was very envious of them.' In Dieppe, and outside on the great meadow, there were many barons on one side and the other; many a blow was struck with lance and shining sword. There was a great combat when Walter was retrieved; the French yelled 'Monjoie!' and the Normans 'God help!'. The Flemish cried 'Arras!' and the Angevins 'Valley!'[127] Count Theobald cried 'Chartres!' and 'Go forward!'. The French were more numerous than* the Normans, but they kept close to the river, for it was protected by infantry, and by archers and squires who did not spare anyone. He who fell amongst them had no concern for his life; he had no chance of getting away without being killed. (3912–32)

The battle above Dieppe was fierce; all day long the duke's lance was the very first to be seen. The king was distressed and his countenance was very downcast, for he could do no further harm to the Normans and had no hope of making any more gains. He found the land filled with archers and villeins, protecting the river in hundreds and thousands, some carrying bows, some axes and some great infantry lances. They killed many horses to the front and to the rear. Marauders grabbed* horse-cloths, sweat-cloths, shields, swords, helmets and cruppers; the losses were not easy to recoup. Many dead and wounded were carried away on biers. The king saw what he had lost and then withdrew his banner. (3933–46)

The king withdrew, angry and puffed up with rage; he was grief-stricken that Richard was not dead or killed and that his body was not maimed or battered. Now his treason was known and proven; for the rest of his life he would be blamed for it and he had not made any progress or improved things. He repeatedly swore to God and His holy goodness, so much had the struggle now increased and intensified, saying* that there would never be peace or an end to

---

[126] A tryst here is an appointed station in hunting. It is from this notion that the sense 'mutual appointment' developed.

[127] Holden identifies this battle-cry as referring to the Valley of Beaufort between Angers and Tours (vol. 3, p. 305). In the Middle Ages the names of important local features or place names were often adopted as battle-cries.

things.* One of them would be condemned completely and shown to be in the wrong; either Richard would be dead or he would remain alive and be disinherited. The king could do no more. He returned to France and Richard went to Rouen with* his men; he was utterly exhausted and overcome by the battle. In Rouen, when he arrived, he was very much in demand, for the people had been told, and they were beside themselves, that Richard had been betrayed and taken to France; there was great joy in the town when he arrived, for everyone had been distraught and worried. Richard gave thanks to the Lord God, through whom, he said, he had escaped the king's men. He cherished and loved all his men very much, thanking and praising them all for the battle. He gave them equipment and rid them of their debts; to many he gave land and increased their inheritances. (3947–71)

When he returned from Dieppe, the king was very distressed; he threw down his shield and his lance and tore up his banner, letting go his reins repeatedly and then pulling them back. He kept on quarrelling with his men and often lamented and sighed, repeatedly swearing by God and Saint Giles the good,[128] saying that he was dead if he could not capture and kill Richard. You would have seen Theobald, contorted in anger and grief, frequently tearing at his own flesh. All day long he came* to the king, urging him and telling him he should not hold any land or be lord over a kingdom if he did not bring grief and suffering to the Normans, or if he did not destroy them all through death or famine. As a result of Theobald's advice, the king had letters and charters written and sealed in wax; he had the barons come from all over his empire. In Laon[129] in France the king held his council; when they were all together there were more than ten thousand men. They did as the king commanded, not wishing to oppose him. (3972–89)

The king assembled a very large number of barons; everyone willingly did what the king asked. As a result of Theobald's advice, he entered Normandy, came straight to Évreux and besieged the city; the king took the city without delay, thanks to Gilbert Machel, who planned the affair.[130] He handed the city over to Theobald, so that he could wage war against the Normans, and Theobald promised he would serve him well. Suddenly Richard came spurring up, but the king had already captured the city. The king had too many men and Richard did not dare join battle with him; he took up his position in a wood, as did his men. When the king entered the wood, the duke emerged from his ambush and diminished* the king's army by thirty knights, in addition to the rest of the equipment, which amounted to a great deal. Then he entered the Chartrain, destroying and seizing everything, and next he set fire to and burnt the Dunois: with prisoners and booty he returned to Rouen. Theobald was so taken by surprise that he never approached him. He intended to avenge himself later and thought he could do so; Richard had brought shame to him, so he would do the same to him,

---

[128] Saint Giles was a hermit (d. *c.* 710) who founded a monastery at a place in Provence later to be called Saint-Gilles. His shrine became an important centre of pilgrimage for travellers to the Holy Land and Compostela. He is the patron saint of cripples, lepers and nursing mothers.

[129] The reading of the manuscript here is *Meleun* 'Melun', which is presumably an error for *Monleun* 'Laon'.

[130] Gilbert Machel is mentioned by the *GND* (I, pp. 124–25), but not by Dudo.

burning all his land right up to the bridge at Rouen. Theobald was strong, fierce and very successful; he called earnestly upon his friends, his men and his neighbours and secretly and swiftly advanced towards Rouen. As soon as Richard found out about this, he sent a spy to find out where Theobald was and how many men he had; the spy managed to get close to Theobald and estimated that he had three thousand knights in his army. When Richard heard this, he was astonished, but he was wise and brave and trusted in God; not wanting to show himself, he hid in Rouen. Theobald was arrogant and displayed great pride. He did not stop, day or night, until he had reached Émendreville, and he lodged his great army between the wood and the Seine. Richard told his men that if anyone emerged he would suffer harm. (3990–4024)

Richard saw the French encamped on his land; he saw the towns burning and the houses smoking. He saw his neighbours captured and their wives killed; he saw Theobald taking up quarters and putting up tents. He began to tremble with anger and distress; you would have seen him puffed up with wrath and anguish, but since he did not know what else to do he sensibly restrained himself. He did not want to attack the army or start a fight, so he allowed Theobald and his knights to feel secure, take up quarters in peace and eat in peace. He summoned all his friends from the region and had his guards shout out all night and blow their horns, as if he was going to have Rouen defended in fear. But quietly and silently he gathered his men together, and as many barges and ships as he could find. All night long he had his men cross over the Seine. At daybreak, when he saw the dawn, he said:

'We must put a great deal of effort into overcoming our enemies who are to be found here. They have invaded our land and have no business here. This war is not about stealing land, taking away cloaks or removing fine clothing, rather it is about losing lives and cutting off heads. They wish to capture or kill us, or disinherit us during our lifetime. If they are more numerous than ourselves, we should not fear them, for unarmed men cannot win the day over armed men. We will find them lying down, unable to defend themselves; we will kill many of them before they can arm themselves. If you lack swords, do not waste time because of this; you can attack them with pickaxes* and crooks. By shattering their lances and piercing their shields and fighting them with our swords, we shall overcome them. This will prove to me today whom I should love most, whom I should pay first and best and to whom I should give lands and a fief. I want to forbid and prevent everyone, if they wish to have my love, from concerning themselves with plunder or removing booty. I will share out the gains later, so that we will all be companions and peers. Let us entrust ourselves to God; I wish to delay no longer.' They all shouted to Richard:

'We are waiting here too long!' It was still early and not easy to see clearly. Richard arranged his men in three squadrons and sent them in amongst Theobald's army on three sides. Then you would have heard Normans shouting 'God help!', and seen them striking and jousting vigorously, and the agitated French calling upon their men-at-arms, hanging shields round their necks and putting hauberks on their backs, lacing on their helmets and mounting their horses. They wanted to withdraw to the woods and escape; none of them was in any mood to joke. (4025–75)

It was at daybreak, when dawn was appearing, that Richard was amongst the tents, shouting out 'God help!', and the Normans behind him did not delay. They struck with their swords and thrust with their lances, seeking out the enemy in their quarters; they did not wait for them to emerge. Theobald was still sleeping in his tent; the French dashed for their arms, trembling with fear, and the Normans struck them in front and from behind. Theobald jumped on to his horse, rallying his men, but many of them were heading for the woods; disarmed, they had been taken unawares and were afraid of the weapons. It is right that someone who seeks shame should find shame himself, and a man who seeks to cause harm to others must endure harm himself. Theobald had displayed so much arrogance and now he would not depart without shame and great losses. Richard's company went on increasing all the time, for burgesses and peasants came running up from Rouen, carrying clubs, pikes and axes; anyone they could attack did not remain on his feet. Theobald's company went on diminishing in number, as many men went and hid in the woods. Theobald sat on his good, swift horse. When his men deserted him, he took flight; before doing so, he struck many blows with his sharp sword. He left behind six hundred and sixty men with no one to protect them and they never saw their wives or children again; they asked for no more than a piece of land to lie in forever. When Theobald came to Chartres, lamenting his losses, he found his dwellings burned, his towns burning and one of his sons dead and lying on a bier; his wife and his men were grieving terribly. (4076–4107)

Theobald was badly harmed and damaged; one loss attracts another and one sorrow is soon doubled; they do not come alone,* this can be proved. Theobald was in Chartres, dreadfully discomfited. In one day he had lost seven hundred and sixty of the men he had brought, dead and wounded;[131] on the same day they burned Chartres, his city. Theobald was so grief-stricken that he almost went out of his mind. The Duke of Normandy was not concerned by this; he gave thanks to Almighty God. He had the dead sought in woods and ditches and nobly buried in churches. He handed over the wounded to doctors and servants; until they were cured, he looked after them all. Then he gave them leave and freed them; for this he was greatly cherished, esteemed and loved. (4108–23)

The Count of Normandy was very brave and courtly. He maintained his peasants well and held his burgesses very dear; to his barons he gave lands, fiefs and equipment and to the sons of vavassors he gave clothing and equipment, arms, palfreys and Spanish horses. Throughout the whole of Normandy he established good laws. The Flemish and the French envied him, and Lothar, who was King of France, hated him greatly; Theobald, Count of Blois, felt great envy for him. Geoffrey, Count of Anjou, made war on him in the Passais, and those in Maine repeatedly robbed him of the Alenchinnois. Rotrou, Count of the Perche and those in the land around Bellême . . .[132] Against these men Richard set the men from the Auge and those from the Hiémois, and against the others he

---

[131] Dudo states that 640 men died (trans., p. 150).

[132] *Rocto* in the manuscript has been interpreted with Andresen as *Rotro* 'Rotrou'. There seems to be a line missing, which would give details of the pillaging perpetrated by Rotrou.

opposed the men from Avranches. Against the Flemish and the inhabitants of Amiens he placed men from the county of Eu and from the Talou, and those from the county of Arques together with those from the Pays de Caux. The Bretons, who were keen to joust, he kept with him, and also those from the Bessin and the Cotentin; each month mercenaries came to him in droves from Hainault, Poix,[133] Brittany and England. He had lost Évreux and made no gains of any value there. He saw his towns laid waste in large numbers, saw the great losses he had sustained and it was no laughing matter; he had no wish to laugh or to go hunting. He spent no time on jokes or on composing *serventeis*. He sent his ships and his boats to Harold, telling him to send the Danes very swiftly to his aid, for Theobald was holding Évreux and defending it againt their will. (4124–52)

Count Richard sent his messenger to Harold, informing him of the emergency and of his losses; he told him about the reckless behaviour of Theobald and Lothar. He sent him word and begged him in the name of his lineage to send him his men by sail and by oar, to gain vengeance over Theobald for his shame and his losses; they should come in safety when they had a strong wind. He would look after them and they would not leave any debts behind them; he and his whole family would be held responsible* if he allowed him to lose his inheritance for lack of help. The king was well disposed towards helping Richard, for he considered him a worthy and a wise man. Soon he sent him the finest of his barons and those who were at the right time and age for fighting. He had ships fitted out and made ready for the crossing; the fleet which set out to make the crossing was very large. (4153–68)

On the orders of the king the Danes made preparations, loading the ships and boats with shields and equipment. They emptied Denmark of its strong, bold men and sailed so successfully that they came to Normandy and sailed up the Seine. When the Danes approached, Richard went to meet them; following his advice, they went up the Seine, heading for Jeufosse, where they took up quarters and attached their ships to the river bank. Then the Bretons came and the Normans joined forces with them and they conferred about how they would do harm to Theobald. They did not spare churches, altars or houses; those they could find they burned and demolished. (4169–81)

The Danes were evil-doers and quick to do harm; in the Chartrain and the Dunois they left no cottage or house standing outside the castle. They left no ox or cow, heiffer or bull, pig or sheep, ewe, goat or lamb, cock, chicken, hen, old dog or pup and no wheat in the barn or good wine in the barrel. Theobald was greatly afraid of this new race; too many of them had come and they were a very great curse. They made a very grievous slaughter of men and women, and no one dared attack or challenge their army. The Angevins and those from Le Mans withdrew, and robbers and thieves slipped away into the woods. (4182–94)

The Danes were doing a huge amount of harm; they were not Christians and did not believe in God. They set churches alight, demolished altars, killed peasants and violated women; this was something the French hated very much.

---

[133] The manuscript reads *Polut*, which may be an error for Pohier 'the inhabitants of the county of Poix in Picardy' (Holden, note to v. 4144, vol. 3, p. 212). It could also be an error for Ponthieu.

The peasants fled from the villages to the cities. Those whom the pagans caught died painful deaths and the king and Theobald could not help them; they did not dare look at them and feared them greatly. There were so many pagans, as many people have said, for they captured Maine, Anjou and France and would have done the same as far as the Great Saint Bernard Pass if they had wanted to go there. They set out from Jeufosse and remained there, taking there whatever they had captured.* The Normans, who shared in the booty, were with them; they captured equipment and plunder without paying a high price. (4195–4210)

When the Normans and the Danes had laid waste the Chartrain and destroyed and robbed the Dunois, they forced their way into the king's lands. They brought great wealth back to Jeufosse and gave it to the Normans very cheaply, and they duly bought it dirt-cheap. Then there was great famine throughout the whole of France and remarkable plenty in Normandy, where men ploughed in safety, sowed in safety and harvested fruit and corn in safety; from the wealth of the French they were rich and well equipped. The peasants in France were very fearful; knights and villeins were not safe except in castles or fortified cities. The king and the bishops conferred and assembled a council at Laon;* they explained to the king the harm and great cruelty which had come upon the whole kingdom because of him, the destruction of the churches and the slaughter of people. Many women had been dishonoured, many made widows and many young children in cradles made orphans.* (4211–31)

'My lord', said some, 'what is your advice? Look at your land being destroyed, inside and out, look at the houses and provisions burning and look at the men who have taken flight and been defeated and ransomed. The Duke of Normandy is not foolish or slow; he has attracted to him so many pagans, amongst others, and he can bring grief to you, to Theobald and to ourselves. Theobald has a hundred towns, nay, more than two hundred, in which he has not ploughed or sown a hundred acres. We have played a number of tricks on many people and broken agreements, fealty and oaths; he will never trust you or any of your family. It would be an illusion and of no use to seek peace with Richard, for we will never have peace unless we hand Évreux over to him. What are you doing, what are you delaying for, what are you thinking, what are you waiting for? You are not seeking peace for us or defending us. In whatever you say to him, you lie and tell untruths.' (4232–48)

'The whole land is destroyed', they said, 'and many towns are laid waste, many churches demolished, many wives dishonoured and many ladies violated. The peasants are not in the vineyards or at their ploughs; France will never prosper through those who are left. If Theobald holds Évreux, Richard has sold it at a good price; Theobald has lost the profit from his land and his revenues. No woman remaining, however old and white-haired, can avoid being violated if she is caught. Theobald, who started the war, is acting wrongly by not defending himself or fighting hard; you are not helping him and neither is he bothering you. Such a fleet, filled with brave men, has come to Richard that the whole of Normandy is covered with them, as if by birds; anger has grown and war has increased so much that peace will never be maintained day or night until a race of people is destroyed and overcome.' (4249–65)

So much did the bishops of France blame the King of France, advising and urging him, that the king summoned the Bishop of Chartres; he was highly regarded for his wisdom and intelligence and was a noble man of good family.[134] He sent the bishop to Richard and he found him in Rouen; Richard served and honoured the bishop greatly, lodging him and looking after him well, and the bishop said everything he wanted to say to Richard.

'Richard', said the bishop, 'you have behaved badly in handing this country over to pagans and destroying churches and Christianity. The whole world is astonished that a man of your goodness would behave so cruelly to Christian people.'

'Upon my word', said Richard, 'I have remained here.[135] If the land has been destroyed, I have done this on purpose in order to destroy Theobald, who had deserved more, and to rid the king of his arrogance and pride, for they have willingly harmed me as much as possible, and I will take my revenge, if God has destined it.' (4266–85)

'Friend', said Richard, 'I do not intend to lie to you. I would rather demolish churches than die in dishonour, and abandon Normandy to pagans rather than be forced out of it shamefully by the king. I recognise that I should hold my land from the king, but since he wants to take it from me without due judgement I will hold on to it, if I can, and bring sorrow to them all. Pagans come to serve me from another land; they come because I need them, should I then fail them? The king wanted to dishonour me through Bruno, the archbishop. Then he had me come to the parley on the Seine; if he could have captured me, he would have put me to death. He wanted to have me destroyed, but did not succeed. The king caused me to flee from the Eaulne to the Dieppe. Since he could not destroy me or get hold of me, on Theobald's advice he came to seize my lands; he took Évreux, my city, then fortified it and handed it over to Theobald to the humiliation of my men. I will yet see them repent for this, please God. Then Theobald came back to attack me in Rouen. One night he came and lodged near the river; he was hardly able to enjoy the gains he had made. For the rest of his life he will remember this. Let the king get an agreement between myself and Theobald, decide who owns the lands legally and share them out; if he does not stop what he is doing, you can pledge to him that I will repeatedly make him hear news such as will not be to his liking or his pleasure.' (4286–4313)

'Richard', said the bishop, 'listen to me and trust me. Remember God and His holy faith. He will soon have completely confounded your reputation and your arrogance.* You are destroying the Holy Church wrongly and unjustly and making poor people destitute, without knowing why; those who have done no wrong are paying a severe price.[136] Take pity on the poor and give the king a truce. He will come and speak with you at Jeufosse. He will make peace as you wish, this he tells you through me; from this time forward, he will remain absolutely loyal to you.' Richard replied thus:

[134] Neither Dudo nor the *GND* mentions the Bishop of Chartres.
[135] The meaning of this line is uncertain.
[136] The meaning of this line is unclear.

'I grant him this, but there will be no peace in this matter, this is my clear understanding, as long as Theobald holds a finger-length of my land. Because of my city which he holds, he is behaving with great pride.' Richard and the bishop conferred and the bishop spoke successfully until Richard showed mercy and pity to the poor. He confessed his sin and error to the bishop and agreed to the truce, granting secure friendship between himself and the king in front of all the barons and the clergy; otherwise, he would consider everything to be mockery and deceit. (4314–35)

'My friend', said Richard, 'you may leave. After a short while, come to me in Jeufosse and bring me a number of the bishops of France and I will have my men gather to meet you. In your presence, I will speak, if you are willing to hear me, and if those who do harm and whom you fear so grant the peace just as you request, I will grant it also and not be blamed for it. If they do not grant it, your words are in vain, for I will do nothing unless it is their will.' The bishop took leave of Duke Richard; he went to the king and told him how he had fared. All the clerics and laymen were delighted by the truce; the peasants went back to the towns and the burgs and the merchants went to the fairs and the markets. (4336–50)

Count Theobald of Chartres heard the news that the king and Richard were to be friends and that the king had left him out of the truce. He took a monk from Chartres, a learned man who had been brought up there, and sent him to Richard, who received him well.

'My lord', said the monk, 'on Theobald's behalf I beseech you to give him a truce until he comes here to you. He will give you back Évreux, which the king took from you, and will put himself at your mercy for his other crimes.'

'Let him come', said Richard, 'I pledge my loyalty to him.' Theobald did not ignore the message. He rode to Rouen with a small number of companions. At the gate he called out and the porter opened it to him. Richard heard the news* and considered him foolhardy for intruding on him without any other protection, and yet, because he did not distrust him in any way, he granted what he wanted and agreed to everything. They kissed each other and rejoiced greatly.

'Richard', said Theobald, 'I have come to you. I have done wrong by you and hated you wrongly. If you have done wrong by me, I have fully deserved it. I am ready to do right by you in accordance with your mercy. I will give you back Évreux, which the king took from you, and I will never hate you; rather do I swear to you and affirm that I am ready to help you if you have need of aid, and let it be the same if I need help.'

'Upon my word', said Richard, 'I grant it thus.' Then Theobald swore to Richard and pledged the accord and the peace as he offered it. (4351–79)

On the day when the bishops were to come and speak with the duke, the duke had the Danes removed from Jeufosse. He had the quarters made over to the bishops of France and had an abundance of bread, wine and provisions brought; he had the French stay for a week at his expense, for the Danes refused to grant the peace. You would have heard them calling out loudly in Danish and shouting and quarrelling violently with Richard, trying to increase the antagonism between Richard and the French; they did not deign to hear or listen to a word, nor could Richard win the day over all of them. You would have seen the

French twisted and contorted in anger; they did not think they could ever find a truce.

'Richard', said the Danes, 'leave us in France. We want to conquer the whole land for your use. We wish to make you lord of it, if you want to defend it, and if you do not want to take control of it . . .'[137]

'I will not do so, I prefer to make peace.' (4380–97)

The peace was confirmed, without obstacle, between the King of France, who was called Lothar, and Count Richard, a very noble warrior. Just as the Normans were able to establish peace more successfully, thus they made the king swear and pledge it. They returned to their lands without any further delay. Then you would have heard peasants rejoicing in the marches. The Duke of Normandy was confident and proud. To the Danes, who had come from Denmark to help him and who had had themselves baptized for love of him, he gave revenues and lands and fields to plough; he had them richly accommodated throughout the lands. The others, who refused to abandon paganism, he had laden with clothing, money and silver, as much as they wanted; he did not want to make any of them angry. He had boats, barges and ships fitted out and laden with provisions and other goods; he had good helmsmen given to them from the Cotentin, who knew how to sail and row over the sea. They headed for Spain, to a fertile country, and captured eighteen cities which they destroyed; I do not know what became of them and I will not attempt to find out. We have to return to the Duke of Normandy. But one can become tired by a long journey and fine songs can become wearisome.* He who sings must drink or take some other reward. He who can should progress in his profession; Wace* would gladly accept bounty, for he needs to take something. (4398–4425)

---

[137] There seems to be quite a substantial lacuna after v. 4396. The end of this *laisse* and perhaps the whole of the following *laisse* are missing.

PART THREE

To remember the deeds, words and ways of our ancestors, the wicked deeds of wicked men and the brave deeds of brave men, books, chronicles and histories should be read out at festivals. If documents were not composed and then read and recounted by clerics, many things which transpired in times gone by would be forgotten. Over time, as the years go by, through changes in language, many towns and regions have lost their original names. England was called Britain and its first name was Albion; London was called Trinovant and before that New Troy. Everwic [York] was called Eborac and firstly Kaer Ebrac. South Wales was Demetia and North Wales Venedocia. Scotland used to be called Albany, Poitou and Gascony Aquitaine; Brittany was Armorica and Alemainne Germany. Cologne was called Agrippina, Thérouanne Morine, Paris Lutetia, the land of Greece Pelasge, Apulia and Lombardy Italy and Constantinople Byzantium. Bethlehem was called Effrata, Jerusalem Gebus, Burgundy Allobroga, Autun Cacua; Judea was Palestine, Sebastye Samaria, Orléans Genabés, Valognes Nantus, Rouen Rothoma, Avranches Ausiona, France Gaul, Wales Cambria and Normandy Neustria.[138] (1–44)

Neustria lost this name and I will tell you why this happened. Whatever there is towards the north, which we call the Chariot in the Sky [the Great Bear], whether it is sky or air, land or sea, everyone is accustomed to call north, because from the north there comes and rises a wind from where the sky holds its chariot. The English say in their language, according to their usage: 'We are going to the north, we come from the north, we were born in the north, we live in the north'. They say the same about a wind from the east, from the south and also from the west. In English and Norse 'man' is equivalent to 'homme' [*hume*] in French. Bring together 'north' and 'man' and together you say Northman, that is 'man of the north' in the vernacular, and from this came the name Normans. Those who were born where the north wind comes from are habitually called Normans, and from the Normans is derived the name Normandy, which they have populated. It used to be called Neustria, as long as it belonged to the French, but because of the men who came from the north it retained the name of Normandy, because the Normans, who lived in that land, populated it. The French say that Normandy is the land of beggars from the north [*north mendie*]. The Normans, people say in jest, came begging from the north, because they came from another land to obtain better possessions and make conquests. (45–80)

---

[138] Where there is no obvious English equivalent, place names are given here according to the form used by Wace. A reading of this passage is complicated by the existence of a number of variants (see Holden, vol. 1, pp. 161–62) and by the fact that in vv. 30–37 Wace reverses the normal order, presenting the earlier name of the location before the later. In addition, the reading of v. 36 is uncertain (see Holden's note, vol. 3, p. 214).

Concerning the twists and turns of these names and the deeds of which we are speaking, we would have been able to say little or nothing if someone had not had them written down. There have been many cities and many rich domains about which we would now have known nothing if we had not had something in writing. Thebes has a great reputation and Babylon had great power; Troy had great power and Nineveh was long and broad. Anyone who went in search of these locations now would find scarcely any trace of them. Nebuchadnezzar was king and he built a golden statue, sixty cubits high and six cubits broad; if anyone wanted to see his body now, he would not, I believe, find anyone who could explain or state where one could find his bones or ashes. But through the good clerics who wrote things down and committed the deeds to books we can speak of ages past and tell of many great works. Alexander was a powerful king; in twelve years he captured twelve kingdoms. He had a great deal of land and wealth and was a king of very great power. But if he did made conquests, this did him little good; he was poisoned and died. (81–112)

Caesar, who did so much and had such ability and who conquered and possessed the entire world – never has any man before or since, I believe, conquered so much – was then treacherously killed in the Capitol, as we read. Neither of these two men, who conquered so much, had so many lands and captured so many kings, when he died had any more of his own domain than his own length. What good has all this done them? What have they achieved by their fame and conquests? Only what people say about who Alexander and Caesar were, according to what they have found in books; all that remains of them is their names. They would have been forgotten if they had not been written about. Everything turns to decline, everything fails, everything dies, everything comes to an end. A tower collapses, a wall falls down, a rose withers, a horse stumbles, cloth grows old, a man dies, iron wears out, wood rots, everything made by hand perishes. I understand completely and am fully aware that all men die, cleric and lay, and that after their death their fame is short-lived unless it is set down in a book by a cleric; it cannot survive or live on in any other way. (113–42)

Those who wrote chronicles and composed histories used to be greatly honoured and very much praised and loved; they often used to receive handsome gifts from barons and noble ladies for setting down their lives in writing, so that they would be remembered for all time. But now I can put in a great deal of effort, write and translate books and compose romances and *serventeis*,[139] but I will scarcely find anyone sufficiently courtly to give me and present me with enough money to employ a scribe for a month, or who would do me any other favour than to remark: 'Master Wace says this very well. You who are skilled in fine and elegant speech ought to keep on writing.' I am content with this and put every effort into it; I will never get more than this from many people. I speak to rich men, who have money and a good income, for through them books are composed and good deeds written down and properly recounted. (143–66)

---

[139] On the terms *rumanz* and *serventeis* in v. 153 see II, v. 4149, III, v. 5311 and Introduction, p. xxiv.

What used to be nobility is dead, and largesse has disappeared along with it; however near or far I may travel, I cannot find anyone who upholds its customs. I can scarcely find anyone who bestows anything on me apart from Henry the second. In Bayeux, and may God reward him for it, he gave me a prebend and he has given me many other gifts as well. May God show him gratitude for all this! He was born of the first Henry and was father to the third; I saw all three of them. I saw and knew three king Henrys; in their time I was a *clerc lisant*.[140] All three were kings of the English and all three were dukes and kings; they were kings of England the Rich and dukes of Normandy. In honour of the second Henry, who was born of the lineage of Rou, I have spoken at length of Rou and his powerful family, and of Normandy which he conquered and of the acts of prowess he performed there. We have dealt with the history of William Longsword, up to the time when the Flemish, as the wicked do, killed him treacherously. We have spoken of his son Richard, whom his father left behind as a small child. Louis, that is Louis Outremer, harassed him greatly after William was killed, but he never managed to bring matters to an end. Louis was brought up in England and that is why he was called Outremer. After the death of Louis, who for a long time was strong and powerful, Lothar, his son, took up the war and attempted to take land away from Richard. Richard, who wanted to maintain his rights, recruited from Denmark Danes and good warriors who were of such great assistance to him that the king and the French became very anxious to have peace with him. Then for the whole of his life Richard held Normandy in joy and peace. He was a man of excellent upbringing and splendid conduct, who took a great interest in birds and hounds; many an adventure befell him. He was skilled in legal matters and rational argument; many of the surrounding lands abided by his judgement and came to him for advice. As his wife he had Duke Hugh's daughter, who was called Lady Emma and very beautiful and comely, but he was not able to have a child by her. She died without his having any heir and he gave all her wealth, gold and silver, clothing and coins, to poor people and churches; he grieved sorely for his wife, but grief does not provide any remedy. The living to the living, the dead to the dead; from the living one can take comfort.[141] (167–233)

In this country* there was a maiden by the name of Gunnor; she was very beautiful, well educated and very courtly. Her father and mother were Danish and she was born of noble Danes, with good lineage on both sides. She was kind and friendly, very generous and honourable; she knew all a woman could know about women's work. The count loved her and made her his beloved; their love was very fine. He had five sons by her; the first one was called Richard and they cherished him greatly. Through the advice of his mother, Gunnor, this first child took his father's name. The second was given a good education: his name was Robert. He was very learned and became Archbishop of Rouen after Archbishop

---

[140] On the expression *clerc lisant* see Introduction, pp. xiv–xv.

[141] For remarks on the prologue to Part III see Bezzola, vol. 3, part 1, pp. 184–90, who states that this prologue and those of the *Roman d'Alexandre* and the *Roman de Thèbes* constitute a 'défense du clerc' (p. 184).

Hugh. After Robert, Malger was born; there is no need to name the others. Richard had three daughters. Emma, the eldest, was highly esteemed and honoured; she was taken to England and married to King Æthelred. King Æthelred had two sons by her, one called Edward and the other Alfred. The second daughter was called Hawise and on the advice of his friends she was given in lawful marriage to Geoffrey, Duke of Brittany. From her he had Alain and Ywun;[142] both were powerful men. The third was Matilda by name and she was given in France to Count Odo, who held Chartres and the Chartrain and had power over Tours and Blois.[143] (234–72)

Richard loved clerics and learning, knights and knighthood. He travelled at night just as by day, having no fear of anything; he saw and encountered many an apparition without ever being afraid of anything. Nothing he saw, either by night or by day, caused him any fear. Because he travelled so much at night, people used to say of him that he could see as clearly at night as someone else could do during the day.[144] When he travelled, at each church he encountered he was accustomed to go inside, if he could; if this was not possible. he prayed outside. One night he came to a church and wanted to pray and entreat God. He went off at a distance from his men, deep in thought, while they rode to and fro. He tied up his horse outside; inside he found a body on a bier. He went past this bier and knelt before the altar; he threw his gloves on to a lectern, but when he departed he forgot them. He kissed the floor and prayed, afraid of nothing. He had not spent much time there and not prayed* there for long when behind him in the church he heard the body moving and the bier grating. He turned round to look at the body:

'Lie there', he said, 'do not move! Whether you are a good or a bad thing, lie in peace and rest!' Then the count said his prayer, I do not know whether it was long or short; then he said, crossing himself: 'By this sign of the Holy Cross, free me from evil things, Lord God of Salvation.'[145] When he turned round, he said: 'God, I entrust my soul to your hands.' He took his sword, looked round and the Devil rose up. He was standing over towards the door; he stood in front of it with his arms outstretched as if he intended to seize Richard and bar his exit. Richard drew his sword and cut his body in half. He knocked him down across the bier; I do not know whether he uttered any sound or cry. Richard came to his horse and had left the cemetery when he remembered his gloves; not wanting to leave them, he returned. He came to the chancel and picked up his gloves; there are many men who would not have gone back there. He gave orders to churches and had it announced and proclaimed in markets that no body should ever be left alone before it had been buried.[146] (273–336)

---

[142] Ywun was in reality Odo, Count of Penthièvre. In v. 267 this same personage is called Johan ('John').

[143] For Gunnor's innumerable relatives see the *GND*, where, in one of his genealogies, Robert of Torigny states that many later Norman leaders were descendants of Gunnor's female relatives (II, pp. 267–75).

[144] This information concerning Richard's special ability is new.

[145] The text here is in Latin.

[146] On Richard's encounter with the devil see Gouttebroze, 'Le Diable dans le *Roman de Rou*', pp. 217–20. Gouttebroze stresses the originality of Wace's account of the way in which Richard

Another adventure befell him, which was considered a marvel and would scarcely have been believed had it not been known by so many; I have heard it related by many people who heard it from their forebears. But many a time, through lack of interest, idleness or ignorance, many a fine deed is not committed to writing which would be fine and good to relate. In the abbey of Saint-Ouen there was at that time a sacristan who was regarded as a loyal monk and had a very good reputation.[147] But the more worthy a person is, the more he is assailed by the Devil, the more he lies in wait for him and tempts him in a variety of ways. The sacristan I am telling you about, under the influence of the Devil, was one day going through the church, taking care of his business, when he saw a lady and fell in love with her, desiring her exceedingly. He thought himself as good as dead if he did not have his way with her; he would not fail to do this for anything he owned. He spoke to her so eloquently and promised her so much that the lady agreed a time with him, that he would go that night to her lodging and cross the plank over the Robec, a stream which ran beneath it; he could not cross anywhere else or speak to her in any other way. (337–70)

That night, when it was completely dark and the monks were asleep, the sacristan was fearful; he had no companion with him and had not sought one. He reached the plank and climbed on to it; I cannot say whether he stumbled, slipped or lost his footing, but he fell and drowned. A devil seized his soul as soon as it left his body, intending to carry it away to hell; but an angel tried to take it away from him; each of them attempted to pull his soul towards him and each gave his reason for doing so. The devil said:

'You do me wrong in taking away this soul which I am carrying. Do not you know that this soul became mine as soon as it embarked on a wrong track? It had started out on the wrong track and I found it doing wrong; it had set out on the wrong path and I caught it on the path of wrong. Wherever I find you, said God, there will I judge you. I found the monk doing wrongful work; the path he was following gave him away and there is no need for any other proof, as soon as he is discovered doing wrong. The path of sin he was following, when he fell, has pronounced judgement over him.' (371–400)

The angel of God replied to him:

'Be quiet', he said, 'things will not be like this. The monk lived a good life as long as he was in the abbey. He lived well and loyally; we have not seen him do any wrong. It is the testimony of scripture, and it is true reason and justice, that everything will be well rewarded and each wrong will be punished. He should be rewarded for the good things we know him to have done. What will become of all the good he has done if he is destroyed? And he has not yet committed the sin for which you have now taken and judged him. He had left the abbey and come to the

---

I, faced with the disturbing presence of the devil, displays determination and faith and shows that he can protect his followers both physically and spiritually. In the eleventh and twelfth centuries there was a movement to attribute saintly powers to Richard. See J. Bédier, 'Richard de Normandie dans les chansons de geste', and N. Cazauran, 'Richard sans peur: un personnage en quête d'auteur'.

[147] Saint-Ouen was an important abbey, which Wace mentions on several occasions (especially III, vv. 701–28, but also *Chronique Ascendante* (*CA*), v. 241, II, v. 3140, and III, v. 2288).

plank; he might still have drawn back from committing the sin if he had not fallen. As he had not committed any wickedness, it is very possible that he would not have done so. Merely because of his foolish thoughts and a modicum of desire, you wish to judge him and condemn him; you are committing a great wrong, let his soul be! To put an end to this dispute, so that neither of us can complain about the other, let us go over to Count Richard and submit ourselves to his judgement; he will make a loyal judgement, as he never makes a false one. Let us stand by what he says without contradiction and without quarrel.' (401–34)

The Devil replied:

'I agree. Let the soul be judged between you and me in this way.' They came at once to Richard, to a chamber where his bed was; he had been sleeping, but at that time was awake, going over many things in his mind. They explained the situation to him, as it had transpired between them, about the monk who in such folly had left his abbey. He was on the way to commit sin, but had not yet done anything sinful; he had toppled off the plank and drowned in the water beneath. Let him come to a judgement and pronounce truly on who should have the monk's soul. Richard said to them curtly:

'Go at once and put the monk's soul back into his body and pull him out of the water. He should not be deceived or caught out, but repositioned on the plank in the very spot from which he fell, when he stumbled and perished. If he takes a full stride forward, either a foot or a full pace, however it might be, let the Devil have him and take the soul without contradiction or objection. If the monk steps back and turns round, let him have his peace.' Neither of them objected to the judgement Richard made. They took the soul back to the body and the monk recovered; then he got up and came back to life and was replaced where he had fallen.[148] As soon as the monk became aware of what was happening and stood in peace on the plank, he took a step backwards quicker than a man who had stepped on a snake. He went back home swiftly, like a man who was afraid of death, and those who held him let him go; he did not take leave of them. He fled to the abbey, wrung out his clothing and hid. He was still afraid he would die there and he was uncertain whether he would go on living. (435–82)

When Richard rose at dawn, he went to pray at Saint-Ouen; he gathered together all the occupants of the convent and asked for the monk. The monk came, with his clothes wet; he had not yet dried them. The count summoned him and made him come before the abbot. 'Brother', he said, 'how do things seem to you? How did you get yourself into that situation? Take better care next time when you cross the plank. Tell the abbot the truth about where you were last night.' Because of his abbot and the count, the monk blushed and felt ashamed, but nevertheless he confessed everything, how he went and how he perished, how the Devil tricked him and how the count freed him; he told the whole truth and the count bore witness to it all. That is the way things became known and the

---

[148] For *en pais* 'in peace' (v. 472) other manuscripts have *en piez* 'on his feet'.

truth acknowledged. This joke was told throughout Normandy for a long time: 'Lord monk, go quietly and mind how you cross the plank!'[149] (483–510)

There was some moorland called Corcers, close to Lyons-la-Forêt. In this area is a valley, neither very broad nor very long; in the forest there is an open space with fields all round it. The month of August was just about over when the duke rose early. Having had his foresters explore where he might find large stags, and had his bows and arrows and his bloodhounds transported there, he went hunting. He had the hunters and servants bring hunting dogs, brachets and lymers[150] and made them take another route in order to avoid being seen. He carried his sword by his side, as he never travelled without it, and came swiftly to Corcers. Hear now what misfortune befell him! He tried to look down into the undergrowth below, I do not know whether he hoped to see anything. In the distance he saw a knight, well dressed and attired; beside him on the ground was his sword, which was equipped with a belt and well decorated. Also at his side was a maiden who was very noble and beautiful, well dressed and attired, with her wimple thrown over her head. The knight could not take flight when he saw the count coming. God, what a sin, for with his sword the knight cut off the maiden's head! The count cried:

'Evil-doer, evil-doer! Women should live everywhere in peace.' Then he spurred towards the knight and cut the head off his body. Afterwards he stopped and stared, seeing and gazing on their beauty; never before, he said, and this was his impression, had he seen such handsome people together. On the fourth day he had them buried, but was never able to find anyone who knew them or knew who either of them were. Because of the sin the duke committed in killing the knight, this was not set down in writing, but it has been handed down from the father to son. (511–60)

Another remarkable adventure took place at the edge of this moorland, to one of the count's hunters. Consider whether it was a matter of honour or shame! They had caught a stag and captured and killed it. They had skinned it and fastened its best parts to a forked stick. One of the hunters made haste; wanting to leave, he turned to go, intending to go to his lord along a path he knew. In the wood he discovered, near the entrance, a maiden who was very well dressed and well shod, well attired with her hair nicely bound. He came to her and greeted her; she returned his greeting and stood up. When he saw her on her feet, he dismounted at once, asking her who she was and what she was doing alone in this wood; she said she was waiting for a man, who was to come and meet her. The hunter took her by one of her sleeves, saying that he was entirely at her service. I cannot relate his precise words, nor how she reacted to him, but people say that

---

[149] This story of the monk from Saint-Ouen is not found in Wace's sources, but it belongs to a well-known tradition. Wace claims to have heard it told by many people (vv. 341–42). Gouttebroze points out that Wace's treatment of the story is different from other accounts and he stresses the subtlety of the debate in Wace's version ('Le Diable dans le *Roman de Rou*', pp. 220–27).

[150] Brachets and lymers are types of hunting hounds. The lymer had the task of detecting the whereabouts of a hart on the morning of a hunt. The brachet or scenting hound was a smaller dog, but it was used in a similar way to the lymer. See John Cummins, *The Hound and the Hawk: The Art of Medieval Hunting* (London: Weidenfeld and Nicolson, 1988), pp. 22–23, 47.

he took hold of her and placed her down on the ground beside him. She suffered and permitted him everything, forbidding him nothing; he made up his mind to do to her what a man should do to a woman. When he had done what he pleased with her and wanted to get up from her, intending to leave her, she hurled him with such force, I do not know whether it was with her feet or her hands, that he flew high into the air amongst the branches and boughs and ended up perched in the fork of a tree. When he tried to look at her and was about to speak to her, he did not know what had become of her; he neither heard her nor saw her. The hunters who were carrying the stag and making their way along this path saw their companion in the tree and got him down with great difficulty.[151] (561–610)

Richard kept Gunnor for a long time, it is generally said, before he was willing to marry her and take her as his wife. But as a result of entreaties by the clergy, who had begged him to do this many a time, and on the advice of his barons, who had many a time exhorted him to do so, Richard married Gunnor; before and afterwards he loved her dearly. When Gunnor first retired to bed on the night of their wedding, she lay down in bed beside the count in a different way and a different manner from her usual one, as if she were resisting him; she turned her back on him and pushed him with her shoulders.

'How is it', he said, 'that you are behaving like this? You have lain with me frequently and never done this to me; you normally turn your face towards me.' Gunnor replied with a laugh:

'My lord, my lord, things are not like that. I have been accustomed to lying in your bed and to doing your bidding. Now I am lying in my own bed and will lie on whichever side I like. I am a married woman and lying in my own bed; I will lie for my own pleasure. Hitherto, the bed was yours, but now it is mine and yours. I never lay in it with confidence and was never with you without fear. Now I have some security.' With these words, she turned round. They turned to look at each other, laughing and joking; for a good long time afterwards, what Gunnor had said and done was recounted.[152] Gunnor was a highly-esteemed lady of good character and well educated; she honoured clerics and knights, spent generously and gave away a great deal. (611–54)

At that time Lothar, who was King of France and strong and fierce, died. He had no son, daughter or other heir who should have the kingdom as a fief. With Lothar, the lineage, which had been admired for a long time throughout the world, came to an end; it was the lineage of Charlemagne, who held Saxony, Germany, Rome, France, Lombardy and a very large part of Spain. Because of the lack of good lineage and on the advice of the most senior barons, Hugh Capet was accepted and made king of France. Capet was the son of Hugh the Great, duke and ruler of Paris; because of his prowess, and because of Richard who had married his sister, through his advice and his love, the French made Hugh lord.[153]

---

[151] This anecdote concerning the count's hunter is not found elsewhere.

[152] This story of Richard and Gunnor is unique to Wace.

[153] The sister referred to here is Emma, whose early death without an heir is narrated below (III, vv. 223–30). Emma's death ended the hoped-for alliance between Normandy and France.

The Flemish tried to oppose him, not wanting him to become their lord, and Hugh mounted a campaign against them. He came to Arras and besieged them; he laid siege to the city all around, but not for long as he had soon taken it. Count Arnulf saw that he was losing and could not defend himself, so he begged Richard for a reconciliation which would avoid both his disinheritance and his death. Richard undertook the peace; he wanted it and went ahead with it. Then he took his leave and departed, returning to Normandy. (655–88)

Richard loved good vassals, good knights and good clerics and held them dear. He had the church of the archbishopric of Rouen, his wealthiest see, knocked down and a larger one erected for the mother of our Lord; he made it longer and broader, taller and better paved. He built Mont-Saint-Michel, placed monks there and honoured it greatly, paying much attention to its construction and devoting a lot of money and income to it. In Rouen he spent a large amount of money on the abbey of Saint-Ouen and frequently visited it to see how everyone was faring. He had stone brought from many parts and in the name of the Holy Trinity constructed the church at Fécamp, which has great prestige. He equipped it well and richly with everything a splendid church requires, books and vestments, crosses and other equipment. He settled clerics there, who would serve, and prebends on which they could live, and he had the bishops of Normandy, over whom he had lordship, come to the dedication and took care of them very well. He had a sarcophagus, in which his body would be placed after his death, prepared beside the church wall, beneath the outside gutter. Then, every Friday, as long as he lived after that, he had it filled to the brim with wheat to share out amongst poor people, along with five shillings of money from Rouen, for the sick and the needy.[154] (689–728)

He fell ill at Bayeux; he was already an old man and became weak. When he saw that death was upon him, that no doctor could cure him and that he was no longer capable of standing up, he gave orders that he should be carried to Fécamp. Then he summoned his barons, his sons, his daughters and his companions, and also his brother Count Ralph, who was from the same mother as himself. He made his son Richard his heir; he was already a powerful man. With regard to the other sons, he asked Richard repeatedly, told him and commanded him that he should maintain them, take care of them and give them some of his land, so that each of them would be able to support himself; he would be served by them. Everything he asked for was granted; Richard did not oppose him in any way. As was his duty, he confessed to the bishops, the abbots and many ordained clergy; he said his *mea culpa*, recognised God and received the body of our Lord, remaining curled up in the bed where he lay; his pain was great and he had to die. When he died, there was great sorrow; at that time you could have heard the weeping and wailing of men, daughters and sons. They carried the body to the sarcophagus which he had prepared a long time ago. When he was buried, you could have heard men and women lamenting; one should mourn a good lord, for finding another one is a hard thing to do. Above him they constructed a chapel to Saint Thomas, which is very beautiful. (729–66)

---

[154] This story is found in Dudo (p. 170).

When the first Richard died and Richard the second received the honour, a thousand years less four had passed since God was born on earth. Richard was the father and Richard the son; each was very brave and noble and each was Duke of Normandy.[155] The father was a good man, the son more so. Through his goodness, his nobility, his valour and his largesse, this one was called Richard the Good; he was greatly esteemed and greatly loved. He made a great effort to serve God and hear God's service. He loved the religious and devoted much care to the love of clerics and monks, doing his best to honour them. He sent for monks from Dijon who were of great piety, the most honourable, the best educated, the most highly esteemed and the best loved; they came from an abbey of excellent repute in Burgundy. He removed the clergy from the churches his father had built and placed monks there. In Fécamp he built an abbey, the most splendid in Normandy, putting so much into it and giving so much to it that the people were astonished. (767–96)

He did not want to put the affairs of his household in the hands of any but noble men. The chaplains were noble, the scribes were noble and the constables noble, very powerful and able-bodied. The stewards were noble, the marshals noble, the butlers noble and the almoners noble; the chamberlains and ushers were all noble knights.[156] Each day they had their rations, and on the principal feast-days clothing and gifts. In this way the court was well served. Each person was treated with courtesy and each did his best to behave nobly and perform acts of honour and largesse. (797–814)

He had scarcely reigned or been duke for any length of time when there arose in that land a war which was to cause great misery. The peasants and villeins, those from the woodlands and those from the plains (I do not know through whose instigation it happened or who started it in the first place), held a number of councils in groups of twenty, thirty and a hundred. They were devising a plan such that, if they could succeed in it and bring it to fruition, harm would be done to the highest noblemen. They discussed this in private and many of them swore between themselves that never again would they willingly have a lord or a governor. Lords did them nothing but harm and they could get nothing out of them, from either their produce or their labours; each day they were experiencing great suffering. They were enduring pain and hardship. Things used to be bad, but now they were worse; every day their beasts were being taken to pay for aids and service. There were so many complaints and legal actions and so many old and new customs that they could not have an hour's peace. Every day they were subject to lawsuits, lawsuits about forest laws, lawsuits about coinage, lawsuits about enclosure payments,[157] lawsuits about pathways, lawsuits about the construction of canals, lawsuits about payments for milling corn, lawsuits

---

[155] Wace states that both Richard I and Richard II were dukes of Normandy, but in reality Richard II was the first Norman ruler to style himself 'duke' (Latin *dux*). On the difficult issue of the relationship between the titles 'count' and 'duke' see David Bates, *Normandy before 1066* (London: Longman, 1982), pp. 148–51.

[156] This point about the nobility of Richard's household is not found elsewhere.

[157] On the term *purprises* in v. 846, translated here as 'enclosure payments', see Holden's note (vol. 3, p. 217). The sense could also be 'encroachment' or 'trespass'.

about broken obligations and about theft, lawsuits about snares,[158] lawsuits about corvées,[159] lawsuits about quarrels and lawsuits about aids.[160] (815–50)

There were so many provosts and beadles, so many bailiffs, old and new, that they had no peace for a single hour; all day long they descended on them. They could not defend themselves in court; each one of them wanted his due. These men had their beasts taken by force and they did not dare take a stand or defend themselves. They could not go on living like this; they would have to abandon their lands. They could get no protection against either their lord or his men, who did not keep any agreement with them.

'Son of a whore!' said some, 'why do we put up with all the harm which is being done to us? Let us free ourselves from their control! We are men as they are; we have the same limbs as they do, we are their equal physically and are able to endure as much as they can. The only thing we lack is courage. Let us unite on oath, defend our goods and ourselves and stick together. If they wish to wage war on us, against one knight we have thirty or forty peasants, skilful and valiant. Thirty men in the flower of their youth will be cowardly and shameful if they cannot defend themselves against one man, providing they are willing to join forces. With clubs and large stakes, arrows and staffs, axes, bows and pikes,[161] and stones for those who have no arms, let us defend ourselves against knights with the large number of men we have. In this way we can go into woods, cut down trees and take what we will, catch fish in the rivers and venison in the forests. We will do as we wish with everything, with the woods, the ponds and the meadows.' (851–94)

With such talk and such words, and other even more foolish remarks, they all agreed on this plan and all swore they would join forces and defend themselves together. They chose I do not know which or how many of the most intelligent amongst them and the best speakers who would go round the country receiving oaths. But a plan transmitted to so many people could not be concealed for long. Whether it was from vassals or men-at-arms, women or children, through drunkenness or anger, Richard very soon heard that the peasants were forming a commune and would take away what was rightfully his, from him and the other lords who had peasants and vavassors. He sent for his uncle Ralph and related the whole affair to him; Ralph was the very valiant count of Évreux and very skilled in many things. (895–917)

'My lord', he said, 'do not worry; leave the peasants to me, for you would only regret taking action yourself. But send me your household troops, send me your knights.'

---

[158] Buttry translates *aguaiz* as 'robbery and murder' ('Contempt or Empathy?', p. 35) and refers to the fact that the term can designate crimes by stealth (stemming from the notion of ambush or lying in wait). However, the other 'crimes' listed by Wace all seem to be those in which the peasants, if found guilty, could claim to be unjustly treated by their lords.

[159] A *corvée* was a day's work of unpaid labour.

[160] Wace's remarks are interesting because he is obviously guessing what sort of complaints the peasants might have had two hundred years previously. On the peasants' revolt see also Arnoux, pp. 45ff.

[161] The term translated here and elsewhere as 'pike' is *gisarme*, a weapon rather like an axe, sometimes with a curved blade and fixed to a lengthy staff.

'Willingly', Richard replied to him. Then Ralph sent his spies and his couriers to many places. He did so much spying and had his spies make so many enquiries, with both the sick and the healthy, that he caught and captured the peasants who were arranging the meetings and receiving the oaths. Ralph was very angry and did not want to bring them to trial; he gave them all cause to feel sad and sorrowful. He had the teeth of many of them pulled out and others' feet cut off, their eyes put out and their hands cut off; yet others he had branded on the hamstrings. He did not care who died as a result. The others he had roasted alive and others plunged into molten lead.[162] He had them all so well dealt with that they were hideous to behold. Henceforth, they were not seen anywhere without being easily recognised. Then the commune[163] came to an end and the peasants made no more moves; they all withdrew and abandoned what they had undertaken, as a result of the fear caused by seeing their friends injured and maimed. The rich peasants paid for all this, but they settled their debt from the own purses; they were left with nothing which could be taken from them while they could still be put to ransom. They reached the best agreements they could with their lords.[164] (918–58)

Richard had brothers and sisters and a number of fine, brave knights. He made some of them counts and barons, giving them lands and dwellings. To William he gave Exmes and he swore fealty to him for it; he pledged his faith to him and became his vassal. William should have kept the peace, but did so for only a short time. Being such a brave knight, William was very proud, and because he trusted deceitful people he served his brother Richard badly; he attracted traitors to him and protected them. He loved war and hated peace, allied himself with men from the borderlands and waged war on Richard's men. Richard often admonished him and frequently threatened William; since William refused to change his ways for him, he had him admonished by others. But he refused to listen to any requests for peace or the maintenance of a truce. When Richard saw he would not have peace and that William would not do anything for him, he managed to capture him and placed him in the tower in Rouen. He mutilated his foolish counsellors, cutting off their testicles and having their eyes put out.[165] When William had been

---

[162] The punishments mentioned in vv. 941–42 do not correspond with those referred to earlier. This couplet was probably not written by Wace. The punishments meted out are more elaborate than those in the *GND* (II, pp. 8–11), which does not refer to mutilation.

[163] Wace uses the term *cumune* in vv. 911 and 947. By the time Wace was writing, this word was employed to describe the movement of townspeople who were given rights of self-government by the kings. This movement had started in northern France *c.* 1115 and it swept through most of the country, including Normandy, until *c.* 1180–90. Wace's use of the term may have been inspired by political fashion.

[164] This portrayal of the peasants' revolt has often been discussed. Wace certainly embellished the account he found in the *GND*. Discussion has centred on whether Wace, who may have been of aristocratic birth, manifested sympathy for the peasants. Gaston Paris thought that he showed no pity for the peasants (pp. 594–95), but it can be argued that, while having no wish to support a rebellion, with its threat to social order, Wace was sensitive to the grievances of the peasants (see Buttry, 'Contempt or Empathy?'). Although peasants in Wace's day doubtless had grievances concerning baronial treatment of them, they were unlikely to revolt. Wace seems to be saying that everyone, peasant and baron, was subject to the jurisdiction of the crown.

[165] These details concerning mutilation are not found in the *GND* (II, pp. 10–11).

in the tower for five years, never able to leave it for a single day, with the help
of a knight who had prepared a rope for him which he had hidden he escaped,
thanks to the rope; he got out of one of the windows and used the rope to climb
down. As soon as he could, he entered the wood, sleeping during the day and
remaining awake at night, fearful about where he should go and where he might
find protection. Richard was a man of such great power and the King of France
loved him so much that he would not wish to quarrel with Richard in order to
help his brother; he could not put his trust in the king as he would not be willing
to harbour him. He did not dare go to Brittany, Anjou or Poitou. (959–1006)

He thought carefully about what he would do and decided to go to his brother
Richard; he would ask him very humbly for mercy and place himself in his
power. He would prefer to place himself of his own accord in the hands of
Richard, his lord, than to be held there against his will; he thought that in this way
he would be pardoned more swiftly. He kept to this way of thinking and
journeyed day and night until he came to Vernay, that was where he was heading,
a forest in the Bessin;[166] he concealed himself under his cape to avoid being
captured or recognised. The count had gone hunting and entered the wood to take
his pleasure. William pursued him through the forest until he dismounted and fell
swiftly at his feet, begging very humbly for mercy. Richard asked:

'Who are you?' As soon as he recognised him, he had him remount and
took him away. He abandoned his anger against him and for a long time retained
him honourably. On the advice of Count Ralph (he was the only one from
whom he took counsel), he gave him Eu and the county along with it and William
swore fealty to him. Then he gave him as a wife a maiden called Lescelina,
daughter of Turketil, a man of great power, rich in lands and possessions and with
no heir apart from his daughter; she had great intelligence, great renown and
great goodness in the way she gave alms and loved God. On the Dive she built
the abbey of my Lady the Virgin. She had three sons by her lord. The eldest they
called Robert; he became Count of Eu after his father. They called the second
brother John; he became a priest and was ordained Bishop of Lisieux, where he
carried the crozier; he was a very well-educated and learned man.[167] (1007–54)

At that time there arose a war between Æthelred, King of England, and the
lord of Normandy; I do not know whether it was through anger or envy. Æthelred
was not prevented by being married to his sister from trying to harm, destroy and
discomfit Richard. He gathered his ships together and summoned his barons
and his knights; when all the men had arrived, the fleet in Portsmouth was
huge.[168] The king called his barons and the vassals he had summoned.

'You will cross this sea and destroy Normandy', he said. 'Capture Richard,
if you can, and bring him to me seized and bound.' They said they would do
his bidding, as best as they were able. Just as the king had ordered, as soon as

---

[166] The GND has Vernensi 'Vernon' (II, p. 10).
[167] Wace's information concerning Lescelin's children is rather garbled. The GND states correctly
that there were three sons: Robert, later Count of Eu, William, later Count of Soissons, and
Hugh, later Bishop of Lisieux (II, pp. 10–11). Wace may have confused John, Bishop of Rouen,
who was the son of Count Radulf of Ivry, with Hugh of Lisieux, son of William and Lescelina.
[168] There is no mention of Portsmouth in the GND.

they had a favourable wind, they quickly boarded their ships. They reached the Cotentin just where the Saire flows into the sea, on the shore where Barfleur lies. They disembarked, each trying to outdo the other, and made their way swiftly over the shore. They captured booty and food, took sheep and cattle and burned and destroyed houses. Women wept and peasants fled; many of them fled to Nigel of Saint-Sauveur, who was vicomte of the area. He summoned vassals and supporters, knights and peasants, burgesses, villeins and men-at-arms. Such was the emergency that they came, well equipped and without delay. Even the old women came running up with stakes, cudgels and clubs and their skirts and sleeves rolled up, ready to deal good blows. They uttered many threats against the English. They would rue the day they came, the people said; if they could encounter them on land, they intended to deal them great blows. (1055–1102)

The English had landed, and from both woodlands and plains they seized and carried off booty, gathered and hunted prey; they beat and killed peasants and thought they could have the entire region. But a man's expectations can falter very quickly and he very soon loses what he expected to possess. For suddenly the men of the Cotentin arrived and did not waste time threatening them, but attacked them fiercely. Then you would have heard the sound of blows and shouting as they called out to each other, but they did not know what they were saying to each other. As they clashed, there was a great clamour and the clash was grievous; once they had come together, they could not be separated. They killed and slaughtered them all, as long as any Englishman remained on his feet. Not a single one escaped, and not one got back to the ships apart from one who was suffering greatly and lying on a mound. Because of the great pain he was suffering, he had not been able to go any farther. He saw the great misfortune, the scene of mortal defeat; out of sorrow and fear, he forgot all his own hardship. He fled to the ships, to those who had remained on board to look after them. As soon as he was able to speak to them, he put the fear of death in them, as he spoke to them in English.

'Flee!' he said, 'flee, flee! You are all dead if you delay at all. If you are found here, you will be killed liked sheep. Even if there were only women fighting against us there, no one would survive to be ransomed. Those you are waiting for are dead; protect yourselves if you can. Draw out on to the high seas if you wish to save your skins.' They were all frightened when they knew the truth; they turned their thoughts to protecting themselves, as nobody is willing to die. (1103–52)

They chose six of the best ships, those which were the best prepared and the best equipped; in great fear and terrified they jumped into them, raised the anchor, untied the ropes, spread the sails and strove to get away from the land, watching very frequently to see if the Normans were pursuing them. They sailed day and night until they reached England, where they gave the king news which was neither good nor favourable.

'You have lost all your men', they said, 'apart from ourselves who are here. You sent them to be slaughtered and will never see any of them again.'

'Were they drowned at sea?' he said.

'Rather they were violently cut to pieces.'

'What!' he said. 'Was there a fight?'

'There has never been one so terrifying. There was a battle, a truly dreadful one, and misfortune came upon us.'

'What men were they?'

'They were good knights, good peasants and good archers and huge, dishevelled old hags who seemed like mad women.' When the king realised that they and the others who came with them were telling the truth, he was filled with grief and sorrow for his barons and his men. He repented of his folly and then left Normandy in peace. There was great sorrow throughout the land for sons, fathers and friends. Sons and daughters wept for their fathers, mothers for their sons, sisters for their brothers. What made Duke Richard happy caused the king great distress. (1153–90)

At that time the treachery took place (I do not know whether you have heard of it) which the English perpetrated on the Danes; they killed and murdered so many of them that no one could count the number of dead and many remained unburied. In England Danes lived side by side with the English; they took English women as their wives and had many sons and daughters. They had spent so much time there and had been there so long that they had greatly increased in number and become much more powerful. The English hated them very much, but they could not get rid of them; they could not rid themselves of them, but did not dare engage them in battle. They took a wicked decision and killed them all, at one and the same time. The day of this slaughter was the festival of Saint Brice.[169]

The discussions were so conducted and the treachery so well concealed that they were all killed at one and the same time, wherever they were in the land; with large knives and axes they cut their throats. They dragged children out of their cradles and smashed their heads against the doorposts, sending their brains flying out; some of them they disembowelled. The ladies and maidens they buried in the ground right up to their breasts. Then they brought their mastiffs, chained dogs and hounds, who tore out their brains and rent apart their breasts. They left no Dane there alive, man, woman or child, except for two youths who slipped away and crossed over to Denmark; they went to tell King Svein about the deaths and the slaughter which had befallen their people. Svein was filled with sorrow; he was a strong king with many men, many friends, many lands and many possessions, and he was a man of great power. He was very angry and upset; never would he have any joy, he said, and he would humiliate the English who had murdered his Danes. Svein had a large number of men and ships; by oar and by sail he sailed into the Humber and headed for York, laying waste the land. The barons of Yorkshire had no intention of letting themselves be destroyed, their towns laid waste and their dwellings burned, but they had no hope of getting help. King Æthelred was too far away and could not come to help them in their emergency; I fully believe that, if he had been there, he would not have been much use to them. (1191–1256)

They achieved what peace they could; they sought peace and received peace, promising and giving so much that they swore peace with Svein; he took

---

[169] The date referred to here is 13 November 1002.

hostages from amongst the most powerful of them and sent them back to Denmark. Afterwards, he left the Humber and went from port to port, reaching the Thames with his fleet; on this river London is situated. Svein besieged it on the river side and seized the surrounding land; he took away from them the goods which used to come by land. He attacked them frequently and took away their provisions. The inhabitants of London saw the war which was developing on land and sea, and Æthelred, who was in Winchester, could not help them. They handed London over to Svein, through the peace which was sworn between them. Æthelred, who was in Winchester, saw that he could not remain in his own land; he crossed over to Normandy, taking his wife and two sons, Alfred and Edward; they all came to Count Richard. Richard took pity on his sister, her sons and her husband; he had them received with honour wherever they wished to stay. Svein made his way through England, which was not difficult to conquer; there was no one to oppose him or do battle with him and there was scarcely a fortress or stone tower or brattice, unless it was in an old town which had been fortified from antiquity. But when the Norman barons had made themselves masters there, they built castles and fortresses, stone towers, walls and ditches.[170]
(1257–1300)

Svein brought harm to many people and was greedy for gold and silver; he took pity on no one, not even on monks or clergy. He went about holding people to ransom and destroying churches. Svein did harm and would have done more if he had lived longer, but it is true what the peasant says: 'A mad dog does not live long'. Svein became weak and had to die; he met with his fate. The monks of Saint Edmund, who wrote about this in their books, say that Saint Edmund had punished him, for he was wreaking damage on his territory.[171] The Danes took away his body and buried it in Denmark. King Æthelred, when he heard this, came back to England, bringing with him his wife Emma, who was highly prized and loved; he left his two sons with Richard, who brought them up willingly.
(1301–24)

After Svein, Cnut reigned; he held Denmark and no one did him any harm. He took homage from his Danes and gave them back their inheritances. Whatever his father Svein held in the year and on the day he came to his end, Cnut wanted to have and hold, not wishing to give it up for any man. Cnut was a man of great courage; on the advice of his barons, he set sail for England with his large band of men. He sailed up the Thames until he came to London on the rising tide; he besieged the city with no intention of departing until he had taken it. King Æthelred, who was inside with a large number of his relatives, thought he could defend the city, but he fell sick; I do not know what illness he was suffering from, but it became much worse and the king died after only a short time in bed. Because he had died at the time Cnut was attacking the city, many thought and said he died of fright. Londoners saw their lord dead and saw how fierce and strong Cnut was, so they decided they should make peace with him and receive

---

[170] Seemingly a reference to the building of castles in England by the Normans after 1066.
[171] The remark about the mad dog and the statement about the punishment of Svein by Saint Edmund are unique to Wace.

him as their lord. They did as they had said and received Cnut in London, without any weapons being used or any harm being done to anyone within. (1325–58)

Edmund, the king's son, left and fled towards Gloucester.[172] I cannot and do not wish to tell you, nor do I wish to waste time on it, how Edmund, the noble baron (I have heard him called Ironside) waged war against Cnut and his men, how he was reconciled with him, how someone later killed him treacherously in his own dwelling and how, cutting off his head and presenting it to Cnut, he received for it the reward due to a traitor. Cnut loved the queen; he paid her weight in gold for her. He held her very dear and she pleased him greatly. He had a son and daughter by her, Harthacnut and then Gunhild, a noble maiden. Gunhild was given in marriage to Henry, King of Germany; she could not have gone to a nobler man than the Emperor of Rome. Now may each person hear and take note of the nobility of Richard the Old and of how his noble lineage was honoured and enhanced. Emma, his daughter, became queen, and England was subject to her; Edward, his grandson, became King of the English and Harthacnut King of the Danes. Gunhild was taken to Rome and married in Rome; she became the emperor's wife and could not have had a nobler husband as her lord. (1359–94)

Richard was a very powerful man with a fine company of men. Geoffrey, Count of the Bretons, accompanied by a number of his barons, came to Richard in Normandy to form an alliance and association with him. He asked him for his sister Hawise, whom he had loved. Richard gave her to him willingly, for with him she was very well placed; the period of engagement was not long and the marriage soon took place. Throughout his land Richard sent for horses, garments and jewels and vessels of gold and silver, making a present of them all to Geoffrey and giving him a number of fine warhorses, gold and silver, garments and money. Then he gave his companions horses and garments and other gifts; there was no Breton, however lowly, squire, man-at-arms or groom, who did not receive his gift from Richard, whether garments, money or other valuables. He escorted them as far as the Couesnon and entrusted them to the Lord God. Geoffrey went to his own land, accompanied by his wife, Hawise. They had two sons; the elder was Alan and the younger one they called John.[173] They lived together for many a day in great joy and honour. Richard had another sister, who did not yet have a husband: her name was Matilda, a noble maiden; there was none more beautiful in many a land. The Count of Chartres asked for her and Duke Richard gave her to him and also part of Dreux, which belonged to Normandy, just where the River Avre divides it; Odo took her willingly. He loved her and cherished her greatly, but she did not last long; she lived for only a short time. She was not with the count long enough to have a child; at her death both the Normans and the French felt great sorrow. (1395–442)

Duke Richard repented of having given Odo possession of his castles and his land. On a number of occasions he beseeched him to give him back willingly what he had given his sister; he should have his land back, he said, since his sister

---

172 This information is new.
173 In reality the name of Geoffrey's son was Odo not John.

had died without heir. Odo refused to do anything of the sort and responded with arrogance and hostility, saying that he would hold and did hold Dreux and was not afraid of his threats or of him. Richard sent word to his barons and summoned all his vassals, both on horse and on foot; they assembled near Dreux. Beside the river named Avre he built and made a fortification. He did so much and worked on it so hard, with fences and ditches, mortar and paving stones, that he had built a strong castle and had no fear of catapults or stonethrowing machines; he gave it the name Tillières. When Richard had to leave there and had equipped the castle with corn, meat and wine, he placed in it Nigel of the Cotentin, and with him Ralph of Tosny, both of them bold and brave men. With Ralph was his son Roger, a noble vassal and a fine warrior, and a number of other knights, chosen from the finest and the best; all the others took their leave and returned to their homes. (1443–78)

Count Odo was furious, for Tillières seemed to be too near him. He hated it greatly and it displeased him greatly; he wanted to destroy it, but was unable to do so. He assembled the men from his territory and sent word to all his good friends, including Waleran of Meulan and also Hugh of Maine; they came with alacrity and in secrecy on the day he had indicated. They intended to attack Tillières, but misfortune was to come upon them in this, for those inside caught sight of them, saw them coming and recognised them; they decided to come out and wait for them outside on the plain. It would be shameful and cowardly for as many fine knights as the duke had placed there not to appear in such an emergency; never again would they have any renown or fame if they remained enclosed, as it were, in a sheepfold without emerging openly and displaying their prowess. They selected those who would remain behind and take care of the gates, those who would take their stand on the battlements and defend the brattices and those who would receive them inside on their return, if need be. (1479–1508)

They created three constables and set up three companies of warriors. Nigel was one of the captains and in charge of one of the companies. Ralph had the other company, and Roger his son had command of the third. These three each had a banner to rally their companions; they emerged in three troops and took up position in three places, on horseback and with their helmets laced on, their shields hanging round their necks and their lances raised. Beside their lords were the squires and along the hedgerows the archers. Nigel's company took up its position in front of the castle gate; Ralph led his men to the right and Roger made his way to the left. He rode a little way forward and stopped beside a hedgerow, getting his troops to hold fast there, with their lances firm and ready to strike, so that when the French joined battle with Nigel they would attack them from the side.[174] (1509–32)

Suddenly those from Le Mans arrived, then the French, those from Chartres and Blois and those from Meulan along with Waleran, who suffered greatly in the struggle; those from Chartres followed Odo and those from Le Mans went with

---

[174] This account of the battle of Tillières is much more elaborate than the few lines devoted to it in the GND (II, pp. 22–25).

Hugh. Waleran led his men, who all came with their lances raised. When they were near a spot from which stones could be hurled, they dropped their reins and charged, raising their shields and lowering their lances, turning towards Nigel's troop and dealing them great blows and great thrusts. They thought they could penetrate beyond them and get past the other troops, but the Normans maintained their positions, receiving them with the iron of their lances; they did not push them back in any way at all or make any progress. The Normans received the blows and thrusts squarely on their shields. When Roger saw the French joining battle and clashing with Nigel's troops, he could not restrain his companions; he summoned them to strike good blows. They rode as a group, all together in close array, and surprised the French with a transverse attack, putting many of them on the ground and knocking down a hundred, in truth, or more, who never rode again; as they fell and lay on their backs, the squires dragged them away. (1533–66)

When the French retreated, on seeing Roger and his men, Ralph of Tosny spurred his horse in his turn; he cut through the ranks of the men from Meulan, joining up with his son Roger and with the Normans, whom he loved dearly. Then you would have seen tough battles, blows from lances and blows from swords, lances broken and shattered, men falling and saddles emptied. You would have seen many warriors fighting, clashing with each other, one horse coming into contact with another, cutting across each other and twisting, the stumps of lances flying high and sparks flying from helmets, men kicking helplessly on the ground and horses dragging their reins. So many Frenchmen were struck down there, so many killed, so many captured, so many taken prisoner; there were so many cowards who fled, so many weaklings who left the scene and many good, bold men impaired and enfeebled. The Normans strove constantly, killing and slaughtering many opponents. The French thought they could withdraw, but even the bravest of them did not know what to do, for the Normans came up so close to them and kept so near them in close array that they could not get away, nor could they maintain their position. (1567–98)

Then suddenly a band of peasants from the region arrived; they had come running up at the shouts which at a distance they had heard from those who were inside with the responsibility of guarding the castle. Because of the booty they had seen, they came out and joined in the battle together, shouting loudly 'God help!', the Duke of Normandy's battle-cry. Because of the dust they created, and the great increase in men and the cry which they heard, the French became fearful and were afraid that Richard was arriving with a large army, which had been hidden nearby; they turned their backs on the Normans, leaving themselves uncovered and exposed. When they turned in this way, their opponents seized a great many of them and put them in the castle. The French set off at a trot and then entered into a gallop; then they departed at top speed, for they had delayed too long. The Normans came chasing after them, shouting time and again 'God help!' and showing no reluctance to deal fine blows, wherever they could reach an opponent. (1599–1626)

The Count of Chartres took flight, as did Waleran; they made their way quickly to Dreux, having almost delayed too long. Their rearguard was greatly reduced and they lost the finest men in their household. Hugh, who had left the battle at a later stage, went off in another direction; the men from Le Mans followed him and he sped away in front of them. He had a good, fast-moving horse, but as he rode he pressed it so hard that he caused it to pull up; it could not go forward or back. On a mound beside a valley his horse's heart burst and it fell dead beside a ditch. Hugh threw off his hauberk and covered the horse with soft earth; he was very upset to lose it. He threw the spurs off his feet and departed in the company of a shepherd. He went into his little cottage with him and dressed in the shepherd's clothing, putting on poor garments and covering his head with the hood. To avoid prison and for fear of being ransomed, he adopted the guise of a shepherd and dressed in poor garments. With the cape around his shoulders, he took up the staff and busied himself with the sheep, driving them in front of him and picking up those which fell; he was there a whole day. When those who were chasing him found him, they asked him:

'Where are they? Where are they?' He replied:

'There they are! There they are! Spur on, spur on! You will soon find them.'

With his hands and his fingers he showed them what was not true, I believe, in order to send them far away from him; he changed his voice and his manner of speaking and chased and drove the sheep. When those who had been hunting him in that direction had left, in the evening, at nightfall, the count left on foot. Barefoot and disguised as a shepherd, he effected a dishonourable escape. (1627–76)

Odo was distressed at the way Normans had captured, shamed and slaughtered the French, for things had turned out very badly for him. But whatever losses might occur, so great was the anger unleashed between them that he would never give up the attempt to destroy Tillières, no matter who would later suffer the unfortunate consequences. Richard swore and declared that neither for poor man nor for rich, for loss or threat which he or anyone else could make against him, would Tillières ever be destroyed and Dreux would be handed over to him. Both sides had in their households fine knights who often went on expeditions. Richard rode into the Chartrain and captured everything he found on the plain. He demolished houses and destroyed towns; all the peasants fled. (1677–96)

Odo entered Normandy and did a great deal of harm in many places, burning towns, capturing men and causing sorrow to the poor; they were strong on both sides and all the bravest men suffered great losses. Richard was very anxious about how to harass his enemies. In order to avenge himself on Odo of Blois and on those from Le Mans and France, and to humiliate those from Chartres, he had two kings come from overseas, King Olaf of Norway and King Laman[175] of Sweden, who had joined forces with Cnut to conquer England; they were all still pagans and not Christians. Through them and the help they gave, Cnut had gained victory over the English; he gave them gold, silver and a large quantity of other goods. In their great fleet they had brought their great vassals and fine warriors, the finest from their regions, with the intention of going to Normandy; but a high wind thwarted them and drove them to straight to Brittany. The

---

[175] In the *GND* the form of the name is *Lacman* (II, pp. 24–25).

Bretons were terrified of them and had no desire for them to remain, so they decided they would do battle with them and drive them out of the country. They gathered on all sides, thinking they could conquer and destroy them; they could not get away or sail their ships against the wind. But all over the nearby fields, which the Bretons had to cross, the pagans dug ditches, deeply hollowed out, narrow at the top and broad inside. The earth which they threw up was all carried to the other fields and they covered all the ditches over with the branches and grass they had gathered. When the Bretons arrived on horseback, ready to strike blows and looking out for the pagans, they came stumbling through the fields, falling from one ditch into another; some fell face down, others on their back, some on their side and others crosswise. As they rose to their feet, the pagans came running up and sent many a head flying. They killed many of the Bretons, wounded many and captured many; the Bretons were badly discomfited and lost many of their men. (1697–1752)

Salomon, who was lord of Dol, was very angry and sorrowful that the pagans had killed the Bretons who had stumbled into the ditches. He fled to his castle in Dol and the pagans pursued him, burning the town and capturing the castle; they killed Salomon inside it. They captured booty, plundered and took everything away to their ships. The Bretons were left in a distressed state and for a long time had no joy. As best they could, and as soon as they had good weather and a good wind, the pagans sailed towards the rising sun, passing lands and ports; they came to the Seine in Normandy and went on up towards Rouen. Richard, who had desired them greatly, honoured them greatly. The whole of France was shaken by the arrival of the pagans; there was no baron or vavassor who was not afraid of them; those who owned castles secured them well and those with possessions concealed them. Robert, the King of France, discovered this, heard about it and found it very displeasing that two kings were coming to Rouen and were to come to France and destroy the whole of it, together with the Normans who would lead them. He had heard of Salomon and the great destruction which the pagans had wrought at Dol. If he let them come to France, they would do the same, he feared, or perhaps even worse. The king saw the harm which would come from this and that the land would be reduced to sorrow if he did not make peace with Richard for the wrongs which Odo had done him. He summoned the barons, gathered the bishops together and made peace between Richard and Odo in such a way that each of them agreed to it; after the agreement and the deliberation Richard retained Tillières. (1753–1800)

They made the agreement in this way – it could not be done otherwise – that Odo retained Dreux and offered service for it to the King of France, and Richard would have Tillières, which would belong to his heirs for ever more, along with the land he captured; there should be a clear boundary between them. Thus the land remained in peace and for a long time there was no war. Richard held the two kings very dear and gave them a large amount of clothing and money; he paid them to their liking and sent them away happy. Robert, who was archbishop, had seen the pagans and did his very best to convert them and make them inclined to serve God. He said and preached so much that he turned Olaf into a Christian and baptized him himself; he gave him his name and sponsored him in baptism. He was baptized and believed in God, then he returned to Norway;

afterwards, those in that country martyred and killed him because of his love for God. (1801–26)

Richard took the sister of the Count of Brittany as his wife and companion. Her name was Judith; she was Geoffrey's sister and Richard loved her in true faith. He had three sons by her: out of affection the eldest was named after his father and given the name Richard at the baptismal font. The second was called Robert and the third William, who took monastic vows at Fécamp. With the three sons he had three daughters, the first called Adeliza; she was married in Burgundy and given to Count Reginald. The first son born to them was called William and the second Guy. Baldwin, who held Flanders and was an hereditary count, took the other sister as his wife and held her in very great honour. The third sister was the most beautiful, but she died as a young girl. Judith died during her husband's lifetime, while in full vigour; she went the way everyone will go, those who have been born and will be born. After her death Richard married Papia and by her had William and Malger; one of them he made a cleric, the other a knight. William was Count of the Talou, between the Pays de Caux and the county of Eu. Malger, who was ordained a cleric, was consecrated archbishop after the death of his uncle Robert; he who serves God acts very wisely. (1827–62)

Once when the duke wasstaying at Bayeux, I cannot say on which day, he sat at dinner with a number of his vassals and friends. I do not know what they had to eat, but they needed spoons; a chamberlain had the spoons and he handed twenty of them to the knights. A noble, valiant knight was sitting at dinner, joking a great deal; he had been in the castle a long time and served as a member of the garrison. He took the spoons and passed them round, concealing one up his sleeve. At that time men had large sleeves and wore white chemises; they fastened them round their waist with laces and their clothes hung down behind them a good way. The man who had stolen the spoon easily stuffed it into his clothing. No one saw him apart from the duke, but he clearly noticed what the knight did; he noticed, but said nothing and made no sign that he knew. The man who had handed out the spoons counted them when they were gathered in. He collected the spoons by number, and when he found one missing he made a lot of enquiries about it; the man who had it did not say a word. The duke said:

'Let this matter be! There is a time to keep quiet and a time to speak. Keep quiet! Do not mention it again or you will regret it. I am quite sure you miscounted.' As soon as the duke ordered him to keep quiet, the man did not dare do anything more. (1863–98)

That night, when it was dark and the knights had eaten, he called the* chamberlain and named the knight who had stolen the spoon, which was still hidden away.

'Go quickly', he said, 'without delay, to that knight's lodging and see what he is doing.' The chamberlain went at once and found the knight drinking; many of his companions, whom he had invited to supper, were eating and drinking with him well and enjoying themselves. The chamberlain watched what they did, but did not stay there long; he told his lord everything he had discovered there.

'Take some of my money', said the duke, 'and confer with his squires. Have yourself taken to his pledges and say that you want to pay off his debts. Keep everything secret so that their lord does not know anything about it.' The chamberlain did the duke's bidding very cleverly. He came to the serving men, spoke to them, took the pledges and paid them off; amongst the pledges he saw the spoon he had lost.[176] The chamberlain was amazed to find the spoon; he came back to the duke and told him how he had paid off the pledges. Then he whispered in the duke's ear that he had seen a great marvel and told him of the spoon he had found, which he had lost at the meal.

'Do not worry about this', said the duke, 'keep quiet about it! Do not mention it to anyone but myself.' (1899–1940)

The squires were very pleased and told their lord that their pledges had been paid off and taken back to their lodgings.

'Was the spoon found?' he said.

'It could not be concealed', was the reply.

'You have dishonoured me', said the knight. 'This reproof will never leave me, wherever I go. I will never go back to the duke. Oh, I have never had such great shame! I will never again appear before the count.' The knight lamented, slept little and rose early, taking leave of those he loved and telling each of them he was going away. He refused to tell any companion, however good, the reason; nothing that any man or woman could have said to him would have stopped him from going. Thus he made his move and left. Count Richard soon discovered this and asked for a horse and mounted; spurring his horse, he caught up with the knight and brought him back. If the duke had not gone himself, no one else could have made him return. The duke brought him back into the hall and in the sight of his men gave him enough money to support himself thereafter, without needing to take or steal from others. He was then on very good terms with his lord and there was great love between the two of them; the knight was never the subject of any ill-intentioned reproach for this folly.[177] (1941–74)

Throughout all Christendom Richard and his excellence were the subject of much talk and discussion. He lived a life of splendour. At that time, in Lombardy, Master Bernard, a man of great learning, held classes in many places and was much talked of; he wanted to know whether Richard was such as he was said to be. He came to Rouen in Normandy from a place beyond Lombardy. He took lodgings with a burgess and the burgess honoured him greatly. That night, when they had eaten, Bernard addressed his host:

'Fair host', he said, 'I would like to speak to the duke, if I could. I have an urgent matter to discuss with him and have to speak to him. I have come here from a great distance to discuss something very urgent with him.'

'Upon my word', he said, 'I do not know how you could speak to him quickly. As far as I know, you will not be able to speak to him at all for a week. He remains in that high tower and does not leave it night or day; no one can enter the tower unless he is summoned by name. He has brought together all the provosts,

---

[176] Presumably the knight stole the spoon in order to pay off his debts, perhaps because, unlike the duke, he did not have the necessary currency.

[177] This story of the spoons is new information, but it may be a version of anecdotes found in the *GND* (II, pp. 58–61).

bailiffs, tax-collectors and vicomtes in this land; he is doing his reckoning and his accounts. After dinner, when he is tired, he leans out of a window which overlooks the Seine and sits there for a good long time, gazing at the woods and the people crossing the bridge.' Bernard spent that night there; next day, when he had dined and knowing the duke had eaten, he put on a cape and beneath it had a belt tightly girt around him. He took a bow in his left hand and an arrow in his right, which the burgess had acquired for him, and placed it in his belt, pulling his hood over his eyes like someone who has to pass through undergrowth. He went along the Seine, strolling along and walking first backwards then forwards, until Richard came to the window in his normal way; he was standing beside a knight and leaning his head out, looking at the river. (1975–2032)

When Bernard spotted him, he drew the bow taut with his knee and inserted an arrow, which he had prepared. Then you would have seen a man taking aim, stretching and pulling taut his bow, palms placed on his brow and aiming high up towards Richard, going down on his knees and getting back up again, his head raised and his arms outstretched. One minute he moved forward, the next he came back, constantly looking up, raising his arms and stretching his bow. When he had taken a long look and stretched his bow for a long time, the count looked and caught sight of him; he saw the arrow and recognised the bow. He thought it was aimed at him and intended to do him harm. He crouched down, stepped back and took cover behind the wall.

'Go at once', he said to his men-at-arms (I do not know how many he had there), 'and bring me a scoundrel down there by the riverside. He keeps on aiming to shoot at me all day long; he intends to hit me, I do not know why.' They said they would kill him and the duke told them not to. They were to bring him there alive and well and not manhandle him or touch him; he wanted to hear from his own mouth who he was and what he wanted. They all ran off, each trying to outdo the other, until they caught sight of Bernard. They removed his hood and pushed and shoved him a great deal, giving him many a blow and thrust, but the fellow submitted to them all. Anyone who could not strike him threatened him, but he was not concerned about what was being done to him or about where he was being taken, providing he was being brought into court. (2033–76)

Bernard was taken to the duke and his cloak was then removed. Richard asked him what he wanted, what his name was, what sort of man he was, why he wanted to shoot at him and why he wished to harm him. Bernard told him everything: that because of his reputation for goodness he had come from a great distance to see him and had not come for any other purpose. He had not made as if to shoot at him because he intended to do him any harm, but to get himself brought to him so that he could speak with him. He complained of the thrusts he had had and about the blows he had received, but he would rather have been beaten than not have come to him. (2077–96)

The duke thought he was very clever and considered this a courtly action; he receiving him with great honour and retained him in his household. He cherished him greatly, loved him greatly and did a great deal of what he advised, until death, which takes many a man from his friend, separated them. In Cherbourg on the Cotentin the duke was praying one morning. Master Bernard came to him and said to him very humbly:

'I have loved you very much, my lord, and you have honoured me greatly. Give me a boon, if you please. I beg you for mercy, do not refuse it to me in the name of holy charity and for the holy love of God.'

'Brother', said the duke, 'you will have it. Tell me what you want.'

'My lord', said Bernard in tears, 'I will tell you what I am asking for. In this place, where you pray and where you call upon God, have my body buried and placed deep in the ground, for on the third day I must die and I want to lie in this spot. This will, I believe, be better for my soul.'

'My friend', he said, 'I grant this.' I do not know how it happened or what it meant, but on the third day Bernard died and his body was carried and placed where he had requested it of the duke.[178] (2097–2128)

Hugh, Count of Chalon, a strong man amongst the Burgundians, was at war with Count Reginald; I do not know whether it was for money or for land. Reginald was count beyond the River Saone, and between them there was no peace or harmony. But in war there are many ups and downs. Through ambush and a surprise attack Reginald was taken and captured and Hugh put him in prison. He kept him in prison for a long time, for he did not wish to ransom him, nor did he want to hand him over scot free or take a reasonable ransom. Reginald's wife, Adeliza, was reluctant to lose her husband and she sent word to her father, the Duke of Normandy, asking him, if he could, to help them. The duke sent word to Hugh, as a token of love and as a reward, asking him to hand over his son-in-law to him freely or to ransom him for an equitable price. Hugh replied arrogantly that he would not do anything for him and Richard saw that he had to do more if he wanted to free Reginald from prison. He summoned his men-at-arms and knights (I do not know how many hundred or how many thousands) and sent them to Burgundy under the command of his son; his son Richard was already grown up and Robert was a very brave and valiant man. He who lends does well and he who gives does better. Richard gave one of the counts of Peronne, who possessed great power within France, two good manor houses as a fief for him and his heirs in order to obtain his help at that time: they were Elbeuf and Chambois and he had them for a long time, I know.[179] (2129–68)

Robert, who was King of France at that time and greatly trusted by Richard, allowed them to pass through his land and go everywhere freely, until they had crossed through France. They bought straw and food at the price charged in each region, until they came to Mimande. Without a stone-thrower and a catapult they took the castle by force; they destroyed Hugh's land, except for the part where they themselves settled. In the land belonging to Count Hugh, who was holding Reginald in prison, they left no plough working, no house standing and no cock crowing. They destroyed towns and houses and then attacked Chalon. They were already breaking down the gates – no pike or wall could resist them – when they found Count Hugh with a saddle round his neck. He offered Richard his back to ride on; he could not humble himself any further. At that time it was the usual way of seeking mercy from one's lord. Hugh returned Richard's brother-in-law to

---

[178] On this anecdote concerning Bernard see J. Marx, 'Les Sources d'un passage du *Roman de Rou*'.

[179] This information concerning the gift to one of the counts of Peronne is unique to Wace.

him and humbly begged him for mercy. He gave his pledge that he would do right and he provided hostages in order to confirm peace; he swore he would come to Rouen and do right by him there. When Count Reginald was handed over and came back to his wife, Richard and his men returned to their regions after some days of riding. On their return you would have seen a great deal of joy expressed throughout Normandy. Duke Richard was filled with joy because of his sons and their prowess; he was delighted by his sons' valour, but in himself he was unwell. There was grief when he fell ill; he was in pain and lingered for a long time. (2169–2212)

When he was close to death, he had himself taken to Fécamp, where his father lay. He confessed to bishops and then spoke to the barons:

'You have loved me greatly', he said, 'and given me a great deal of willing service. I have held you very dear and honoured you very gladly. On your advice, and may you be loyal to him, I want to give my land and my fiefs to Richard. Make him your lord and strive to love him, for he is very noble and brave. I give the Hiémois to my son Robert, and if he serves his brother well, as one should serve one's lord, I wish and advise that things should be better for him because of it.' They replied:

'We grant this. We shall never do anything which displeases you.' When the duke had divided up his lands and rewarded those who had served him in his court, his soul left his body. He had maintained his land for twenty-nine years and at that time he came to his end. He was prepared for burial with great honour and interred with great honour. His body and that of his father, as I saw it, and I was there, were removed from the ground and placed behind the main altar. They were taken there and are there still; the monks hold them very dear. (2213–46)

When Richard the Good was dead, the third Richard, who was his son, did homage to the King of France and took possession of his inheritance from him. To Robert, his younger brother, as his father had asked him, he gave the Hiémois, and other fiefs which he assigned to him in a number of places. But Robert was not content with this and, thinking he could take Falaise away from him, quickly entered the castle and garrisoned it with men and arms. But he was not there long, for Richard arrived swiftly and caused him to abandon the castle and forced all his men to leave it. The two of them had a parley in order to effect a reconciliation, thanks to their friends. Little time had elapsed since this reconciliation when Richard was in Rouen with his large troop of men. I do not know what he ate or what he drank, but he fell ill and died, as did a number of his companions and the finest of his barons. They never knew whom to accuse, whom to hate and whom to blame, but they said and swore, and the French bore witness to this, that there was never again in that land a lord of such worth as he, however long his life lasted; but he had been killed because of envy. He had held the country for two years since his father Richard had been alive. This Richard had a son, Nicholas, who was sent to school at a young age at Fécamp, and later became a monk;[180] he

---

[180] It is possible to interpret vv. 2284–85 as stating that Nicholas was sent to school at Fécamp, where he later became a monk.

loved the life of a monk and maintained it. Later, because of his goodness, he was elected abbot at Saint-Ouen. (2247–88)

Robert was duke after his brother and in character he took after his father to a certain extent. He loved god-fearing men, honoured clerics and priests and cared greatly for the poor and especially lepers. He put much effort into providing food and clothing for lepers and went further than all his ancestors in largesse and noble habits. He completely doubled the number of his servants and had gifts given to everyone. At Cerisy he founded a religious house and church, placing monks and an abbot there and giving them villages and towns; and he gave them the same jurisdiction the duke had in his land, covering murder, theft, kidnap, homicide and arson.[181] It was at an annual feast, but I cannot tell you which one, that the duke went to hear Mass. When it was time to make offerings, the duke offered first and then everyone else together. The duke looked across the church and saw a respected knight who had not been to make his offering. He called a chamberlain and had him bring him a hundred pounds, which he then had given to the knight by way of a gift. The man who received the money came to the altar and offered it all. When he was asked how it came about that he was giving so much money at the same time, for considerably less would have sufficed for him, the knight spoke, saying that this money was given to him to make an offering and that he should not retain any of it. This was considered an act of great nobility and the duke performed another generous act, giving him another hundred pounds to keep for his own use. There was much talk and discussion of his largesse and his gifts. (2289–2334)

The duke loved competitive games,[182] the pleasure of chess and winnings from backgammon. One day he was sitting with a knight at the backgammon table, along with a cleric – I do not know whether he wanted to speak with the duke – and he was concentrating on the game and on the look-out for points. Suddenly a youth arrived, with a vase beneath his cloak; his father had recently died and he wanted to take over his lands. The vase was very fine and splendid; it would not have been easy to buy, as the whole thing was expertly made from gold. The man who held it drew it out and handed it to the duke as a present. The duke said to him:

'Thank you very much.' He said to the cleric:

'Lord cleric, take this, the vase is yours, have it.'

Now hear what marvel took place! As soon as the cleric held the vase and was about to draw it towards him, he fell prostrate and died. He did not utter a word or stir; his soul departed and his body lay there. Everyone marvelled at this occurrence and for a long time it was much debated. The physicians in their schools discussed it at length. Many of them came to this conclusion and they uttered this judgement: just as with very great sorrow many men have died

---

[181] The information concerning Robert the Magnificent's care for lepers comes from the *Brevis relatio* (p. 25); that on Cerisy is new, but Wace is probably quoting from charter material at Cerisy.

[182] The word *covenables* in v. 2335 is difficult to interpret. The normal meaning of this adjective is 'suitable' (see Holden's note to this line, vol. 3, p. 223). The information concerning Robert's love of games is new, as is the following story about the vase.

suddenly, likewise with very great joy a man can die in accordance with reason. When very great grief takes hold of a man, his heart locks fast and grieves greatly. When it cannot open again soon, he has to die at once. When very great joy takes hold of him, then his heart opens and enlarges; if it cannot close again, he must die at once. Because of the great joy the cleric felt at the present he had suddenly received, his heart was filled with joy and it grew so much that it could not be constricted when necessary. The duke had the body removed and ordered the table to be put away. (2335–84)

A man from Beauvais came to the duke and presented him with two knives which he had made, very good and fine; the duke gave him a hundred pounds. The man thought he had been well paid and came to his lodgings very happy. He was counting his money in front of him when a messenger came with two warhorses and gave them to him on the duke's behalf (I do not know who had given them to him). The man who had received the money and the two horses mounted one and took the other, setting off quickly on his way, keen to be on the move so that he would not suffer any harm. Swiftly, and filled with great joy, he left with the two horses he was taking with him. Then the count received a present of a splendid silver cup and as soon as he held it in his hands said:

'Where is and what became of the man who brought me the knives?' Some people said to him:

'He is already far away'.

'Why has he gone so soon?' he replied. 'This upsets me. I did little for him. If he had stayed with me for a little while, he would have left a rich man.' The duke had a custom, as his men well knew, that when someone brought him a present, if he gave it to anyone, he would not receive another present that day, unless it was something to eat, without the same person who had had the earlier present having this one at once. He could become satiated, he used to say, by anything apart from giving, and however great the gift it always seemed very small to him; he would never have given one so great that he would subsequently regret it. (2385–2426)

At that time, as I reckon it, William of Bellême fortified Alençon and thought he could hold it. He became known as an evil traitor, for out of love for him Duke Robert had entrusted it to his safekeeping. The duke summoned all his men, his friends and his family and besieged Alençon, putting guards on all sides so that William could not leave or get out of the castle. He attacked him and assailed him until William came, barefoot, with a saddle around his neck, to ask for mercy; then he could consider himself a fool. The duke took pity on William, who was walking barefoot, carrying his saddle and humbly begging for mercy; he abandoned his anger against him. Then the duke entrusted the castle to him, on his fealty, his faith and his oath, and William placed within it anybody he liked. But William never kept faith with Robert and, as soon as he could, made him angry. Because of William and his lineage there was on many occasions a great deal of suffering and damage in Normandy; they never kept their word. Tremendous harm was done by his four sons, whom he had trained and raised: Waryn, Fulk, Robert and William; there were no greater traitors in any kingdom. Many of them came to a bad end through their treachery. The eldest, who was called Waryn, was the first to end his life badly. Gonthier, a very fine knight, who performed many praiseworthy actions and was one of his friends, was suddenly killed by Waryn, without him ever having challenged him or displayed any sign of hostility; the evil wretch swiftly strangled him, in the sight of his men. On their father's command, Robert and Fulk, the two brothers, with large forces and many men from his household with whom he had provided them, rode through Normandy, collecting great booty. When the duke's household knights arrived, they had their hands full of booty and plunder, which they had taken from peasants. There was no talk or other discussion; the duke's men pursued them as far as the forest of Blavou, discomfiting and defeating them. Fulk was immediately knocked down and fatally wounded through the body, and with Fulk lying there in the field Robert took flight, even though he was severely wounded and had great difficulty escaping. Those who could flee did so, abandoning the booty and the plunder. William lay ill and had done so for a long time. When he learned the truth about the death and wounding of his sons, the soul was separated from his body. I do not know whether it departed well or badly, for he lived badly and finished badly; he did not seek peace and did not love peace. (2427–2500)

Then the territory remained in the hands of Robert and William the younger. If the father before them was a traitor, these men were more so, or at least the same. But later Robert was captured in Ballon during a war and imprisoned; there his head was completely smashed in with a club. After Robert came William, who held Bellême for a long time. This was William Talvas: if anyone was unfortunate enough to fall into his snares, he could not extricate himself with any joy unless he could slip away furtively. This one surpassed his whole family in evil and cruelty. The Bellême family was always evil and arrogant; the man who took Bellême from them rid them of this great arrogance. (2501–20)

At the time I am speaking of, King Robert fell ill and had his son Henry crowned. He invested him with the whole of France, and to Robert the younger he gave the territory of Burgundy, which has the status of a duchy. The brothers agreed to this, but after the death of their father the king, Constance, who was their mother, hated her eldest son Henry and loved Robert greatly. She hated Henry as a stepmother hates and envies her stepson; no reconciliation could be reached, neither through friend nor family. She wanted to strip Henry of the kingdom and give everything to Robert. Through the castles which she controlled and the great wealth she had, and through the barons who loved her and supported her, she inspired great hostility towards Henry and led the whole of France astray. Henry was very much afraid of being disinherited; he came to Robert in Normandy, one day before Palm Sunday.[183] The king found Robert in Fécamp and the duke honoured him greatly; the king came with few companions, just twelve men-at-arms. He explained his difficulty to the duke and how he was hated, and he promised the duke, without any delay the whole of the Vexin as far as Pontoise, if he could perform a task for him; he did not care whether his mother was upset by this.

---

[183] The detail concerning Palm Sunday, the statement that Henry spent a week at Fécamp and the promise of a gift of the Vexin are new information.

'I shall do my best', he said, 'with my person and my wealth.' (2521–60)

The king spent a week there and greatly enjoyed himself; the duke honoured him as he was obliged to do for such a lord. He honoured him greatly and served him greatly; he gave him a great deal and offered a great deal, a large amount of clothing and money, splendid vessels and fine warhorses. He escorted him as far as Gisors and sent him on his way to France. He summoned all his household knights, who were soon ready, and made them wage war in the borderlands, from where he could approach France; he was with the king in France against Queen Constance. The duke was so successful, and so was the king, and they waged war so well against the French that Henry retained his power and remained in his territory. On account of the acts of honour and service he had performed for him in many ways, when they parted the king invested Robert with the Vexin and also with Pontoise, Chaumont and other towns there, which Robert held for the whole of his life and which the French greatly envied. (2561–88)

Duke Robert ruled his land well and wished to conquer all the territory which was rightfully his. He wanted to enter Brittany by force and refused to let Alan remain in peace; Alan was not willing to come to his court and did not deign to obey him, as his ancestors, who had ruled Brittany earlier, had done. Alan and Robert were very close cousins, each being the son of an uncle and an aunt; since they were of one family, one high estate and one lineage, Alan did not deign to serve Robert and in this way the hatred between them grew. Alan did not deign to bow down to him and Robert refused to let the matter drop. He strengthened a castle on the Couesnon, some say at Pontorson, others at Chéruel; the peasants know this well.[184] When he had strengthened the castle, he put Nigel and a valiant knight by the name of Alfred the Giant in charge of it. The duke with his other household knights advanced to Dol, burned the city and destroyed and laid waste the region. From there he went to Normandy and dispersed his barons. Count Alan was strong and fierce, a valiant and noble knight. Those in Brittany honoured him and for this reason called him the Breton king, for in their opinion he was King of Brittany, for no one before him, since Charlemagne, had ruled the whole of Brittany so firmly. He scorned anyone else's power and was keen to avenge himself; but now let him be careful that harm does not come to him! He who increases his misfortune avenges himself poorly. Many men through their great courage have often been harmed; in courage anyone without prudence can soon find that things go wrong. (2589–2634)

Alan was very bold and brave and he assembled all his knights, summoning as many men as he could raise and thinking he could lay waste Normandy. He set out for the Avranchin, wanting to win, but he lost. Nigel and Alfred heard of the gathering of the Bretons and they assembled the men from the Avranchin and summoned all those they could, men on foot and on horseback.

'Noble and well-born barons', they said, 'now we will see who does this well and who loves his lord. Protect your domain this day and protect your lord's advantage. These people, who are coming for what is ours to land which is ours,

---

[184] This information on Pontorson or Cherrueix is new. Holden rejects the identification Cherrueix for Carues (vol. 3, p. 223), but see the *GND*, II, pp. 56–57.

think we are cowardly; they are striving to obtain booty; if they, before our eyes, take any away, because we cannot protect our own possessions, our heirs will be greatly reproached for this. Attack them fiercely and you will soon have put them to rout. Strike knights and horses, strike lords and vassals, kill whatever you can kill; if you spare anyone there, you will rue the day!' They cried out:

'Let us go, let us go! What are you doing? We are delaying too long!' (2635–64)

Then a spy came to tell them that their men had dispersed; they were burning towns, looking for booty and capturing peasants. Then the Normans rose up from a little valley; they made Nigel go on ahead and he would be the first to strike, along with those he wished to take with him and select; Alfred was to lead all the other men in close formation. Beside him he had a standard borne to which their men could rally. The Bretons, who had spotted them, set off towards them holding their shields. The Normans cried: 'God help!', the Duke of Normandy's battle-cry, and the Bretons cried 'Maclou, Maclou' and gathered around Count Alan. The Normans struck the Bretons and the Bretons countered them well. Anyone who fell amongst them was in a sorry plight; he was filled with fear before he got back on his feet. You would have seen a very fierce assembly, a dense battle and a violent fight. Many men on both sides fell, more brave men than cowards, for the brave pushed forward and the cowards held back. Alan had no Bretons with him apart from the principal barons; they had all rushed off in search of booty and were dispersed throughout the towns. Yet they held very firm until Alfred and his men arrived. But then they were forced backwards; they could not support the battle or hold their position. Anyone who could not take flight was killed. Because of the great booty they sought and the plunder they captured from where they had remained, the Bretons were discomfited. Before those who had gone looking for booty were assembled, the Bretons were so badly treated, knocked down and wounded that they could not remain there or participate in any combat or joust; they could only turn and flee, and the Normans pursued them. The peasants of the Avranchin did not keep to the main roads or highways. Without being summoned or asked to do so, they took to the paths and the undergrowth. They struck down those taking flight and killed those who had fallen; the flight was great and the pursuit was great. The trail of dead bodies was very great, the loss was great, and the slaughter was great; the booty was great, as was the plunder from the dead, who lay over the whole area, and from the wounded who later died. Count Alan was defeated and he remained unwell for a long time. When the duke discovered the news, I think and believe that it pleased him greatly.[185] (2665–2730)

The duke had with him Alfred and Edward, Æthelred's two sons; they had been thrown out of England and disinherited very wrongfully. The duke sent a messenger to King Cnut, who was married to their mother and held their father's inheritance, telling him to give them back their inheritance; he had had the land for a long time and it ought to be given back to them. Cnut said they would not have any of it, unless they conquered it by force, and the duke was very upset that he did not respond differently. He had all the ships in Normandy and the best

---

[185] The battle as described here is much more elaborate than in the *GND* (II, pp. 56–59).

knights, helmsmen and good mariners, good men-at-arms and good archers assemble quickly in Fécamp; he intended to cross to England and take from Cnut the land which he was refusing to hand back to the rightful heir. The wind was fair when they departed and they expected it to remain so. But hear now about a cruel occurrence. The night became dark and black, the sky turned black and the sea became turbulent; the weather changed and the wind turned. They were unable to reach land or harbour; I do not know whether they were heading east or north. God had arranged things in this way, before worse befell them, for there would have been very great slaughter before the land was conquered. The storm and the north wind, which blew violently, harassed them so much that they could not reach land or return to Normandy. Yet they remained so close together that they came to the island of Jersey. Jersey is close to the Cotentin, where Normandy comes to an end; it is in the sea towards the west and it belongs to the territory of Normandy. (2731–74)

For a long time Robert and Edward suffered greatly in Jersey and they remained there for a lengthy period, waiting for the wind to blow so that they could travel to England; but God would not allow them to have this. As they could not wait any longer, they had to adopt another strategem. The duke handed one section of his fleet and part of his men over to a vassal by the name of Tavel, who was an expert in both good and evil.[186] He was very brave, courageous on land and courageous at sea; this was the reason why the duke called upon him. He asked him and commanded him to cross the sea to Brittany and destroy and lay waste Alan's land. He himself, he said, would go by land and wage war by land. Tavel put his ships to sea with the men who had been left with him and the duke delayed no longer. He sailed to Mont-Saint-Michel and crossed into Brittany, striving to capture lands. The whole of Brittany was greatly agitated until Alan decided to make peace with his cousin; he had done him wrong and would do right by him. He sent word to Robert that he would speak with him and submit to his counsel. If he would accept it, he would send for the archbishop, who would advise them loyally, for each of them was his nephew. Robert granted this and they then sent for the archbishop. He came very quickly and duly arranged peace between them; he reconciled his two nephews, making them both promise peace and grant peace. Alan did homage to Robert openly, in the sight of all his men, and Robert freed him and pardoned him his misdeed; in this way the war came to an end. The duke returned to his own land. (2775–2822)

The duke had been staying in Falaise; he had visited it on several occasions and fallen in love with a maiden there by the name of Arlette, daughter of a burgess.[187] She was still a maiden and a virgin and to him she appeared comely and beautiful; she was taken to his bed and he did with her what he wanted and took his pleasure with her. When she entered the duke's bed, wrapped in her shift, she undid her shift at the top and ripped it open all the way down to her feet. She

---

[186] The correct name is Rabel (*GND* II, 78–79, see especially p. 78 n. 2).

[187] Wace does not identify Arlette (the Latin texts call her Herleva) as the daughter of a tanner (or tawer), but see below, vv. 4317–24.

was thus able to expose herself fully without rolling up her shift. The duke asked her what she meant by tearing her shift right down.

'It is not decent', she said, 'for the lowest part of my shift, which rubs against and touches my legs, to be turned towards your mouth, nor for what is placed on my feet to be turned towards your face.' The duke appreciated this gesture and considered it to be to her credit. When they had lain awake together for some time – I do not wish to say anything more about the way a man disports himself with his beloved – the maiden fell asleep. She slept beside the count and the noble baron lay there patiently. When she had slept for a short while, she let out a lament because of a dream she had had and started in such a way that the count felt it. He asked her why it was that she lamented so and started.

'My lord', she said, 'I do not know, unless it is because I dreamt that a tree, which was growing upwards towards the sky, was emerging from my body. The whole of Normandy was covered by its shadow.'

'All will be well', he said, 'if God pleases.' He comforted her and drew her towards him.[188] (2823–66)

From this Arlette a son was born who was called William; when he was born and emerged from his mother's womb, he was placed in a litter of straw and left alone in the straw. The woman who first picked him up – I do not know how it happened or what was meant by it – laid him in a bed of straw while she went somewhere else. The child tossed and turned until he was covered by the straw; he had his arms full of straw, pulled it towards him and placed it over himself. The old lady came and took the child, whose arms were full of straw.

'Come on now', she said, 'what a man you are going to be! You will conquer so much and have so much! You have soon got hold of your rightful property with your hands and your arms full of it.' The child grew, for God loved him and set him on the road to good deeds.[189] The duke did not cherish him any less than if he had had him by his wife. He had him brought up in splendour and just as nobly as if he had been born from his spouse; he was soon grown up and strong. As a young boy, William was brought up for a time in Falaise. One day Old William Talvas, who held Sées, Bellême and Vignats, passed through Falaise; I do not know where he was going. One of the burgesses called to him, saying to him with a smile:

'My lord', he said, 'come here and go into that dwelling and see your lord's son, as a gesture of goodwill and friendship.'

'Where is he?' he said, 'show him to me.' He had him brought before him. I do not know what the child did or whether he laughed or cried. When Talvas had looked at him, seen and examined him at close quarters, he said to him:

---

[188] A brief mention of a similar story about Arlette is given by William of Malmesbury, *Gesta regum Anglorum*, Book III, c. 230, vol. 1, pp. 426–27, and vol. 2, pp. 219–30). Krappe, 'Le Songe de la mère de Guillaume le Conquérant', finds a similar prophetic image in the *Gesta Theodorici* and some Scandinavian sagas, the origin of which in his view lies in a Byzantine source, and Braet traces Arlette's image to a number of sources, especially the Bible ('Le Songe de l'arbre chez Wace'). See also Belletti, 'Il sogno di Arlette'.

[189] Holden takes the view that the couplet in vv. 2887–88, found only in the base manuscript, is inappropriate in the context and was thus not written by Wace (vol. 3, p. 224).

'A curse on you, a curse on you!'

And he said a third time:

'A curse on you! For through you and your lineage mine will be much debased and through you and your lineage my heirs will be greatly harmed.' He would have gladly harmed him with his words, if he could; then Talvas left and said nothing for a long time.[190] (2867–2922)

The boy was quite young when his father made up his mind to visit Jerusalem and pray at the Holy Sepulchre. He summoned all the bishops, the abbots and the barons, the most powerful, the most senior and those he regarded as the wisest. He told them what his thoughts and intentions were, that he wished to go to Jerusalem if God were willing to give him the strength to do so; he wanted to expiate his sins, he said, dressed as a pilgrim and with bare feet. They all cried out in unison that if he went they would be in dire straits; if he left them without a lord, shame would come upon the land. They feared the power of the Bretons and the Burgundians, for on both sides there were lineages which claimed it as their rightful inheritance, and if things went wrong for him each of them would put in a claim. 'My lords', he said, 'you are right, but I have no child or heir, except for a small son of mine. I will hand him over to you, if you like, on the advice of the King of France who will protect him as well as he can. He is small, but he will grow and, God willing, become strong; I recognise him fully and consider him mine. Accept him and you will be acting wisely, and if God grants it, I may yet come back. This boy has been brought up among you; you will be acting in accordance with nature and honour if you love him in true faith and I leave him to you in my place.' They replied:

'We agree to this and will serve him very willingly.' Then they went to the youth and became his vassals; they took many oaths and swore fealty and alliance to him, just as barons and vavassors should do to their liege lord. To confirm the matter and make it lasting, the duke took him to the King of France and presented him to him by the hand. He made him become his vassal and take possession of Normandy. Through the Archbishop of Rouen, he handed over his land to Alan, who was his vassal, to govern as steward and justiciar. But he did not have the land for long, for through poison which attacked his kidneys, causing his followers great sorrow, Alan died in Normandy; he lies in the abbey of Fécamp.[191] (2923–86)

What more shall I tell you? The duke set off, taking with him from amongst his most noble vassals both fathers and sons. With him he had many knights, chamberlains and squires, quartermasters and hirelings, who led the horses and chargers;[192] he went past Langres and Besançon. One morning, on his way, when he had stayed in a castle in Burgundy (I do not know its name), he roused one of the hirelings, whose task it was to guard the gate. He got up and opened

---

[190] The story of Talvas's encounter with William is unique to Wace. Nothing further is known about William's time at Falaise.

[191] The information concerning Alan's burial at Fécamp is new.

[192] The reading *destriers* 'chargers' in v. 2994 is suspect. The other manuscripts read *sommiers* 'packhorses'.

the gate and had to wait and wait until all the travellers, pilgrims and merchants were outside. The duke sent all his men before him; he himself intended to pass last of all. The procession was large and lengthy and they could not all pass quickly; it took them a long time to get out. The hireling, who wanted to sleep, chivvied the pilgrims along, shoving many of them with the stick he held in his hand. He angrily struck the duke, who came last, in the back; the blow could be heard from a distance away. The duke bowed low to him with great humility and the Normans all sprang up as one. Even with a thousand lives, he would not have left with one; they would soon have brained him and disembowelled him with their staffs. But the duke went amongst them, protecting and guarding him.

'Barons', he said, 'keep moving, keep moving! Leave the fool alone, do not touch him! We are pilgrims, we should not start a skirmish or a quarrel. Anyone who begins a skirmish does wrong; let us accept everything patiently. We ought to suffer a great deal worse in order to expiate our sins. If the wretch struck me, I have deserved much worse. I prefer the blow he gave me to the whole of my city of Rouen.'[193] (2987–3036)

This is the way things remained; the duke did not want any more harm to come to him. He passed safely over the Great Saint Bernard Pass and through Lombardy with his company. He went to talk to the pope, for he wished to carry the cross with his blessing. He saw the statue of Constantine, which was in Rome, made out of copper in the image of a human, with a copper horse as well, immovable by rain or wind. Because of the power and the honour of the Emperor Constantine, in whose name the image was raised and after whom it was named, he had it dressed in a mantle, the most precious he could find. Then he left there, joking about the barons of Rome who left their lord without a cloak, winter or summer; they ought to have honoured him and given him one mantle per year. He was conducted with great honour through the emperor's lands and had the four hooves of the mule he was riding, the most precious of those he had brought with him, shod in gold. Then he strictly forbade any of his barons from ever picking up the gold when it fell from its hooves. He passed through Constantinople and made his way to the emperor. While he was talking with him, in the fashion of that place he placed his mantle on the ground and sat down without it. When he departed and set off from there, he did not deign to pick up his mantle. One of the Greeks saw him without his mantle and picked it up for him, telling him to take it and put it back round his shoulders. He replied nobly:

'I do not carry my seat with me'. (3037–80)

Each of the Normans also left his mantle on the ground, doing just what the duke had done and leaving their mantles in the palace. The duke gave them much more splendid and more handsome mantles; this was considered to be a noble act on his part. The emperor gave orders that, as long as he was in the city, the duke should receive a large amount of his money, for he wished to honour him. But the

---

[193] This story of the duke's stay in Burgundy is also found in the *Brevis relatio* (pp. 26–27), but Wace recounts it with variations.

duke refused to accept this, not wanting to be provisioned by him; he had, he said, plenty of money to spend. As long as he was a pilgrim, he wanted to live off his own money; but when he returned, if he came back, he would take provisions and other things from him. The emperor sent out a proclamation and issued an edict to merchants everywhere in order to prevent him from finding firewood or logs with which to cook his food; but the duke bought all the nuts he could find and cooked all his food with them and did so more abundantly and more sumptuously than he was accustomed to do, because of the firewood he lacked. The emperor laughed at this a great deal and said to his men with a laugh, speaking in Greek, that the duke was a very courtly man; now he should do whatever he wanted, he would never deny him anything. Because of the nobility of the Normans, who made benches out of their mantles, the emperor had benches and seats made in the palace, all round the hall; before that time, everyone who wanted to be seated in the palace sat on the floor. (3081–3120)

Duke Robert was about to depart joyfully and take his men away joyfully when an illness, which lasted for two weeks or more, overtook him; he could not mount his horse nor travel on foot, yet he did not want to remain where he was or upset his men. So he hired poor Saracens and had himself carried shoulder high; he had himself carried on a litter, just as a body is carried on a bier. Then suddenly a pilgrim, born in Pirou on the Cotentin, arrived; he was on his way from Jerusalem and had been to the Holy Sepulchre. He met his lord and, very distressed by his pain, wept profusely in his presence. When he left, he asked what news of him he should give when he returned to Normandy.

'Tell my friends', he said, 'and the people in my country, that, alive and well, I am having myself carried to paradise by devils; pagans, who are carrying me to the Lord God, have raised me up shoulder high.' The pilgrim left and the duke was carried onwards.[194] (3121–50)

At that time and in those days Jerusalem belonged to the pagans; throughout the entire kingdom of Syria the power lay in pagan hands. All the land was theirs and there were scarcely any Christians there; those who dwelt there at that time were totally subject to the pagans. No pilgrim could enter Jerusalem to pray without giving a besant or the equivalent in gold or silver before doing so. There were many people in that region to whom the gate was forbidden because they could not get hold of besants; they remained outside the gates. When the duke entered the land and approached the Holy Sepulchre, he found many such people, poor, wretched and forsaken. You would have seen wretches coming to him in their hundreds and thousands, crying and shouting that in God's name he should get them into the city. The duke was a man of great charity and he swore an oath, swearing by the heart in his body, that if he entered the city no one would remain behind him, as long as the besants lasted. 'May God help you', they all cried. 'Welcome to you', they said. He did as he promised them and had them all enter in front of him. The man who was lord of the city, a pagan of great nobility, heard of the great acts of honour which the duke was performing for many people and of the great wealth he was spending and the good deeds he was

---

[194] The story of the pilgrim from Pirou is unique to Wace.

doing. He exempted from the besants the duke himself and all those he wanted to bring in; neither on leaving nor on entering did they have to pay a penny.[195] (3151–94)

The pagan was a man of great worth and he had the whole of that day's offerings, which had been taken to the Holy Sepulchre, given and handed over to the duke; he refused to have or take a penny and had everything given and handed over to the duke, who immediately distributed everything to the poor. The duke had safe conduct everywhere and everywhere was honoured by all. I cannot tell you of the acts of nobility, honour and good faith he performed, nor of the money he spent or of the offerings he made to the Holy Sepulchre in Jerusalem and to the crib in Bethlehem. He made his way back as far as Nicaea and was killed there by a poison given to him treacherously by a scoundrel (may God curse him!).[196] With great honour the body was placed in the bishop's church by the bishop and the clergy, in the manner befitting such a noble lord. The tomb is still there; it can still be seen and it still remains. Count Drogo died with him; he drank from the same drink as the duke. Because he was courtly and learned, the duke had given his precious holy relics, which he had obtained earlier in Jerusalem, to Turstin, his chamberlain, chief guardian of his chamber (he was my grandfather on my mother's side*). Through Turstin he sent them to Cerisy, an abbey he had built in Normandy, between the Cotentin and Bayeux, three leagues from Saint Lô. The sorrow was great and rightly so, but this is what pleased the Heavenly King with respect to Duke Robert, who died in this way. The sorrow was great and long-lasting; Robert had lived for eight years after taking possession of the fief. (3195–3240)

William his son, who was still very young, was grief-stricken. He had many men, but few friends, for he found many of the men very hostile; the men held dear by his father he found very arrogant and proud. The barons waged war amongst themselves and the strong damaged the weak, not wanting to leave anything for him, and he was unable to bring them all to justice. They burned and destroyed towns, captured and robbed peasants and did harm in many ways. Between Walkelin of Ferrières and Hugh, lord of Mont-Saint-Michel – I do not know who was in the right and who was in the wrong – there was a violent conflict and there could be no reconciliation through bishop or lord and no peace or alliance. They were both good knights, both strong and fierce. On one occasion they encountered each other; their anger was great and they joined battle. I do not know who was more successful or who killed the one or the other of them, but that was the end of the fighting. Hugh was killed and so was Walkelin; they both died in the battle at the same time and on the same day. William grew up and became stronger; he heard many stories which distressed him in his heart, but at that time he could do nothing else. The barons fought each other and in spite of him refused to stop; each of them built a castle and a fortress in accordance with his wealth. As a result of the castles, wars sprang up and there was destruction of land, great skirmishes, great hatred, great seizures and great

---

[195] This story about Jerusalem and the Holy Sepulchre is new.
[196] On the poisoning of Richard see William of Malmesbury, II, p. 163.

challenges; as regards their misdeeds and other activities, they paid scarcely any heed to the duke's wishes. (3241–84)

William had not yet left childhood behind when King Henry, son of Constance, came to Dreux with large numbers of men and did great damage in the area around Évreux. He sent word to the duke, accompanied by great threats, that, if he wanted his peace and his favour, he should hand over or demolish Tillières before he entered it by force; if he refused, there would never again be any truce or peace with him. He did not want William to have a castle there; people were complaining and he was causing great harm to them. If he demolished it, as he asked, it would not be rebuilt for four years; he would confirm this loyally by fealty and oath. The duke told the Normans what the king had said to him. A number of them advised him to do the king's bidding; he had to suffer many wrongs until he had greater strength. They accepted what the king said and the king swore on holy relics that within four years the castle would not be rebuilt by any vassal of his, as far as he had the power; in that time he would maintain peace with him. When Gilbert Crispin heard what had been said, he was very distressed and it displeased him greatly. He came to the castle as fast as he could and had his men gather and make their way there. He wanted to hold it against the king; Duke Robert had given it to him and he had been warden of it for a long time. He blamed the duke and considered his barons to be cowardly and treacherous to have given him such advice; they had not been faithful to him. (3285–3324)

The king summoned his men and assembled all his troops. He besieged Tillières at once and the duke did the same; they did so with one accord, but they found the castle to be strong. However, they begged this Crispin so much, and those on the other side threatened him so much, that he abandoned the castle to them; but he gave it back to William in order, he said, to discharge his fealty. The duke handed it over to the king and at once the king set fire to it in their sight; the castle was all ablaze, the gates destroyed and the walls demolished. You would have seen many Normans in tears and calling upon their ancestors; the king, in spite of their grief, went and joked with his friends. Then he returned to France; he was delighted at the destruction of the castle. It was not long before he forgot the oath and broke the agreement he had made earlier with William. With his noble knights he returned to Normandy; he took his men as far as the Hiémois, burnt Argentan and destroyed everything, doing the same for many other towns and distressing all the peasants. He went back via Tillières and rebuilt and strengthened the castle; he had utterly belied the faith he had pledged to William. You would have seen many Normans contorted and demented with grief and anguish when they saw the castle rebuilt. They cursed those, whoever they were, whose advice to destroy the castle had been accepted. (3325–66)

Turstin, who was vicomte of the Hiémois, saw that the king and the French were in the process of capturing the land, seizing possessions and burning towns, and that the duke's power was declining; no one was receiving protection from him. He abandoned the duke like a traitor, fortifying Falaise, of which he was warden, and bringing mercenaries from France, good men-at-arms and fine archers; he intended to take the castle from the duke and did not deign to offer him service for it. The duke very speedily summoned his men to come to him, those from the Auge and the Cinglais; those who were close by came quickly. They immediately attacked Falaise and knocked down a large section of its wall and, if daylight had not failed them and night not come so soon, those inside would have been greatly distressed; but in the dark the enemies were separated. Turstin was stunned and dismayed by the great assault, by the wall he saw dismantled and by the people he could see. He asked permission to leave the castle and obtained a truce to get away. In this way Turstin departed, disinherited by his own pride; I do not know whether he later returned or whether he was later reconciled. (3367–99)

William of Arques was very fierce and a good, bold knight; he was brother to Archbishop Malger, who loved him deeply and cherished him. On one side he was brother to Robert, and he was the son of Pavia and Richard and uncle of William the Bastard, who knew many a trick and many a ruse. Because he belonged to the lineage which was laying claim to the inheritance, and because he was born in wedlock, he was causing harm to the duke. To honour his family and secure his fealty, the duke gave him Arques and the county of Talou as a fief; he accepted this and became his vassal. He swore fealty to him, but did not uphold it for long. In order to do damage to his lord, he built a tower above Arques; the tower was built on the top of the mountain and had a deep valley on several sides. Because he had a good castle and was born of a legitimate spouse, and because the king said he would give him help when he needed it, he told William he would hold on to the castle and never serve the duke. The duke was ruling Normandy very wrongfully; he was a bastard and had no right to it. The duke was a man of very great power and also of great wisdom – he who has intelligence is not poor – he summoned William of Arques to come to him and serve him. But William refused completely; he pledged his faith to the King of France and opposed the Bastard. Throughout the land he robbed and pillaged, not caring who saw him, and he provisioned his tower and his castle. But the duke did not stand for this for long; unexpectedly, he summoned his men at once from all parts. At the foot of the mound in the valley, which overlooked the whole region, he built a small castle with a ditch, a spiked stockade and a palisade; then the inhabitants of the castle could not capture ox, cow or calf. The duke built such a castle that, with so many knights and such men, they could defend themselves well, so that neither king nor count could capture them; he put there the finest knights in all Normandy. (3400–54)

Then the duke left to attend to his affairs elsewhere. It could not be concealed from the king that the duke had built a castle and was having the tower watched so that no provisions could get in. He assembled a large number of knights and obtained equipment and arms with the intention of supplying the tower of Arques, for their corn would be running out. The king at that time was at Saint-Aubin and was carrying with him a large amount of corn and wine. He had them stop there and prepare their provisions and packhorses to carry their equipment, as well as knights to act as convoy. Those in the duke's castle soon heard about the provisions and about the large army which was waiting in Saint-Aubin and was to bring supplies to the castle. They took one section of the Normans, the strongest and best fighters, and secretly set up an ambush over towards

Saint-Aubin. Afterwards, they took another section and stormed the king's men; then they cunningly withdrew, as if they were taking flight. When they had gone past the ambush created from their own men, they turned to face those who were pursuing and insulting them and the French joined battle with them; those in the ambush emerged and attacked the men from France. The French, who had strayed a long way from the army, were greatly deceived and the Normans surprised them greatly, capturing and killing many of them. Hugh Bardulfus was soon captured and the Count of Abbeville, who was called Enguerrand, was killed. They all endured a great deal of suffering and the King of France was grief-stricken; he grieved and suffered deeply for the knights who had been caught unawares and for the barons who died in that way. He had the packhorses prepared, the provisions taken and loaded up and carried to the tower of Arques; he himself was part of the convoy. Then, I believe, he returned to Saint-Denis in great shame.[197] (3455–3508)

Because of the woods and the rivers, which were plentiful in that land, and for a number of other reasons, the duke was staying in Valognes when a messenger came up, spurring his horse in great anguish.

'You would be better off elsewhere', he said. 'Those responsible for protecting your borderlands need your assistance, for your uncle, William of Arques, has made an alliance with King Henry of France and sworn an oath of allegiance. The king is to provision Arques for him and William is to serve him.' The duke did not wait long enough for the boy to say any more, or even to finish what he was saying; he demanded his good horse.

'Now I will see', he said, 'who will come and follow me.' He did not make any other preparations. He crossed the rivers at once, passed through Bayeux and Caen and made as if to go to Rouen. When he came to Pont-Audemer, he went on to Caudebec and from there to Baons-le-Comte – what use is a long account of this? – the duke spurred and hastened his horse so much and changed it so often that he quickly came to his men in Arques. He could not find any of the men he had had mount their horses in Valognes; everyone was amazed he had come there so soon from such a distance. No one could keep up with him;* none of the men in Valognes who left with him managed to catch up with him. The duke was delighted by what had happened, about the great discomfiture which had befallen the French and also about their men who had been captured. William of Arques guarded and held the tower firmly for a long time; he would have held it for longer if provisions had not failed him. But, because of the lack of provisions, he abandoned the land, the castle and the tower; he gave everything back to Duke William and fled to the King of France. (3509–60)

Alfred the Giant saw wars and misfortunes spreading throughout the lands; he had lost Duke Robert, who had held him very dear, and saw his inexperienced son William, who was unable to defend his land. He had no regard for any of his own possessions; he wanted to abandon everything and did so, giving his brothers the fiefs he had in a number of places. He gave his silver and gold to the abbey of Saint-Vigor in Cerisy; for love of the Creator and for love of his lord,

---

[197] The information about the king's return to Saint-Denis is unique to Wace.

who had founded the abbey, he loved and supported it.[198] There was a town called Le Lièvre, which was in his possession, and with all its appurtenances and the church of Saint-Laurent, together with the church of Tessy, he united it with Cerisy; then he became a monk in the abbey and lived a very good life. (3561–84)

William grew and gained in strength and was active on several fronts. He was now fully grown to adulthood and had held the land for twelve years when, through Nigel of the Cotentin and Ranulf of Bessin, two vicomtes of great power, who were very capable of stirring up trouble, there arose a conflict in the region which caused a lot of damage to the land. William had with him Guy, son of Reginald the Burgundian, who had married Richard's daughter Adeliza and had two sons by her; Guy had been brought up with William since he was a young boy. As soon as he could ride and was able to feed and dress himself, he was taken to Normandy to be prepared for knighthood with William. William cherished him greatly, and when he had dubbed him a knight he gave him Brionne and Vernon and other lands surrounding them. When Guy was given possession of the castles and had strengthened and improved them, he began to display arrogance and lay claim to Normandy. He was very envious of William, who had power over him; he rebuked him for his bastardy and as a result treacherously set a war in motion. But things turned out badly for him, for he wanted to capture everything and lost everything. He brought together Nigel and Ranulf and spoke to Longtooth Haimo and to Grimout of Le Plessis who served William unwillingly, saying that there was no closer heir who should have Normandy.[199] Richard was his mother's father. He was born of the spouse and was not a bastard; if anyone were willing to do right by him, Normandy would belong to him. If they wished to support him, they would share it with him. He said so much to them and promised them so much that they took an oath that to the best of their ability they would support him and wage war against William; by force or by treason they would seek to disinherit him. Thus they fortified their castles, strengthened ditches and raised palisades; William knew nothing of all their preparations. (3585–3640)

To enjoy himself and conduct his business William went to stay in Valognes; I do not know how many days he spent there hunting in the woods. One evening those in his household had left the court late and gone to bed. Apart from William's closest advisors, they were asleep in their lodgings; William himself was lying in bed, but I do not know whether he was asleep. During the first part of the night a fool by the name of Goles suddenly arrived, with a stick round his neck, shouting at the door to the chamber and beating on the walls with his stick.

'Open up', he said, 'open up, open up! You will all be killed, get up, get up! Where are you lying, William? Why are you sleeping? If you are attacked here, you will soon be killed. Your enemies are arming themselves. If they can find you

---

[198] Alfred the Giant's gifts to Cerisy are recorded in charters. See M. Fauroux, *Recueil des actes des ducs de Normandie de 911 à 1066* (Caen: Société des Antiquaires de Normandie, 1961), no. 195.

[199] On Grimout of Le Plessis see van Houts, 'Wace as Historian', pp. xxxviii–xxxvix.

here, you will never get out of the Cotentin and not live till the morning.' William was very much afraid, and as a terrified man does, he did not ask for news, for it would scarcely have been good. He was in breeches and chemise and he put a cloak round his shoulders, grabbed his horse very quickly and set off; I do not know whether he had any spurs or whether he sought any companion. He made haste until he reached the fords, found them ready and crossed over; in great fear and great distress he crossed the ford over the Vire by night. He bowed to the monastery and ardently prayed God to conduct him, if it pleased him, and let him go in safety. He did not dare go in the direction of Bayeux, for he did not know whom to trust. He chose his path because he wanted to pass between Bayeux and the sea and was passing through the town of Ryes when the sun was rising. (3641–86)

Hubert of Ryes was at his gate, between the church and his castle; he saw the unkempt William and his distinctly weary horse.

'How come you are travelling, fair lord?' he said.

'Hubert', he replied, 'dare I say it?'

'Yes', he said, 'certainly, come forward fearlessly.'

'My enemies are looking for me and threatening to kill me – I am not hiding anything from you – some men whose names I do not know have sworn to have me killed.' Hubert took him to his castle, asked for his good horse and called his three sons.

'My fair sons', he said, 'mount up, mount up! Escort this lord of yours until you have brought him to Falaise. You should go this way and that, and woe betide you if you visit any town.' Hubert pointed out the highways and byways to them clearly; they understood what he said very well and obeyed his command well. They travelled across the entire country, passing Foupendant,[200] which is on a ford,* and getting William into Falaise. If he was there, a curse on anyone who was upset by this! Hubert was still on his drawbridge, looking up and down, very anxious to receive news, for he expected to hear a great deal. When the men who were looking for William came spurring up, they called him to one side and urged him to tell them whether he had seen the Bastard, which way he was going and in which direction. He replied to them:

'He passed this way, not long ago. You will soon catch him! But wait, I will take you and strike the first blow. By my faith I swear to you that, if I find him, I will be the first to strike if I can.' Hubert took them so much out of their way and sent them to such a distance that he no longer had any fears concerning William, who was going another way. He told them a great deal about one thing and another and then went back home. (3687–3736)

The Cotentin and the Bessin were at that time in great confusion; very fearful news about William, who had been betrayed, soon went all round the regions. That night he was supposed to have been murdered; some said he was dead, others that he had been captured and a number of people said he had fled.

---

[200] The location of Foupendant (MS *Folpendant*) remains uncertain. Perhaps Foupendant south of Caen, on the Orne (near the forest of Cinglais and above Harcourt), or Folpendant in the forest of Souleuvre, near Vire (Calvados). See Holden, vol. 3, p. 226.

'God protect him!' they all said. Between Bayeux and the fords, you would have seen the roads travelled by those who came from Valognes; they considered themselves dead and shamed because of the lord they had had that night and lost. They did not know where to seek their lord; it would have been better for him not to have any land. They made so many enquiries for news, not knowing where to go and look for him and cursing Grimout of Le Plessis and those who trusted him; they had a deep suspicion that he had committed this treachery.[201] (3737–60)

Because of what had happened, Normandy was very much afraid and troubled. The vicomtes hated the duke. They took and seized his lands, leaving nothing they could get hold of in any place they could reach; they took so much from William that he could not do anything about it. He could not enter the Bessin or ask for his rights or his revenues, so he went to King Henry in France, whom his father Robert had served. He made his complaint against Nigel, who was serving him badly, about the revenues he was losing and about Longtooth Haimo. He also complained of Guy the Burgundian and of Grimout, who wanted to betray him – there was no man he should hate so much – and of Ranulf of Briquessart, who was taking and sharing out his revenues, and of other barons in the region who had turned against him. As a result of William's complaints and what he had said, the king summoned his army and came very swiftly to Normandy. William summoned the inhabitants of the Pays de Caux, those from Rouen and the Roumois, those from Évreux and the Évrechin, the men from the Auge and the Lieuvin. They had gathered in the Hiémois all the men they had summoned from all sides. Those from France set up camp on the River Laison, between Argences and Mézidon, and the Normans, who supported William and came in his hour of need, camped beside the River Muance, which runs through Argences.[202] (3761–3800)

When the vicomte of the Cotentin and the vicomte of the Bessin knew that William was coming, that he intended to fight and was bringing the King of France, thanks to whom he expected to defeat them, as a result of the bad advice they had accepted and the arrogance they had shown, they did not deign to restore his property to him or to seek peace or accept it. They summoned their vassals from all sides and their friends and relatives, calling for and summoning all the vavassors and the barons who were on oath to do their bidding. They crossed the Orne at several points and assembled at Val-ès-Dunes, which is in the Hiémois, between Argences and the Cinglais; from Caen one can reckon about three leagues, by my estimation. The plains are long and broad, without great hills or great valleys, very close to Gué Berengier; there are no wooded areas or rocks, but the land slopes down towards the rising sun. A river surrounds it

---

[201] The account of what happened in Valognes is unique to Wace.

[202] Details concerning the location of the battle of Val-ès-Dunes in 1047 are more precise in Wace and William of Malmesbury (Book III, c. 230, vol. 1, pp. 428–29, vol. 2, p. 221) than in the GND (II, pp. 120–23) or William of Poitiers (pp. 10–11). See also the Chronica de Hida, p. 286, and the Brevis relatio, p. 27. In general, Wace's account of the battle of Val-ès-Dunes is more elaborate than that of either the GND or William of Poitiers. For a discussion of the battle see D. C. Douglas, William the Conqueror (London: Eyre and Spottiswoode, 1964), pp. 48–62.

towards the south and south-west. At the church of Saint-Brise in Valmery, Mass was sung to the king on the day of the battle; the clergy profited greatly from this. In Valmery the French armed themselves and prepared for battle; then they entered Val-ès-Dunes and assembled the common troops. They occupied the whole of the riverbank, fully equipped like fierce troops. William set off from Argences, passing through Gué Berengier and making his way along the river until he joined forces with the French. William's men were on the right and the French on the left; they turned their faces towards the west, for they knew their enemies were over there. Ralph Taisson of the Cinglais saw the Normans and the French; he saw William's men increasing in number and took a stand at a distance, over to one side. He had a hundred and forty knights with him, as many as he had in his troop; they all moved along with their lances raised, all with a wimple secured to them. (3801–56)

The king spoke to Duke William; each of them was armed, with his helmet laced on. They divided their troops and made preparations for their battles, each with a staff in his hand. When the king saw Ralph Taisson, who was standing so far from the others with the large number of men he was bringing, he did not know and was not aware which side he was on and what his intentions were.

'William', said the king, 'who are those men over there with the wimples? They are all very splendidly equipped: do you know anything about their plans? Be aware that those to whom these men commit their loyalties will win the day.'

'My lord', said William, 'I believe that all of these men are on my side. The lord's name is Ralph Taisson; he has no quarrel or conflict with me.' (3857–76)

Much was done and said there and I have not written it all down. Ralph Taisson was in a quandary about whether to support William. The vicomtes were beseeching him and making great promises to him and he had confirmed and sworn on the holy relics in Bayeux that he would strike William wherever he might find him. But his men begged him and advised him for honour's sake that, whatever he might do elsewhere, he should not let his rightful lord down in battle; William was his natural lord and he his vassal, this he could not deny. Some time ago he had done homage to him in the sight of his father and his barons; he who fights against his lord has no right to the fief or the honour.

'He is the one we support', said Ralph. 'You are right; this is we what we will do.' He was in the midst of his men and rode away from them, spurring his horse and shouting 'Thury!'. He made all his men stop and went to speak with Duke William. He went spurring over the field and struck his lord with his glove, saying to him with a laugh:

'I am acquitting myself of what I swore. I swore I would strike you as soon as I found you. I have struck you in order to acquit myself of my oath, because I do not wish to perjure myself. Do not be upset! I do not do it for any other treacherous reason.' The duke said:

'My thanks to you'. Then Ralph departed. William made his way over the field with a great company of Normans, searching for the two vicomtes and asking for the traitors. Those who knew them pointed them out, over on the other side, where their men were. You would have seen troops and captains moving across the great expanse of fields. There was no rich man or baron who did not have his banner beside him, either a banner or some other standard, as a rallying point for his troops, with blazons and ensigns and shields variously painted. You would have seen these fields shuddering greatly, horses spurred and prancing, spears raised and lances brandished, shields and helmets gleaming. As they spurred their horses, they shouted out whatever battle-cries they had. The French shouted 'Montjoie!'. It pleased them to be heard. William shouted 'God help!', that is the Norman battle-cry. Nigel cried 'Saint Sauveur!', the battle-cry of his domain, and Ranulf cried very powerfully 'Holy Saviour, Holy Saviour!', and Longtooth Haimo called 'Saint Amand, Lord Saint Amand!'. There was a great deal of noise as they came together; the entire earth shuddered and trembled. Then you would have seen knights spurring their horses, some turning, others joining battle, the bold spurring forward, the cowards quivering and trembling. (3877–3950)

The men from the Cotentin did battle with the King of France and the French; they attacked each other in tight formation, striking each other with lances lowered. On both sides they received blows on their shields from the lances. When the lances shattered and broke, they attacked each other with their swords, not seeking jousts but striking each other in the battle itself, just as champions do when they are alone on the battlefield, one against one. They strike and hit each other and turn aside when they are afraid. Each man is ashamed to flee and each wants to win the day; each advances as best he can. The men from the Cotentin and the French were similar in strength, each of them withstanding the other. The press of battle was great and they suffered greatly, drew their swords and shattered their lances. They struck each other well and came to blows, damaging each other in many ways. You would have seen much fighting between vassals and horses and knights struck down. The king himself was hit and knocked from his horse. A Norman, whose name was not known, came amongst them, thinking that, if the king fell, confusion would reign in the whole army. He struck the king sideways and knocked him down sideways. If his hauberk had not been a good one, in my opinion, he would have killed him. The peasants spoke about this and still say jokingly: 'From the Cotentin came the lance which struck down the King of France'. (3951–90)

If this man had then left, he could have joked as he departed, but as he was leaving and trying to turn his horse, a knight spurred his horse and attacked him; he thrust him forward with such violence that he knocked him down flat. But everyone strove so hard for the king, trying to get him back into an upright position, that he clung on to his horse. He was still holding on to the saddle-bow when the throng surrounded him and pulled him off his saddle, making him fall on to his back; he was soon trodden underfoot by the horses and left there for dead. There was a great crowd of men trying to get the king back on his feet and they soon succeeded in getting him back on his horse; he had fallen between his men and was not jostled or torn to pieces. He remounted easily; before this he had been bold, but afterwards he was more so. As soon as the king was on his horse, you would have seen vassals striking with lance and sword, Frenchmen attacking Normans, and Normans turning, parrying and moving away from each other. The king frequently made himself visible, because they had seen him fall. Then Longtooth Haimo was struck down, as well as I do not know how many of his relatives, who never returned from there unless they were carried away on a bier. Longtooth Haimo was a Norman, a powerful man on account of his fiefs and vassals; he was lord of Torigni, of Évrecy and of Creully.[203] He went about striking the French repeatedly, crying out 'Saint Amand!'. A Frenchman frequently saw him behaving in this arrogant manner and he stopped and stared at him; he waited until he approached him. At one of the turns which he had seen Haimo make when he had struck a Frenchman, he spurred his horse very rapidly; on his shield and over his saddle-bow he struck Haimo with great power and Haimo fell on to his shield; I do not know how he was wounded, but he was found dead on his shield. From there he was carried to Esquay and buried in front of the church. There were many people who, having seen his brave deeds, thought that Haimo had struck the king and knocked him off his horse and that this was the reason why the French killed him, taking their revenge on behalf of the king.[204] (3991–4050)

Ralph Taisson waited, watched and remained patient until he saw the two armies joining battle and the knights coming together. Then he made his move and rode forward; it was very apparent where he was heading. I do not know how to relate all his great deeds or how to name those whom he struck down. Together with Ranulf the vicomte – I will not say much about this – there was a man by the name of Hardret, who was born and raised in Bayeux; he rode out in front of the others, trusting to his own prowess.[205] William rode at full speed towards him and, holding his lance, took aim and sent the sharp iron right through his neck, next to his throat, between his throat and his chin; nothing could save him. William pushed him and he fell, his body toppling backwards and his soul departing. The duke had left his lance in him and he drew out his naked blade. He fought nobly and well, bringing down and felling many men. Ranulf saw the great struggle and all the unhorsing of men; he heard the uproar, the cries and the sound of clashing lances. He came to a stop as if stunned, like a man who was somewhat lacking in bravery; he was afraid that he may have been betrayed and that Nigel had taken flight. He was very much afraid of William and of all the men who accompanied him. He would be badly treated if he were captured, and it would be worse for him if he were killed; if one of these things was bad, the other was worse. He did not seek any distinction in arms. When his men spurred forward, he pulled back, disliking the battle very much; they went forward and he went backwards, still afraid that someone would strike him. He left his companions; he wanted to flee and did so, throwing down his lance and then his shield. Off he went at full speed and the cowards went with him; many men who suffer no injury still lament bitterly. (4051–4100)

Nigel fought like a brave man. If the king had found them all like this, the French would have rued the day they came; they would have been discomfited and vanquished. He gave and received many a blow and fought well as long as he was able; but he saw that his strength was failing and that many of his men were

---

[203] Longtooth Haimo is also known as Haimo Dentatus. On this personage see *The Domesday Monachorum of Christ Church Canterbury*, ed. by D.C. Douglas (London, 1944), pp. 55–56.

[204] The story concerning Haimo is new information, but it has elements in common with material in William of Malmesbury (II, p. 221) and the *Chronica de Hida* (p. 286).

[205] Hardret of Bayeux remains unidentified.

dead. The French surrounded him in growing numbers and Normans were failing and diminishing in number. Some of them who were wounded fell and others who were afraid took flight. He himself was frightened and did not know what to do or which way to go. He thought he could find Ranulf on the battlefield and that in his company he could recover his strength; but when he realised that Ranulf was taking flight and would not be coming back to him, he began to move away from the battlefield, having no other recourse. He joined up with those who were taking flight and abandoning their arms. When Nigel left the battle, Ranulf was already two leagues away, as if he had been forced to flee; never in his life had he known so much sorrow. Because of his valour and his speed, his bravery and his prowess, he was called Falconhead [Chief de Falcon]; Nigel Falconhead was his name.[206] I do not wish to tell you which of them fought better, nor can I, and I have not found it in writing; I was not there and did not see it, but I know that the king won the day and that Ranulf fled the battlefield. The throng of men taking flight was huge, as was the throng of those striking. You would have seen many paths travelled and knights spurring their horses; you would have seen many weapons hurled and hauberks flung from backs, fields of corn crossed, horses exhausted and weary. They wanted to head for the Bessin, but they were very much afraid of crossing the Orne. They all fled in great confusion between Allemagne and Fontenay, seven here and six there, five here and three there, all terrified to cross the Orne. Those who pursued them did not take pity on them;* they tore them to pieces and routed them. They threw so many into the Orne and so many were killed and so many drowned that the mills in Borbeillon, it is said, were brought to a standstill. The king had his men assemble, intending to take them back to his land. They carried the sick and the wounded with them and buried the dead in the cemeteries in the region. (4101–62)

William remained in that land and for a long time afterwards there was no war. The barons made peace with him, promising and giving him so much that he kept faith with them, preserved the peace and let them off their wrongdoing. But no reconciliation with Nigel was possible and he did not dare dwell in that country; he was in Brittany for a long time before he made peace. Guy escaped from Val-ès-Dunes and fled to Brionne. William hastened after him and besieged him in a strong castle. At that time the fortress was on an island in the Risle, which completely surrounded the fortress and the dwelling. Guy was enclosed within Brionne, but he had no peace or repose there, fearing greatly for his person. The duke built two castles outside it. Because of the lack of provisions and the attack launched by the duke's men, Guy handed over Brionne and Vernon. There was no other stipulation, other than that he would remain with the duke and the duke would provide him with equipment. But he had not been there long, and he was not greatly cherished, when he went to Burgundy, to the region where he was born. (4163–94)

When the Normans saw that the duke had the upper hand over everyone to such an extent, they sent hostages in order to preserve peace; they did fealty and

---

[206] Vv. 4113–24 are omitted from the editor's base manuscript. For this and other problems affecting vv. 4113–30 see Holden's note (vol. 3, p. 227).

homage and obeyed him like their lord, destroying their newly-built castles. If they had thoughts of doing harm, they kept them secret and served either willingly or unwillingly. The duke captured Grimout of Le Plessis and imprisoned him in Rouen. If he did capture him, he was right to do so, for he would, it is said, have murdered him treacherously at Valognes, when a fool, named Goles, warned him of it. Grimout acknowledged the treachery and named as an accomplice a knight by the name of Serlo, from Lingèvres, father of Hugh; Serlo offered to defend himself and this necessitated a battle. On the day of the battle, when it was to take place without fail, he was found dead in the gaol and there was a great deal of talk about this; just as he had been in chains, he was buried in fetters. When the church in Bayeux was dedicated, part of Grimout's land was granted to it in the name of the Virgin Mary; part of it, whatever one says, was granted to the abbey in Caen.[207] (4195–4226)

Geoffrey Martel, a count of Anjou, did much harm through his deceptions and his ruses to people in the Touraine and Poitou and also to his neighbours on several sides, putting men to ransom and seizing castles. From Count Theobald he took Tours and also many cities and castles. From William the Poitevin, who held Poitou and Limousin, he took by force Mirebeau and Loudun, a splendid castle. From those of Bellême he took Alençon and Domfront without good reason; Alençon is part of Normandy and Domfront part of Maine.[208] He fortified Domfront and against their will he held the Passais against the Normans, placing knights and men-at-arms there, very arrogant and evil men who moved rapidly through Normandy, where they inflicted much harm. William wanted to see Domfront, where Martel had his troops: they were coming and going through his land and he would suffer great anguish if he did not defeat them. He took a large number of armed men with him, but one of the men he had taken informed those in Domfront that the duke was coming to see Domfront; they could benefit greatly if they were able to decide what to do in this matter. Those who would have gladly made such gains jumped quickly on to their horses, thinking they could catch William unawares and capture some of his men. When they had left Domfront, they assembled beside a mound. But the duke caught sight of them, saw their lances and shields and made his companions spur towards them; he himself wanted to do battle with them, but they turned and fled, refusing to turn round. There was not one of them who wanted to turn round or who dared to do battle with the duke; he had a very swift horse and pursued them right up to the gates; he drew near to one of them, held on to him and the man behind him captured him. Nothing more happened on that occasion and William had his men turn back. He saw the land and the regions, saw the roads and the valleys, saw the

---

[207] After his defeat Grimout was put in prison in Rouen, where he remained, chained in fetters, until his death thirty years later (1074). During his imprisonment his estate was confiscated and granted to Odo of Bayeux. Van Houts points out that Grimout's case shows that Wace consulted 'documentary, narrative and oral material for the compilation of his *Roman de Rou*' ('Wace as Historian', p. xxxviii).

[208] The statements that Alençon is in Normandy and Domfront in Maine, and later that the river Sarthe acts as boundary (vv. 4299–300), provide helpful information concerning the contemporary frontier.

defiles and the rocks, saw the paths and the tracks and saw the castle which was situated up above; it was not subject to assault. William had three castles built in the vicinity and took away their means of subsistence. (4227–86)

While he remained there to build the castles he was establishing, a spy arrived from Alençon; I do not know whether or not he was a Norman. He gave Duke William some advice; the duke, when nones sounded, had food given to the horses and made his men mount them that evening. In the twilight he passed through Mehoudin and headed straight for Alençon, through Couptrain to Saint-Samson and from there to Alençon. Alençon is situated on the Sarthe, which creates a division between two areas: the Normans are over towards the castle and the inhabitants of Le Mans on the other side of the river. Over that side, at the far end of the bridge by which people come and go, there was at that time a ditch, high, deep and reinforced. On the ditch there was a spiked stockade with a dwelling-place enclosed within it; around it brattices were raised, made from good planks and crenellated; there were knights and men-at-arms there, quarrelsome and slanderous. The duke arrived there first in order to see what they were doing. They behaved arrogantly and spoke basely, insulting William a great deal and repeatedly shouting out to him: 'The hide, the tailor's hide, that is what belongs to his trade!'. Because he was born in Falaise, where there were many tailors, they reproached him with that trade by way of insult and opprobrium.[209] The duke, who heard everything, swore by God's splendour – that was an oath he often used – that, if he could catch them, these words would be painfully bought; they would be pruned of their limbs, bear no hand or foot and be unable to see near or far. Then he had squires and vassals join the knights, sending some to attack and others to fill in the ditch. The roofs of the houses, the laths, the beams and whatever they found nearby they piled up in the ditch. Then they set fire to it all down wind; the wood was dry and the fire spread. Between the fire he lit and the assault he made on them some were burnt and others captured, and there were those who were put to death in shame. The duke wanted to have the prisoners and to know all their names; those who had insulted him and abused him he had taken before Alençon and had their hands and feet cut off. He had their feet thrown into the castle in order to frighten those inside. They were terrified and the duke swore on holy relics that they should expect a similar reward if they failed to hand over the castle to him at once. (4287–4359)

Then the duke told them that, if they handed it over to him, they could go free; he would let them all depart with their limbs and their persons safe. They could go in safety wherever they liked throughout Normandy. Totally defenceless and frightened by the threats, they handed over the castle to the duke and he received it from them, placing in it men-at-arms and knights, sentinels and porters; then he returned to Domfront. He harried those inside so much that they sent word to Geoffrey Martel to come and assist the castle; they had nothing to eat and no

---

[209] On the question of whether the insult involved the profession of tanner (*parmentier*) or tawer (*peletier*) see Holden's note to v. 4319 (vol. 3, pp. 227–28). See also E. van Houts, 'The Origins of Herleva, Mother of William the Conqueror', *English Historical Review*, 101 (1986), 399–405, and the *GND*, II, pp. 124–25.

money to spend. He should give them leave to hand over the castle or he should provide them with supplies or rescue them; if he lost the castle, the shame would be his. They had defended the castle for so long and waited for his help for so long that they would not be in the wrong if they handed it over, since they did not expect help from anyone. They all knew for certain that, if the duke captured them by force, he would not take any ransom from them other than the one he took from those on the bridge at Alençon. (4360–86)

Geoffrey Martel was anxious that Domfront should be rescued. He summoned men from Le Mans and Anjou and sought lords and neighbours; he had come close to Domfront and could easily be seen from there. William knew he was coming with the intention of protecting Domfront. He called three of his men, who were very sensible and courtly, FitzOsbern, his steward (his name was William, a noble vassal), and Roger of Montgomery, and William FitzThierry.

'Get on your horses', he said, 'you know how to count knights. Find out how many men are being brought by Martel, who is doing all he can to protect Domfront. Tell him I am guarding the gate and will receive what he brings with him. I am in my own land and protecting what is mine; let him leave me what is mine and he will be acting wisely. He has put the inhabitants of Touraine and those of Poitou to the test; he has done with them what he wanted, as appears from the lands he is taking from them. Tomorrow he can put the Normans to the test, either army against army or in single combat. Whatever he says or does, we are ready here and now. He will not pass, let him know this, and more than a thousand men will be killed in the process.' The three barons rode until they found Geoffrey Martel. Many words were exchanged there and many complaints made, large and small. There was much discussion about pleas, pillage and other matters, but the upshot was that Martel said and made a verbal promise that the next day he would go to Domfront and see who would wait for him there; he would be on a white horse and have a golden shield, so that William would identify him easily and recognise him by his arms. They replied mockingly that he would make his way there to no purpose, torment himself to no purpose and go there for nothing; for William, if he waited for him, would be with him at daybreak. They told him what arms he would have and what horse he would be riding. Martel said that he would go to Domfront and attack him in Domfront. They did not argue with him and listened to whatever he said, except to say that, if he came, they would see him and do the best they could; they would wait for him if he attacked them and, when he left, he would see how things were. (4387–4448)

They took their leave of Geoffrey Martel, all expecting there to be a battle. William said:

'Let everything rest with God and his will'. That night they remained awake a long time and watched the castle closely. The bold wished that the battle would take place and the cowards that it would not; they would not have minded whatever agreement they reached, provided they departed in peace. The next day, they all armed themselves amidst great tumult and great clamour. Martel made his men ready; I do not know whether he intended to advance. He was making as if to fight, dividing up his troops, both those from Anjou and those from Maine, when Geoffrey, the lord of Mayenne, arrived, spurring across the fields with his men following close behind him. Then he said to Geoffrey Martel:

'My lord, you should not advance! You could soon do something foolish and lose more than you gain. You have started out a little too late, the castle has been handed over to the duke.' Martel thought he was telling the truth and was doing so for his advantage; he left the region, angry and sorrowful. (4449–78)

When those guarding Domfront found out they were not going to get help and that Martel, who was abandoning the region, would be doing nothing more, they handed over the castle at once, safeguarding their limbs and their equipment. The duke had his banner carried and raised within the keep; he razed to the ground the castles with which he had besieged Domfront, having the brattices carried away and reconstructed at Ambrières; he had a castle fortified there in order to discomfit Count Geoffrey. When he had fortified the castle and entrusted it to the guards, he came to Rouen in Normandy; on the advice of his barons he took a wife of high lineage in Flanders, daughter of Baldwin and niece of Robert, King of France (she was the daughter of his daughter by Constance). She was related to many noblemen and her name was Matilda; she was very beautiful and noble. The count gave her to him joyfully along with a good deal of splendid apparel. He took her to the castle at Eu, where the duke married her; from there she was taken to Rouen and was very well served and honoured. She had three sons by him whom she raised: Robert, William and Henry. In between the sons were two daughters, Adela and Cecily, very noble girls. Cecily became abbess at Caen and Adela became countess of Chartres and wife of Count Stephen, a fine man and a noble baron; they had children, so the lineage increased very well and was enhanced.[210] Malger, who held the archbishopric, placed an interdict on Normandy, on William and his wife, excommunicating both of them; they were of such close lineage, he said, that they should not have got married. In order to make amends, and so that God would give him true pardon and the pope allow him to hold on to his relative, the duke had a hundred prebends established to feed and clothe a hundred poor people, the maimed, the powerless, the infirm, the blind, at Cherbourg, Rouen, Bayeux and Caen; they still exist and remain just as they were established.[211] Then they built in Caen two very splendid abbeys, in two churches, very close to each other, one for monks, the other for nuns. (4479–4540)

Malger behaved foolishly. Often the things he said were nonsense; one was sensible, but another foolish. In Rouen he committed many evil acts, leaving no book or chalice there, no cross or good linen in the cupboard which he did not have dragged out. He spoilt and destroyed everything; no one knew what was happening. He did so much harm and was rebuked so much that he was rightly deposed; he gave up the Rouen crozier and handed it over to William, who, by common assent of the council, gave it to Maurilius. Maurilius was a professed

---

210 Cecily became abbess of Sainte-Trinité at Caen, which was founded by her mother; Adela married the Count of Blois in 1080 and became the mother of the future King Stephen of England (reigned 1135–54).

211 This information about the hundred prebends is unique to Wace.

monk in Fécamp; he was good before this happened and good after it. Malger did not want to remain there; he hated seeing his family and went far away from the region. He crossed over to the Cotentin and came to the isles of the Cotentin; he lived there and settled there until the end. Of the life he lived there, of the woman Gisla whom he loved and of the children he fathered on the island where he lived we are able to relate a great deal, but this is not our concern. From them came a man who was very honoured, called Michael of Baynes. Many people said in truth that he had a devil as familiar, I do not know whether or not it was a type of goblin; I know nothing about it. It called itself Toret, and Toret it was called. When Malger wanted to speak with it, he called out 'Toret' and it would come. Many people could hear them, but no one managed to see them.[212] (4541–82)

Malger dwelt on the islands, often moving from one to the other; when he wished to do so and it pleased him, he went hither and thither. Wanting to cross over to Normandy and reach the Cotentin, at the port called Wincant, he sailed across the sea. He called to the sailors:

'My lords', he said, 'look out! For I know well and am telling you that one of us, I do not know who, must perish today, I do not know how, either by drowning or by some other means.' They heard him, but did nothing more about it, putting their minds to steering their ships. It was summer and very hot. Malger sat next to the pilot; he had his breeches bound to his feet and wore no leggings. They had just lowered the sail and made harbour. Malger made a move, I do not know why, but when he tried to move his feet, they became entangled in his breeches and could not go forward; thus he stumbled and fell into the sea, headfirst. Despite all their efforts, he could not be pulled out before he had drowned. At low tide, many people went looking for him and he was found between two rocks, wrapped in his breeches; then he was carried to Cherbourg and buried there. (4583–4618)

At that time, says the author of the history of the Normans,[213] Cnut died in Winchester. He was the father of Harthacnut and had as his wife Emma, the wife of Æthelred and the mother of Edward and Alfred. During his father's lifetime, Harthacnut, on the advice of his mother Emma, had gone to Denmark and was a very honoured king. Because of Harthacnut, who was a long way away and attending to other business, England passed to Harold, a bastard son of Cnut. Edward and Alfred heard of the death of Cnut and were filled with joy; they thought they could have the kingdom, for there was no closer heir. They obtained knights and ships and prepared two fleets. Edward set off from Barfleur, taking with him forty ships, and arrived at the port of Southampton, expecting to have the entire land. But the English, who were well aware that the brothers were on their way, had no intention of welcoming them or retaining them in the land.

---

[212] Orderic Vitalis, in an interpolation in the *GND*, states that Malger was sent off to the isle of Guernsey (VII, pp. 142–43, see p. 130 n. 2). Wace is the only source for Malger's stay in the Channel Islands, for the reference to his woman Gisla and the story of his son Michael of Baynes and his familiar Toret. Wace's source is presumably oral tradition in the Channel Islands. Gouttebroze, 'Le Diable dans le *Roman de Rou*', associates Toret with the god Thor (pp. 228–31); Toret would thus be a survival in the Channel Islands of Viking heathenism.

[213] This is a reference to the *Gesta Normannorum Ducum* of William of Jumièges.

Either they were afraid of Harold, Cnut's son, or it may be that they loved him. They refused to let Edward have the country and the Normans joined battle with them, capturing and killing a large number of them and placing a good many of them on their ships. But the English had soon increased in numbers and come running from all sides. Edward saw that he would not conquer his inheritance without great losses; he saw the rapidly increasing number of men and feared the loss of his own people; he himself, if he were captured, would be killed without ransom. He had his men return to the ships and all the equipment loaded up. (4619–62)

At that time he could do nothing more, so he went back to Barfleur. Alfred, meanwhile, set out from Wissant[214] with a large number of ships and arrived safely at Dover, from where he went on to occupy Kent. The very low-born Count Godwin came to oppose him; his wife had been born in Denmark and she was of good Danish family. She had Harold, Gyrth and Tostig as sons, and because of the children I am telling you about, who were born of the Danes and loved by the Danes, Godwin loved the Danes much more than he did the English. Hear what devilry, great treason and great felony he committed! He was a traitor and committed treason, following in the footsteps of Judas. The traitor deceived and betrayed the son of his natural lord and the heir to the domain, as Judas had betrayed Jesus. He had greeted him and kissed him, eaten from his bowl and assured him that he would bear him faith and loyalty. One night, when he was about to go to sleep and had already gone to bed, Godwin captured and bound him and sent him off to London, to King Harold, who was aware of this treason and expecting him. He had him taken to Ely and then had his eyes put out; they put him to death in such a shameful fashion and in such pain that I dare not describe it. Those who came with Alfred were taken to Guildford; they lost their heads in great sorrow, apart from one man in ten. The English had counted them, sat them in rows and divided them into tens; then they sent every tenth man away and cut the heads off the other nine. Because the tenth part was so large and there were so many left, they further divided them into tens once again and every tenth man was spared.[215] (4663–4712)

Very soon afterwards, Harold died; he went the way he had to go. Those in England gathered together and thought about the question of kingship. They feared Edward, the rightful heir, because of the Normans whom they had decimated and because of his brother whom they killed. The upshot was that they agreed to summon Harthacnut and to make him King of England. So Harthacnut, who was the son of Emma and Cnut, was summoned; he came back from Denmark and the clergy crowned him. He summoned his brother Edward, who was the son of his mother Emma and retained him with great honour; all he lacked was the title 'king'. He was king for two years, then fell ill; he did not languish

---

[214] The form Wincant in the text must be interpreted here as the port of Wissant between Calais and Boulogne. Earlier (v. 4589), the form Wincant represents an unidentified port on the Cotentin.

[215] Wace's story of the killing of nine men in ten can also be found in the *Chronica de Hida* (p. 287) as well as in William of Malmesbury (pp. 336–37), who states that it was not in the Anglo-Saxon Chronicle.

long and soon died. His mother was grief-stricken by this, but it was a great comfort to her that her son Edward had come and been welcomed into the kingdom. The English found no other heir who should have the kingdom. Edward was noble and courtly and he established peace and good laws. He took a wife, the daughter of Godwin, Edith by name, a beautiful maiden, but they had no children; people said that he had not lain with her carnally or known her carnally. But no one ever saw this and there was no dispute between them. He loved the Normans very much, cherished them and treated them as friends. He loved Duke William just as much as he would his own brother and child. (4713–52)

The discord and the great envy which the French have towards Normandy have lasted for a long time and did last for a long time; they will never, I believe, come to an end.[216] The French abused the Normans both through bad deeds and bad words. They often reproached them, calling them 'bigoz' and eaters of pigswill[217] and often setting the king against them, saying:

'My lord, why do you not take the bigots' land away? Their ancestors, brigands who came by sea, took it away from your ancestors and from ourselves.' Because of traitors, who hated the duke and said such things, the king undertook a task which inflicted harm on many men. He said he would go to Normandy and conquer it; he would divide his men into two armies and enter from two sides. He intended to achieve what he had said he would do and summoned his men from everywhere; he summoned men from two regions divided by the Seine. He gathered together in the Beauvaisis those from Rheims and those from Soissons, those from Laon and from Noyon, those from Meaux and from the Vermandois, those from the Ponthieu and from the Amiénois, those from Flanders and from Beaumont, all those from beyond the Seine, those from Brie, those from Provins, in their hundreds, thousands and twenties; from that direction they were to enter the Pays de Caux. As constable and leader, he gave them his brother Odo and ordered them to go by way of the Pays de Caux and lay waste the entire land. Using his seigniorial jurisdiction, the king had all the rest of the men on the other side of the Seine summoned and told to come to him in Mantes; those from the Touraine, those from Blois, those from Orléans and from the Gâtinais, those from the Perche and those from the Chartrain, those from the woodlands and those from the plains, from Bourges and from the Berri, from Étampes and Montlhéry, from Gïen and from Châtillon, from Sens and from Château-Landon, all these the king summoned to Mantes. He threatened the Normans and boasted that he would destroy the Évrechin; he would destroy the Roumois and the Lieuvin and ride through them as far as the sea and return via the Auge. (4753–4810)

William, who had a great fear of the king's arrogance, was very alarmed; he arranged his men into two sections and from them established two companies.

---

[216] This comment on the animosity between the French and the English continues a theme found as early as the opening lines of the *Chronique Ascendante*. See note 1 above.

[217] The term *bigoz* seems to represent *bi got* 'by God'. See Stephen de Ullmann, 'Anglicisms in French: Notes on their Chronology, Range and Reception', *Publications of the Modern Language Association of America*, 62 (1947), 1153–77 (p. 1155). On the term *draschiers*, translated here as 'eaters of pigswill', see Holden's note to v. 4760 (vol. 3, p. 229).

Towards the Pays de Caux he took Walter Giffard and those on that side, the Count of Eu, Robert by name, and Hugh of Gourney the Old; with them he put William Crispin, who owned a large area of land in the Vexin. These men commanded the men in their territory, their relatives and friends. The duke kept the rest of the men with him to oppose the king. He summoned those from the Bessin and the barons from the Cotentin and those from the valley of Mortain and from Avranches, which is farther away, Ralph Taisson of the Cinglais and the knights from the Auge and the Hiémois; these men the duke had with him. He would, he said, be very close to the king and camp near him, watching out for the foragers; they would not get far with their foraging without, if possible, suffering losses. He had foodstuff removed from where the king would pass and had the livestock taken into the woods and looked after by the peasants. The barons, who were over towards the Pays de Caux and were to defend that region, stayed in the woods and forests until the men from that area arrived; they moved from wood to wood and hid in the copses. The men from France rode along and camped in Mortemer; the lodgings were so comfortable that they remained there for a night. They thought they could go everywhere in peace and did not expect to find any knight who dared to oppose them or bear arms against them; they thought and said that all the knights were over in the direction of Évreux with their lord, who was very much afraid of the king. The French were very arrogant, very cruel and very destructive; wherever they passed, they destroyed whatever they found, laying waste towns and manors, burning dwellings, capturing booty and peasants, violating women and holding on to those they selected. They remained in Mortemer where they found good lodgings; during the day they devastated the land and they spent the night carousing, asking for wine, killing beasts and eating and drinking in safety. Through their spies, the Normans discovered their whereabouts and their behaviour and all night long assembled their men, summoning their allies and their companions. (4811–76)

In the morning, at daybreak – they were still sleeping – suddenly the Normans surrounded Mortemer and set the town alight. The fire took hold of one lodging then another, and the flames spread throughout the town; then you would have seen frightened people, a town in disarray and a bitter struggle. Throughout their lodgings the French stirred, grabbing such weapons as they could find and thinking themselves defeated since the Normans had caught them in their beds. One man thought he could mount his horse who could not get hold of the bridle, another thought he could escape from the dwelling who could not reach the door; the Normans guarded the exits and the paths at the ends of the streets. The fighting there was very fierce and many extraordinary happenings took place there. From morning, at sunrise, until nones, as the day wore on, the full-scale fighting and the fierce, harsh battle continued. The French could not escape and the Normans refused to leave them; the first to abandon the battle was Odo, who fled. The Normans captured Guy, Count of Ponthieu, armed and alive, but they killed his brother Waleran, a very strong and valiant knight.[218] There was scarcely a lowborn groom there who did not take Frenchmen prisoner and capture fine

[218] The correct name of Guy's brother is Enguerrand.

horses, even two or three, in addition to other lesser equipment; there was no prison in the whole of Normandy which was not filled with Frenchmen. You would have seen many Frenchmen taking flight, hiding in woods and bushes. In burnt patches,[219] dunghills, fields and paths you would have see heaps of dead bodies and many wounded men dying. That very night, fairly early, news came to the duke in the army that the French were defeated and he had some respite in respect of his land. News is a remarkable thing; it travels very fast and speedily and the man who carries good news knocks on a door with confidence. The duke was delighted by what had happened and delighted by the defeat. To the place where the king was lodged – he was already in his bed – he sent a man (I do not know whether it was a valet or a squire) and made him climb a tree and call out loudly all night: 'Frenchmen, Frenchmen, get up, get up! Be on your way, you are sleeping too much! Go and bury your friends who have died in Mortemer!' (4877–4940)

The king heard what the man was shouting and was amazed and very frightened. He sent for his favourite counsellors, earnestly asking them whether they had heard any news of what the man in the tree was shouting. While they were speaking to the king and asking for news, suddenly the news arrived and was spread throughout the army that the finest of their friends had been killed in Mortemer; those who remained alive were prisoners in Normandy, placed in chains and in gaols. At such words and news, the French were stirred into action; they got moving, yelling that they were delaying too long. They took their palfreys and warhorses and loaded up their jades and their packhorses, setting fire to the shelters and the huts; they had soon abandoned everything. They sent their equipment on ahead and the king followed behind them to watch over it. If the duke had wanted to attack, he could have done the king much damage, but he did not want to discomfit him any further; he had, he said, already enough cause for grief. The king had enough misfortune, he said, so he did not want to create any more for him at that time. The king withdrew to Paris and the barons to their own lands, and the huge numbers of men he had taken with him returned to their own regions.[220] The king felt great anguish and anger towards the Normans; he was upset about those who had been captured and more so about those who had been killed. Since he could not recover the dead, he intended to free those who had been captured. He sent word to the duke, saying that if he freed the prisoners he held he would offer him a truce and peace, unless any other quarrel arose; in respect of whatever Geoffrey Martel was taking from him, and whatever he could take, he would never wage war against him and never be the cause of any sorrow for him. This happened as I am telling you and the duke returned the prisoners, but they left all their equipment to those who had won it; the prisoners paid and settled for whatever they had consumed. (4941–94)

---

[219] The reference here is to the practice of burning grass and spreading its ashes in order to improve the soil (see Holden, note to v. 4917, vol. 3. p. 230).

[220] Wace's account of the battle of Mortemer is more elaborate than that in the *GND* (II, pp. 142–45) and in William of Poitiers (pp. 48–51).

Geoffrey Martel hated the duke. He was very upset because he heard that everything was going well for him and because he had to come to terms with the king. The king had made the taking of his land one of the points of the agreement. He was very upset and displeased, very angry and irate; if he did not defend himself again the duke, he said, he would consider himself very indolent; if he left the Passais in peace, he had no right to any of the lands he may possess. He who does not dare to defend his own rights has faint hope of taking someone else's. He spoke to the Count of Poitiers and brought him into this affair, as well as the vicomte of Thouars and a number of others from other areas, some from the Touraine, some from Poitou, some from Le Mans and some from Anjou, using his power of summons and entreaty. With a large army he arrived before Ambrières. He thought he could catch the inhabitants of the castle unawares, using intelligence and cunning to capture it, but those inside defended themselves so they were not harmed by those outside. Many projectiles were hurled and discharged, but no great harm was done. Those inside the castle taunted Martel's men greatly for not daring to attack them, and this caused them to abandon the assault completely. To demonstrate their boldness, they had a stretch of fence quite deliberately torn down so that they could all see the entrance; but Martel made no further gains there and found no one willing to attack them. Those from Étouteville were there, whose task it was to guard the castle. Martel was forced to delay so long in setting up his war machines that the duke came spurring up, summoning his men from all sides. Martel knew the duke would come and that he would fail to take the castle. He abandoned the Passais and Ambrières; I do not know if he returned there later. But he had greatly damaged the land, burnt and destroyed many a town, captured booty, ransomed peasants and caused sorrow to men and women. (4995–5046)

Those from Le Mans took Martel's side and came with him to oppose the duke; the duke was very angry with them. Herbert, their lord, had now died childless, but he had said on his deathbed that once he was dead they should protect themselves and take the duke as their lord, for if they sided with Martel they would never in their lifetime have peace and would live in pain and suffering; they would never be safe from his machinations. Herbert spoke well, but they did not believe him and a number of them regretted it. They joined forces with Martel against the Duke of Normandy. The duke showed no reluctance to harm them, driving them so hard and pressing them so hard because of the castles he conquered and the barons he captured that they handed over the city against the will of many people. He had stone and lime brought there and constructed a tower; he took their fealty and homage and took secure hostages from the barons so that they would keep the peace, maintain the peace and serve the duke loyally. Geoffrey, lord of Mayenne, the strongest man in Maine, had as his wife the sister of his lord, Count Herbert. Through her he thought he could have Le Mans, because Herbert had no heir. He opposed the duke for a long time and waged war on him a great deal and caused him such harm. The barons who were from his family supported him. On one occasion, he entered Le Mans, but he was not there for long and soon abandoned it; he did not dare wait for the duke and would not have been able to protect himself. In this hour of need he could easily have summoned a thousand knights without going far; he was a man who held extensive lands and possessed very great power. I cannot tell of the combats, the battles or the skirmishes, or of the expenditure or the costs, the blows from lances or the thrusts which William suffered in order to bring peace to poor people; but with his incursions and ambushes Geoffrey greatly upset the peace. William saw he would not have peace as long as Geoffrey held the castle. He summoned and sent word to his men, leaving no one of fighting age, asked the Bretons, the Flemish and many others from a number of directions and rode straight to Maine, burning and setting fire to burgs, burning the entire town and its dwellings, demolishing walls and spiked barricades. A long time afterwards, when he saw his opportunity, he rebuilt them without more ado, placing guards there who equipped the castle and kept and protected the peace. (5047–5114)

Duke William was very brave; he did harm to all his enemies and was loved for his generosity and feared for his prowess. He won and conquered a great deal, gave away a great deal and spent a great deal. Because of his reputation for chivalry the French were very envious, both with regard to the households over which he ruled and the lands he conquered. The king could not love Normans; he preferred to perjure himself, he said, than not to make them pay for the battle of Mortemer. On the advice of Geoffrey Martel, around August, when the corn was new, he summoned all his barons and assembled the knights, all those who held fiefs from him and owed him service. They entered Normandy and passed close to Exmes, making a great assault on it, but they did not stay there long, as they wanted to cross the whole of the Hiémois and the Bessin as far as the sea. They burnt the towns and the burgs, making many men sorrowful; there were many unfortunate women there. They came to Saint-Pierre-sur-Dive; the town was completely protected, for the king lay in the abbey there. The duke's men were in Falaise and he received news which distressed him greatly; the king, it appeared to him, was doing wrong by him. He summoned and assembled his knights and strengthened all his castles, reinforcing his ditches and rebuilding his walls; he would allow the open land to be laid waste. If he could protect his castles well, he said, he could rally properly and restore all the open land. He did not want to reveal himself to the French and allowed them to go anywhere in the region; but he thought he could drive them out in shameful fashion when they returned. (5115–60)

The king prepared his men, saying he would go towards Bayeux and destroy the whole of the Bessin; on leaving there, he would pass through Varaville and lay waste all of the Auge and the Lieuvin. The French went swiftly though the Bessin as far as the River Seulle. From there they returned to Caen, where they crossed the Orne; Caen still lacked a castle and had no wall or battlement. When the king left Caen, he passed through Varaville. There was a long and broad procession of men, which could not pass quickly in its entirety. When they were crossing the bridge, there was a huge throng with each man wanting to advance.[221] The duke soon found out, through someone or other, when and which way the king would be going and he set out after the company, with the great numbers of household

---

[221] The *GND* speaks of a 'ford' not a 'bridge' (II, pp. 152–53). This account of the battle of Varaville is more elaborate than in the *GND* (see II, p. 152 n. 1) or in William of Poitiers.

knights he led. He directed his men in close array through the valley of Bavent and let the word be known throughout the region, and had it said and announced to the peasants, that with such arms as they had they should come to him as soon as they could. Then you would have seen peasants making haste, with clubs and cudgels in their hands. The king had crossed the Dive, the river which runs through the region, together with the bulk of the army which was doing its best to make speedy progress, but the throng behind them was long, with no interruption at any point along its length. (5161–96)

The duke saw he had the upper hand over those who were in the tail. When he entered Varaville, with his men growing in number from one town to another, he discovered Frenchmen holding fast and making up the rearguard. There you would have seen a fierce combat, many a blow struck by lance and sword; knights struck with their lances, the archers shot their arrows and with their clubs the peasants dealt them blows, overthrowing and stunning many of them. They pushed them on to the causeway, killing and knocking down many of them; the Normans, who came running up in great crowds, went on increasing in numbers. Then you would have seen the French troops making haste, one pushing another forward. The causeway, which they found to be long and in bad repair, caused the great distress; they were weighed down by the plunder they had taken. You would have seen many of them leaving the road, stumbling and being propelled off the path, so that they could not pick themselves up or get back on to the right path. When it came to crossing the bridge, there was a great throng, with everyone struggling to make progress. The bridge was old and the weight substantial; the planks gave way and the smaller ones fell down. The sea rose and the waves were high. There was a heavy weight on the bridge and it collapsed and fell down; whatever was on it was lost. Many men fell with the bridge, which sank right down to the bottom. When the bridge collapsed, the shouting was agonising and frightful. You would have seen a great deal of equipment floating away, men plunging into the river and sinking to the bottom; no one could escape alive unless he was a gifted swimmer. When they had failed to cross the bridge, there was none courageous and bold enough not to fear for his life, for they had no way of escaping. The Normans behind them were taking them prisoner and they could get no farther. They groped their way along the river banks, looking for fords or crossing-points, throwing away their weapons and booty; they regretted having so much with them. They stumbled through the ditches, dragging each other along. The Normans pulled them out, showing them no mercy or pity. (5197–5252)

All those who had come to a halt and not crossed the bridge were captured and bound, or else they were killed or drowned. Never, they said, was so much booty obtained in Normandy without more loss of life. William gave thanks to God. The river and the sea took away a great many; the king, who saw them, was disconsolate. He climbed above Bastebourg,[222] saw Varaville and Cabourg, saw the marshes and the valleys, long and broad on several sides, saw the great river and the broken bridge and saw his men being destroyed. He saw some captured

---

[222] Bastebourg is a hillock near Dozulé (Calvados), on the right bank of the Dive.

and bound and saw others drowning in the sea; those who were drowning he could not help in any way and he could not rescue the prisoners. He breathed hard and sighed with anger; his grief left him speechless. You would have seen his body badly twisted and his countenance discoloured with anguish; he would gladly have gone back, he said, if he had thought he could make it, if his barons recommended it,* but none of them advised him to cross there.

'My lord', they said, 'you would not get across. You will come back on another occasion, destroy the entire land and take from the wealthiest men what is rightfully yours.' Then the King of France departed, filled with anger and sorrow. Henceforth, he never carried sword or lance – I do not know whether he did so as a penance – and he never went back into Normandy, nor did he reign for much longer. He did what each man will do: he came from the earth and returned to the earth. When the king had died, it was Philip, his eldest son, who was crowned after him; the duke was a very close friend of his. (5253–96)

The history of the Normans is a long one and hard to set down in the vernacular. If one asks who said this, who wrote this history in the vernacular, I say and will say that I am Wace from the Isle of Jersey, which is in the sea towards the west and belongs to the territory of Normandy. I was born on the island of Jersey and taken to Caen as a small child; there I went to school and was then educated for a long time in France. When I returned from France, I stayed in Caen for a long time and set about composing works in the vernacular; I wrote and composed a good many.[223] With the help of God and the king – I must serve no one apart from God – a prebend was given to me in Bayeux (may God reward him for this). I can tell you it was by Henry the second, the grandson of Henry and the father of Henry. (5297–5318)

The story is a long one before it comes to an end, about how William became king, about the domain which came to him and about who held his land after him. His deeds, his words and his adventures, which we find in writing, would be good to recount, but we cannot speak of everything. A brave and courtly knight, he established good laws throughout his lands and held firmly to justice and peace for poor people, wherever he could; he was never able to love a thief nor the company of an evil-doer. In Caen he built two abbeys on which he lavished a great deal of wealth. One abbey he built in the name of Saint Stephen, in which he placed monks. His wife Matilda took the other in hand, which was dedicated to the Holy Trinity; she placed nuns in it and for love and charity was buried there, as she had indicated in her lifetime. The duke did things I cannot find anyone else doing, before or since. He summoned all his bishops and had them assemble in Caen; he had counts, abbots and priors, barons and rich vavassors all come to Caen and listen to his commands. He had holy relics brought there wherever he could find them, whether in a bishopric or an abbey over which he had lordship; he had the body of Saint Ouen brought from Rouen to Caen in a casket. When the clergy, the relics and the barons, of which there were many, were assembled in Caen, on the day he had ordered, he had everyone swear on the

---

[223] In v. 5311, as in v. 153, Wace uses the term *romanz*, which could possibly be translated as 'romances'. See Introduction, pp. xxiv, xxxi, and note 139 above.

relics to hold and maintain peace, from Wednesday at sunset to Monday at sunrise; they call it a truce, I believe, and there is nothing like it in any other country. Anyone who fought another person within that period, who performed a clearly wicked act or who stole anything from someone else, was to be excommunicated and receive a fine of nine pounds in favour of the bishop; this he established. The duke swore out loud, and all the barons likewise swore, that they would keep the peace and maintain this truce.[224] (5319–76)

So that the peace, which was to last for ever, would always be remembered, the duke immediately had a church built there out of blocks of stone and mortar; in it the relics, which had been brought to the council, lay together. Many of those who founded the church called it All Saints church, because of the relics, of which there were so many. But many people preferred it to be called Holy Peace and to turn it into Holy Peace, because of the peace which was sworn there when it was first created; I have heard many people call it Holy Peace and All Saints.[225] Beside it they built a chapel named after Saint Ouen, where the holy relic reposed as long as the council lasted. William was a man of great goodness. People from foreign parts loved him very much; he was very noble and courtly and King Edward cherished him. The duke went to visit Edward to find out how things were with him; he crossed over to England and Edward honoured him greatly. He gave him many dogs, birds and other fine and beautiful things, and whatever he could find which suited a nobleman.[226] The duke did not stay there long; he returned to Normandy, having business with the Bretons who were opposing him. (5377–5412)

Godwin, rich in possessions, wealthy in land and behaving with great arrogance and pride, was in England. Edward had his daughter as his wife, but Godwin was cruel and treacherous and did a great deal of harm in the country. Edward feared and hated him for having betrayed his brother, for having decimated the Normans and for many a harmful deed which he had perpetrated. Their ever-growing exchange of words and their manifest activities led to a great quarrel between them, in which reconciliation was difficult. Edward feared Godwin greatly and drove him out of his land; he swore that Godwin would not remain there and that he would not have him in his kingdom unless he swore fealty towards him and handed over hostages for him to keep in perpetuity as a guarantee that during his lifetime he would maintain peace. Godwin did not dare refuse him; partly to reassure the king, partly to support his family and partly to protect his men, he gave the king as hostages one of his nephews and one of his sons, whom he had brought up together. The king sent them to Duke William in Normandy, as someone in whom he trusted greatly. He sent him word to look

---

[224] On the Truce or Peace of God see n. 12 above. In reality the Normans rejected the Truce of God for many years. See Bates, *Normandy before 1066*, pp. 53, 163–64, 179. The story of the Truce and the relic displayed at Caen is not in the *GND*; in William of Poitiers it is very brief (pp. 80–81). See also Maylis Baylé, *La Trinité de Caen, sa place dans l'histoire de l'architecture et du décor romans* (Geneva and Paris: Arts et Métiers Graphiques, 1979), p. 81 n. 36.

[225] These details concerning the church are unique to Wace.

[226] The information that William visited Edward in England (*c.* 1050) is found in the Anglo-Saxon Chronicle (version D only), but nowhere else.

after them until he himself asked for them; it appeared as if he wanted him to hold on to them permanently, people said, until he could have his kingdom if he died before him. Matters with respect to Godwin then stayed calm and the king left him in peace. I do not know how long he lasted, but I do know that in Odiham, where he was eating, he choked on a morsel of food over which the king had made the sign of the cross.[227] (5413–56)

King Edward was of good disposition and had no wish to harm anyone; he wished to show true justice to everyone without pride or covetousness. He built a number of abbeys, providing them with fiefs and other possessions, and particularly Westminster. Hear with what intention! Because of a personal need – I do not know if he did it because of an illness, to recover his kingdom or because of his fear of the sea – he vowed he would go to Rome to pray and seek pardon for his sins; he would speak to the pope and take penance from him. At a time he specified, the king prepared his journey; the barons, the bishops and the abbots were gathered together. They spoke as one person and told and advised him that in no way would they let him go and that this vow had to be overturned. He could not in their opinion live much longer if he had to endure great suffering. It was too lengthy a pilgrimage, for the king was very old; so if he went to Rome, he might not return, as death or illness could keep him there. Great harm would befall them if they lost the king. They would send someone to the pope and get him to absolve him of the vow; he could easily get absolution and perform some other penance instead. They sent someone to the pope, who released the king from the vow, but he enjoined and advised him, in order to secure release from the vow, to seek out a poor abbey, which had been be founded in the name of Saint Peter, and give it so much of his own wealth, honour it so much and assign so much of his income to it that it would always be wealthy and honoured in the name of Saint Peter. (5457–5502)

Edward received the pope's command gladly. Near London, towards the west, and it still appears and stands there, was an abbey dedicated to Saint Peter, which had been impoverished for a very long time. It was situated on a little island by the name of Zornee [Thorney], near the Thames. We call it Zornee because there was an abundance of thorns there and because it was surrounded by water. *Ee* in English we call *isle*; *ee* is *isle*, *zorn* is *espine*, either branch or tree or root. Zornee in English is the *isle d'espines* in French; it was later called Westminster, when the church was founded there. King Edward saw Westminster, which was in need of much improvement, and he saw the place, which was getting poorer, and the church, which was dilapidated. On the advice of clerics and laymen, in view of the peaceful times he was enjoying, with great care and great endeavour, with his money and his income he established Westminster properly, giving it so much of his property, fine towns and good dwellings, crosses, books[228] and good possessions; the place would never want for anything if matters were conducted loyally. But when each monk takes charge of finances, the common good comes to grief and deteriorates; a monk who seeks control wants to lay his hands on

---

[227] All English sources say that Godwin died at Winchester or Windsor.
[228] The word translated here as 'books' is *textes*; see note 39 above.

money.* The king established Westminster, cherished the place and loved it dearly; afterwards, he gave the church of Saint Edmund so much that the monks there are wealthy. (5503–42)

King Edward had lived on and ruled his kingdom for a long time. He was upset by the fact that he had no child or close relative belonging to him who could have his kingdom after him or who could maintain it. He thought about who would inherit his kingdom when he died; he thought hard and often said he would like to give his inheritance to Duke William, his relative, the finest of his lineage. Robert, his father, had raised him and William had served him a great deal. All the advantages he had enjoyed had been through this lineage; whatever impression he had given, he did not love anyone as much. For the honour of the good family with whom he had been raised, and because of William's valour, he wanted to make him heir to his kingdom. In the land was a steward by the name of Harold, a noble vassal. Because of his reputation and his courage he had great power in the kingdom; he was the strongest man in the country, strong in men and strong in allies. He had England in his power, as a man does who is possessed of the office of steward. Through his father he was English and through his mother Danish; his mother Gytha was Danish, born and raised in great wealth; she was a very noble lady and rightly so; she was sister of Svein, aunt of Cnut,[229] mother of Harold and wife of Godwin, and her daughter Edith was queen. Harold was on good terms with his lord, who had married his sister. When his father, who had choked on the morsel of food, had died, he wanted to cross over to Normandy and free the hostages, for whom he felt a great deal of pity. He took leave of King Edward; Edward openly refused him permission, forbade him and entreated him not to cross over to Normandy or speak to Duke William; he could easily be tricked there, for the duke was very astute. If he wished to have his hostages back, he should send other messengers. I have found this in writing, but another book has informed me that the king, to ensure that the kingdom passed to Duke William, his cousin, after his death, asked Harold to go to him.[230] I do not know which is the correct explanation, but we can find both in writing.[231] (5543–5604)

Whatever business he was pursuing and whatever he intended to do, Harold set out, no matter how things would turn out for him; an event which has to take

---

[229] See Holden's note to v. 5578 (vol. 3, pp. 231–32). The Svein concerned is Svein I Forkbeard.

[230] Edward the Confessor, King of England 1042–66, was the son of Emma, daughter of Duke Richard I of Normandy; William's father, Robert I, was Edward's first cousin.

[231] On this passage see Rollo, pp. 155–61. What Rollo describes as the 'official Norman truth', that Edward sent Harold over to William to ensure the succession by swearing to accept William's claim to the throne (*GND*, II, pp. 158–61, William of Poitiers, pp. 70–71, Orderic Vitalis, II, pp. 134–37), is undermined by Wace, who mentions an account of events which has Edward telling Harold not to go to William because of the possibility of trickery. Wace recognises the existence of the Norman view ('another book tells me . . .', v. 5598), but he is drawing principally on the view of the Anglo-Saxon chronicler Eadmer who, in his *Historia novorum* (ed. Rule, p. 6, trans. Bosanquet, p. 6), has Edward point to Duke William's astute mind and the likelihood that William would want to gain considerably from the return of the hostages (his brother and his nephew). In Rollo's opinion, by reproducing Eadmer's account, Wace is subverting 'any irreproachably defensible Norman claim to the Britain of the past and the England of the present' (p. 161).

place cannot be prevented, and something which has to happen cannot fail to do so for any reason. Harold had two ships prepared and set sail at Bosham. I cannot tell you what mistake he made, either concerning the helmsman or the crosswind, but I know he went astray. He did not manage to enter Normandy and had to sail to the Ponthieu; he was unable to turn back and could not conceal his arrival there. One of the fishermen in that region, who had been to England and often seen Harold, caught sight of him and recognised him by his face and his speech. He went in secret to tell Guy, the Count of the Ponthieu – he did not want to speak to anyone else – that he would bring great gain to him if he were willing to accompany him. If he gave him just twenty pounds, he would make him gain a hundred, for he would hand over to him such a prisoner as would give him a hundred pounds or more. The count assured him he would do his bidding and the man who desired gain showed him Harold. They took him to Abbeville, and through an associate Harold sent word to the duke in Normandy to inform him of how things had gone, that he was coming to him from England, but was unable to reach a true port. He was coming to him as a messenger, but had failed to find good passage. The Count of the Ponthieu had captured him and put him in prison without his having committed any crime; he should free him, if he could, and then he would do whatever he wanted. (5605–52)

Guy guarded Harold with great care, greatly fearing a mishap; he sent him to Beaurain to get him a long way away from the duke. The duke thought that, if he himself held Harold, he would be able take advantage of this; he promised and offered the count so much, threatened and entreated him so much that Guy handed Harold over and he took possession of him; the duke let him have a fine dwelling near the River Eaulne.[232] William held Harold in great honour for many a day, as was right and proper; he sent him in very noble fashion to many a rich tournament. He gave him weapons and horses and took him to Brittany, three or four times (I do not know how exactly many) when he had to fight against the Bretons. Meanwhile, the duke held discussions with him until Harold agreed to hand England over to him as soon as King Edward died, and to take his daughter Adela as his wife if he wished; if it pleased him, he would swear this to him and William accepted it. In order to receive this oath he arranged a parley; he convened a great council in Bayeux, as people are accustomed to say. He ordered all the holy relics to be assembled in one place, having an entire tub filled with them; then he had them covered over with a silk cloth so that Harold neither knew about them nor saw them, nor was it pointed out or explained to him. On top of it he placed a reliquary, the finest he could choose and the most precious he could find; I have heard it called 'ox-eye'.[233] When Harold stretched out his hand, his hand trembled and his flesh quivered. Then he solemnly swore and affirmed, according to the text someone dictated to him, that he would take Adela, the duke's daughter, and hand England over to the duke; after Edward's death, he

---

[232] This information concerning the gift to Guy of Ponthieu of a manor on the Eaulne is unique to Wace.

[233] Although the 'ox-eye' story can be found in the *Brevis relatio* (p. 28), the story about the tub containing relics, and the brocade covering it, is unique to Wace.

would do his very best in this respect, in accordance with his strength and knowledge and providing he were alive and that God and the relics present assisted him truly. Many people said: 'May God grant him this!'. When Harold had kissed the relics and was back on his feet, the duke drew him towards the tub and made him stand beside it. From the tub he removed the brocade, which had covered everything, and showed Harold the relics inside, over which he had sworn; Harold felt great fear at the relics which he showed him. When he had made preparations for his journey, he took leave of Duke William; William escorted him and begged him to act properly. As he departed, he kissed him in the name of faith and friendship; Harold crossed rapidly and safely to England. (5653–5724).

The day arrived, which could not fail and which no man can escape, because each person must end up dying. King Edward had to die. It was very much his wish that, if possible, William should have his kingdom. But he was too far away, tarried too long and could not extend the time. Suffering from the illness from which he would die, Edward lay sick; he was very close to death and already very weak. Harold gathered his family together, summoned his allies and other people and entered the king's chamber, taking with him those he wanted. An Englishman spoke first, as Harold had commanded:

'My lord', he said, 'we are very distressed that we must lose you. We are frightened by this and very much afraid of being forsaken. We cannot lengthen your life or exchange your death for someone else's. Each man has to die his own death; no one can die on behalf of another. We cannot protect you from death and you cannot escape death; whatever happens, you have to die, earth must return to earth. After your death, no heir of yours remains to comfort us. You are an old man now and have lived for a long time without having any children, son, daughter or any other heir who can remain behind in your place, who could protect us or support us and become king by virtue of his lineage. Throughout this land people are weeping and wailing, saying that if you are no longer with them, they are dead. They never expect to have peace and I think they are telling the truth, for we will never have peace without a king and never have a king except through you. Give your kingdom while you are still alive to someone who can bring peace in the future; may God never grant it, and may it not please Him that there should be a king who would do worse by us! A kingdom is bad and worth very little as soon as justice and peace are lacking; he who does not bring justice and peace has no right to any kingdom he may have. You are good, you have done good and will do good. You have served God and will have God. We are distressed that you are going, except for the fact that you will have God. The finest of this land are here and the finest of your friends. All of them have come to beg you, and you should grant this to them since they all come to make this request of you, that Harold should be king over your land. We cannot advise you better and you cannot do better.' (5725–88)

As soon as he had named Harold, throughout the chamber the English shouted out that he had spoken well, that he had said the right thing and that the king should believe him. 'My lord', they said, 'if you do not do this, we will never have peace as long as we live.' The king then sat on the bed and turned towards the English.

'My lords', he said, 'you are very well aware and have heard many times that I have given my kingdom after my lifetime to the Duke of Normandy. What I have given him some of you have sworn to him on oath.' Then Harold, who was on his feet, said:

'Whatever you have done, my lord, allow me to be king and let your land be mine. I seek nothing more than your acquiescence. You would never do anything for me which you would regret.'

'Harold', said the king, 'you will have this, but I know that you will die. If I ever truly knew the duke and his barons who are with him and the great forces he can summon, nothing can protect you other than God.' Then Harold said he would do what was right and the king should say what he wanted; he would do what he had to do and not fear a Norman or anyone else. The king then turned and said (I do not know whether he did so with a willing heart): 'Now let the English create a duke or a king, Harold or another, I grant this.' In this way he made Harold his heir, since he could not have William. There had to be a king for the kingdom; a kingdom cannot be without a king. He allowed his barons to do what they wished. The king died, he could not go on living; as a result the English had much to bewail. The body, which was greatly honoured, was buried in Westminster; his tomb, which was built and still remains, was sumptuous. As soon as King Edward was dead, Harold, who was wealthy and powerful, had himself anointed and crowned; he refused to speak to the duke. He took homage and fealty from the wealthiest and most senior men. (5789–5840)

The duke was in the hunting-park in Rouen, holding a bow in his hands. He had strung it and stretched it, pulled it and shot it; he had given it to a servant and wanted to go hunting, I believe. With him he had many knights, youths and squires.[234] Suddenly there arrived at the gate a servant who had travelled from England. He came straight to the duke and greeted him; to one side he informed him that King Edward had died and Harold had been made king. When the duke had heard what he said and knew the full truth, that Edward had gone to his end and Harold had been made king, his expression became one of anger and he abandoned completely his intention to hunt. He repeatedly laced up his mantle and repeatedly untied it; he spoke to no one and no one dared speak to him. He crossed the Seine by boat, came to his hall, entered and leant on the edge of a bench, turning this way and that, covering his face with his cloak; he laid his head on the arm-rest. In this way the duke reflected for a long time, without anyone daring to speak to him. Many people behind him asked:

'What is the matter with the duke, for him to look like that?' Suddenly the steward, who was coming from the park on horseback, arrived. He passed by the duke and went through the hall, humming; many people went and asked him why the duke was looking as he did. He replied:

'You will hear news, but will regret being over hasty to hear it, for what happens with news is that, if you do not hear it new, you hear it old'. Then the duke rose from where he was sitting and the steward said:

---

[234] This story of William being at hunt when the news of Edward's death arrived is not found elsewhere.

'My lord, my lord, why are you hiding the news which you know? If we do not hear it when it is new, we will perhaps learn it when it is old. There could be no advantage to you in concealing it and you would lose nothing in telling it. Be kind enough to us to tell us what everyone throughout the city knows. Throughout this city people say, everyone knows it, great and small, that King Edward is dead and has passed from this world. Harold has become king and received the kingdom.' (5841–5900)

'I am distressed by this', said the duke, 'but I can do no more. I am distressed because of Edward and his death and because of Harold who has done wrong by me. He who has taken the kingdom, which was given and promised to me, does me wrong. Edward had given it to me and Harold had sworn this to me.' To these words FitzOsbern, with the brave heart, replied:

'My lord', he said, 'do not delay. You should set about taking vengeance at once on Harold, who has broken his word to you. Unless courage fails you, the land will not remain with Harold. Summon as many men as you can, cross the sea and take the land from him! A worthy man must not begin anything or set anything in motion only to abandon it, either start something and bring it to fruition or leave everything without more ado.' In this way, news about King Harold passed through the region. (5901–24)

William sent word repeatedly to Harold that he should maintain his oath and Harold sent word back shamefully that he would do nothing for him; he would neither take his daughter nor hand over the land to him. William challenged him and sent him a challenge; Harold always replied that he had absolutely no fear of him any longer. The Normans, who lived in that country and had wives and children there who had been taken there by Edward and given great castles and fiefs, were thrown out of the country by Harold; he did not want to leave a single one there. He expelled fathers and mothers, sons and daughters, sisters and brothers. Harold took the crown at Christmas, but it would have been better for him to have done something else! He did nothing but harm to his own cause and to the entire region; he perjured himself over the kingdom and his rule did not last long. He caused harm to the whole kingdom and brought sadness to his lineage. He refused to take the duke's daughter or keep or observe his promise, but he paid for this wretchedly, he and the people he loved most. (5925–54)

From the news he heard, William discovered and learned that Harold would do nothing for him and would not keep his promise to him. He made up his mind to cross the sea and do battle with Harold; if the Lord God supported him, he would avenge himself on the traitor. Duke William was very upset that Harold was so contemptuous of him* and that he did not deign to speak to him before being crowned. He had taken from him what Edward had given him and what he himself had sworn to him, completely falsifying and contravening his oath. If he could harm and damage him, he said, without crossing the sea, he would gladly do him such harm; he would rather cross the sea, he said, than not avenge himself on Harold and not obtain what was his by right. The duke said he would cross the sea and take vengeance on Harold. In order to take a decision on this matter before revealing his plans to anyone else, he summoned Robert, Count of Eu, whose territory was alongside that of the inhabitants of the Vimeu, and Roger of Montgomery, whom he regarded as his staunch supporter, and the son of Osbern of Breteuil, William by name, a very arrogant man; he also summoned Walter Giffard, who at the time was a man of great goodness. He summoned Bishop Odo, his brother, and Robert of Mortain; Robert was the duke's brother and he loved him dearly. They were both his brothers, but on his mother's side. He summoned Roger of Vieilles, who performed many honourable deeds, for he was thought to be a very wise man and was already well on in years; he had six sons who were already knights, very noble and fierce men. He was lord of Beaumont-le-Roger and had jurisdiction over a large amount of land. He summoned Odo au Chapel, whose wife was Muriel, the duke's sister by his mother;[235] her father was Herluin. I do not know whether a child was born from them, but I never heard of one. Before beginning full preparations, he told these barons his plan, telling them how he was losing what was rightfully his and how Harold had taken it from him. If they dared advise him properly, he would cross the sea to avenge himself. If they were willing to expend the effort, with the large number of men he could summon, and if God were willing to grant it, he could recover what was his by right. They told him they were all willing to go with him, if need be. Not even if they had to mortgage their lands, or sell them, if need be, would he lose anything he should have, but he should trust his vassals and his clerics.

'You have', they said, 'a powerful body of men, many valiant and wise men, who are all of great power. They think they are just as worthy as ourselves to whom you are speaking. Say these things to them; they who are to share in the hardship should come to the council.' (5955–6032)

In this way the barons were summoned and they all assembled on one day. The duke told them and explained to them the way Harold had tricked him and that he had taken from him what Edward had made him heir to; he could not get possession of it. He wanted to avenge himself, if he could manage to do so, but he needed a great deal of help; without their help he could not obtain a large number of men or ships. Let each man say what he would do for him, how many men and ships he would bring. They said they would discuss it and respond to him after their deliberations; the duke agreed to this. They were in council for a long time and their discussions lasted a long time; there was concern amongst them for a long time about what they would say, what they would reply and what help they would provide for him. They lamented the situation amongst themselves at great length; they were often burdened with taxes, they said. They went on lamenting amongst themselves and discussing the matter in groups, twenty here and fifteen there, or forty, a hundred, thirty or sixty. Some said they would build ships and cross the sea with the duke, others said that they would not go, for they had large debts and were poor. Some wanted to go, others did not; there was a great dispute going on between them when FitzOsbern came forward.

'What are you quarrelling about?' he said. 'You should not fail your natural lord, who is endeavouring to seek honour. With your fiefs you should serve

---

[235] This information about Odo (or Eudo) 'au Chapel' is unique to Wace. Wace is correct in identifying the half-sister of Duke William as Odo's wife. See van Houts, 'Ship List', p. 161 n. 5.

him, and since you must serve him, serve him enthusiastically! Do not wait for him to ask you and do not ask for any delay. Go forward and offer him much more than you can manage. Do not behave in such a way that he can complain that his campaign is being halted because of you. If he failed to cope with this emergency, he would perhaps soon say, being quarrelsome, that he had lost everything because of us. Do so much for him that he cannot say that his campaign has failed because of you.' (6033–84)

'My lord', they said, 'we are afraid of the sea. We are not obliged to serve beyond the sea. Speak on our behalf, this we beg you. We make you our spokesman and you will say whatever you like. We will do whatever you say.'

'Are you making me responsible for this?' he said.

'Yes', said each one, 'I agree to this. Let us go to the duke. You speak for us, as you know what our capabilities are.'* FitzOsbern then left them; he went ahead of them and spoke for them.

'My lord, my lord, look this way! There are no men on earth', he said, 'whom a lord should love so dearly, or who perform so many honourable deeds as the men you have; you should love and protect them. To further your cause, they say, they would let themselves be drowned at sea or thrown into a burning fire; you can trust them completely. They have already served you for a long time and followed you at great cost and will serve you gladly. If they have done this well, they will do so better. They will cross the sea with you and double their service to you. The man who is accustomed to bring twenty knights will voluntarily bring forty; he who normally serves with thirty will serve you with sixty, and he who normally serves with a hundred will gladly bring two hundred. As a sign of true affection, I will bring for my lord's hour of need sixty fully-equipped ships laden with warriors.' (6085–6122)

The barons were all amazed and protested most fiercely at the words he spoke. Many of them were critical of the promises he was making, for which he had no guarantee. You would have heard great confusion at court, much noise generated and loud protests from the barons. They feared that the service, which had been doubled, would become an hereditary obligation, be regarded as a custom and be passed on as a custom. The entire court was soon thrown into great confusion and there was a great deal of noise and shouting; no one could understand anyone else, hear what was said or make a reply. The duke withdrew to one side because of the noise, which he disliked; he summoned the barons one by one, telling and begging each one in this emergency to do enough to receive his love and his good will. Since the matter had been handled in that way, they should double their service to him, unless of their own volition they did more. They would, he said, be doing him a great service; never from that time onwards – this he promised them – would they be required to serve him apart, from what was customary in that country and according to what their ancestors were accustomed to give their lord. Then each one said how much he would do for him and how many ships he would bring; the duke had everything put into writing and the ships and knights enumerated; the barons agreed to this. Then each one agreed and nominated how many knights he would find and how many ships he could bring. From his brother, Bishop Odo, he formally received forty ships. The Bishop of Le

Mans[236] had thirty ships equipped with mariners and sailors; he was very keen to help the duke's cause. Each of the barons promised ships, but I do not know what each one said. Then he asked his good neighbours, the Bretons, those from Le Mans and Anjou, those from the Ponthieu and from Boulogne, to come with him at this time of need. To those who were willing he promised land if he managed to conquer England and to many he promised regular rations, generous pay and fine gifts; from everywhere he summoned mercenaries, who willingly seek gain. (6123–80)

He told the King of France,[237] his lord, out of love and commitment, that he intended to cross the sea and attack Harold, who was cheating and failing him in every respect. The duke went to speak with the king at Saint-Germer in the Beauvaisis; he sought him there, found him there and explained his situation to him, saying that if he were willing to help him, to the extent that with his assistance he would get what was rightfully his, he would receive England from him and he would do service to him for it; the king replied that he would not do so and that the duke would not make the crossing with his permission. The French had begged the king, telling and advising him that he should not assist William nor allow him to gain in strength. William was very strong and this ought to worry him; he would be a fool to let him become any stronger. For if he allowed him to bring the great wealth from beyond the sea, the property and great riches, together with the fine body of knights and the pride of Normandy, he would never have any peace as long as he lived. For that reason the king should do his best to thwart Duke William, so that he could not rise any higher or cross over to England.

'If you want to help the duke', they said, 'you cannot do so without cost. The whole of France will be harmed and it will all be reduced to poverty. No Frenchman will follow you there and none will cross the sea; if any misadventure occurred to you there, it would redound greatly to your shame. The duke is seeking from you something to his own advantage, but it will never improve things for you. Once he has conquered England, you will never again receive service from him. He gives little service, but will give less; when he has more, he will do less for you.' (6181–6224)

Because of what the French said – and they said even worse, if they could say worse – the king refused to help the duke; in fact he thwarted him whenever he could. I do not know what the king replied, but I am well aware that he let the duke down. When the duke took leave of the king, as a man whose heart was filled with anger, he said:

'My lord, I will depart and do the best I can. If it pleases God, I will seek what is my right. If I get it, may God grant this to me, you will never thereafter see me acting with harmful intent, nor will you ever enter my territory with harmful intent. If I fail to get what is my right, through the ability of the English to defend

---

[236] The Bishop of Le Mans can be identified as Arnald (1065–81). Originally from Avranches, he became a scholar at Le Mans and was appointed bishop shortly after Duke William's conquest of Maine. See van Houts, 'Ship List', p. 168 n. 50.

[237] The king referred to here is Philip I (1060–1108). The information given here is unique to Wace.

themselves, I will lose only my head over it; it will be all up with me. My children will have my land; you will never go and conquer it from them. Whether I live or die, whatever I do, I care nothing for other people's threats.' William left him then and made no further demands on him. He asked the Count of Flanders to accompany him in this emergency, as one should a father-in-law[238] and friend. The count replied that, if he wanted to have his assistance, he would first of all like to know for certain how much of England he would have and what part of it he would get. The duke said he would go and speak to his barons about this, discuss it with them and let him know by letter what their advice was. The duke went away and did nothing more. Then he did what no one before him had ever done: he took a small amount of parchment, without any letters or writing on it and, completely blank, sealed it in wax, writing at the very end that he would have as much of England as stated within the letter. Through a well-educated servant, who had been with him a long time, he sent the letter to the count and the man gave it to him. The count broke the seal and unfolded the parchment; he looked inside but saw nothing. He showed it to the servant, and the servant, who was courtly, said to the count at once:

'There is nothing there. You will have nothing and should expect nothing. The duke wants to seek honour for your sister and your nephews. If they could have had England, they would have had no more control over it than you. They would have made you lord over everything; everything would have been yours and everything theirs. If is pleases God, he will conquer it and not have any help from you.' I do not know what reply the count made, but the servant departed.[239] (6225–92)

The duke wished to make his preparations in a very sensible fashion. He sent word to the pope through clerics skilled in speech, telling him how Harold had served him, broken his oath and lied; since he was not taking his daughter and would not hand over to him the kingdom which Edward had given him and Harold had sworn to him, let him punish the perjurer in accordance with the judgement of the Holy Church. If it happened that God wanted him to conquer England, he would receive it from Saint Peter and serve no one other than God as a result. The pope granted him this and sent him a banner, a banner and a ring, very costly, splendid and fine; as he said, beneath the stone was one of Saint Peter's teeth.[240] By these tokens, he sent him word, and in God's name agreed, that he should conquer England and hold it from Saint Peter. On the date fixed for this, a great star appeared and shone for fourteen days with three long rays towards the south; such a star is accustomed to be seen when a new king is to have a kingdom. I have seen many men who saw it, who lived before it and long after it; anyone wanting to speak of stars should call it a comet. (6293–6328)

---

[238] The term *serorge* (v. 6251) means 'brother-in-law'. In reality Baldwin V (1035–67) was William's father-in-law and he also acted as regent for young Philip I of France. Baldwin V was succeeded by Baldwin VI (1067–70), brother of Matilda; he was thus brother-in-law to William.

[239] This story of the blank letter is unique to Wace.

[240] The pope referred to here is Alexander II (1061–73). The information about the ring and the tooth's relic underneath its stone is new.

The duke was filled with joy at the pennon and the permission which the pope had given him. He summoned smiths and carpenters. Then you would have witnessed building materials and wood being brought energetically to all the ports throughout Normandy, pegs being made and edges trimmed, ships and skiffs prepared, sails raised and masts put up. With great effort and at great cost, the whole of one summer and one August they spent getting the ships ready and assembling the troops. There was no knight in the land, no good man-at-arms, no good archer, nor courageous peasant of fighting age, whom the duke did not request to accompany him to England; he promised payments to the vavassors and fiefs to the barons. When the ships were ready, they were anchored on the Somme and taken to Saint-Valery, where they were handed over to the barons. There were many ships and boats on the Somme – it is this which gives the river its name. The Somme divides the Ponthieu and the Vimeu, which stretches as far as Eu. Eu divides the Vimeu and Normandy, a land under different jurisdiction. Eu is a river and a walled town, which sits on the river Eu in fine style. The duke had men from many regions; Aimery, the vicomte of Thouars came, a man of very great power who could raise a large number of men. Alan Fergent, who had a large company of Bretons, joined in the crossing; from Le Pallet[241] came FitzBertrand, and the lord of Dinan came, and also Ralph of Gael and many Bretons from many castles, as well as those from the region of Brocéliande, about which the Bretons often tell stories, a very long, broad forest which is highly praised in Brittany. To one side, the fountain of Barenton emerges beside the stone slab. Hunters used to go to Barenton during great heat and scoop out the water with their horns and moisten the top of the stone; in that way they used to get rain. Thus in days gone by it would rain, in the forest and all around, but I do not know for what reason. People used to see fairies there, if the accounts of the Bretons are true, and many other marvels. There used to be hawks' nests there and a huge quantity of stags, but peasants have destroyed everything. I went there in search of marvels; I saw the forest and the land and looked for marvels, but found none. I came back as a fool and went as a fool. I went as a fool and came back as a fool. I sought foolishness and considered myself a fool.[242] (6329–98)

News about the Duke of Normandy soon spread to many places, that he intended to cross over and oppose Harold, who had taken England from him. Then mercenaries came to him, one by one, two by two, four by four and five and six, or seven or eight or nine or ten. The duke retained them all, giving and promising them a great reward. Many arrived as a result of the promise

---

[241] For *Peleit* Andresen suggests the reading *Poreeit* 'Porhoet' (one of the former counties of Brittany), but it is probably Le Pallet near Nantes, the birthplace of Peter Abelard.

[242] Much has been written about this passage concerning the fountain of Barenton. There is an evident link between Wace's remarks and the magic spring in Chrétien de Troyes' *Yvain*. At one point Chrétien has Calogrenant use very similar language to that of Wace: 'Einsi alai, einsi reving,/ Au revenir por fol me ting' (ed. by M. Roques, Paris: Champion, 1960, vv. 577–58). Rollo suggests that by demonstrating at first hand that Breton marvels are pure fancy, Wace is dismissing his past career, as in the *Brut* he himself had helped to create this Brythonic world of fantasy (p. 163).

they had made earlier; many wanted lands from the duke if they could capture
England. Some demanded pay and desired provisions and gifts; they had
frequent expenses and could not wait long. I do not wish to set down in writing
for you, nor do I wish to expend any effort on this, how many barons and how
many knights, how many vavassors and how many mercenaries the duke had
in his company when all his ships were ready. But I heard my father say – I
remember it well, though I was a young lad – that when they set off from Saint-
Valery there were seven hundred ships less four, either ships, boats, or skiffs,
carrying weapons or equipment. I have discovered in writing – I do not know
if it is true – that there were three thousand ships under sail. With so many ships
it is obvious that there would have been a large number of men. They remained
in Saint-Valery for a long time, waiting for a good wind; this upset the barons
greatly. Then they begged the monastery so ardently that the reliquary of Saint
Valéry was placed on a rug in the fields. All those who were to cross the sea came
to pray to the relic, and they all made such offerings of money that the relic was
covered with it. After that day, they very soon had a favourable wind and breeze.
The duke had a lantern placed on the top of his ship's mast, so that the other ships
could see it and hold their course behind him; he had a gilded copper weather-
vane hoisted to the top. On the head of the ship at the front, which sailors call
the prow, he had a child carrying a strung bow and arrow made out of copper.
He had his face turned towards England and looked as if he were firing in
that direction, so that, wherever the ship sailed, he looked as if he were firing
in front of him.[243] Of the fleet, which was so large, and the men, who were so
numerous, only two ships perished; I do not know whether they were overloaded.
(6399–6464)

The duke had a great many knights and many ships in his fleet, many archers
and men-at-arms, bold and brave men, carpenters and engineers, fine smiths and
farriers. The ships headed for one port, all together in close formation, all side by
side, all anchored together, all drawn out of the water together and all discharging
the men together. They arrived near Hastings and first found land there; they
gathered their ships all together, putting one ship up against another. Then you
would have seen fine sailors, fine men-at-arms and fine squires issuing forth
and unloading the ships, throwing anchor, pulling the ropes, carrying forth the
shields and saddles and leading out the warhorses and palfreys. The archers
disembarked first and reached land first, at which time each of them stretched his
bow, with their quivers hanging at their sides. They were all shaven and tonsured
and all dressed in short garments, ready to attack and ready to flee, ready to
turn and ready to escape; they all travelled the length of the shore and found no
armed man there. When the archers had disembarked, the knights then did so, all
armed and wearing hauberks, with their shields around their necks and their
helmets laced on. They came ashore together, each armed and on horseback, all
with their swords girt about them; they reached the open land with their lances
raised. The barons had banners and the knights had pennons; they stationed
themselves next to the archers, having first taken possession of the terrain. The

[243] On William's flagship see van Houts, 'Ship List', pp. 172–73.

carpenters, who came next, held great axes in their hands and they had adzes and mattocks hanging by their sides. When they had joined the archers and got together with the knights, they decided on a good spot to establish a strong fortress. Then they threw down from the ships and dragged on land the wood which the Count of Eu had brought there, all pierced and trimmed.[244] They had brought all the trimmed pegs in great barrels. Before evening, they had built a small castle with it and made a ditch round it, creating a great fortress there. Then you would have seen kitchens built, fires lit and food brought out, at which time the duke sat down to eat; the barons and the knights had plenty to eat. The duke had brought a great deal with him; they all ate and drank a lot and were very happy to be on land. (6465–6534)

A cleric had come to the duke before he had left the Somme. He knew about astronomy, he said, and about necromancy and considered himself to be a diviner and practised divination in many things. He had foretold and cast lots about the fact that the duke would cross the sea safely and achieve his purpose without having to fight, for Harold would promise him so much and say and do so much that he would hold the land from the duke and become his liegeman; the duke would return safely. He had foretold the safe passage well, but was wrong about the combat. When the duke had crossed over and arrived safely, he recalled his diviner, asking for him and seeking him urgently; one of the sailors replied that things had gone wrong for the diviner because, he said, he had drowned in the sea and perished in one of the ships.

'This is not important', said the duke, 'he was not a man of great learning. The man who could not prophesy with respect to himself would have prophesied badly with respect to me. If he had been able to tell the truth in everything, he should have predicted his own death. He is a fool who trusts a prophet who knows the outcome of someone else's business and does not know when his own end will come; he takes an interest in others and forgets himself.' Nothing more was said about the prophet, and the ships were drawn up on to dry land.[245] (6535–72)

When the duke first disembarked, he fell forward on to the palms of his hands; at once a loud cry arose and everyone said:

'This is a bad sign!' But he cried out to them:

'My lords, by the splendour of God! I have taken possession of the land in my two hands. It will never be abandoned without a challenge. Whatever is here is ours. Now I will see who is bold.' Then a man ran on to the land and stretched out his hand over a cottage; taking a fistful of the roof, he ran quickly back to the duke:

'My lord', he said, 'come forward, receive this investiture! I invest you with this land, the country is yours without doubt.' The duke replied:

'I accept it and may God be with me.'

---

[244] For a discussion of whether the Normans brought with them wood for palisades see E. A. Freeman, *The History of the Normans*, and J. H. Round, 'Mr. Freeman and the Battle of Hastings'. Freeman's suggestion of an English palisade at Hastings is now commonly rejected. See R. A. Brown, *The Normans and the Norman Conquest*, 2nd ed. (Woodbridge: Boydell Press, 1985), p. 145 n. 129.

[245] This section on the cleric's prophecy is mostly unique to Wace, although he does draw to a certain extent on stories told by William of Poitiers and found in the *Brevis relatio* (p. 31).

Then he had the news relayed and shouted to everyone and the command given to the sailors that the ships were to be broken up and pulled up on land with holes in them so that the cowards could not return and use the ships to take flight in. I cannot write everything down at once or say everything at once, but, whatever I do say, one way or another, the truth is that, when he arrived, the duke made all his men arm themselves. The first day they arrived there, they stayed close to the shore and the next day they came to the castle called Pevensey; the squires, the foragers and those intent on gain took booty and supplies, before what was in the ships ran out. Then you would have seen the English fleeing, chasing their animals, abandoning their houses, all withdrawing to the cemeteries where they remained in terror. (6573–6616)

One of the knights in the area heard the noise and the shouting coming from the peasants and villeins, who saw the great fleet arrive. He was well aware that the Normans were coming with the intention of taking possession of the land. He took up position behind a mound so that no one could see him; he stood there watching how the great fleet arrived. He saw the archers emerging from the ships and afterwards the knights disembarking. He saw the carpenters, their axes, the large numbers of men, the knights, the building material thrown down from the ships, the construction and fortification of the castle and the ditch built all round it, the shields and the weapons brought forth. Everything he saw caused him great anguish. He girded on his sword and took his lance, saying he would go to King Harold and give him this news.[246] Then he set out, sleeping late and rising early. He travelled extensively night and day in search of Harold, his lord, and found him beyond the Humber, where he had dined in a town. Harold was acting with great arrogance. He had been beyond the Humber and defeated his brother Tostig; things had gone very well for him. Tostig was Harold's brother, but they had quarrelled. Tostig had asked Harold and had his supporters ask him, since things had turned out for him the way they had, and rightly or wrongly he was king, to give him his father's fief and grant him the land which their father had inherited; he was not asking for anything unreasonable and would become his vassal, recognise him as his lord and serve him just as he had served King Edward. Harold refused to grant this to him, to give it to him or anything else in exchange. Tostig, who was very angry, crossed over to Denmark and, bringing Danes and Norwegians with him, arrived near York. Harold discovered this and made preparations; he rode against Tostig and fought with his brother. He overcame him and his knights. Tostig was killed near Pontefract and Harold had many other evil deeds performed there. (6617–74)

Harold was returning from Pontefract and gloating over what he had done. But the man who gloats is a fool; one joy soon comes to an end. Bad news soon comes; he who kills another can soon die. A man's heart often rejoices at the approach of his own misfortune. Harold was returning joyfully and behaving with great arrogance, when a messenger gave him news of the sort which

---

[246] This scout is probably Robert FitzWimarch, a man of Breton or Norman origin who was established in Essex by 1052. See William of Poitiers, pp. 116–17 (esp. p. 116 n. 2).

made him think differently. Suddenly the knight who had come from Hastings arrived.

'The Normans have arrived', he said, 'and established themselves in Hastings. They intend to take the land from you, unless you can defend it. They have already built a castle with brattices and a ditch.'

'I am very distressed', said Harold, 'that I was not there when they arrived. Things have gone very badly for me in this respect. It would have been better for me to have lost whatever Tostig asked for than not to be at the port when William came to the shore. I would have protected this point of entry properly. I would have caused so many of them to dive into the water and so many of them to drown that they would never have come ashore and never taken anything of ours. They would have had no escape from death unless they had drunk the entire sea. But this is what pleased the Celestial King; I cannot be everywhere.' (6675–6710)

In the land there was a baron, but I do not know his name, who had loved the duke greatly and become one of his close advisers; he would never have wanted things to go wrong for William, if he could manage it.[247] He sent him word privately that he had come with insufficient forces; he had few men, he believed, to accomplish what he had undertaken. There were too many people in England and it was very difficult to conquer. In true faith he advised him, and in sincere love sent him word, that he should withdraw from the country and go back to his land before Harold arrived; he was afraid that things would go badly wrong for him. He would be very upset, he said, if things turned out badly for William. The duke sent him word in brief that he should not be concerned for him; he should not be afraid for him, but believe and be well aware that, if he only had ten thousand noble knights just like the sixty or more thousand he had, he would still fight. He would not depart, he said, before taking his revenge on Harold. (6711–40)

Harold spurred on until he came to London, summoning Englishmen from all parts to come at once, fully armed, on the date he had announced to them, with none excused other than for ill-health. He would have attacked the duke at once or fixed a day for combat, but he was summoning and awaiting the arrival of his large army of men who would be coming. Those who heard the summons came with great haste. The duke very soon heard that Harold was assembling a great army and had come to London from the north, having killed his brother Tostig there. He asked for Hugh Margot, a tonsured monk at Fécamp.[248] Because he was very learned, knowledgeable and highly esteemed, the duke sent him to Harold and Margot set out. He found Harold in London and spoke to him as follows:

'Harold', he said, 'listen to me. I am a messenger, hear in what respect. The duke sends you word, and I say this to you, that you have very soon forgotten the oath you made him in Normandy some time ago. You have been untrue to your oath. Put things right and give him back the crown and the lordship which is not

---

[247] This story of the baron is unique to Wace.

[248] The information on the name of the monk (Hugh Margot) is unique to Wace. The fact that messengers were sent is known from William of Poitiers (pp. 120–23) and the *Carmen de Hastingae proelio* (pp. 14–21).

yours by right of inheritance. You are not king through inheritance nor through the men in your lineage. King Edward, when he was well and had full legal power of disposition, gave his land and his kingdom to his finest relative, William, giving him the best gift he could, as the finest man he had. While in good health, before his death, he gave it to him, and you do him wrong, for you heard this and accepted it. You did not oppose it, rather you swore an oath to him. Give him back his land, do right by him before any more harm comes of it. Such great armies as you and he can muster cannot fight without great harm and great loss; this will be entirely your responsibility. I am well aware that some people will pay for this without being in any way at fault. Give him back his kingdom, which you have; if you keep it from him, you will be doing so wrongly.' (6741–96)

Harold was very arrogant. Someone who saw him said that he had reddish hair.[249] He became angry at these words and at the threats which Margot made against him in this way. I believe he would have harmed him, but Gyrth, his brother, jumped up and stood in front of the king, sending Hugh Margot away. He left without taking leave, for he did not want to stay there any longer. He said no more and did no more; I heard nothing more of what he was aiming to do. He went back to Duke William and told him how badly Harold had treated him. Then Harold chose a messenger who knew the language of France and sent him to Duke William, entrusting him with his message:

'Tell the duke I send him word that he should not accuse me with regard to any promise or oath, if I foolishly made one to him. If I ever promised him anything, I did it to secure my own release. I swore the oath to him in order to be released and granted him whatever he wanted from me. I should not be reproached for this, for I did not do it of my own free will. Strength was on his side and I was afraid that, if I did not do his bidding, I would never return home and would remain there for ever. If I have done any wrong by him, I will take it upon myself to procure absolution. But if he wants any of my money, I will give him some to the best of my ability. I will rebuild all his ships for him and give him safe-conduct. If he does not accept this offer, tell him truly that, if he waits long enough for me, I will attack him on Saturday and do battle with him on Saturday.' (6797–6838)

The messenger went to see the duke and told him on Harold's behalf that he should go back to his own land and let England go. He would rebuild his ships for him, give him safe-conduct and provide him with so much gold and silver that he would be able to pay all his men. Duke William replied:

'My thanks to him for these fine words. But I have not come to the country with so many shields in order to obtain his sterlings, but to take possession of the entire land, just as he swore it to me and as Edward gave it to me, handing over to me as hostages two young men of noble lineage, one the son and the other the nephew of Godwin.[250] I still have them in my possession. I took possession of

---

[249] The information that Harold had reddish hair is unique to Wace.

[250] The hostages are referred to by William of Poitiers as the son and grandson of Earl Godwin (pp. 20–21, 120–21). They are normally identified as Wulfnoth (*GND*, II, pp. 160–61), and Hakon, who may have been a nephew rather than a grandson of Godwin. See Frank Barlow, *Edward the Confessor* (new ed., New Haven and London: Yale University Press, 1997), pp. 303–05.

them and will hold on to them, if I can, until I have what is rightfully mine.' Then the messenger replied:

'My lord', he said, 'you ask too much of us. You ask much too much of my lord. You want to take away his reputation and honour, because you are asking him to give up his kingdom as if he would not have dared to defend it. He is still hale and hearty; he is not wounded or injured, nor is he afflicted by war in such a way that he has to abandon his land to you. It is not appropriate, if you please, that he should let you have his kingdom in this way. Harold is not willing to abandon anything to you, nor can you take anything away from him. But for love of you and your grace, and without fearing your threats, he will give you whatever you want, gold and silver, money and clothing. Return to your country before you come to blows. If you do not accept this offer, you should know, if you wait for him, that on Saturday he will be on the battlefield and on Saturday he will do battle with you.' The duke agreed to this date and the messenger took his leave. When he wanted to go, the duke had him given a horse and clothing. Dressed in his new clothes, the messenger came to Harold and told him everything, showed him everything the duke had given him and told him how he had honoured him and about everything he had discovered from his visit to him. Harold regretted very much that he had not done the same for Margot. (6839–96)

While Harold and William were speaking through clerics, messengers and knights, the English were gathering in London. When they were to depart from London, as I have heard it said, one of Harold's brothers, Gyrth by name, began to speak to him.

'My fair brother', he said, 'stay here, but let me have your troops. I will take the risk and do battle with William. I have no agreement with him, through oath or pledge. I am not his vassal through allegiance and I do not owe him anything on oath. Things could turn out in such a way that there would no longer be any necessity for blows to be struck. I am afraid that, if you do battle with him, in view of the fact that you are perjuring yourself, worse will befall you as a result of your perjury and that he who is in the right will win. But if I am conquered or captured, you, who would still be alive, could, if it pleases God, gather your troops together to do battle, or come to such an arrangement with the king that you could rule your kingdom in peace. While I am going there and doing battle with the Normans, go through this land setting fire to everything, destroying houses and towns, capturing booty and food, swine, sheep and cattle, so that the Normans cannot find any food or anything off which they can live. Get the food a long way away so that they cannot find anything to eat; in this way you can frighten them greatly, and the duke himself will leave since his food will run out.'[251] Harold said he would not do this, nor would Gyrth go to the duke without him, nor would he do battle without him. He would not set fire to dwellings or towns, nor would he rob his vassals or take away their possessions.

'How', he said, 'could I harm the people it is my duty to govern? I must not destroy or harm the people to whom I owe protection.' (6897–6948)

---

[251] Gyrth's speech is first given by Orderic Vitalis in his interpolations of the *GND* (II, pp. 166–69) and later also in his *Historia ecclesiastica* (II, pp. 170–72).

Everyone supported this advice and wanted to act in this way. But Harold swore an oath in order to demonstrate his great courage, stating that they would never go on to the battlefield without him and never fight without him. They would consider him a coward, he said, and many would rebuke the man who sent his good supporters to a place to which he did not dare go himself. In this way he left London, because it was not possible to keep him there. He led his men forward, as troops who were fully armed, to a place where he raised his standard; he had his pennon fixed at the very spot where Battle Abbey was built. He would, he said, defend himself against anyone who attacked him in that place. Harold looked at the place and had it enclosed by a good ditch; he left three entry points on three sides, giving orders that they should be guarded.[252] (6949–72)

That night the Normans were on their guard and they stayed awake all night, fully armed. All night they were fearful, for they had been told that the English would come to them that night and attack them that night. The English themselves feared the Normans would attack them that night; in this way they spent the whole night awake, each side watching out for the other. In the morning, at daybreak, which people normally call dawn, Harold mounted his horse together with Gyrth; they were both noble vassals. The two of them left the tents and came out of the fortress. They did not take with them any knights, foot-soldiers or squires, and neither of them carried any weapons except for a shield, a lance and a sword. They wanted to get a sight of the Normans and find out where they were. The two of them rode along, keeping a close eye on things, until from a lookout point where they stopped they could see the enemy, who were close by. They saw a large number of shelters and huts and well-equipped tents and heard a large number of horses whinnying and saw weapons gleaming. They stayed there a long time without saying a word to each other. I do not know what they did, what they said or what decision they reached between them, but when they were leaving and returning to their shelters, Harold spoke first.

'My brother', he said, 'there are many men here. The Normans are very good knights and they are accustomed to bearing arms. Tell me what you advise me to do with respect to such huge numbers of men as you can see. I dare not do anything other than return to London. I want to go back to London and assemble more men.'

'Harold', said Gryth, 'you wretched coward! That decision has come too late. This is not the time for cowardly action, you must ride forward. Wretched coward! When I told you, and had your barons beseech you, that you should remain in London and let me fight, you would not do anything of the sort. Misfortune may come upon you as a result of this. When I said this to you, you refused to do it and did not believe me or anyone else. Now you want to do this and I do not; you have very soon lost your pride. As a result of what you have seen, you have lost your courage. If you turned back, it would be said that you were taking flight; if you were seen to be doing so, who could control your men? If they once departed, they would never be re-assembled.' Harold and Gyrth argued until they quarrelled verbally; Gyrth tried to strike Harold, but Harold

---

[252] This information on three entry points is unique to Wace.

spurred his horse, making him miss, and Gyrth struck his horse behind the saddle-bows, near Harold's shield. If he had struck Harold, he would easily have pushed him down to the ground. Gyrth spoke some very foolish words to him and reproached him with cowardice.[253] (6973–7050)

They spurred on towards the tents, but thereafter gave no indication of their quarrel. When they came amongst their men, they showed no resentment towards each other. Harold's brother Leofwine, born after Gyrth, rose early and went into Harold's and Gyrth's tent.[254] Not finding his two brothers where he had left them in the evening, he did not think he would ever see them again; they had, he said, been captured treacherously and handed over to their enemies. Then you would have seen a grieving man crying and howling like a madman. When he found out where they were, that they were trying to get a glimpse of the Normans, he and his companions, counts and barons, mounted their horses at once and left their lodgings. Suddenly there were the brothers returning and the barons reproached them for having gone off so foolishly and without taking precautions; in this way they returned to the tents, all ready for battle. Harold sent two spies to discover what companies and what barons and armed men the duke had brought with him. They had just reached the army when they were spotted and brought to William. They were very fearful, but when he found out what they wanted and that they had come to count his men, he had them taken through all his tents and showed them the whole of his army. Then he had them well looked after, well fed and watered, then let them go free; he had no wish to harm them or treat them badly. When they came to their lord, they were full of praise for the duke. One of the Englishmen, who had seen the Normans all shaved and tonsured, thought they were all priests and could sing Mass, for they were all tonsured and shaved; no whiskers remained on them. He told Harold that the duke had more priests with him than knights or other men; as a result he marvelled greatly that they were all shaved and tonsured. Harold replied that these were valiant knights, bold, brave and warlike.

'They have neither beard nor whiskers', said Harold, 'as we do.' (7051–7110)

Then the duke chose a messenger, a wise and well-educated monk, knowledgeable and learned, and sent him to King Harold. He put three choices to Harold and asked him which he preferred: he should hand England over to him and take his daughter as his wife, submit to the judgement of the pope and his men, or come out one to one and fight with him in single combat. Whichever of them killed the other or could overcome him and live would have the whole of England freely, so that the other's men would not be harmed. Harold said he would do none of these, not keep any promise to him, submit to any judgement or fight with him single-handed. (7111–30)

Before the day of the battle, when it was sure to take place, the duke spoke to his barons, telling them part of what was on his mind. He wanted, he said, to speak to Harold, who was depriving him of what was rightfully his; he wanted to accuse him in person and find out what he would reply: he would accuse him

---

[253] Wace's references here to Gyrth, clearly an elaboration of his previous speech, are new.
[254] This reference to Harold's brother Leofwine is unique to Wace.

of perjury and require him to fulfil his obligation. If he were not willing to make amends and did not wish to be reconciled with him, he would challenge him at once and do battle with him the next day. If he were willing to make peace with him and accept his advice, he would give him everything he had beyond the Humber, over towards Scotland.[255] The barons said and advised that things should be just as the duke had stated; some said to him:

'Fair lord, we want to say one thing to you. If there is no alternative and we have to do battle, let us do so promptly. There should be no postponement. Any delay could harm us; we have no need to delay. Harold's men are growing in numbers each day; they are constantly arriving and becoming more numerous.' The duke replied to them in truth that there could be no more delay. He and nineteen companions mounted their horses, all with their swords girt about them; squires who accompanied them carried the other weapons. Afterwards, a hundred knights mounted and rode behind them, but without getting too close. A thousand knights also mounted and followed the hundred. They were positioned so that they could constantly see what the hundred and the twenty men were doing. (7131–74)

The duke sent word to Harold – I do not know whether through a monk or an abbot – that he should come to speak with him in the meadows: he need not fear anything. He should bring with him in safety whomsoever he wished and they would speak of peace. Gyrth did not wait until Harold had replied; he did not let Harold speak or go and speak with the duke. He jumped to his feet at once.[256]

'Harold', he said, 'will not be going. Tell your lord this much, that he should let us know what he wishes to say, what he would like to take and what he would leave us, what sort of agreement he would like to make.' While the men who had to take these words to the duke were returning, Harold summoned his companions and all his counts by name to hear what the duke would say and what information he would send.

'Let him tell us whatever he likes', said Gyrth. The duke sent word to Harold, saying that if he kept his promise he would give him Northumberland and whatever he had belonging to this kingdom beyond the Humber; then he would give his brother Gyrth the land of their* father Godwin. If they were not interested in this, he accused Harold of perjury with respect to his daughter whom he was to take and the kingdom which he ought to hand over to him. He had completely broken his promise to him; if he did not make amends, then he challenged him. The English should know in truth, he wanted everyone to know it, that those who oppose him along with Harold and support Harold in this affair are excommunicated by the pope and the clergy. The English protested bitterly about this excommunication.[257] They feared this greatly, even more than the battle. You would have heard them protesting greatly, each advising the other; no one was so brave that he did not want the battle to be called off. (7175–7224)

---

[255] This reference to the gift of land beyond the Humber is new information.
[256] The following contributions on Gyrth's part are unique to Wace.
[257] This reference to excommunication is new information.

'My lords', said Gyrth, 'I know and can see that you are very much afraid. You fear the battle and want harmony. I too want this, truly much more so, I believe, but I am very fearful of William, who is full of trickery. You have heard what he has said, how he wants to humiliate you. Of the land he does not have he will leave us as much as he likes. If we accept what he offers and cross to the other side of the Humber, he will send us even farther away and not leave us as much as that, constantly showing himself to be cleverer than us and destroying us. When he has the upper hand over everything and has most of the land, he will allow us to rule very little of it, because he expects to take it away from us completely. In his cunning he intends to remove us from a great land to an impoverished part of it; he would like to have the entire land. There is another worry, more for you than for me, for I will, I believe, be able to survive. He has promised all your lands to knights from other regions. There is no count or baron to whom he has not promised a great gift; there is no county or barony, castle or castellany which William has not entirely given away. I say to you in truth that he has taken homage from a number of men to give them your inheritances. They will drive you out of your lands and, worse, will kill you. They will destroy your households and ruin your sons and daughters. They are not coming for your possessions, but to damage you and your heirs. Defend yourselves and your children and all the other things you own. William never gave my brother any orders concerning the distribution of your great fiefs, great domains or ancestral lands. But if counts were to remain counts, if barons had what was rightfully theirs and if their sons took their place and inherited their fathers' fiefs, I assure you I would not speak of this or ever disturb the peace on this account. If this were so, we could tolerate this and it would be preferable to accept. But if you lose your dwellings and your other possessions, your residences and your domains, where you were raised day after day, what would become of you and what would you do? To which land would you flee? What would happen to the children, to the wives and sons, to everyone, great or small? To what land will they go begging and in what land will they seek their fortune? When they lose here what is theirs, how will they be able to seek anyone else's land?' (7225–94)

As a result of these words which Gyrth uttered, and others which ensued, and because Harold told the barons that he would increase their fiefs, promising the others more than he could give them, you would have heard a great stir amongst the English, who swore to God and solemnly declared that the Normans would rue the day they came. They had been very foolish to make their way there. Those who had earlier desired peace and who feared the battle were inspired with great courage and desire to do battle. Gyrth had so disturbed the council that no one who spoke of making peace was listened to thereafter without being rebuked by the most powerful men there. (7295–7312)

The duke and his men did no more; they returned to their camp, all certain and convinced that they would be doing battle next day. Then you would have seen lances raised, hauberks and helmets prepared, stirrups and saddles made ready, quivers filled, bows strung and everything which was required for the fight made ready. When battle was to be engaged, the night before, I have heard tell, the English were very happy and there was much laughter and merriment. They ate and drank all night long and that night they never went to bed. You would have seen them moving about a great deal, dancing, jumping up and down, and singing. 'Be happy', they cried, 'and let us drink together. Let the cup keep coming and let us drink. Drink this way and that; drink to my health. Drink an entire cup, then half a cup; drink to your health'.[258] This is the way the English behaved. The Normans and the French spent the night in prayer and in acts of contrition. They confessed their sins and avowed them to the priests; those who had no priest near them confessed to their neighbour. Because it was a Saturday on which the battle was to take place, the Normans promised and vowed, as the cleric had advised them, that if they lived they would never eat meat or fat on that day. (7313–48)

Geoffrey, Bishop of Coutances, enjoined penances on many of them; he heard confessions and gave blessings. The Bishop of Bayeux, who conducted himself very nobly, did likewise. He was bishop of the Bessin and his name was Odo FitzHerluin, the duke's brother through their mother. With his brother he brought a great force of knights and other men, being very rich in gold and silver. It was on the fourteenth day of October, which was the festival of Saint Calixtus, which fell at that time on a Saturday, that the battle I am speaking of took place. The priests in their chapels, which had been newly established throughout the army, spent the whole of the night awake, calling on God and praying to Him. They fasted and did penance, saying their own private prayers and reciting psalms, the *Miserere*, litanies and petitions; they beseeched God and begged for mercy, saying their *Paternosters* and Mass, one the *Spiritus domini*, the other the *Salus populi*, many of them *Salve sancta parens*, which was appropriate for that occasion.[259] It was appropriate for that day, for that day was Saturday. (7349–80)

When the Masses, which came to an end early in the morning, had been sung, all the barons assembled; they came to the duke and decided they would form three divisions of armed men and attack the enemy in three places. The duke stood on a mound, which gave him the best vantage over his men. The barons stood round him and he spoke to them in a loud voice.

'I must love you all', he said, 'and I put great trust in you. It is my duty and my wish to thank you for crossing over the sea for me. You have come to this land to seek my advantage and my honour. I cannot, and this upsets me, thank you as I should, but when I am able to do so I will, and you will have what I have. If I am victorious, you will be so as well; if I capture land, you will have it. But I say in truth, I did not merely come to take what I am asking for, or to have what was

---

258 The text here contains a number of English words: *bublie, weisseil, laticome, drincheheil, drinc, hindrewart, drintome, helf* and *tome*. Woledge points out that in this passage 'Wace is trying to convey the impression of the jabberings of foreigners' ('Notes on Wace's Vocabulary', p. 21, see also n. 3). William of Malmesbury also contrasts the behaviour of the English and the Normans the night before the battle (Book III, c. 242, vol. I, pp. 452–55, vol. II, pp. 232–33).

259 The *Miserere* is the fifty-first psalm; the *Paternoster* is the Lord's Prayer. The *Spiritus domini* is a votive Mass beginning *Missa votiva de Spiritu sancti*. The *Salus populi* and the *Salve sancta parens* are also votive Masses, beginning respectively *proquacumque necessitate* and *de Sancta Maria a Purificatione usque ad Adventum*. This specification of the prayers is unique to Wace. On this passage see Woledge, *ibid.*, pp. 21–22.

promised me, but to avenge the crimes, treacheries and faithless acts which the inhabitants of this country have constantly perpetrated against our people. They have done much harm to my family and much harm to other people. They do whatever they do by treachery; they will never do harm any other way. The night of the festival of Saint Brice[260] they performed a dreadful act of treachery; they inflicted great pain on the Danes and killed them all in one day. They had eaten with them and then they killed them while they slept; I do not think it is a sin to kill people whose beliefs are no better than this. You have heard about Alfred, how Godwin betrayed him. He greeted him, kissed him, drank and ate with him, then betrayed him, captured and bound him and handed him over to the treacherous king, who placed him on the Isle of Ely; he put out his eyes, then killed him. He had all the Normans taken to Guildford and tithed, and when the tenth was separated out – just listen to this crime – because there seemed to him to be a large number of them, he at once took a tenth of the tenth. Such crimes, and many others they have perpetrated against our ancestors and our friends as well, who conducted themselves nobly, we will, if it pleases God, avenge. When we have overcome them, which we will do with ease, we will have their gold, their silver and their possessions, of which there is an abundance, and their dwellings, which are splendid. In the entire world there are no men as strong and valiant as you who are gathered here. You are all proven vassals.' (7381–7450)

They began to shout:

'You will never see a single coward here. No one is afraid of dying for love of you, if need be.' He replied:

'My thanks to you! In God's name do not be taken by surprise. Strike them well, right from the start. Do not make any attempt to seek booty; it will be shared between us. Each man will have plenty of it. There could be no protection for you in peace or flight. The English will never love the Normans and never spare Normans. They were criminals and remain criminals; they were false and will remain false. Do not show any weakness, for they will have no pity on you. Neither the cowards for taking flight nor the bold for striking well will be any more praised by the English, nor spared any the more. You can flee as far as the coast, but you cannot go any farther. You would not find there either ship or bridge. Both helmsman and ships will be lacking and the English, who will kill you shamefully, will catch up with you there. You would die a finer death in combat than you would in flight. Since you would not escape by fleeing, fight and be victorious. I am in no doubt about victory. We have come to have glory, and victory is in our hands, you can all be certain of that.' (7451–86)

While William was speaking and still wanting to say more, William FitzOsbern, arrived, with his horse completely covered in iron.[261]

---

[260] The date concerned is 13 November. On the murder of the Danes see the Anglo-Saxon Chronicle 1002 and the *GND*, II, pp. 14–17 (esp. p. 15 n. 4).

[261] The notion of a horse covered in iron is anachronistic for the battle of Hastings. Even in Wace's time the practice must have been in its infancy as it is not generally attested until the beginning of the thirteenth century. See Holden's note to v. 7490 (vol. 3 p. 236).

'My lord', he said, 'we are delaying too long. Let us all arm ourselves, come on, come on!' Thus they went to their tents and armed themselves as best they could. The duke was greatly agitated; everyone was following his advice. He honoured all the vassals greatly and gave away many weapons and horses. When he was preparing to arm himself, he asked for his good hauberk and a vassal raised it on his arms. He brought it to the duke, but, as he lifted it, he turned it round, although he did not do so on purpose. The duke put his head into it and had nearly got it on. Then he turned the part at the back to the front and swiftly threw it backwards. Those who had seen the hauberk were very fearful.

'I have seen many a man', he said, 'who, if this had happened to him, would never again have borne arms and never again entered the field of battle. But I never believed in fate and I never will. I trust in God, for He does what He likes with everything and makes what He wants come about. I never liked soothsayers and never trusted diviners; I entrust myself fully to the Lord God. Give me my hauberk! Do not be afraid! The hauberk which was turned round and then given back to me the right way round signifies the turning round of things which will be altered.[262] The name which was derived from 'duchy' you will see turned from duke into king. I who have been duke will be king. Do not have any other thoughts.' (7487–7530)

Then he crossed himself, took his hauberk, lowered his head and placed it inside, lacing on his helmet and girding on his sword, which a servant had brought. He asked for his good horse: no one could find one better. A king had sent it to him from Spain as a mark of great friendship; if its lord spurred it, it would fear no weapon or throng of men. Walter Giffard, who had been to Santiago de Compostela, had brought it.[263] William held out his hand, took the reins and placed his foot in the stirrup; he spurred the horse, darted forward, turned round and then caused his horse to rear up.[264] The vicomte of Thouars saw how the duke bore his arms and said to his men around him that he had never seen such a fine warrior who rode so nobly or who bore his arms so well, nor

---

[262] This story of the hauberk is found for the first time in William of Poitiers (pp. 124–25). In William's account the duke laughs off the incident, seeing it as mischance rather than as an evil omen. Wace alone links the incident to the unreliability of soothsayers. The story occurs elsewhere, e.g. in the *Brevis relatio* (p. 31) and also in the *Chronicle of Battle Abbey* (pp. 17–18, 36–37), where the author adopts Wace's version.

[263] Confirmation of this story concerning Giffard and the Spanish horse is found in Gaimar's *Estoire des Engleis*, vv. 6077–78. Gaimar knew that a member of the Giffard family had taken part in the battle of Barbastro in 1064 (Gaimar's editor, A. Bell, in his note to vv. 6077–78, misunderstands the reference to Barbastro). A Norman contingent fought at Barbastro and Walter Giffard may have picked up the Spanish horse there for William the Conqueror.

[264] On the interpretation of the verb *s'esterchir* in v. 7546 see Sayers, 'OFr *s'esterchir*: Horses Rearing and Rearing Horses'. Holden translates this verb as 's'affermir' ('to steady oneself'), but Sayers links it to the English *stretch* and sees the rearing of the horse as contributing towards William's pre-battle activity; the latter was 'a staged scene intended to give the host a signal and a sight of their leader, much as the ducal standard would function in the battle itself' (p. 220). There is no equivalent to this scene in Wace's Latin sources.

whose hauberk suited him so well, nor who brandished his lance so well, who sat so well on his horse, nor who turned or held on so well.

'There is no such knight on earth. He is a fine duke and will be a fine king. Let him fight and he will win. Shame on anyone who fails him.' The duke asked for horses and had a number brought along behind him. Each one had a good sword hanging in front from its saddle-bows and the men bringing the horses carried lances of steel. Then the barons armed themselves, as did the knights and the foot soldiers. They set off in three companies and formed three companies of warriors. In each of the three companies there were many lords and chieftains, who would not have displayed cowardice even at the cost of their limbs or their lives. (7531–74)

The duke called to a servant and had his standard, which the pope had sent him, brought forward; he brought it and unfolded it. The duke took it, raised it up and called to Ralph of Conches:[265]

'Carry my standard', he said. 'I want to do for you only what is right. By right and through your ancestors, your family should be the standard-bearers of Normandy. They were all very fine knights.'

'Many thanks', said Ralph, 'for recognising our right. But, by my faith, the standard will not be borne by me today. Today I give up my right to perform this service for you. I will serve you in another manner, I will serve you in something else, I will go with you into battle and do battle with the English as long as I can remain alive. I will have you know that my hand will be worth more than that of twenty other men.' The duke looked in another direction and called to Walter Giffard:

'Take this standard', he said, 'and carry it into battle.' Walter Giffard replied:

'My lords', he said, 'for God's sake! See how white and hoary my hair is. My strength is in decline. It has weakened and I am easily out of breath. The ensign should be held by someone who can sustain long suffering. I will be in the battle. You have no man who will be of greater use to you in it. I expect to strike so many blows with my sword that it will be stained with blood.' (7575–7614)

Then the duke said very fiercely:

'My lord, by God's radiance! You want to betray me, I believe, and fail me in this great need.'

'My lord', said Giffard, 'we will not do such a thing and we will never commit treason. It is not treachery which makes me refuse, for I have a large company of knights and men from my own fief. I have never had such a good opportunity to serve you as I do now. Now, if it pleases God, I will serve you. If need be, I would die for you. I would put my body in jeopardy for you.'

'Truly', said the duke, 'I loved you before and now I love you more. If I can escape alive, things will be improved for you for ever more.' Then he called a knight of whom he had heard great praise. His name was Turstin, son of Rollo the White; his dwelling was in the Bec-aux-Cauchois. He handed him the standard and Turstin was very grateful to him for it; he bowed low and carried

---

[265] Ralph of Conches is better known as Ralph of Tosny.

it willingly and well. Members of his family still hold their inheritances freely: all his heirs must have their inheritances freely. William sat on his horse. He had Roger, called Montgomery, come forward.[266]

'I have great trust in you', he said. 'Go over there and attack them from that side. William FitzOsbern, my steward, a good vassal, will ride with you and attack them with you. You will have men from Boulogne and from Poix and all my mercenaries. On the other side, Alan Fergent and Aimery the warrior will lead Poitevins and Bretons and all the barons from Maine. With all my great forces, with my friends and my family and my noble vavassors, from whom I expect very great assistance, I will do battle amidst the great throng, where the battle will be at its most violent.' (7615–66)

All the barons, the knights and the foot-soldiers were armed. The men on foot were well armed, each carrying a bow and a sword. On their heads they had hats, and tied to their feet they had pieces of material. Some had fine leather jerkins, which they had tied to their waist, many had on a doublet and they had quivers and sheaths girt about them.[267] The knights had shining hauberks and swords,* iron leggings, gleaming helmets, shields around their necks and lances in their hands. They had all constructed cognizances, so that one Norman would recognise another; no mistakes would be made, no Norman would kill another Norman and no Norman strike another. Those on foot moved forward, in close formation, carrying their bows and the knights, who protected the archers, rode behind them. Those on horse and those on foot, from the time they set out, kept to their route and their circuit, in close formation and at a slow pace. No one outstripped the other, came too near or went too far away; they all in close formation and all with great ferocity. The archers, who had to shoot laterally, were on both sides. (7667–98)

Harold had summoned his men, those from the castles and those from the cities, ports, towns and burgs, his counts, barons and vavassors. The peasants came in throngs, bringing such weapons as they could find; they carried cudgels and great pikes, iron forks and clubs. The English had occupied a field. Harold was there with his friends and with the barons from that country, whom he had summoned and demanded. They had come at once, from London, Kent, Hertford, Essex, Surrey and Sussex, from Bury St Edmunds and Suffolk, from Norwich and Norfolk, from Canterbury and Stamford, and men came from Bedford. Men came from Northampton and those who were from Huntingdon, from Warwick,[268] Buckingham, Derby, Nottingham, Lindsay and Lincoln came when they received the message. Towards sunset you would have seen a huge number of men over there, from Salisbury and Dorset, from Bath and Somerset. Many came from the direction of Gloucester and many from Worcester, Winchester, Hampshire and the county of Berkshire. Many men came from other regions which we have not named; we cannot name them all and do not want to

---

[266] There is some doubt about whether Roger of Montgomery took part in the battle or whether he stayed in Normandy. He certainly crossed with the Conqueror to England in December 1067.

[267] This description of the knights' outfit is unique to Wace.

[268] For 'Warwick' the base manuscript reads *Evrowic* 'York'.

enumerate them all. All those who were able to bear arms, who had received the message about the duke, went to defend the land against those wanting to take it away from them; scarcely any came from beyond the Humber. They had had other difficulties; the Danes had caused them harm and Tostig had made things worse for them. (7699–7744)

Harold knew that the Normans would come and that they would attack them next morning. That morning he had occupied a field, where he had placed all his English troops. In the morning he made them all arm themselves and equip themselves for battle; he had weapons and equipment befitting such a lord. The duke who intended to conquer England was going to attack him, he said. He also said that the man who intended to defend the land against him was going to be waiting for him. He told and commanded his men, and advised his barons, that they should all stand firm together and defend themselves together, for if they left that spot they would find it very difficult to regroup.

'The Normans', he said, 'are good warriors, valiant on foot and on horse. They are good knights on horseback and used to doing battle. If they can make inroads amongst us, there will be no chance of retrieving our position thereafter. They have long lances and swords, which they have brought from their country, and you have sharp axes and great sharp pikes. Against your weapons, which cut so well, I do not think theirs are worth much at all. Cut whatever you can cut and never spare anything, or else you will regret it.' (7745–76)

Harold had many bold men and they came in great numbers from all directions, but a multitude is not worth much if the favour of heaven is lacking. Then person after person said that Harold had few men because things had gone against him. But many people say, and so do I, that if pitted one to one against each other, the duke's men would not have been numerous. But the duke had in truth many courageous men and better men; he had plenty of good knights and a huge number of good archers. The English foot soldiers carried axes and pikes, which were very sharp; they had made shields for themselves out of shutters and other pieces of wood. They had them raised before them like hurdles, joined closely together; from them they had made a barrier in front of themselves.[269] They left no gap through which any Norman, intent on discomfiting them, could get amongst them. They surrounded themselves with shields and small planks, thinking they could defend themselves in that way. If they had held firm, they would not have been beaten that day. No Norman would ever have broken through without losing his soul shamefully, whether from an axe or a pike, from a club or some other weapon. They had small, short hauberks and helmets on top of their heads. (7777–7810)

King Harold said, and had it said and announced as their lord, that each man should hold and turn his face straight towards the enemy. No one should leave the spot where he was, and anyone coming there should find them ready. Whatever a Norman or anyone else might do, let each man defend his position well. Then he asked those from Kent to go where the Normans were to fight, for people say

---

[269] This idea of a wall or barrier of shields is known from other sources, e.g. the Bayeux Tapestry and William of Poitiers; the technical detail provided here is unique to Wace.

that the men from Kent were to strike first; wherever the king might go in the battle, the first blow should be theirs.[270] The men from London, in true faith, were to protect the king's person, stand all round him and protect the standard; they were placed at the standard, which each man should defend and protect. When Harold had made everything ready and given all the commands he wanted, he came amidst the English, dismounting beside the standard; Leofwine and Gyrth were with him, both of them Harold's brothers, and around them were many barons. Harold was beside his standard; it was very valuable, shining with gold and precious stones.[271] William, after this victory, had it taken to the pope to show and ensure the memory of his great conquest and his great glory. All keen to fight, the English held their positions in close formation; they had made a ditch to one side which ran through the fields. Meanwhile, the Normans appeared; they rose up from a hill where they had been. From a valley and a hill a body of men rose and came forward. King Harold saw them from a distance and called to Gyrth, saying:

'My brother, which way are you looking? Have you seen the duke arriving? Our men will not be harmed in any way by those men I see there. There are very few men to conquer ours, and in this land there is a large number of men. I still have all these warriors, whether knights or peasants, a hundred thousand warriors times four.'

'Upon my word', said Gyrth, 'you have many men! But I have very little regard in battle for a collection of peasants. A large number of men you certainly have, but I am very much afraid of the Normans and fear them very much. All those who have come from across the sea do much that is to be feared and dreaded; they are well armed and on horseback. They will destroy our knights. They have many lances and shields, many hauberks and pointed helmets, many spears and swords, bows and barbed arrows. The arrows are very swift; they move much faster than swallows.'

'Gyrth', said Harold, 'do not be afraid! God can come to our aid, if He wishes. You do not need to be afraid of the men I can see there.' (7811–82)

While they were talking, from those Normans they could see there arose a troop in which there were more men, following the other in close formation. They made for one part of the battlefield, so that they did not join forces with the others. Harold saw them and looked at them. He called to Gyrth and pointed them out to him:

'Gyrth', he said, 'our enemies are increasing. Knights are coming and getting more numerous. A great many of them are arriving and I am very much afraid; I have never been so fearful. I am very much afraid of the battle; I am feeling great fright.'

'Harold', said Gyrth, 'you were wrong to nominate the day for the battle. I am distressed that you came here and did not remain in London, either in London or in Winchester. But now it is too late; things cannot be otherwise.'

---

[270] This information concerning the men from Kent is new.

[271] Wace's information concerning the jewels in the standard is new, as is the statement that William had the standard taken to the pope after his victory.

'My lord brother', said Harold, 'advice which looks back is not worth much. Let us defend ourselves, if we can. I do not know any other way of escape.'

'If you had been in London', said Gyrth, 'you could have gone from town to town and the duke would never have attacked you. He would have been afraid of the English and feared you; he would have retreated or made peace and you would have kept hold of your kingdom. You refused to believe me and did not value what I said. You specified a day for the battle, fixed this day for it and sought it here according to your own will.'

'Gyrth', said Harold, 'I did it for the best. I fixed a day for it and made it Saturday because I was born on a Saturday. My mother used to tell me that things would go well for me on that day.'[272]

'He who trusts fate is a fool', said Gyrth. 'No worthy man should ever trust it. No worthy man should trust in fate; each man has his own day on which to die. You say that you were born on a Saturday and on that day you can be killed.'[273] (7883–7928)

Then a company of men, covering the entire countryside, rose up. The standard, which had been brought from Rome, was raised there; the duke moved alongside it. The best and finest men, good knights, good vassals and good warriors were there. Noble barons, good archers, good foot-soldiers, who were to guard the duke and surround him, were there. Knaves and other riff-raff, who had no place in battle and were looking after the small items of equipment, made their way over to a hill. The priests and the ordained climbed up to the top of a hill to pray God, say their prayers and watch the battle. (7929–48)

Harold saw William coming and saw the fields covered with warriors. He saw the Normans, who intended to strike on three sides, divide off into three. He did not know which ones he should fear most. At that time he could scarcely speak:

'We are in a sorry plight', he said, 'and I am very much afraid we will be shamed. The Count of Flanders has betrayed me; I acted foolishly in trusting him.[274] For in his letter he sent me word, and assured me through his messenger, that William could not have so many knights. For this reason', he said, 'I delayed getting hold of better men. It distresses me that I did not act differently.' He drew his brother Gyrth to him; they positioned themselves beside the standard. Each of them prayed for God's protection; all around them were their relatives and the barons whom they knew. They had urged them all to perform good deeds; no one could escape from there. Each man had donned his hauberk and had his sword girded on and his shield around his neck. They held shoulder high great axes with which they intended to strike great blows. They were on foot and in close formation; they behaved very fiercely, but if they had been able to foretell the future they ought to have been weeping and wailing at the sorrowful adventure which was upon them, wretched and harsh. They often

---

[272] This reference to Saturday as Harold's birthday and the allusion to his mother (Countess Gytha of Wessex) are unique to Wace.

[273] These interventions on Gyrth's part are unique to Wace and are presumably a further elaboration of Gyrth's earlier contributions.

[274] This allusion to the Count of Flanders is unique to Wace, but it is probably an elaboration of an earlier story.

called out 'Alierot!' and called on 'Godemite!'[275] Alierot [Holy Rood] in English is Sainte Croiz in French, and Godemite is the same in French as Almighty God. (7949–88)

The Normans had three companies in order to attack in three parts; they divided off into three companies and formed three companies of warriors. The first and the second came, then the third, which contained the most men. That was the duke's company, with his large number of men; they all moved forward boldly. As soon as the two armies caught sight of each other, they created a great deal of noise and tumult. You would have heard many bugles sounded and many trumpets and horns blown. You would have seen many men settling themselves securely on their saddles, lifting their shields, raising their lances, stretching their bows and taking their arrows, ready to attack and defend. The English held firm and the Normans kept on coming. When they saw the Normans coming, you would have seen many English shaking. Men were roused, and the whole army was in a state of agitation, with some men going red and others pale. Weapons were seized and shields lifted and the bold dashed forward while the cowards trembled. (7989–8012)

Taillefer, a very good singer, rode before the duke on a swift horse, singing of Charlemagne and of Roland, of Oliver and of the vassals who died at Rencesvals.[276] When they had ridden until they drew close to the English, Taillefer said:

'My lord, I pray you! I have served you for a long time and you owe me a debt for all my service. Discharge your debt to me today, if you please. As my only reward I beseech you and want to beg you earnestly for this. Grant me, and let me not fail in it, the first blow in the battle.' The duke replied:

'I grant it.' Taillefer spurred his horse impetuously and positioned himself before all the others. He struck an Englishman and killed him beneath his feet, passing his lance right through his belly. He laid him out dead on the ground. Then he drew his sword, struck another knight, then cried:

'Come on, come on! What are you doing? Strike, strike!' Then, when he struck his second blow, the English surrounded him. There was suddenly noise and shouting, with people being roused to action on both sides. The Normans set about attacking and the English defended themselves well, some striking, others

---

[275] Cf. the use of English words in vv. 7331–34 and later in v. 8058.

[276] Taillefer is also mentioned in the *Carmen de Hastingae proelio* (vv. 391–408), in the *Estoire des Engleis* (vv. 5265–302; in v. 5268 he is called a *juglere* 'minstrel') and in Henry of Huntingdon, who states that the English were amazed when they saw him juggling with swords (Book VI, c. 30, pp. 392–93), but only William of Malmesbury (*Gesta regum Anglorum*) mentions the *Chanson de Roland* (Book II, c. 242, see the note in vol. 2, pp. 233–34). Wace is the first to combine the two traditions. See Sayers, 'The *jongleur* Taillefer at Hastings', who suggests that the allusion to Charlemagne's ultimate victory over the pagans on behalf of Christian right serves to legitimise William's cause in the same way as the reign of Arthur in Geoffrey of Monmouth's *Historia regum Britanniae* and Wace's own *Roman de Brut* justifies Henry II's rule over England, by stressing the principle of continuity and right (p. 84). See also D. C. Douglas, 'The *Song of Roland* and the Norman Conquest', *French Studies*, 14 (1960), 99–116, and Andrew Taylor, 'Was there a Song of Roland?', *Speculum*, 76 (2001), 28–65.

thrusting; they were so bold that they had no fear of each other. So the battle, which is still greatly renowned, was suddenly joined. You would have heard a great deal of noise from the horns, great clashing of lances, great striking of clubs and great fighting with swords. At times the English retreated, at others they rallied; those from across the sea attacked and withdrew repeatedly. The Normans cried out 'God help!', and the Englishmen shouted 'Out! Out!'.* Then you would have seen between men-at-arms, English and Norman infantry, great struggles and mêlées, thrusts from lances and blows from swords. When Normans fell, the English cried out; they insulted each other and very frequently issued challenges to each other. But they did not understand each other. The bold struck blows and the cowards became fearful. Because they did not understand what they said, the Normans said that the English barked.[277] Some men lost their strength, others gained in strength, the bold struck and the cowards took flight, as men do when in combat. The Normans were intent on attack and the English defended themselves well. They pierced hauberks and split shields, receiving great blows and returning great blows. These men advanced, those withdrew; they tested each other in many ways.[278] (8013–78)

In the fields there was a ditch. It was behind the Normans, who had passed round the side of it; they had taken no notice of it. The English pressed the Normans so much, and shoved and pushed them so hard that they forced them back into the ditch, causing men and horses to kick helplessly. You would have seen many men falling, some tumbling on top of others, stumbling and falling flat on their faces, unable to get up. A good number of the English, whom the Normans pulled down with them, died. During the entire day the English had not killed as many Normans in the battle as perished in the ditch; this is what those who saw the dead bodies said.[279] The squires, who were with the equipment and whose task it was to protect it, wanted to abandon it all because of the loss of the Frenchmen whom they saw stumbling into the ditch, unable to stand up again. They were very much afraid and on the point of leaving; they intended to abandon the equipment, but did not know any means of escape, when Odo, the good priest, who was ordained in Bayeux, spurred his horse, saying to them:

'Stand still, stand still! Calm down and do not move! Do not fear anything, for, please God, we will win the day.' In this way they were reassured and did not stir. Odo went spurring back to where the battle was at its fiercest; that day he had truly shown his worth. He had donned a short hauberk over a white shirt. Its body was broad and its sleeves were broad; he sat on an all-white horse and everyone recognised him. He held a club in his hand, made the knights head for where the need was greatest and brought them to a stop there. He often made them attack and often made them strike. (8079–8128)

---

[277] Here the English are referred to as 'barking' (*abaier*). In v. 8231 they are said to 'howl' (*glatir*).

[278] In other manuscripts vv. 8077–78 appear after v. 8066.

[279] The story of the ditch is probably a reference to the Malfosse, mentioned by Orderic Vitalis in his interpolation in the *GND* (II, pp. 168–71), but named only in the *Chronicle of Battle Abbey* (pp. 38–39, see also pp. 14–15).

From the hour of tierce,[280] when the battle commenced, until past nones, things went this way and that, so that no one knew who was going to win the day or conquer the land. They held firm on all sides and fought so fiercely that no one could guess who would overcome the other. The Norman archers, who held their bows, discharged a thick hail of arrows at the English, but the latter covered themselves with their shields so that they did not manage to strike them in the flesh; neither by their aim nor their fine shooting could they cause them any harm. They decided to shoot the arrows higher; when the arrows descended, they would fall straight on to their heads, striking them in the face. The archers adopted this plan and shot high above the English. When the arrows came back down, they fell on to their heads, piercing their heads and their faces and putting out the eyes of many of them; they did not dare open their eyes or reveal their faces. Arrows flew more densely than raindrops in the wind; they flew very thickly and the English called them mosquitoes. It happened in this way that an arrow which had fallen from the sky struck Harold right in the eye, removing one of his eyes. Harold pulled it out violently and threw it away, but breaking it before he did so. Because of the pain in his head, he leant on his shield. For this reason the English were wont to say, and still say to the French, that the arrow which was shot into Harold's eye was well made. The man who took out Harold's eye greatly increased the Normans' pride.[281] (8129–74)

The Normans noticed and saw that the English were defending themselves in such a way and had such great capacity to do so that they managed to make only slight progress against them. They secretly conferred, and made preparations amongst themselves, to move away from the English, making it look as if they were taking flight, until the English pursued them and become dispersed throughout the fields. If they could divide them, they could attack them more easily; their strength would be much weakened and they could defeat them more easily. They did just as they had decided and attacked them from a retreating position, making it look just as if they were taking flight. The English pursued them and the Normans kept on moving away little by little with the English following them, so much so that the more the Normans moved away the closer the English drew to them. Because the French were moving away, the English thought and said that those from France were taking flight and would never return. The feigned flight deceived the English and because of this flight great harm accrued, for if they had stood firm, without moving, they would have defended themselves very well and been very difficult to overcome; but they dispersed like fools and pursued the Normans like fools. You would have seen the Normans withdrawing with great cunning, slowly retreating to make the English come forward. The Normans fled and the English pursued them, with their lances outstretched and their axes raised. When the English had become emboldened

[280] Tierce or terce was the third hour of the day (about 9.00 am). The first hour of the day was prime (around 6.00 am). None was the ninth hour (around 3.00 pm).

[281] On this episode see David Bernstein, 'The Blinding of Harold and the Meaning of the Bayeux Tapestry', in *Anglo-Norman Studies V: Proceedings of the Battle Conference 1982* (Woodbridge: Boydell Press, 1983), pp. 40–64 (p. 47).

and spread throughout the fields, they mocked the Normans and hurled insults at them:

'Cowards', they said, 'you who wanted to have our lands came here in vain. You thought you could have our lands and were fools to come here. Normandy will be too far away for you. You will not get back there at this time of need. It will be no use going back, unless you can jump up and fly away. You have lost sons and daughters, unless you drink the whole of the sea.'[282] (8175–8228)

The enemy listened patiently, not knowing what they were saying. They thought they were just howling, for they did not understand their language. When the Normans came to a stop and turned round, intending to rally, you would have heard barons calling out and yelling loudly 'God help!'. The Normans recovered their ferocity and turned to look the English straight in the face. Then you would have seen Normans turning and doing battle with the English, each encountering the other and striking and dealing blows at one other. This one struck, another missed, this one fled, another pursued; this one finished off his opponent, another threatened him. The Normans took their stand against the English and made ready to strike forcibly. In many places you would have seen fine flights and fine pursuits. The number of men was huge, the battlefield broad, the combat dense and the fighting harsh. On all sides they fought well; the blows were great and the fighting was good. The Normans were doing well when an Englishman came running up, with a hundred armed men in his company, equipped with many weapons. He held a very fine Norwegian axe, its blade more than a full foot in length. He was well armed in his own manner and big and strong with a bold countenance. In the battle, right at the front, where the Normans were at their densest, he came dashing up, swifter than a stag; that day he knocked over many a Norman. With the company of men he had he came straight up to a Norman, who was armed and on horseback. He intended to strike him on the helmet with his axe of steel, but the blow slipped right past him. The axe, which was very sharp, skidded on to the front of the saddle-bows and sliced crossways through the horse's neck, so that the blade of the axe, which was heavy, went right into the ground; the horse fell forward on to the ground along with its master. I do not know whether he struck him any more blows, but the Normans who saw the blow gasped in amazement. The Normans had completely abandoned the assault when Roger of Montgomery came spurring up, with his lance lowered. Despite the long-shafted axe which the Englishman held shoulder high, he did not hesitate to strike him in such a way that he laid him out flat on the ground.[283] Then he cried:

'Strike, Frenchmen! We have the field against the English!' Then you would have seen a violent mêlée with many blows from lance and sword, and you would have seen the English defending themselves, killing horses and splitting shields. (8229–94)

There was a mercenary there from France, who conducted himself nobly and sat on a wonderful horse. He saw two very arrogant Englishmen, who had stayed

---

[282] This story of the mockery of the Normans by the English is unique to Wace.
[283] This story of the bold Englishman is new information.

close to each other because they were highly thought of and should be together, protecting each other. They held two long, broad pikes at shoulder height and were doing great harm to the Normans, killing men and horses. The mercenary looked at them, saw the pikes and feared them; he was afraid of losing his good horse, for it was the best he had. He would gladly have turned aside, if that would not have appeared cowardice. But soon he had quite different thoughts. He spurred his horse, pricking it and dropping the reins, and the horse carried him swiftly. He raised his shield by the straps, for fear of the two pikes, and struck one of the Englishmen cleanly with the lance he was holding, beneath the chin, on the chest; the iron passed right through his spine. While this one was being struck down, the lance fell and shattered, and he seized the bludgeon which hung from his right arm and struck the other Englishman an upwards blow, shattering and breaking his head. (8295–8328)

Roger the Old, the lord of Beaumont,[284] attacked the English from the front rank.* Remarkable fame accrued to him from this, as is apparent from his heirs, who are rich. Many people will tell one that they had good ancestors and that these men were on good terms with their lords who gave them such domains. Descending from this Roger came the lineage of Meulan. William, who is called Malet, went boldly amongst the English, and with his gleaming sword he engaged them in fierce combat. But they pierced his shield and killed his horse beneath him; they would have killed him as well, when the lord of Montford and Lord William of Vieux-Pont arrived. With the large number of men they had with them they rescued him boldly, but lost many of their men there; they immediately put Malet on to a completely fresh horse. (8329–52)

Those from the Bessin performed well, as did the barons from the Cotentin, and Nigel of Saint-Sauveur attacked the English with great vigour; he strove hard to have the love and goodwill of his lord. Using his horse's chest he sent many men tumbling that day, and as they struggled to their feet you would have seen him doing good work with his sword. The lord of Fougères, who had many fierce troops from Brittany, gained great fame from this battle, as did Henry, the lord of Ferrières, and the man who at the time was warden of Tillières; he assembled a large number of men, together with his barons. Any man who did not escape was killed or captured; they struck the English all together, making the entire ground shake and tremble. On the other side, there was an Englishman who greatly damaged the French; with his sharp axe he went about attacking them very severely. He had a helmet made entirely out of wood, such that a blow to the head would not harm him; he had attached it to his clothing and laced it around his neck. A Norman knight saw the outrageous and reckless treatment he was meting out to the Normans. This knight was seated on a very worthy horse, which neither water nor fire would have restrained if his lord spurred it well. He spurred the horse and it carried him swiftly. The Norman struck the Englishman on the helmet, knocking it down over his eyes. It hung over his face and the Englishman

---

[284] The name Roger here is an error for Robert, son of Roger the Old. For a detailed discussion of the list of names of the men and their localities found in vv. 8329–707 see van Houts, 'Wace as Historian', pp. xlviii–lxii, and the notes in Holden's edition (vol. 3, pp. 239–40).

raised his hand, intending to lift up the helmet and free his face. But he gave him a blow which cut off his right hand and his axe fell to the ground; another Norman dashed forward and with his two hands picked up the axe, for he had coveted it greatly. But he had it for a very short time, for at once he paid a heavy price for it. For when he bent down to take hold of the axe, an Englishman with a long-handled axe struck him in the middle of the back, shattering all his bones; one could see all his entrails, his lungs and his innards. The knight on the fine horse turned round unharmed, but he encountered an Englishman and shoved him so hard with his horse that he very soon knocked him down and trampled him under foot. (8353–8414)

All these men were in the battle:[285] the good citizens of Rouen, the youth of Caen, Falaise, Argenton, Anisy and Mathieu, and the man who was lord of Aumale, Lord William of Roumare, the lord of Lithaire, the lord of Touques and the lord of La Mare, the lord of Néhou, a knight from Pirou,[286] Robert, the lord of Beaufour, the man who was lord of Aunou, the chamberlain of Tancarville, the lord of Étouteville, Eustace of Abbeville, the lord of Manneville, William called Crispin, the lord of Saint-Martin, Lord William of Moulins and the man who was lord of Le Pin. None of them failed to display great valour. That day a vassal from Grandmesnil was in very great danger, for his horse carried him away and almost threw him to the ground as he was jumping over a bush; because of the reins he broke the bridle and the horse darted forward and went running towards the English. Catching sight of him, the English ran towards him with axes raised, but the horse took fright, retreating, then turning again. Geoffrey the Old of Mayenne and Humphrey the Old of Bohun, Humphrey of Carteret, and Malger, who was a new knight, and William of Warenne came – the helmet on his head suited him very well – and Old Hugh of Gournay, together with his men from Bray. With all the troops which these men brought they killed and put to death many opponents. Engenulf of Laigle came, with his shield around his neck and holding his lance. He struck the English with great violence and strove mightily to serve the duke; because of the land he had promised him, he did his very best to serve him. The vicomte, lord of Thouars, did not display cowardice that day. Richard of Avranches was there and with him the lord of Les Biards, and the lord of Soligny, and the butler from Aubigny, the lords of Victrié and of Lassy, of Vaudry and of Tracy; they were in the same company and struck the English impetuously,* not fearing pike or ditch. They knocked down many men that day and killed many a good horse, and many of them were wounded. Hugh, the lord of Montfort, the lords of Épinay and of Port, of Courcy and of Jort killed many men that day. The man who was lord of Reviers had a large number of knights with him and they struck out at the front, trampling the English with their horses. Old William of Moyon had many companions with him; Ralph Taisson of the Cinglais and Old Roger Marmion conducted themselves like brave men and later received a great reward for it. Next to Nigel's company rode Ralph of Gael; he was Breton and led a troop of Bretons. He was serving because of the land he owned, but he did not

---

[285] In order to facilitate comprehension of this passage, v. 8435 is translated first.
[286] The manuscript here reads *Peitou*.

hold it for long, for, it was said, he forfeited it.[287] Avenal of Les Biards was there and Hubert Paynel of Moustiers, Robert Bertram, who was deformed but very strong on horseback; he had a large number of troops with him and many men were killed by him. (8415–8504)

The archers from Vaudreuil, who were men of great arrogance, and with them the lord of Breteuil, put out the eyes of many Englishmen with the arrows of steel they had brought with them. You would have seen the lords of Soules and of Orval, the lords of Saint-Jean and of Bréhal and the lords of Brix and of Le Hommet, striking at very close quarters, placing their shields on their heads and receiving blows from axes; they preferred to die there rather than fail their rightful lord. The lords of Saint-Saens and of Cailly and the lord of Sémilly and Martel of Bacqueville were there; next to him was the lord of Presles and the lord of Gouvix and of Cintheaux, the lord of Le Molay and the lord of Monceaux, the man who was lord of Pacy, the steward of Courcy and a knight from Lassy, and with them the lord of Gacé, the lords of Ouilly and of Sassy and the lords of Vassy, of Tournebu and of Perrières, William of Colombières and Gilbert the Old of Asnières, the lords of Cahagnes and of Cornières, the Old Hugh of Bolbec, Lord Richard, who held Orbec, the lord of Bonnebosq, the lord of Le Sap, the lord of Glos and the man who held Troisgots at that time. He caused two Englishmen to think they were fools; he knocked one over with his lance and brained another with his sword, spurring his horse and turning so that no Englishman touched him. The lord of Montfiquet, who was responsible for protecting the woods (he was the ancestor of Hugh Bigot, with lands in Maltôt, in Loges and Canon, and who used to serve the duke as steward in his household) had a very large company of men with him. He was the duke's steward by hereditary right and a very noble and bold vassal; he was small in stature but very bold and valiant. Nevertheless, with the numerous troops he had brought with him he clashed with the English. (8505–58)

There you would have heard commotion, shouting and a great crunching of lances. The English were opposing them in the lists and splintering their lances; with pikes and axes they shattered their lances and the Normans drew their swords and broke up all the lists. The English withdrew to their standard in great dismay; there they were all assembled, the maimed and the injured. Then the lord of La Haye spurred his horse. He spared no one and showed no pity; he struck no one without causing his death and no one he wounded was able to survive. The lords of Vitré and of Ivry, of Montbray and of Sai and the lord of Ferté felled many an Englishman; many of them did great harm and they lost many of their own men. The lords of Botevilain and Trussebut, men who feared neither blow nor thrust, caused themselves to be greatly hated that day, receiving blows and dealing them.[288] William Patrick of La Lande called upon King Harold fervently, saying that if he saw him he would accuse him of perjury. He had seen him in La

---

[287] This forfeiture took place in 1075. Ralph of Gael was implicated in the so-called earls' rebellion and sent into exile. He later returned to his patrimony in Brittany.

[288] Botevilain and Trussebut are more likely to be toponymns than patronyms, even though the locations have not been positively identified.

Lande; Harold had stayed there and passed through La Lande when he was brought to the duke, who was then in Avranches and had to go to Brittany. There the duke dubbed him a knight and gave arms and equipment to him, and also to his companions; then he took him with him to attack the Bretons. Patrick was beside the duke, fully armed, and he was on very good terms with him. There were many knights from the Pays de Caux there, who were involved in the fighting and the attacks. (8559–8602)

The English were not skilled in jousting or in bearing arms on horseback. They held axes and pikes and did battle with such weapons; a man who intends to strike with an axe cannot give his mind to protecting himself, as he has to hold it in both hands if he wishes to strike with great vigour. To strike well and protect oneself at the same time is impossible, it seems to me. Over towards a mound they took their stand and the Normans stationed themselves over towards the valley. The Normans attacked them courageously on foot and on horse. Then Hugh of Mortemer spurred his horse;[289] he had with him the lord of Auvilliers and the lords of Les Oubeaux and of Saint-Clair. They overthrew many Englishmen. Robert FitzErneis extended his lance, took his shield and spurred his horse towards the standard. With his sharp spear he struck an Englishman in front of him, knocking him down dead at once; immediately he drew his sword and delivered many a blow against the English. He went straight to the standard, because he wanted to knock it down, but the English surrounded him and killed him with their pikes. When he was sought, he was found there, dead and slaughtered beside the standard. Count Robert of Mortain was not far from the duke; he was the duke's brother through his mother and he rendered his brother great assistance. Sitting on a very swift horse, the lord of Harcourt spurred it and helped the duke as much as he could. The lords of Crèvecoeur and Drucourt and the lord of Brucourt followed the duke whichever way he went. The lords of Combray and Aulnay and the lords of Fontenay, of Rubercy and of Le Molay went about asking for King Harold, saying to the English:

'Look here! Where is the king whom you serve and who has broken his word to William? He is dead if he can be found!' There were many other barons there, whom I have not yet named, but no one can deal with each one or give an account of each one. I cannot recount all the blows and do not want to compose a long work. I cannot name all the barons and do not know the full names of all the men from Normandy and Brittany whom the duke had in his company. There were many men from Maine and Anjou, from Thouars and Poitou, from Ponthieu and Boulogne. The number of men was great and the need great; there were mercenaries from many lands, some wanting land and some wanting money. (8603–68)

Duke William fought and entered the thickest part of the fray, knocking down many men so that no one could rescue them; it was clear that the opportunity was now his. The man who held his standard – Turstin, son of Rollo the White,

---

[289] The reference to Hugh of Mortemer is an error for his father, Ralph. See van Houts, 'Wace as Historian', p. lvii.

was his name, born in the Bec near Fécamp, a brave and renowned knight – rode next to the duke and went whichever way he went; when the duke turned, he turned and when he stopped he stopped. He entered the thickest press, wherever he saw the most English; the Normans were killing them, slaughtering them and cutting them down. With the duke was a large company of vavassors from Normandy, who would have let themselves receive blows to their own bodies in order to protect their lord. Alan Fergent, Count of Brittany, led a large company of Bretons;[290] they are fierce and warlike men who are keen to seize and acquire what they can. He killed and maimed many men and no Englishman he struck remained standing. Alan Fergent, a brave and valiant knight, fought very well, bringing the Bretons with him and doing a great deal of harm to the English. The lord of Saint-Valéry and the Count of Eu struck well, and Roger of Montgomery and Lord Aimery of Thouars conducted themselves like brave men; anyone they struck was in a sorry plight. (8669–8704)

Duke William strove very hard and broke his lance on the English; he made every possible effort to reach the standard with all the forces he had brought with him. He did his best to find Harold, for the entire war stemmed from him. The Normans protected their lord and surrounded him carefully; they went about dealing great blows against the English and they defended themselves very well. They put in a great amount of effort and defended themselves, exchanging blow for blow. There was a man there with great strength who was reputed to be a champion wrestler; with an axe he held he did great harm to us Normans. Everyone feared him, for he destroyed a great many Normans. The duke, who went to strike him, spurred his horse, but the man parried and caused him to miss; he jumped sideways with a great leap, raising his axe shoulder high. When the duke turned round for fear of the axe, he charged up with great power and struck the duke on the head, damaging his helmet severely; but he did not wound him greatly. However, he did make him bend well forward, almost causing him to stumble, but he duke had fixed himself firmly in his stirrups and quickly recovered his position. When he thought he could avenge himself and kill the wretch, the fellow drew back, for fear of receiving a blow from the duke. He came dashing in amongst the English, but still failed to get protection, for the Normans, who had seen him, pursued and followed him, piercing him with the iron of their lances and knocking him down dead on the ground. Where the press of battle was at its densest and the lords of Kent and Essex were fighting marvellously, pushing back the Normans and making them retreat, the Normans were unable to do them great harm.[291] (8705–52)

The duke saw his men retreating and the English regaining confidence; holding on to his shield by the straps and making sure he was firmly in the saddle, he took and raised a lance given to him by a squire. Next to him he saw his standard and around him more than a thousand armed men, who were watching over him carefully and fighting where he fought. In close formation, as was their

---

[290] Alan Fergant, also mentioned earlier in vv. 6367–68, is an error for Alan Rufus. See Van Houts, 'Wace as Historian', p. l.

[291] The syntax of vv. 8747–52 makes this passage difficult to translate.

duty, they made a move to strike the English.[292] With the strength of their good horses and the blows of their knights they completely broke through the throng and sliced through the crowd before them. The good duke led them forward; many men fell* and many took flight. You would have seen many English falling, lying on the ground and kicking their legs; those unable to get up were trampled by the enemies' horses. You would have seen brains flying out in great number and bowels lying on the ground; many men fell in this attack, from amongst the wealthiest and the most noble. The English rallied in places and killed those whom they attacked; they strove as best they could, cutting men down and killing horses. An Englishman saw the duke and was intent on killing him. He intended to strike him with a lance he carried, but did not manage it, for the duke struck him first and knocked him down to the ground. (8753–88)

Great was the noise and great the slaughter; many souls were driven out of their bodies and the living had to jump over the dead. On both sides they became weary of fighting. Anyone able to make a sudden attack did so and anyone who could not strike made a thrust. The strong strove mightily against the strong. Some died, others lived; the cowards kept on withdrawing and the bold advanced. Anyone who fell amongst them was in a sorry plight and knew great fear before he picked himself up; many men fell who never got up, for the great throng split many of them open. The Normans had pushed forward so much that they reached the standard. Harold was with the standard, defending himself as best he could, but he was suffering great pain from his eye, as it had been put out. While he was suffering pain from the blow to his eye, which was hurting him, an armed man came through the fighting and struck him on the ventail, knocking him to the ground. As he was trying to get up again, a knight, who struck him in the thigh, through the fleshiest part, knocked him down again and the wound went right through to the bone. Gyrth saw that the English were thinning out and that there was no way of escape; he saw his lineage falling and had no hope of protecting himself. He wanted to flee, but could not, for the throng was increasing all the time. Then the duke spurred his horse and reached him, pushing him forward very violently; I do not know whether this blow killed him, but it was said that he lay there for a long time. The Normans knocked the standard to the ground, killed King Harold and the finest of his allies and captured the golden pennon; there was such a throng when Harold was killed that I cannot say who killed him. (8789–8834)

The English suffered great sorrow because of the loss of King Harold, and because of the duke who had defeated him and knocked down the standard. They fought for a very long time and defended themselves for a long time until finally the day drew to a close. Then they realised, and many became aware, that their standard was no longer visible. The news went round and grew that Harold was truly dead. The English did not think they would receive any further assistance; they left the battle and those who could take flight did so. I cannot say, and do not say, nor was I there and did not see it, nor have I heard any authority say who

---

[292] In place of *Engleis* 'Englishmen', manuscripts BD have *Kentois* 'men of Kent', which may be the original reading.

felled King Harold or with which weapon he was wounded. But he was found dead along with the other dead bodies. He was found dead amongst the dead; his great efforts could not save him. Some English who escaped from the field did not stop till they reached London; they said and feared that the Normans were close behind them. There was a great throng crossing the bridge and the water underneath was deep. Because of the throng the bridge broke and many men fell into the water.[293] (8835–66)

William fought well. He entered many a press, dealt many a blow and received many; many men died by his hand. Two horses were killed beneath him, and of necessity he took a third to avoid falling to the ground or losing a drop of blood. However each man performed, whoever died and whoever lived, it is true that William won the day. Many of the English fled from the field and many died on the spot; William offered thanks to God for it. Proudly, Duke William asked for his own banner to be carried to the place where the standard had been and had it raised on high there; that was a sign that he had conquered and knocked down the standard. He had his tent set up amongst the dead, ordered his lodgings to be taken there; he had his food brought there and his supper prepared. Suddenly, along came Walter Giffard, spurring his horse.

'My lord', he said, 'what are you doing? It is not fitting for you to remain with these dead men. Many an Englishman lies here amongst the dead, covered in blood, unhurt or wounded, having smeared themselves with their own blood and intentionally lying amongst the dead. They have in mind to rise up during the night and during the night make their escape. But they are confident that, before they do so, they can avenge themselves and intend to sell themselves very dearly. None of them is concerned about his life and does not care who kills him, provided he has killed a Norman; we do them wrong, they say. You ought to have taken up lodging elsewhere and had yourself guarded by sentinels. Let the guard be made up tonight of a thousand or two thousand armed men, those in whom you trust most; we do not know who is watching us. Today has been a day of fierce fighting for us, but the happy ending gives me great pleasure and joy.'

'Giffard', said the duke, 'thanks be to God, we have done very well so far, and if God is willing to grant it to us and finds it to His liking, we will do well from now on. Let us make God our protector in all things.'[294] (8867–8920)

Giffard then turned away and William disarmed. When he did so, you would have clearly seen him taking the strap from around his neck, removing his helmet from his head and pulling the hauberk off his back, and barons and knights coming up as well as young men and squires. They saw the great blows on his shield and saw the battered helmet; they marvelled at it all. Everyone said:

'No man was ever so brave when spurring his horse or striking blows in such a way or supported such a weight of arms. Since Roland and Oliver there was never such a knight on earth.' They esteemed him greatly, praised him greatly and rejoiced at what they had seen; but they were distressed because their friends had been killed in the battle. The duke stood amongst them, a man of mighty

---

[293] This bridge was probably Robertbridge; the information presented here is unique to Wace.

[294] This story of Walter Giffart's intervention is unique to Wace.

build and great height; he gave thanks to the King of Glory, through whom he had won this victory. He thanked the knights and frequently lamented the dead. That night he lay in the field and ate and drank amongst the dead. The next day was Sunday. Those who had lain in the open and those who had stayed awake in the fields and suffered much hardship, rose early in the morning and made their way through the fields; they buried their friends, those whose dead bodies they could find. The noble ladies in the land went to seek their husbands: some went looking for their fathers or their spouses, or for sons or brothers, and they carried them to their towns and buried them in the churches. Clerics and priests in the country, at the request of their friends, took those whom they were seeking and built mass graves and placed them there. King Harold was taken away and buried at Waltham, but I do not know who took him and I do not know who buried him.[295] Many a man remained lying on the field and many took flight at night. (8921–72)

The bishops sent word to each other and assembled in London; the barons came to them and they all held a great council. By common advice of the clergy, who recommended and advised it, and through the barons, who saw that they could elect none other, they had the duke crowned king and swore fealty to him; he took the fealty and homage and returned their inheritances to them. It was the year one thousand and sixty-six since the birth of Jesus Christ, if scholars have calculated correctly, when William took the crown. For twenty-one years and half a year more, William was then king and duke.[296] To the many people who had followed him and served him for a long time he gave castles, he gave cities, he gave dwellings and he gave counties; he gave lands to the vavassors and gave many other forms of income. Then he had all the barons summoned and all the English assembled, giving them the choice of which law they would uphold and which customs they wanted, either those of the Normans or of the English, and of which lords and which kings. They said they should be those of King Edward; may the king uphold and protect his laws for them. The customs which they knew, which they used to hold at the time of Edward, those were the ones they wanted and those they asked for, those pleased them and those they adopted; this was their will and the king granted it to them. (8973–9010)

William suffered much hardship and much fighting ensued before he held the land in peace, but however distressing it was to him, he dealt with everything very successfully. He crossed over to Normandy; when he arrived there, he came and went as he pleased,* making peace here and peace there, destroying thieves and punishing evil-doers. Where the battle had taken place, he had an abbey built and placed an abbot in it. The King of France requested that he should serve him in respect of England, as was the case for his other fief of Normandy,

---

[295] Wace is the first to mention that Harold was buried at Waltham, although this information is given in the *Waltham Chronicle* (composed shortly after 1177), where the author quotes an eyewitness (ed. and trans. by Leslie Watkiss and Marjorie Chibnall (Oxford: Clarendon Press, 1994), pp. 52–57).

[296] William became Duke of Normandy in 1035, when he was seven years old, and remained duke until his death in 1087. He was King of England from 1066 to 1087.

which he held.[297] William replied to him that he would serve the king in the same way as the king had supported him at his time of need and protected him; in his conquest he had not been of any use to him or helped him at his time of need. With respect to his fief he would serve him well, but with regard to the other fief he owed him nothing. He had conquered England without him and he owed service to no one other than God and the pope in Rome; he did not have to serve any other man. For Normandy, by right, he would serve him as he should. But had he helped him, as he had asked him to do, and participated in the battle with him, he would have said that he had England through the king. In this way a quarrel developed, but they were later reconciled. The King of France did nothing more, nor did William say anything more to him. The French often waged war against him and very often caused him harm. William defended himself well and often damaged the French; many a time things turned out badly for him; one day he won and the next he lost. This is the way it goes in warfare; the man who had lost then gets things back. (9011–55)

William was in Rouen, where he had been for many days. He became ill there, I do not know how long it lasted; he could not mount his horse, bear arms or go to war. The King of France very soon heard that he could not wage war and that he was lying in his bed. He sent him word as an unpleasant joke that he was lying in childbed for a long time, just as a woman does when she has a baby; from now on he ought to get up, as he could be resting for too long.[298] William replied to him that so far he had scarcely lain in bed:

'When I do get up', he said, 'I will go and hear Mass in his land, taking him a rich offering and providing him with a thousand candles. They will have wooden wicks, and iron shining at the top instead of a flame.' This was his message, and when he had recovered he accomplished what he had said. He took a thousand armed men into France, with lances upright and swords raised, and he set fire to dwellings and towns; the king could see the fires. Then William set Mantes ablaze and burnt the whole town to a cinder, setting fire to the burgs and the cities and setting the churches aflame. William rode through the town on a horse of which he was very fond; it set two of its feet down on a burnt part, but swiftly withdrew them and darted forward very violently. The king prevented himself from falling, yet he was severely wounded by his saddle-bows with which he collided. And when the king left there, with the large number of men he was leading, he came to Rouen and retired to bed; because of the injury, which was causing him pain, he had himself carried to Saint-Gervais because he would be more comfortable there. (9056–9100)

William gave his land to his sons, so that after his death there would be no quarrelling. He summoned all his barons:

'Listen to me', he said, 'and take note of what I say! Normandy, my inheritance, where most of my lineage is, I give to Robert, my eldest son. I granted it to him a long time before I became king and now I give him Le Mans in addition.

---

[297] This request for homage and fealty by the King of France is anachronistic. It reflects problems between Henry I and Louis VI of France after 1106.

[298] This joke about William lying in childbed is unique to Wace.

He will have Le Mans and Normandy and will serve the King of France in respect of them. In Normandy there are many fierce men, I do not know any others of a similar kind; they are brave and valiant knights, able to make conquests in every land. If the Normans have a good chieftain, their company is greatly to be feared; if they have no fear of a lord who constrains and represses them, they will begin to give bad service. The Normans are not brave without discipline; it is appropriate to oppress and subdue them. If a king constantly keeps them down and is someone who represses and subdues them well, he will be able to conduct his affairs with them. The Normans are arrogant and proud, boastful and overweening; they should be repressed the whole time, for they are very hard to discipline. Robert, who has to watch over such men, has much to do and to think about. I would like, if God wished to grant it, to advance the cause of William, my son, who is here and who is very noble and well born. He desires England for himself and wants to become king of it, if this were possible; but I cannot do this myself, you know the reason why. I conquered England wrongfully and many men there were killed wrongfully; I killed their heirs wrongfully and took over the kingdom wrongfully. What I stole wrongfully and had no right to I ought not to give to my son, neither should I endow him with it wrongfully. But I will send him overseas and beg the archbishop to grant him the crown, if he can do so by right. If he can do this by reason, I beg that he should give him this gift.[299] To Henry, my youngest son, I have given five thousand pounds and to William here I command, and send word to my other son Robert, that each one in his power, as he holds me dear, should make Henry rich and wealthy, more than any man holding land from him.' (9101–62)

William lay ill for six weeks; the illness was severe and his infirmity grew. He confessed his sins to the bishops, the abbots and the tonsured priests and then he took the *Corpus domini*; he divested himself of everything, dividing it up and sharing it out. He released all the prisoners and had them all declared free, and he had his brother, Bishop Odo, released from prison. If he had expected to live long, he would not have let him go so soon. He had captured him on the Isle of Wight and put him in prison in Rouen. Odo, he used to say, was malicious and as covetous as he could possibly be. He had been his steward for a long time and was cruel and evil to everyone; the whole of England complained of him and he put to ransom both poor and rich.[300] In secret, he had enquired and asked of his friends whether a bishop could ever become king or whether he could ever be king; he hoped he would become king if the king died before him. He put his trust in his great wealth and in the large number of men he led. Because of his eloquent words and speeches and the foolish promises he made, the king regarded him as an outright traitor and was suspicious of him. (9163–96)

---

[299] William's speech is historically interesting in that he states that he has no right to grant England to William Rufus; only the Archbishop of Canterbury can do so.

[300] These remarks concerning Odo echo those of Orderic Vitalis (II, 264–67, IV, 38–45) and William of Malmesbury (I, 506–07, II, 256). For the specific characterisation of Odo as lay lord (Earl of Kent), see *ibid.*, II, 256.

When he had given the order to capture him, because of the accounts he refused to render for the income received from having held England, there was no one who would approach him or dare to lay a hand on him. Then the good king dashed forward and seized him by the fastenings of his cloak, dragging him forward right out of the ranks:

'I capture you, I capture you!' he said.

'You do me wrong', said Odo. 'I am a bishop and carry the crozier. You ought not to lay a hand on me.'

'By my head', said the king, 'yes I should! I will capture the Earl of Kent, my bailiff and my servant, who has not rendered me an account of my kingdom which he has held in stewardship.' In this way Odo was captured and held, and after that he was not handed back for four years. The ship was close by and the wind was good; the bishop was placed in the ship, taken to Rouen by sea and held in the tower for four years, without ever being able to leave it until the king had died.[301] (9197–9222)

At the beginning of September, on the eighth day, the king died and left this world.[302] When prime sounded, which he heard clearly and asked what it was that was ringing at that time, he called upon God as best he could and on my Lady the Virgin Mary. He came to the end of his life while speaking these words and his mind was not impaired or his speech affected. He had lived for sixty-four years and known much hardship in battle. He was still only seven, a small child, not very big, when Duke Robert took the cross and went to Jerusalem.[303] At the time the king passed away and left this world you would have seen many servants moving about, coming and going, taking away velvet and coverlets and whatever they could remove. It took almost the time needed to cover a full league before they placed the body on a bier; they left the king, whom people were accustomed to fear when he was alive, to lie alone. Then the news spread and people came rushing up in large numbers and the bishops and barons came in a great procession. They prepared the body very well, opening it up, anointing it and embalming it. They had the body taken to Caen, just as he had commanded. There was no bishop in the province, no abbot, count or noble prince who was not present when the body was buried, providing he could get there. Many monks were there, dressed in their robes, and priests and minor clerics. When they had prepared the body, they sang out loud *Libera me* and carried the body to the church. But the bier was still outside when a cry arose there which terrified everyone, for the town was on fire. Everyone made their way there and ran over towards it, except for the monks who remained and stayed with the body. When the fire had died down and gone out, the people came back; they carried the body

[301] On Odo, Bishop of Bayeux and Earl of Kent, see Ann Williams, *The English and the Norman Conquest* (Woodbridge: Boydell Press, 1995), pp. 11–12, 27.

[302] William the Conqueror is normally thought to have died on 9 October (the date given in manuscript B).

[303] Holden points out (note to v. 9235, vol. 3, p. 242) that, if William was sixty-four when he died in 1087, he would have been twelve, not seven, when his father died in 1035. The figure seven is in fact correct, as William was born in 1028 or 1029 and was fifty-nine or sixty when he died. See note 296 above.

to the church and the clerics did their duty. With goodwill they all sang the *Requiem eternam.* (9223–78)

While the sarcophagus in which he was to lie was being prepared, and the bishops and the barons were surrounding it, a vavassor suddenly came up, breaking through the crowd. His name was Ascelin FitzArthur. He came confidently through the crowd, climbed up high on to a stone and turned towards the bier, calling upon the clerics and bishops. He stood on high and spoke out loud. Everyone looked at him.

'My lords', he said, 'listen to me! In the name of Almighty Jesus and by the pope in Rome – I cannot invoke any higher authority – I forbid and refuse to let any one of you bury William in the place where you are to put him, or that he should lie in a place which is rightfully mine. For the most part, this church is rightfully mine and belongs to my fief; I have no greater right in any place. I did not sell it or mortgage it,[304] forfeit it or give it away, nor did William have it from me by pledge or give me any surety for it. He took it away from me by force and never afterwards offered to compensate me for it. I call upon Him by name to do me right at the Day of Judgement when everyone will assemble, before Him who does not lie. On that day let him do right by me; in the hearing of everyone I summon him by name.' When he had said this, he stepped down, and suddenly there was great noise and tumult throughout the church, with no one able to hear or listen to anyone else; those who were coming and going regarded this as a great marvel. The king, who had made so many conquests and captured so many cities and castles, did not have any land free of claim in which his body could lie in death. The bishops called upon the man and asked those around them if what he said was true, and they said he was right. The land had been his father's and passed from generation to generation. They told the man to take money and abandon his entire challenge. They gave him sixty shillings and for this sum he released the tomb in which the body was placed; for that reason he took the money. The barons promised him that things would be better for him in the future; Ascelin agreed to this and then they buried the body.[305] (9279–9340)

Robert remained in Normandy and made his lordship effective everywhere. He was a small man, but burly, with short legs and big bones.[306] The king gave him a nickname as a result and called him Curthose; he wore short hose and was called Curthose. William Rufus crossed the sea, was crowned and reigned for thirteen years. In his father's name, he had a sealed letter taken to Lanfranc,

---

[304] See Holden's note to v. 9305 (vol. 3, p. 242).

[305] The story concerning Ascelin comes from Orderic (IV, pp. 104–07) and can be corroborated by charter material from Saint-Étienne at Caen (see also Orderic, *ibid.*, p. 106 n. 1). On the influence of Orderic Vitalis at this point see Holden, vol. 3, p. 111. In Holden's view the account of the death and burial of William the Conqueror is the only substantial example of the influence on Wace of the *Historia ecclesiastica*. On the question of the demand for sixty shillings for the place of burial see William of Malmesbury, II, p. 259.

[306] On Robert Curthose see Orderic, II, pp. 356–57, and IV, p. 107: 'Corpore pingui brevique statura unde vulgo Gambaron cognominatus est et Brevis-ocrea' ('short and stout, he was commonly nicknamed "fatlegs" and "curt-hose"'). For a recent discussion of Robert Curthose's rule in Normandy see J. Green, 'Robert Curthose Reassessed', in *Anglo-Norman Studies XXII: Proceedings of the Battle Conference 1999* (Woodbridge: Boydell Press, 2000), pp. 95–116.

Archbishop of Canterbury, and Lanfranc had the letter read out. Because of his father's goodness he held the son dear and crowned him in Westminster on Michaelmas Day; this was good and it pleased the Heavenly King. Henry had a large amount of money, which his father had given him. He had part of his mother's treasury and a large part of his father's, and he was skilled at investing money, using it well and looking after it. King Rufus was a man of great nobility; he was brave and very generous. He did not hear of any knight whose prowess he heard praised and then fail to mention him in his register and give him some annual reward. In order to make his name distinctive – it resembled his father's, for each had the name William – the son later had the nickname Rufus. (9341–74)

Robert, who was in Normandy, was very envious of his brother and of the fact that he had been raised to the rank of king, although he had been born after him; he was distressed by this and it upset him. He spoke to his brother Henry, who had his father's treasure, and told him he would give him the whole of the Cotentin by way of a pledge, providing he made no permanent claim on it; he should hand over his money to him on these terms.[307] For he did not want to wait any longer before crossing over to England to obtain what was rightfully his from King Rufus, who was acting wrongfully and shamefully with regard to him and who was younger than he, and king. Henry lent him the money, just as he had asked, and received the Cotentin as a pledge; he was to keep it until the duke gave him back his money or acted in accordance with his wishes in this matter. Then Henry asked the duke, and had his friends ask him as well, if a man by the name of Richard of Reviers could become his companion. He should grant him the man and his service and let him remain with him and be with him; he would teach him how to behave in society and take him to tournaments. Richard was courtly and brave and highly praised by everyone; the duke granted him this and released Richard to him. I do not know what Richard thought about this, but he gave the impression of being very upset that he was to leave the duke and serve his brother Henry.

'Richard', said the duke, 'you will do this and serve my brother Henry. I grant him your fief and yourself as well; he is no less noble a man than I. Be his vassal, I command you, serve him well from now on and you will never be shamed by him. We are from the same family.' (9375–9420)

In this way Richard joined Henry and served him all his life.[308] When Henry had lent the duke the money he had asked for and the duke had received all the money, he sought knights and a fleet and crossed the sea with a very large army. The king very soon heard that his brother was coming to attack him and that he wanted to take possession of England. He summoned his men from all parts and

---

[307] For the sale of the Cotentin see Orderic, IV, pp. 118–20. Robert of Torigny points out that some people said that Robert gave Henry the Cotentin and some said that he mortgaged it (*GND*, II, pp. 204–05). For discussion of the transaction referred to here see William of Malmesbury, II, p. 359.

[308] On Richard of Reviers (d. 1107) see Orderic, IV, p. 220, and *Charters of the Redvers Family and the Earldom of Devon, 1090–1217*, ed. by R. Bearman (Exeter: Devon and Cornwall Record Society, vol. 37, 1994), pp. 2–11.

in a very short time gathered together a large army, for he preferred to die on the battlefield rather than to abandon England to the duke. But the barons, who loved William very much, and the bishops, advised him to seek and obtain peace, and to give his brother a sufficient amount of his wealth and an increase in his income, rather than not have peace.[309] The peace was obtained, sought and made in such a manner that the king would give Robert each year from then onwards, as long as he lived, five thousand pounds in money; Robert agreed to this willingly. Thereupon, the duke returned to Normandy with his barons. (9421–48)

At that time, because of the Cotentin, which Robert took away from him, the war which caused great trouble in the land began between Duke Robert and Henry. King Rufus conceived a hatred for Henry because of the money he had lent Robert to wage war on him; he had no desire to help his cause. If Robert had harmed Henry, this would not have angered the king. Robert spent the money and held on to the Cotentin; Henry neither had it nor could he get his money back. To take his revenge he installed himself on the Mount where Saint Michael's monks are [Mont-Saint-Michel]. Henry was on bad terms with the king and likewise with Duke Robert. He was estranged from both of them, as if he were very much hated by them, and he did not dare remain with the duke, nor could he have the Cotentin; he did not know which way to turn and where he could receive protection. He did not leave without companions, taking a large number of men with him; he took with him the brothers and sons of the most noble and the highest born and they all served him very willingly, for they put great hope in him. He did not dare remain in the country and no one dared protect him; he said he would go to Brittany and remain there. Count Hugh gave him hospitality in Avranches and he made his way there.[310] He spent one night there and explained to Count Hugh how his brother had treated him and how he had conceived a hatred for him. The duke was taking the Cotentin away from him and he was unable to get from him what was rightfully his, nor did he dare to remain in the land. He did not know to whom to make his complaint and considered himself very much forsaken; but Hugh comforted him greatly. (9449–94)

The very next day, after dinner, when Henry was due to leave, Count Hugh spoke to him, giving him some advice and pointing out to him Mont-Saint-Michel.

'Do you see that rock there?' he said. 'That is a fine spot and a fortified place; it will never fail, either by night or day. It is surrounded by a rising tide, which gives the place great protection. I have seen the time', he said, 'when, in the event of my being as you are now, from such a great lineage and unable to do better, I would have established myself on that rock, turned the church into a fortress and summoned Bretons and mercenaries, who would willingly have made some profit for themselves. I would have terrified people and no Norman would have had any peace from me. I do not ask you or command you, nor, I believe, do you have it in you to do what I say, but I would have done it in that way.' I do not know

---

[309] Duke Robert planned to go to England in 1088, but did not in fact do so (Orderic, IV, p. 134).

[310] Count Hugh is Hugh of Avranches, Earl of Chester. The discussion here between Count Hugh and Henry is unique to Wace.

whether the count said any more or what impression he gave Henry, but Henry mounted his horse at once and went straight to the Mount. From Mont-Saint-Michel he waged war and challenged his brother Robert; never, he said, would he have any peace with him unless he gave him back his money. He often moved swiftly through the Cotentin and pillaged the whole of the Avranchin, capturing peasants and ransoming them; he left nothing he could capture. (9495–9530)

Henry stayed on the Mount and held it until the King of England arrived. The king and the duke gathered together and summoned men from all sides. They besieged the area surrounding the Mount, from Genêts to the Couesnon and the river Ardevon; only the poor left the Mount. The king stayed at Avranches and the duke was in Genêts. You would have seen a great deal of jousting and dense fighting between the Mount and Ardevon and the river Couesnon. Each day, when the tide ebbed, the knights went forth in search of jousts. The king was knocked off his horse there and struck by a number of lances. The breast-strap on his horse broke and the two saddle-girths as well; he fell off, along with his saddle. But he held on to the saddle well and did not lose it; he freed himself and jumped to his feet, defending himself with his sword. He never let go of his saddle, holding on to it well and protecting it well. He cried out 'Royal knights!' so loudly that a crowd of vassals came, and the Normans and the English who were with him helped him; but before they had come to his aid, he had received many great blows. They led him to safety, then mocked the king a great deal with respect to the saddle he was protecting and the great blows he was suffering. The king said with a laugh that he had to be the protector of what was his; it is shameful to lose and abandon what belongs to one as long as one can protect it. It would have upset him that a Breton could boast of having taken away his saddle. (9531–72)

Henry held the Mount fiercely, I do not know for how long. They had plenty of food, but there was a lack of drink; they had a lot to eat, but found wine very scarce. When Henry had suffered thirst for a long time, he quietly sent word to Duke Robert that he had a desire for wine; he had no other needs. Robert sent him at once – I do not know if he felt pity for him – a barrel full of wine, the best he could find in the army. He granted the whole day and gave permission through a truce for the inhabitants of the Mount to get water and for the Mount to be provided with water; they could take it wherever they wanted it in security, fearing nothing. Then you would have seen servants moving about and bringing water in vessels. Duke Robert was severely reproached for the wine which was taken to the Mount and for having given the truce so that water could be taken there. The king became very angry when he heard this; he was very upset that his enemy was provided with the best wine to be found. He ought to have been starving them, yet he was providing them with drink. He wanted to abandon the siege, but the duke made him stay.

'Do not hold it against me', he said, 'if I have provided Henry with drink. I would have been accused of felony and would have acted basely to deny him food and drink when he himself asked for it.' He had the king stay long enough for him to reconcile his brothers. The upshot of the agreement was that the Cotentin would remain Henry's and he would maintain it and hold it in peace until the duke gave him back his money. (9573–9618)

When this war was over and the agreement reached, King Rufus abandoned the siege and went back to England.[311] The duke went to Caen and from Caen came to Rouen. Henry paid his mercenaries, making promises to some and giving gifts to others. At the agreed date, he followed the duke to Rouen. I do not wish to recount or say any more about how anger or wrath caused Henry to be captured in Rouen and imprisoned in the tower, nor about how he was freed and sent away from that land, and about how he went to the king, who then retained him in France, nor about how Haschier, who had one of his eyes covered with a plaster so that no one could recognise him, found him in Paris and then took him away.[312] I do not wish to say how cleverly Haschier caused to him have Domfront, nor how he was received when he came to Domfront, nor how he conquered the Passais and took everything away from the inhabitants of Bellême, nor how Robert attacked him there and besieged part of Domfront. I do not wish to relate how the duke went back home without doing anything further and how he abandoned his equipment to the knights and the burgesses, not because he wanted to make them a present of it or grant it to them willingly; he left part of his equipment behind, then returned to Normandy. (9619–56)

At this time, as I do wish to tell you, the great crusade to the Holy Land took place, when Antioch was conquered, the city of Nicaea captured and Jerusalem taken. Duke Robert was very much preoccupied with the great crusade he had heard about; he was very keen to participate, but did not have enough money. He informed King Rufus of this, that he wanted to travel and take the cross. He did not want to wait any longer, but he would let him have Normandy and Maine, which he held. The king should give him money against them, by way of a pledge, so that he could depart. King Rufus agreed to this willingly and took the entire land as a pledge; he was not at all niggardly with him, for he gave him a full six thousand six hundred and sixty-six marks against the land Robert had given him.[313] Robert was filled with joy; many barons took the cross with him and many men from other lands, who went with him, assembled. Then the brothers, who never saw each other again, separated. Robert set out for Jerusalem, conducted himself well and performed many fine deeds there; he was there when Antioch was taken and won great renown as a result of his exploits. Then he was present at the capture of Jerusalem; the pagans could not withstand them. As a result of the standard which he knocked down, where Kerboga fought,[314] and the pagans whom he killed and the banner he conquered, which

---

[311] The siege of Mont-Saint-Michel took place between 26 February and 12 April 1091. The geographical specifications, the references to jousting and the story about the wine are unique to Wace. See Orderic, IV, p. 250, and C. W. David, *Robert Curthose* (Cambridge, Mass.: Harvard University Press, 1920), pp. 63–65.

[312] This story concerning Haschier is also found in Orderic (IV, p. 158), where the editor, M. Chibnall, identifies him as Richard Achard, Henry I's former tutor, who was later awarded land in Berkshire.

[313] The principal Latin sources agree that the sum paid by William Rufus was 10,000 silver marks. Wace is alone in quoting the figure of 6,666.

[314] Kerboga was a Saracen prince.

he later gave to the church his mother had founded at Caen, he received great renown and great honour; many people spoke of him. (9657–98)

King Rufus, who was very brave, made himself feared and respected by everyone; he had maintained justice well throughout his land and brought peace to it all when Helias took Le Mans away from him. He entered the city by night and garrisoned it as best he could. When King Rufus found out about this, he considered that Helias, who had taken possession of his city, had acted with great arrogance. When in the past the king had first captured Le Mans, in order to create a lasting peace there and make the land secure, he had the daughter of Count Herbert betrothed to his son Robert, but she had died young and in tender years, before Robert could take her.[315] Then he ruled Le Mans by force and did not hand it over to the rightful heirs, because of the girl who had died; instead, he built a strong tower there. When William died, he left Le Mans to Robert, who left it to King Rufus when he took leave to join the crusade. He left Maine and Normandy to the authority of his brother Rufus; the king was to give it back to him when he returned from the Holy Sepulchre. (9699–9728)

In Langres[316] there was a Burgundian, a nobleman by the name of Hugh; he was the nephew of Herbert, who held Le Mans as his inheritance. Herbert considered him to be his heir and Le Mans should rightfully have been his, but he lost it because of strangers, in such a way that he was not able to go back there. The inhabitants of Le Mans, who knew it was rightfully his, had summoned him in secret and promised to hand it over to him if he wanted it and dared take it. Wishing to have Le Mans, he came, but he did not enjoy being there and could not enjoy the pleasure of dwelling in the land; he would never be free of war, he said. So finally he sold Le Mans to Count Helias, his cousin; Helias was a member of the same family, so he claimed his right to the inheritance. Helias bought it, giving him ten thousand shillings for it;[317] Hugh abandoned his rights to Le Mans and turned it over to the barons. He took the ten thousand sous and returned to his country. Helias was a man of great power with a great deal of land and money; he put in a challenge and a demand for the land he had bought, and the inhabitants of Le Mans supported him and undertook to advance his cause; those who lived in the league around the city were all subject to his orders and the barons in the region had many a battle on his behalf. They thought very highly of him, loved him and wanted him to be their lord, as is the custom with many people who desire new lords. Through the help provided by the neighbouring castles, and the connivance of the inhabitants of Le Mans, Helias entered Le Mans and the residents received him; they handed it over to him, everything with the exception of the city tower. The tower held out and those in Le Mans besieged it and captured the surrounding burg. When the Normans, who defended the tower, saw the strength of the inhabitants of Le Mans, they sent word to England and begged the king for assistance, telling him what had happened and about the treachery of the inhabitants of Le Mans. (9729–82)

---

[315] The daughter's name was Margaret; she died at Fécamp.
[316] The correct place is Liguria in Italy not Langres (Orderic, IV, p. 192).
[317] The sum of ten thousand shillings is also mentioned by Orderic (IV, p. 198).

The king was in England, where there were many Normans and many English. He had asked for brachets, as he wanted to go hunting in the woods. Suddenly, a servant who had come from overseas, came into the hall. The king immediately recognised him; he had left him in charge of Le Mans. He called out to him and said from a distance:

'What is happening in Le Mans? Is there a crisis?'

'My lord', he said, 'Le Mans has been captured. Count Helias has established himself within it. He has captured the city and besieged the castle on all sides. The Normans who are defending themselves inside are awaiting your help and your presence.' The king's mood changed completely when he heard the message; he swore by the crucifix in Lucca[318] that this would be paid for dearly. This was his usual oath: he did not make any other. Then he called to the messenger:

'Go', he said, 'without delay! Cross the sea as fast as you can and speak to my men in Le Mans. I will be in Le Mans in a week's time; then, if it pleases God, I will help them.' The messenger then set off and the king moved very quickly. He summoned his men:

'Tell me', he said, 'if you can, how and what way I could get to Le Mans by the straightest route; let each man turn his face in the exact direction he thinks Le Mans is.' They turned aside and made the calculation, then pointed to a wall, saying that Le Mans was over there, so he said that he would go that way. For a hundred marks of silver, he kept on saying, he would not stray from Le Mans by a hundred feet from the point at which he was standing when he heard about the crisis there. Then he had the wall, which was very fine and complete, knocked down; the wall was knocked down and the exit made so large that King Rufus and the vassals all passed through it on horseback. The king spurred on to Southampton and summoned his people from all sides; he asked for sailors and gave the orders for them to cross the sea.

'My lord', they said, 'have mercy in God's name! We do not have a good breeze; we do not have a favourable wind. It is dangerous to sail against the wind. The sea is cruel and we are afraid of the weather; we do not dare set sail.'

'I have never heard of a king', he said, 'who was drowned at sea. Have your ships drawn out into the deep and see what you can do.' (9783–9846)

To do the king's bidding, they agreed to what he asked. They carried the king into the vessel, along with those he wanted to take with him. They drew in the boats and anchors and had people sit quietly and turned the ship towards the wind. They strengthened the shrouds and hoisted the sail; the man who took up his position at the helm headed directly for the wind. With the corner of the mainsail and the spritsail forward, they sailed to Barfleur and in the early morning they arrived at Barfleur on the Cotentin; then the king continued his journey and did not halt until he reached Maine.[319] Then you would have seen

---

[318] The *vo de Luche*, literally 'the face of Lucca', was a miraculous crucifix venerated in the cathedral at Lucca. See D. M. Webb, 'The Holy Face of Lucca', in *Anglo-Norman Studies IX: Proceedings of the Battle Conference 1986* (Woodbridge: Boydell Press, 1987), pp. 227–37.

[319] For a similar story concerning the capture of Le Mans and the reaction of William Rufus see William of Malmesbury, I, pp. 550–51. William gives the date as summer 1099.

messengers hurrying about, summoning barons and knights to come to Le Mans swiftly, for the king would wait for them there. Then you would have seen the land swarming with men, and knights coming to the king. Those in Le Mans were very scared and amazed that the king had come so far so quickly and that his men were increasing in number so rapidly. There are two rivers in the region, one called the Cul, the other the Con. The king had heard of them and frequently heard their names mentioned. Because of the baseness of the names which he knew, he refused to cross these rivers; because of what was fun and a joke he abandoned his straight path and rode up the rivers until he got up above their source. He rode around until he bypassed the Cul and the Con and in this way passed both rivers without ever touching their waters. The two rivers have these names near Le Mans, over towards Alençon.[320] (9847–88)

The king arrived at Le Mans with fierce intent and encamped near the abbey of Saint-Vincent. With the intention of causing harm to those in the city, he constructed the castle of Mont Barbet.* Those in Le Mans could not withstand this and had to abandon the city; they abandoned the city to the king and he took full possession of it. Then he gave all the dwellings and the other possessions held by the inhabitants of the city to those who had defended the tower. Count Helias departed and returned to Château-du-Loir. Then you would have seen a great war begin in Le Mans, Château-du-Loir and Mayet, a small castle in which the inhabitants of Le Mans had taken refuge. As far as the burg called La Fesse, the war was violent and dense. Through the commotion caused by this war, which was devastating the land, the king besieged Mayet because he was unable to obtain peace. He assembled men on all sides; I do not know how many remained there. Mayet was completely surrounded by a ditch, which was wide and deep. In order to attack it better, King Rufus wanted the ditch filled with debris. With him in the army the king had Robert of Bellême, a baron whom people considered very treacherous, but who was on very good terms with the king. Robert of Bellême was a traitor and knew many forms of treachery and evil; he was an expert in treacherous games and feared on account of the harm he did. He told the king that there was a lack of debris and that it was necessary to look for some; he would never capture the castle if he did not fill the ditch with debris. The king said to him jokingly that from each knight he should demand a packhorse, a mule or a palfrey; no other means of transport was possible, and he should throw into the ditch everything he could lay his hands on. Robert departed with a laugh and jokingly told many members of the army that the king had commanded that everything should be thrown into the ditch, whatever came into the servants' hands, even the horses and the peasants. The look on his face and his words thoroughly alarmed everyone. They fled the siege and many went around crying out jokingly:

'Sons of whores, get away, get away! You will all be dead if you dawdle at all. If you can be captured here, you will all be thrown into the ditch.' (9889–9950)

Then they left the siege; it would have been difficult to restrain them. Because of what had happened, the siege failed and the king felt badly let down that he

---

[320] This information concerning the rivers Cul and Con is unique to Wace.

could not maintain the siege and was witnessing the departure of the army. He could not stop the members of the army and they did not dare return; they fled over the paths and the fields. Then the king came to Le Mans. Those in Mayet rejoiced greatly because these men had left the siege; they were astonished by King Rufus, from whom they were rescued so soon. Those in Le Mans fought with greater vigour and the Normans strove to combat them; they besieged towns and castles, set up ambushes, launched attacks, burnt towns, took booty, captured burgesses and robbed peasants; in front of castles and burgs there was often a violent struggle. The war did harm and would have done worse if it had lasted any longer and not come to an end; a large number of horses were killed and many knights wounded and captured. But in one attack the Normans detained Count Helias; they captured and detained him and handed him over to the king in good health. Those who captured him presented him to the king, who desired him greatly. The king sent him to Rouen and ordered him to be guarded; he gave orders that he should be guarded in the tower and put in stout chains. Helias was a good knight, handsome, noble and very robust. To those who were to guard him and who put him in chains he displayed no displeasure and did not feel humiliated.

'My lords', he said, 'keep hold of me! I am a nobleman, guard me well! I will yet make peace with the king and be on good terms with him, I believe. But I will say one thing to you now, by my lord Saint Julian. If I had not been captured so soon, he would not have acquired much in this land. I would have waged war on the king so forcefully that on this side of the Channel he would not have had an entire foot of land or a tower or a castle which was his. But things have turned out differently; he has won and I have lost.' (9951–10006)

I do not know whether he said anything more, but the king was immediately told about how Helias was behaving and what he was saying. So the king had him brought to him and the chains taken off him; he called for his palfrey and had it splendidly saddled. He said to the count:

'My lord count, get on your horse and go wherever you wish. Do the best you can, but on another occasion take better care of yourself, for if I capture you again you will never get out of my prison. I do not want you to think that you have been a casualty of war, but you will not be able to go anywhere without my watching your back closely.' I do not know whether Helias said a word, or how he departed from the king, but I do know that he made peace with him and did not tarry long afterwards. When the king had a favourable wind, he quickly crossed the sea; there he behaved joyfully, but I do not know how long this lasted. He was a man of great power and had been king for thirteen years when, at the height of his excellence, the end of his days came. (10007–36)

The king went to Winchester and stayed there for a long time. Then he said he wanted to go hunting in the New Forest. He rose one morning and asked for his companions; he gave them all arrows, which had been presented to him. Walter Tirel, a much loved knight from the court, took from the king an arrow with which he killed him, so people say. They went into the New Forest, intending to hunt stags and hinds; they set up their watch throughout the forest, but departed in great sadness. For the king, the knights and those who were his archers took up their positions and stretched their bows just as they saw the hinds coming. I do not know who shot arrows and who did not, nor who made the hit or who stretched the bow, but people say, I do not know if he did it, that Tirel shot and killed the king. Many people say he stumbled, got caught up in his cloak and diverted the arrow, and that the steel penetrated the king. Some say that Tirel intended to hit a passing stag; it was running between him and the king. Having stretched his bow, he shot, but his arrow slipped to one side, brushed a tree and was diverted, striking the king and knocking him down dead. Walter Tirel quickly ran to where the king had fallen and was lying. (10037–74)

Henry, the king's younger brother, had gone into the forest with the king, but when his bow was stretched one of the strands of the strings broke; Henry took the bow in his hand and rode quickly to a peasant's lodging in order to get twine or thread to mend his bowstring. While he was delayed over the mending of his bow, an old lady in the dwelling asked a youth who it was who was holding the bow and wanted to go hunting.

'My lady', he said, 'it is Henry, the brother of the king of this country.'

'My friend', she said, 'I know, I know. I will give you a piece of news. Henry will soon be king if my ability to see into the future does not let me down. Remember what I have said, that this man will be king in a little while. If what I say is not true, you can say that I have lied.' When Henry had prepared the bow, he spurred towards the wood, accompanied by a large number of squires whom he had brought with him. He had just drawn near the wood when a man emerged from it; then two came, then three, then nine, then ten in great confusion. Those who told Henry of the king's death frightened him greatly and he rode very swiftly to the spot where he discovered the great sorrow. Then the grief increased, the tears increased and the confusion and the sorrow increased. They carried the body to Winchester and buried him in the monks' choir; Tirel fled to France and lived for a long time in Chaumont. (10075–10116)

The bishops assembled and the barons sent word to each other. They took Henry and crowned him, handing the entire land over to him, not wanting to wait for Robert, who was involved in the capture of Jerusalem. They did not know what he would do or if he would ever return. It is necessary for a kingdom to have a king, for it cannot exist without a king. Henry had to be begged a great deal before he was willing to accept it, saying that he would wait for his brother to return from Jerusalem. But the barons begged him, and many of them advised him, until he did what they told him to do and granted them what they sought. Henry conducted himself in a noble manner and held his land wisely. In order to acquire military assistance and strength, he married the daughter of Malcolm, King of Scotland; her name was Matilda and she pleased him greatly. They had a son and a daughter; the son was called William and he was highly esteemed and much loved. The daughter had the same name as her mother; through the advice of her father, Henry, she was taken to Germany and given in marriage to the emperor; then she was crowned in that realm and called empress.[321] William,

---

[321] King Henry V (1106–26), Holy Roman Emperor, married Matilda (d. 1167). See Marjorie Chibnall, *The Empress Matilda: Queen Consort, Queen Mother and Lady of the English* (Oxford: Blackwell, 1991).

Henry's son, gave and spent generously and dwelt with his father, who loved him very much. He did what his father asked and avoided what his father forbade. The flower of chivalry from England and Normandy set about serving him and had great hopes of him. The king loved him as his heir and provided him with a very beautiful wife, the daughter of Fulk, Count of Anjou, who was later crowned in Jerusalem by election and summoned* there by virtue of his goodness. After her marriage the girl was taken to England, expecting to be lady and queen. But He who is in control of the destiny of all things had arranged things differently, and they turned out differently, for her spouse perished before he could take possession of the kingdom. (10117–72)

William was to cross over to England and he set sail at Barfleur; he was to follow his father. It was dark and the light was not good; the sailors had been drinking and had not worked out the correct course. They had left the jetty and already spread the sail. O God, what a catastrophe and what sorrow there was! They had started out in a light wind and were still close to the harbour when they ran aground on a rock. The ship banged into the rock, split completely and foundered; the sea entered in several places. The sail was large and the ship capsized and everyone perished. Beroul alone escaped; he grabbed hold of a piece of wood and clung on to it, holding on firmly until he reached the shore when people came who lifted him out. He revealed and explained how the king's son had drowned and how the ship had broken up. This Beroul was from Rouen; he was a butcher and sold meat. To get what was due to him he was following the court, for he had sold his meat to a number of people on credit. He had been wearing a furred robe, which had protected him against the great cold. It was winter and very cold; it was Advent and Christmas was coming. Of the great fleet and the convoy only one ship had been lost. The king with all his other men reached Southampton safely; he was distressed and thought it astonishing that his son and his ship had not arrived. In order to get everyone away from Southampton, the king went to Clarendon. He sent men round all the ports and had the shorelines searched to see whether his son and his ship had come and whether they could hear any news of him; he who was dead could not come, nor could anyone hear news about him.[322] (10173–10218)

The king waited at Clarendon and listened intently until the news was known, which had come from across the Channel, about his son and the members of his household, who had perished entirely in that way; such a thing could not be concealed and he was told how it had happened. He suffered grief; he could have had none greater. He fell back on his bed so that no one dared speak to him, and he spoke to no one. I cannot say whether he fainted, but he was lying there without getting up when his chamberlain,* William of Tancarville, a good vassal, said to him:

---

[322] Wace's account of the shipwreck of the *White Ship* (25 November 1120) is very close to that in Orderic's *Historia ecclesiastica* (VI, pp. 296–306). Orderic calls Beroul Beroldus and also states that he was a butcher (p. 298). According to Orderic, there was a second survivor called Geoffrey, son of Gilbert of Laigle (p. 298), but he died before he could be saved. See Orderic, p. 298 n. 2 and p. 299 n. 4, and William of Malmesbury, II, p. 382.

'My lord, get up! Go and eat, do not delay any longer! You would make your enemies happy if you continued to grieve. They would be delighted by your distress. Women should lament and weep, women should express sorrow, but you should take comfort and advise us all. Those who are dead and have drowned* will not live because one mourns them, a son cannot recover a father, nor a father a son by displaying grief. There is no escape in tears. Get up at once and go and eat! The sorrow is intense, the loss great, but you would regret showing any sign of it.' Because of what the chamberlain said, the king got up and sat on the bed; he ordered his food to be brought and had his barons dine with him.[323] In the sight of other people he showed no sign of his sorrow for his son. He took his pleasure with, and devoted his attention to, noble and beautiful women and courtly maidens; this is a game which brings much pleasure. (10219–62)

When the king had lost his son, he sent his daughter-in-law, the daughter of the Count of Anjou, along with splendid equipment and vessels of gold and silver, palfreys, warhorses and a large amount of money, to her father Fulk and her brother Count Geoffrey, who was called Plantagenet and had a great love of forest and woodland pursuits. He was a very noble knight, well educated and a good warrior. Plantagenet wanted to give his sister a husband, if he could, but she said she would not accept this; she would have no other spouse than God. She did not want to debase herself or demean herself through marriage; she was to be queen on earth, and since she could not be so and had failed in this she did not want to take a lesser husband; since she could not have a king, the son of a king, she would not take a husband of lower rank. She said and avowed that she would have no other husband than God. She became a nun at Fontevrault; she could not marry any higher.[324] She committed herself entirely to God and devoted herself to His service; later she became lady of the abbey and an abbess for the rest of her life. (10263–94)

King Rufus was, as I said, killed in the New Forest and after him his younger brother Henry established himself in the kingdom. No one had waited for Robert, but he did come very quickly; he returned from Jerusalem. He had married a noble lady from Conversano, to which he had gone, and brought her to Normandy. Her name was Sibyl and a great deal was said about her beauty in many places. From them a son, William, was born, who became a noble count of Flanders; he was greatly loved by knights and willingly gave them gifts.[325] But he did not survive long, for he soon died of a wound he received in the arm, at a castle against which he was waging war and where he had besieged by force the greatest of his enemies. Those in Flanders and those in France felt great sorrow at his death. (10295–10318)

Robert came from Jerusalem and there was great joy in Rouen over this. He took possession of the whole of Normandy and had it fully in his power, finding

---

[323] This story regarding the intervention of William of Tancarville is unique to Wace.

[324] Matilda of Anjou had married Henry I's son William in 1120. Wace differs from Orderic in saying that, after his death in November of that year, Matilda returned to Anjou, whereas Orderic has her stay in England for several years (VI, p. 330).

[325] Sibyl's son was William Clito, who was Count of Flanders between 1127 and 1128.

no adversary there and being able to do what he wanted throughout. But he was exceedingly distressed and exceedingly angered by Henry, his younger brother, who was king against his wishes; he himself should have been king of England, he said, through seniority of birth. He summoned barons and knights and entreated neighbours and mercenaries; with a large number of men, ships and noble knights he crossed the sea and came to Portchester. From there he set off to capture Winchester, but was told that the queen, his sister-in-law, was in childbirth, and he said it would be a base act to attack a lady in childbirth. He turned his men towards London, for he expected to find the king there. They were already in Alton Wood when the duke encountered a man who told him that the king was coming and would meet him on the other side of the wood, where he was waiting; he should take care not to advance rashly, for the king was intending to surprise him as he came out of the wood.[326] Then you would have heard the knights asking for their arms and their warhorses, donning their hauberks and lacing up their helmets, girding on their swords and issuing many threats, jumping quickly on to their horses, shields around their necks and holding their lances; they all strove to arm themselves well and sit securely in their saddles. (10319–58)

The king had found out about the duke's arrival and it became well known. The duke knew about the approach of the king, who arrived in great haste; each thought he would encounter the other while going through Alton Wood. They remained like this for a long time and feared each other for a long time, each afraid of entering the wood and no one wanting to go back. On both sides there were sons and fathers, uncles, nephews, cousins or brothers, and no one dared advance for fear of killing his relatives. No one wanted to strike his cousin, his relative or his neighbour. In this way they remained stationary for a long time and for a long time they were all fearful, with no one daring to advance as they were afraid of encountering their relatives; they had greater fear of their friends than they had of their enemies. The king was afraid and the duke was afraid, but I do not know which was more so; they were afraid and fearful that they would be fighting their relatives; on both sides they were afraid and none of them dared advance. The barons realised and were aware that things were going badly, that relative would be killing relative, cousin cousin and brother brother, relative relative and a son his father. They all made up their mind that they would act quite differently and bring about peace between the brothers and never fight for them. (10359–96)

Robert, who held Bellême and was on good terms with the duke, and the lord of Mortain, which belonged to his honour – people say he was called William –, and Robert FitzHaimo,[327] along with other powerful barons whose names I do not know and who held lands from both the king and the duke and owed service to

---

[326] On Robert's invasion of England see Hollister, pp. 88–95, who acknowledges the importance of Wace's account, in particular his information concerning the queen's pregnancy and his reference to Alton in Hampshire (pp. 88–95, esp. p. 88, n. 6, and p. 90).

[327] Robert FitzHaimo was the son of Haimo, sheriff of Kent. The latter was the son of Haimo of Val-ès-Dunes.

both of them, undertook to bring about the peace, because of their fear of the battle. They went back and forth from the king to the duke, carrying messages between them; they sought to achieve peace and spoke of harmony. They told the duke he should make peace and not seek from the king something he should not do or which could not be done, for after he had been crowned he ought not to be deposed; he would rather be struck dead than be toppled from the kingdom. A brother should not do this to his brother or make so many men fight each other; on both sides there were sons and fathers and on both sides nephews and brothers.

'My lord', they said, 'have mercy, in God's name! You who have been to the Holy Sepulchre should instruct us all, teach us and educate us. A battle is greatly to be feared. One cannot bring forces together* in the way you and the king have done without a large number of men being killed. You could lose such good friends that you would never again know joy. Moreover, a man who from the start expects to win and is ready for action can end up departing wretchedly and doing so in great shame. Make peace and, if you are reconciled, be friends as you should be.' (10397–10440)

They said such things to the duke and did the same with the king. They said so much, begged so much and advised the king so much that each submitted to the judgement of the barons on their side. Through their advice they were reconciled and accepted their judgement. Why should I go on relating this to you or delay matters with words? It was established by covenant that from that time onward, each year as long as he lived, the king would give Duke Robert three thousand marks of silver to keep the peace and repress all anger, and that if war broke out against the duke, as soon as he had informed the king, he would find a hundred knights and more for him, as long as the war lasted. The duke would do the same, as soon as the king informed him. The king made this agreement and he had Domfront and the Cotentin in his possession. He had held Domfront for a long time and had control over the Cotentin; he did not want to let these two go, but he had to grant them to the duke. In this way there was an agreement between them, and it was confirmed that the king would pay the money and the duke would abide by this. (10441–72)

Duke Robert went back to his ships* and the king remained at peace. From that time he did not find anyone in England who moved against him or waged war on him. But he was hostile to those who had acted against him and helped the duke cross the sea in order to cause him harm and upset; he never showed any love for these men. He blamed William, the lord of Mortain, his first cousin, son of Robert FitzHerluin, through whose advice the duke had acted and done what he suggested to him. In addition, Robert of Bellême, son of Roger of Montgomery, was on bad terms with King Henry because he had served the duke. Through these men, as the king said, the duke had done whatever he had done; the king could not have loved these men in any way and they were very much hated by him. He had the land each of them held in England taken away from them and refused to allow or agree to anyone exchanging with them. They all complained to Duke Robert that it was through their love for him that they were losing their land; what they had lost because of him ought to be restored to them. A number of other barons also appealed to the duke in this matter. While a number of people who were losing their fiefs the other side of the Channel were making their complaints, the Count of Warenne arrived; his name was William and he held Lewes[328] and a large number of other lands beyond the territory of his county, of which the king had completely dispossessed him. William had abandoned everything to him.[329] (10473–512)

King Henry had hated Count William for a long time and, if it pleases you, I shall tell you briefly the reason for this hatred. When Henry was with King Rufus, who was always very arrogant, his interest, before he had any land or revenues, lay in dogs and woodlands; he had his dogs, went into the woods and delighted in hunting. When he was leading a pack of dogs, you would often have heard him blowing his horn and, if he wanted to go hunting, he had a large number of brachets brought along. Often, when they came to him, he had the greyhounds placed in a hide.* Where forests, dogs and hunting were concerned, he was very skilled; according to the opportunity available, he used to capture stags, hinds and boar. Because of the stags he used to catch and the way he constantly searched the forests, Count William used to laugh at him. As a joke, he called him Stag's Foot and often attributed to him, by way of a joke, the ability to determine from a stag's tracks how many antlers it had. This often made Henry angry, but because of the king, whom he feared greatly, he did not dare quarrel with the count, for the king loved the count very much.[330] Henry would suffer and listen to something which upset him greatly. When he became king, he remembered the old taunts with which the count used to mock him; he could not forget them. For this reason alone – this is what people said to each other – William was hated by the king and dispossessed of his land. Many people say, whatever I myself say, that this dispossession was the product of cunning and deviousness and false and feigned hatred, and that, because the count was so cunning, he was sent to Normandy to speak to the duke, for he was very skilled at plotting to do harm. He complained to the duke that King Henry had hated him because of his love for him; he was afraid he had lost his land unless the duke could restore it to him. Because of the complaints and the outcry which the duke heard from a number of people, he suddenly crossed the sea to Southampton in safety, with a dozen knights, in addition to men-at-arms and squires; he was going to ask the king, he said, to return their land to his barons. (10513–74)

The king, who was in Winchester, heard all about this affair involving the duke, and he soon heard what it was he wanted. He told his men he would capture the duke and throw him into prison; he would never escape. Robert, who was Count of Meulan and considered to be very valiant – he was a wise and very learned man – went forward and spoke to the king.

'My lord', he said, 'have mercy for God's sake! You should not behave in that way. You should not capture your brother or cause him such shame. But if you are willing to trust me, I will release you from the need to return the money you owe

---

[328] To the manuscript reading *qui les maintint* Holden prefers the reading *qui Leswes tint* (note to v. 10508, vol. 3, p. 245). William I of Warenne (d. 1088) was buried in the abbey at Lewes (now in West Sussex), which he himself had built.

[329] This William was William II of Warenne (d. 1137/38). Wace is the unique source for the story given here. Hollister accepts the story (p. 93 n. 5).

[330] Holden has emended vv. 10538–44 extensively, as the original is 'full of incoherences'.

the duke, before he is able to leave. And if you wish to grant it, I want to go and speak to the duke.'

'Go ahead', said the king, 'I agree to this. I do not mistrust you in any way.' The count had just put on his spurs and his horse had been brought when the king called him back; he wanted to talk to him again. I do not know what they said to each other, but they were deep in discussion; then the count sped away again, as if there were an emergency. He found the duke near Southampton. Meeting him on his path, he drew him to one side and asked him how things were going:

'My lord', he said, 'how are you? Who is behind all this and what are you thinking of? Demons are behind it, I believe. What are you doing in this country? You have forsworn all of it and handed it over to the king freely in return for the money he is to give you; you are behaving very reprehensibly. You have received bad advice, believed bad advice and acted very wrongfully, since without safe-conduct and permission you have entered this country without any other forces. The king says he will have you seized and you cannot protect yourself against him. How dreadful it would be if he captured you, since you have no one to protect you. And if he once captures you, you will never get out of his prison.' (10575–10628)

The duke was horrified and terribly afraid. He took hold of his reins and came to a stop, realising for the first time that King Henry hated him and would very soon capture him. He wanted to return to Southampton, set sail there and return to Normandy, but he would be severely reproached for this, nor would he be able to sail a ship immediately against the wind and it would give an unfortunate impression if he turned back in this way.

'My lord count, 'he said, 'what do you advise, given the weather you can see?'

'I advise', he replied, 'in true faith, in view of the evident weather conditions, that you speak to the queen, who has risen from childbed, and place yourself in her safe-conduct, for otherwise all of you will be captured. If she provides safe-conduct for you, you can proceed in safety.' Duke Robert was very worried and terrified of being caught. He went to speak to the queen before daring go to the king. The queen gave him her assurance and received him and honoured him well. The duke came to an agreement with her and entirely relinquished his claim to all the money the king was to give him each year as long as he lived. (10629–62)

Because of what he had done for her, the queen was very well disposed towards the duke, and the king, when he heard of this, tempered his anger towards him. The duke went to the court, and when he did so he spoke to the king, not wanting there to be any suspicions or harmful intent.

'I have not come here', he said, 'with a show of force, or arrived here to diminish your revenues or make a claim on your lands, nor for you to pay me the money you owe me according to our established agreement. You do not have to render me what was agreed, and I do not have to take it from you. We were born of one father and mother; we have the same father and mother. I must maintain my brotherly relationship with you, I to you just as you to me. As you are aware, you should be as noble as I am, and between us there is no advantage, it seems to me, other than seniority of birth; that was bestowed on you as soon as you were crowned. The dignity of the crown gives you a great advantage.

Because I love and trust you, I grant you exemption from the money which you should give me as long as you rule this kingdom. I release you, be free and do not seek anything further as far as I am concerned. I have given the queen everything and released you. I grant it to her for love of you and release you because of my own honour. When you wish and desire it, give me some of your fine possessions, pay me in fine things and I will take them, for that is right.' 'Thank you', said the king, 'you have spoken in true courtly fashion.' When the duke was given assurances and thought he had made peace, he made his request to the king, doing so on the part of his barons; the king said the duke could go when it pleased him. He would do whatever was his duty. The king did not wish to do any more than that and the duke was unable to do any more. He who has lost has lost; the king still held what he had held. The duke came to his own land, very upset and considering himself a fool for making such a foolish journey and releasing the king from all the money he owed him. He could never again recover it,* having given it to the queen and released the king completely; he had not made any gains in anything he had asked of him.[331] (10663–10726)

Duke Robert knew from what had happened that the king had scarcely any love for him and he was very keen to take his revenge on him; he had a great desire to vanquish him and hated whatever the king loved and praised what he blamed. For this reason a great quarrel arose between them which could not be ended peacefully. Because of what was being said by those who were losing their fiefs abroad, the duke did harm to those on the Cotentin and those in Domfront in the Passais.[332] The king frequently sent word to him that he was doing wrong by him and should act better towards him. None of his threats were of any use; he was seizing his revenues, pursuing his men and refusing to maintain the agreement with regard to the Cotentin, which he was accustomed to rule. Complaints were frequently being heard and he refused to tolerate this any longer. The duke often informed him that he ruled the Cotentin and would go on doing so and that he would never let him have Domfront; he would rule it as long as he could. Domfront was his possession and so was the Cotentin; if the duke took something from his own fief, the king should not bear him any ill will, for if the king took heed of what was reasonable the duke was doing nothing but right by him. (10727–56)

When the king had heard everything and the spokesman had fallen silent, a knight, who spoke to the king on the duke's behalf, stood up. He had come from Normandy and was highly esteemed and learned; he held land from both the duke and the king and owed fealty to both of them.

'My lord', he said, 'I have come from across the Channel. I am a vassal of the duke and hold land from him, and I hold land both from you and from him. I belong and have belonged to each of you.* I have to state what is appropriate for me and you should not feel any anger towards me, for you have the whole of

---

[331] This account of Duke Robert's visit to England is remarkably detailed. Of particular interest is the discussion with Queen Matilda.

[332] Being familiar with the Cotentin, Wace would have known from local sources about the quarrels between Henry I and Robert concerning the Cotentin and Domfront.

England and you alone rule all of it. The duke should also have whatever belongs to Normandy; you should have everything on this side and he on that side. Thus each of you will have a great deal; this should suffice for each of you. It would serve no purpose to seek further sovereignty. You wish to take away a part of Normandy which he holds – but you would not do so, I hope.* The duke will certainly not stand for it; he claims the Cotentin and Domfront, which are part of his inheritance. Your father granted them to him when he died and came to his end; he gave him his entire inheritance according to justice and seniority of birth. Therefore, the crown you wear and the land you rule would have come to him, if reason had been maintained with regard to him. But now things have turned out so that you have received the kingdom and you ought to have advanced his cause and left Normandy in peace, through seniority of birth and justice and through what is honourable and natural. You are fully aware that he is the elder and that you would be reproached because of this.' (10757–10800)

The messengers spoke in this way and set about making peace. They would very much have liked, if they could, to bring about peace between the two brothers, but the king refused to accept it; he was not willing to give the duke a truce. He repeatedly blamed the duke for having mocked him greatly and he would never make peace with him; when he could, he would get what was rightfully his. The messengers departed and returned to Normandy; they were unable to make any progress with the king. Now the duke should prepare to defend himself! They told Duke Robert what they had discovered with regard to the king. The duke greatly feared the king, from whom he had received no surety. Throughout Normandy he sent out a proclamation, a command and an edict that no knight who was his vassal, who held land and a fief from him, should cross over to England nor remain with the king, nor should he become a vassal of the king or swear any oath to him; he should remain in Normandy and offer service for his fief to the duke.[333] Those who were from England and lived in England should remain in England and offer service for their fief to the king. For no one, in his estimation, he said – and I am certain he was right – could serve two lords or love them equally without supporting one of them more than the other and wanting more for one than for the other. (10801–38)

So there suddenly began the war which could not be ended peacefully until the duke was captured and the king had won a complete victory. Through traitors and slanderers, flatterers and deceivers – may they take a dreadful tumble! – the king's and the duke's anger increased.* There was a great deal of coming and going and they spoke ill of each other, not caring about any losses, providing each of them did what he liked. The king put his trust in money, which he had in abundance. He crossed over to Normandy and, having a large quantity of money, took a large number of men with him.[334] The lords of the Cotentin received him and were delighted by his arrival. With great barrels and carts he had the money carried with him. To chastelains and barons, who had towers and fortified

---

[333] Wace is the only source for this ducal proclamation.

[334] This probably refers to Henry I's 'invasion' of Normandy in 1105 (see Orderic, VI, pp. 60–61) rather than to his brief visit in 1104 (Orderic, VI, pp. 56–57).

dwellings, and to good warriors and marquises he gave so much and promised so much that they abandoned Duke Robert and waged war on the king's side. Even those who held lands from the duke and owed him fealty left the duke in favour of the king, abandoning their true lord. Suddenly the land was in great fear and people were very much afraid. The war was great and they were dismayed. They took everything to the cemeteries, leaving nothing in their houses for robbers and thieves. The king had a large amount of sterlings and he summoned the men from Le Mans and Anjou and the Bretons who were supporting him, and they came willingly at the prospect of gain. However many mercenaries came, there were not too many to prevent the king from retaining them all; no one who maintained his period of service failed to be rewarded with provisions. (10839–82)

The duke had scarcely any money, for he was spending it freely. His revenues were soon completely exhausted and his feudal aid used up; with all this spending and giving there was no chance of their flourishing. He had his castles rebuilt, the walls repaired and strengthened, brattices and battlements constructed and trenches made in front of castles. At Caen he built a trench which can still be pointed out, stretching from Rue d'Esmeisine[335] to Porte Milet; part of the Orne flows there, where the tide comes in and out. When the duke had mercenaries, he paid them well when he could, and when he could not pay them and did not dare anger them, for they were quick to go over to the king's side and fight with the king, he had his burgesses brought and handed them over to the mercenaries* in due form, this one for twenty pounds, that one for a hundred, this one for thirty, that one for forty, this one for fifty or sixty. The burgesses did not dare serve him and he was hated by many of them. They diverted their possessions and property to abbeys and they themselves fled there, not daring to wait for him in the burgs; for this reason many men failed the duke. When news of this came to him, he said at once:

'Let us forget this! We cannot fight everyone. Let them come, let them go! We cannot retain everyone.' He was not very prudent and indeed was very negligent; people had considered him to be negligent since his return from the Holy Land. Negligence seems like cowardice and many people admonished him for it, but in spite of being thoroughly admonished he showed no improvement. When the duke had nothing to give, being either unable to give or not wanting to do so, he evaded any difficulty with promises; he promised much and gave little. Gonthier, who is said to be from Aunay, was on the duke's side against the king; he was a knight of great nobility and supported the duke in good faith.[336] Gonthier was in charge of the large number of troops and performed many great acts of chivalry.[337] He distributed provisions and it was through him that the duke gave

---

[335] The base manuscript reads *la rue Meisine* 'Rue Meisine'. Holden accepts Andresen's suggested reading *la rue Oismeisine* (literally 'Hiémois Street': see note to v. 10895, vol. 3, p. 247). See also vv. 11318–19. The Rue d'Esmeisine is now the Rue Saint-Jean. On Wace's knowledge of Caen, see Holmes, pp. 57–60.

[336] Gohier de l'Aunei is probably the Gunherius de Alneio mentioned by Orderic as the duke's castellan of Bayeux (IV, 203, VI, 78).

[337] In place of *granz chevaleries* 'acts of great chivalry' in v. 10940 Holden prefers *granz chevaucies* 'great military expeditions' (note to v. 10940, vol. 3, p. 247).

gifts; he was warden of Caen and Bayeux and often went from the one to the other. (10883–10944)

In front of Bayeux, at Saint-Joire – as the man who knows the story states – there took place at that time an encounter between knights from the region who were staying in Bayeux and the king's men who were waiting there. The town was in a state of great agitation; the king's men had attacked it and there were many good knights there, with infantrymen and archers above the ditches. Neither side showed any pity for the other and many inhabitants left the city.[338] The king had a mercenary by the name of Brun, a recently dubbed knight who had come from a far-off land to acquire fame and perform acts of chivalry. He possessed the very finest equipment and his weapons were of superb quality. There was not a single man at court whose accoutrements matched those of Brun; on his horse he sat nobly and very richly attired. He was attached to his saddle with tight bindings round his thighs; he could not have received a blow powerful enough to dislodge him from the saddle. He raised his lance, took his shield, spurred his horse and entered the battlefield; his horse galloped along and Brun was quite clearly seeking a joust. Robert of Argence* had arrived; he had come from Bayeux and was sitting on his horse, well armed and well prepared to joust. He saw Brun on the other side, intent on jousting; with his lance raised he took his shield, very desirous of a joust. The knights, who were on the field and had caught sight of the two vassals who had taken the field in order to joust and were clearly seeking a joust, cleared the area so that they could joust; they issued orders to the archers and the infantrymen not to do any harm and remain at peace, in spite of anything they may witness. The area was cleared and no one did any harm there. (10945–96)

When the area was cleared and the joust arranged, the knights who were to joust came to a standstill, at the far end of the battlefield. On their swiftly-moving horses they soon launched themselves at each other; one rode towards the other, spurring his horse and letting go his reins. They held their shields in front of their chests and came together with lances raised, attacking each other with such great violence that they could be seen from all sides. Lord Brun struck Robert so forcibly that he deprived him of his shield, dislodging it from around his neck and knocking him to one side. But Robert stayed firm in his stirrups, raised himself upright with a great show of strength and hit Brun with such power on his saddle-bows, in front of his shield, that he split them in two and transfixed him on the saddle-bows behind; he could not be knocked down on to the ground, for he was hanging by his thighs. Brun fainted on his horse, but he turned his head downwards. People came running from all sides and took hold of Brun, who was hanging down; they detached him from the saddle and laid him down on the ground. His soul departed; it could no longer remain. You would have heard a great deal of weeping and grieving. Those from the towns and the burgs came running up from all sides, lamenting greatly and weeping profusely, mourning Brun's beauty. Some grieved and wept for him profusely; others, who had never before seen him or known anything about him, lamented him. Men-at-arms,

---

[338] See Holden's note to v. 10956 (vol. 3, p. 247).

whose duty it was to serve him and who were from his country, cried out and grieved a great deal, saying around the body:

'O Brun, Lord Brun, noble baron Brun! We have very good reason to weep for you! We will never return to our own country, since we cannot take you back. Who would dare tell your friends that you have been killed? We ought to die for you, but you cannot be saved by us.' They grieved and lamented greatly, then took the body away from there. Because of Brun's death, they departed and abandoned the field on both sides; no further harm was done that day and there was no more jousting or shooting of arrows.[339] The king conceived a hatred for Robert, as if he had intended to kill him, and he did not dare remain in Normandy. But when the war was over, he returned to Apulia with his equipment, to acquaintances he had there. (10997–11060)

For a long time the inhabitants of Bayeux defended themselves very stoutly, not wanting to surrender to the king; he could not take them by force. Gonthier, who was their constable, a brave and valiant knight, rode throughout the region, bringing prisoners and booty which greatly assisted the town. He spent lavishly and gave away a large amount of money, getting and giving a great deal of credit and borrowing and disbursing a great deal. Robert, who is said to have been the son of Haimo – he was regarded as a noble baron – and who held the honour of Torigni with extensive lands around Creully, had quarrelled with his lord the duke and gone over to King Henry. He was seized one morning in Secqueville-en-Bessin when in the process of capturing the Bessin and taking the entire country. The duke's household knights heard this and forced their way into Secqueville; the men from Caen came up swiftly and those from Bayeux were very soon there. Robert entered the church, climbing up as far as the bell-tower, but he could not stay up there long; whether he liked it or not, he had to come down, for fire was brought there which set the church alight. So, because of the fire, he came down and surrendered to those from Bayeux. Robert was captured, well guarded and taken to Bayeux. The knaves who were taking him could scarcely be prevented from threatening and striking him;[340] they frequently called out: 'The rope, the rope for the traitor who has abandoned his rightful lord!' (11061–1102)

The king, who was very displeased, saw that Bayeux was holding out for so long; because of Bayeux he was losing Caen and all the advantage gained from the Bessin, for a large number of troops, who were an obstacle to them, were in Bayeux. From Le Mans he summoned Count Helias, who brought many barons and was very keen to serve the king; he came with great eagerness. The king and the count assembled and went to Bayeux together, where they set light to the burg. Then you would have seen flames leaping high, chapels and churches burning, houses and food-stores toppling, as well as the episcopal church, in which there were many wealthy clergy; the church was entirely destroyed and its precious possessions taken outside. Count Helias gained great fame from this and performed many acts of chivalry there. The men from Le Mans, who were

---

[339] This story of the joust between Brun and Robert of Argence is unique to Wace.
[340] See Holden's note to this line (vol. 3, p. 248). After v. 11102 MS B adds a further six lines.

with him, took away whatever they found; many things were carried away and the king gave them a large part of them. In this way the king had possession of the city and power over the area; he left nothing as far as Caen and the war grew and became more violent. The duke could not recover anything or return to Bayeux. No one could remain between Bayeux and Caen; the peasants did not dare till the land, join their oxen together or plough the fields and the merchants did not dare go about the town or transport their merchandise. There was war throughout the land, each one wanting to overcome the other. The king was strong and the duke was strong. The war lasted for six years or more before peace could be had there; they were men of great power. I do not wish to relate the adventures, often good and often harsh, which befell the king, the duke and the households they ruled as long as the war lasted. One man lost who later won. This happens in warfare; one man loses today who wins tomorrow. You are well aware that fortune is not always equal for all men; a man who was down can come up again. Things are not the same for all or constant for all.* Because of the gifts he gave, the king had most of the knights and the best of the barons with him; they abandoned the duke for the king. (11103–62)

The king had in his prison a knight by the name of Thierry. His family was from Caen and he was born in Caen, the son of Ralph FitzOgier.[341] His relatives had loved him very dearly. He was a knight of great courage with many wounds on his face; he was bold, as was evident from the great injuries he had received. This Thierry and many more men, the finest in Caen, had been captured by Robert the Old of Saint-Rémy at Cagny in the Hiémois.[342] They were travelling from Argences to Caen with the intention of going to Caen, but this Robert, who was cunning, was lying in wait for them and brought them to a halt. He had assembled* his friends and knights from his region and was pretending to go hunting in order to lie in wait for the men from Caen. When he saw the opportunity, he lay in wait for them and captured them all; none of them escaped. It was easy to capture them; they could not defend themselves as they had insufficient knights and were not riding their warhorses. Thierry fought stoutly and defended himself for a long time, but because of the wounds to his face he was knocked down and captured. When Robert of Saint-Rémy had taken his booty as he pleased, he prepared his prisoners and bound them over by oath not to escape. He took them all to Torigni, not wanting to go to Saint-Rémy. He sold and handed over his prisoners to Robert FitzHaimo, who at that time was of great renown; he bought them very willingly.[343] By way of agreement, in this first instance, he

[341] Ralph FitzOgier is mentioned in several charters from Caen. See *Les Actes de Guillaume le Conquérant et la reine Matilde pour les abbayes caennaises*, ed. by L. Musset (Caen: Société d'Impressions Caron, 1967), nos 7, 14, 18, 25 and 27. See also van Houts, 'Wace as Historian', pp. xxxix–xl.

[342] C. W. David discusses this passage and gives credence to Wace's unique information on Robert (*Robert Curthose*, p. 166 n. 114). David identifies Saint-Rémy as Saint-Rémy-des-Landes (Manche, near La Haye du Puis). Holden (note to v. 11176, vol. 3, p. 248) hesitates between Saint-Rémy-des-Landes and the Saint-Rémy which lies five kilometres south of Thury-Harcourt (Orne); the latter is more likely.

[343] On Robert FitzHaimo (d. 1107) see Douglas, *Domesday Monachorum*, pp. 55–56, and the *GND*, II, pp. 248–49.

gave him the whole of Charbonière and granted him other lands and fiefs in a number of places. Robert FitzHaimo thought that, if he could, he would promote his own cause thanks to the prisoners. He sent a messenger at once to Domfront, informing the king, who was there, that he should come to him without delay, for he thought he could advance his cause greatly. (11163–11214).

The king mounted his horse at once, as soon as he heard the summons, and found Robert at Yvrandes, the place to which he had summoned him. Yvrandes is in a hermitage, surrounded by a great wood called the Lande Pourrie; the church is dedicated to the Virgin Mary.[344] Robert met the king, spoke to him in secret and told him what had happened. The king was pleased and greatly cheered by the prisoners Robert had bought; they were powerful men, born in Caen, whom the lord of Saint-Rémy had captured and placed under his protection. Through these men he could have Caen, if he conducted himself sensibly. The king then granted Robert FitzHaimo the wardenship of Caen as a fief, for himself for all time and for his heir, as soon as he could get possession of it; he also gave him other revenues which Robert had asked of him. The king cherished Robert greatly and Robert served him well; he had abandoned the duke in favour of him, as a result of which he had a very bad reputation. (11215–42)

Why should I tell you any more about this, or dwell on it any longer? Discussion continued, but it was kept between them, until a conclusion was reached concerning an agreement about the king and the prisoners, that the king would hand over the prisoners, declare them entirely free and make them rich men, giving them lands and possessions; the prisoners would hand over Caen and receive the king within it. In order to conceal this discussion, so that no one could create an obstacle for them in this matter, the prisoners provided hostages, sons and nephews from their lineage, in order to pay off their ransoms, for he had made them swear this. Through ruse and cunning, and the enemies' machinations,[345] the ransoms were fixed, established and guaranteed by hostages. In order to deceive the common people, so that nothing would be known about all this, they pretended to obtain what was necessary and pay their ransoms; for if the poor people had known that things were going to turn out this way, the king would never have had Caen without a great struggle. But through Thierry and Ralph, through Nicholas and Aiulf and through their rich families, which had many members, and through their near neighbours, who were captured over towards Argences, this plan was hatched and concealed from the poor.[346] Many men, whose names I cannot tell you, and I do not wish to write down lies, were involved in this affair and consented to what happened. Covetousness is an evil thing and many evil things stem from it; it is the root of sin, and all evils are begun because of it. Through the promises made by the king, who promised lands to many men, and in order to free their friends, whom they could not

---

[344] Yvrandes is six kilometres south of Tinchebray.

[345] See Holden's note to v. 11262 (vol. 3, p. 248).

[346] Of the four men mentioned, Thierry, Ralph, Nicholas and Aiulf, only Thierry, son of Ralph FitzOgier, has been identified. See Chibnall's note to book XI of Orderic's *Historia ecclesiastica* (IV, p. 79 n. 5).

redeem, and because they repeatedly saw that the barons were abandoning the duke, the inhabitants of Caen let the duke down and went over to King Henry. (11243–97)

At that time there was a garden in Caen, near the church Saint-Martin, between the church and the wall next to Porte Arthur; there the gathering took place and the decision was agreed upon to withdraw support from Duke Robert. You can now hear what is clearly a miracle! For never since this meeting – I can say this in truth – has the garden borne fruit; it has produced neither apples nor any other fruit. The duke realised and saw quickly, and was quickly advised and told, how the occupants of Caen were withdrawing their support from him and would surrender Caen to the king. He was advised to depart before worse harm came to him, for the king's men, who were on their way to the Bessin, were close by. The duke was very much afraid of the burgesses and made his way to the Hiémois; he went though Porte Milet with the numerous household knights he was leading. A gate-keeper, by the name of Taisson – I do not know if he had any other name[347] – encountered a chamberlain[348] and robbed him of a bag; the duke moved forward, not wanting to go back for such matters. I do not know whether he later returned it to him, but I do know he took it from him. The rascals who saw what Taisson had done did the same and robbed the squires, knocking them down and manhandling them. The crowd kept going and did not look back; the duke kept going, never to return there. (11298–11336)

The war was great and the anger great – but I cannot relate or tell everything – between King Henry and his brother, born of one father and one mother. The king possessed very great power and he had more men and more money from England, which he ruled in peace; thus he did as he pleased. Why should I go on with this tale? The king continued fighting, taking castles and towns by force and providing gifts from his wealth, until he besieged Tinchebray and set up his siege around it in opposition to the Count of Mortain, who was not far from there.[349] The count and the duke came together and summoned all their good neighbours; they wanted to help the castle and rescue all the equipment inside, but at their time of need they let the duke down and left him on bad terms, because of the promises made and the fiefs granted to a large number of men. The duke put his trust in what was rightfully his and in the men he expected to have on his side; with all the men he brought with him he thought he could get the siege lifted. The battle was soon joined, but it did not last long. Those who came attacked well and the besiegers held out well; scarcely any men were killed. The duke was soon laid low and captured, and with him the Count of Mortain; they were both captured in the battle. The duke was captured and the count was captured; neither of them was rescued by their own men. Many men who held fiefs from them and who should have been with them, abandoned their lord at this time of need; as a result

---

[347] Taisson (Latin Taxo, Taissimus) is the name of the family which founded Saint-Étienne at Fontenay. The family were also benefactors of the monasteries at Caen.

[348] William of Malmesbury refers to him as an *armigero* 'squire' (I, p. 706).

[349] The Count of Mortain was William, son of Robert Count of Mortain, half-brother to William the Conqueror. The battle of Tinchebray took place on 28 September 1106.

of their shameful actions, they received rewards from the king, for which they were severely reproached. (11337–80)

The king had the duke and the count in his power, whoever might be honoured or shamed thereby. He acts very shamefully, no one could do worse who betrays his liege lord. No man, for any reason, should fail his earthly lord; he should protect his life and limb and uphold his earthly honour. He who abandoned his lord did wrong; the duke was captured and the count with him. The lord of Bellême departed; he received no blow and gave no blow.[350] He left with his troops, with neither loss nor gain. The king had his prisoners, the duke and the count, sent across the Channel; no one could bring about a reconciliation with him and they could not escape. Throughout Normandy he commanded that nothing should be removed or taken away; they should go in peace and come in peace and, as they had held lands, so they should continue to do so. Let him whose felony has been proved be destroyed and dismembered. The prisoners, who were transported across the Channel, were well looked after. Robert, Count of Gloucester, who was the bastard son of the king, held the duke in Cardiff in Wales, as long as he lived; he died in Cardiff in Wales, in the prison where he lay for a long time. From Cardiff his body was carried to Gloucester and buried. The Count of Mortain lived in King Henry's prison until the death of King Henry, who reigned for thirty-seven years.[351] (11381–11418)

Let he whose business it is continue the story. I am referring to Master Beneeit, who has undertaken to tell of this affair, as the king has assigned the task to him; since the king asked him to do it, I must abandon it and fall silent. The king in the past was very good to me. He gave me a great deal and promised me more, and if he had given me everything he promised me things would have gone better for me. I could not have it, it did not please the king; but it is not my fault. I have known three king Henrys and seen them all in Normandy; all three had lordship over Normandy and England. The second Henry, about whom I am talking, was the grandson of the first Henry and born of Matilda, the empress, and the third was the son of the second. Here ends the book of Master Wace; anyone who wishes to do more, let him do it. (11419–40)

---

[350] The lord of Bellême was Robert of Bellême. See the chapter 'Robert of Bellême', in George Slocombe, *The Sons of the Conqueror: Robert Curthose, William Rufus, Henry Beauclerc and the Grandson, Stephen* (London: Hutchinson, 1960), pp. 43–50, and K. Thompson, 'Robert of Bellême Reconsidered', in *Anglo-Norman Studies XIII: Proceedings of the Battle Conference 1990* (Woodbridge: Boydell Press, 1991), pp. 263–86.

[351] Robert Curthose remained in prison from 1106 until his death in 1134. The date of William of Mortain's death is unknown.

APPENDIX

LE ROUMANZ DE ROU ET
DES DUS DE NORMENDIE[352]

---

[352] For the status of the Appendix within the composition of the *Roman de Rou* see the Introduction, p. xxiii, above. The first 122 lines of the Appendix correspond to the first 142 lines of Part III. Vv. 7–18 and 95–96 of the Appendix have no equivalent in III and twenty lines of III (plus lacunae after vv. 65 and 68) are not found in the Appendix. For a full list of correspondences see Holden, vol. 3, p. 249.

To remember the deeds, words and ways of our ancestors, books, chronicles and histories should be read out at festivals, and also to remember the wicked deeds of wicked men and the brave deeds of brave men. For this reason great knowledge and great skill were shown by those who were first to write, and particularly by the authors who composed books and writings concerning the noble deeds and fine words of barons and lords in times gone by. They would have been consigned to oblivion had it not been for the degree of remembrance which writing creates for us and which recounts stories for us. There have been many cities with a great deal of wealth and power of which we would have known nothing, if we have not had these writings. Thebes has a great reputation and Babylon possessed great power; Troyes had great power and Nineveh was long and broad, but anyone who now went in search of these locations would scarcely find any trace of them. Nebuchadnezzar was king and he built a golden statue, sixty cubits high and six cubits broad;* if anyone wanted to see his body now, he would not, I believe, find anyone who could explain or state where one could find his bones or ashes. But through the good clerics who wrote things down and committed the deeds to books we can speak of ages past and tell of many great works. Alexander was a powerful king; in twelve years he captured twelve kingdoms. He had many lands and a great deal of wealth, and he was a king of great power. But if he made conquests, this did him little good; he was poisoned and died. (1–46)

Caesar, who did so much, had such ability and conquered and possessed the entire world – never has any man before or since, I believe, conquered so much –, was then, as we read, treacherously killed in the Capitol. Neither of these two men, who conquered so much, had so many lands and captured so many kings, had when he died any more of his own domain than his own length. What good has all this done them? What have they achieved by their fame and conquests? Only what people* say about who Alexander and Caesar were, according to what they have found in books; all that remains of them is their names. They would have been forgotten if they had not been written about. Everything turns to decline, everything fails, everything dies, everything comes to an end. A man dies, iron wears out, wood rots, a tower collapses, a wall falls down, a rose withers, a horse stumbles, cloth grows old; everything made by hand perishes. I understand completely and am fully aware that all men die, cleric and lay, and that after their death their fame will be short-lived, unless it is set down in a book by a cleric; it cannot survive or live on in any other way. Over time, as the years go by and through changes in language, towns, cities and regions* have lost their original names. England was called Britain and its first name was Albion; London was called Trinovant and before that New Troy. Brittany was Armorica and Alemainne Germany. Paris was called Lutetia, the land of Greece Pelasge,[353]

---

[353] The form in the manuscript here is *Pelarge* (cf. III, v. 30, where the form is *Pelasge*).

Apulia and Lombardy Italy and Constantinople Byzantium. Scotland used to be called Albany, Poitou and Gascony Aquitaine, France Gaul, Wales Cambria and Normandy Neustria. (47–94)

You must hear where the Normans came from and how they received this name. Whatever there is towards the north, which we call the Chariot in the Sky [the Great Bear], whether it is sky, air, land or sea, everyone is accustomed to call north, because from the north, from where the sky holds its chariot, a wind comes and rises. The English say in their language, according to their usage: 'We are going to the north, we come from the north, we were born* in the north, we live in the north'. It is the same with the other winds, but we will speak only of the north. In English and Norse 'man' is equivalent to 'homme' in French. Bring together 'north' and 'man' and so together you say Northman, that is 'man of the north' in the vernacular, and from this came the name Normans. The Normans have to be called . . . Normandy, which they have populated, because the Normans, who lived in that land, populated it.[354] The French say that Normandy is the land of beggars from the north [nort mendie], because they came from another land to acquire and seek better possessions. In times gone by the Ortenoiz,[355] men from Norway, the Danes and other peoples from the north used to go about capturing lands and plundering. They were accustomed to do a great deal of harm in many places* along the shore. They called themselves the Normans, who came by sea from the north. These men were responsible for much persecution, destruction, harm and hostility in many lands and they invaded France on many occasions before they conquered Normandy. This belonged to the King of France and he held it as his own; but since it was granted to Rou and settled by the Normans, they removed the name Neustria and called it Normandy. Thereafter, they kept hold of it fiercely and defended it against all others. (95–144)

The first to arrive there was Hasting, who made many people poor and wretched; he was a companion and master of Björn, who was called Ironside. He was called Ironside – I do not know if this is true, but it is said – because the mother who bore him had cast such a spell and enchantment over him that iron could not injure him, neither through a blow or a thrust. He was the son of Lothbroc, a Danish king, who was always a man of bad faith. When Troy was destroyed long ago (this caused the Greeks much joy), many of the men who could escape,* having sought whatever people and ships they could get hold of,[356] with their wives, servants and sons and with great hardship and great perils, spread out through many lands, populating lands and creating cities. One race of people escaped from Troy and reached Denmark. Through Danas, an ancestor

---

[354] There is a lacuna after v. 115 corresponding to III, vv. 66–67, and after v. 116 a lacuna corresponding to III, vv. 69–72. The full passage in III reads: 'Those who were born where the north wind comes from are habitually called Normans, and from the Normans is derived the name Normandy, which they have populated. It used to be called Neustria, as long as it belonged to the French, but because of the men who came from the north it retained the name of Normandy, because the Normans, who lived in that land, populated it' (vv. 65–74).

[355] The Ortenoiz are a Scandinavian people. In v. 184 they are called Olenoix.

[356] On the curious syntax of v. 160 see Holden's note (vol. 3, p. 250).

who had been their lord for a long time, they called themselves Danes, so that their lineage would be remembered; or from the Danube, a very large river, which the *clerc lisant* call the Ister, which divides the kingdoms and flows swiftly in that direction, they were called Dani, who were formerly Dacians.[357] The Danube divides Germany and Scythia, where the inhabitants are very wicked, always fighting and skirmishing and with blood constantly on their hands. (145–80)

There was an island there by the name of Scanza, which divides two peoples. The Danes lived on one side and the Olenoiz on the other. The Alenoiz, who are called the Alans, are neighbours on the Scythian side, closer to Norway.[358] Beyond is Palus Maeotis [the Sea of Azov] and then Jeta and Sarmata. These are very hostile peoples, very hostile and wicked. They used to worship a god they were accustomed to call Thor; they loved him greatly and trusted in him greatly, sacrificing live human beings to him and sprinkling themselves with their blood; but before doing so they broke their fast. Once they had done this, they never let each other down. They stained their weapons with this blood and they also stained themselves when they were to go into battle, for either conquest or food. They travelled with a greater feeling of security when they carried some of this blood with them which they had sacrificed and with which they had touched their god.[359] (181–206)

In times gone by it was the custom for a long time among pagans in Denmark that, when a man had several children and had brought them up, he retained one of the sons by lot to be his heir after his death; and the one on whom the lot fell would go away to another land, for children went on being born* and the number of sons and daughters went on growing. The land could not support them; there was insufficient food for them to survive. Through this custom I am telling you about and through the lot which fell in this way, and through the grant of his father Lothbroc and his mother's advice, Björn prepared his journey, not daring to remain in the land. Lothbroc handed him over to Hasting and entrusted him to Hasting, on whose advice Björn would journey and who would keep watch on his conduct. (207–28)

Hasting was an arrogant pagan, very wicked and unrestrained. He never showed any pity for anyone and was never able to maintain any friendship. He had served Lothbroc for a long time and he then brought up his son Björn; under Björn he became master of his household knights and his ships.[360] They summoned the Danes and the Norwegians, obtained ships and craft and had many men and many ships. There was no one near there with any skill in battle or ability to steer a boat who, on account of the system of lots, or for reward or with

---

[357] On this passage concerning Denmark and Dacia see van Houts, *The Gesta Normannorum Ducum*, I, p. xxxi.

[358] Vv. 185–86 are clearly corrupt and the sense here is not satisfactory. See Holden's note (vol. 3, p. 250).

[359] The meaning of v. 206 is not entirely clear. It would be possible to replace *tout* with *Tour* 'Thor'.

[360] Holden sees the term *desouz* 'under' as indicating that Björn, because of his rank, preserved theoretical authority over Hasting, who later became the authentic leader of the expedition (vol. 3, p. 251).

hope of gain, failed to come to Hasting; each man was well received. Björn and Hasting brought them together and they all took oaths of commitment to each other. They would go to France, they said, and destroy the whole of it, sharing out its wealth and giving it to their knights. They had great faith in Thor, their god, as if he were possessed of great power. You would have seen a great deal of food being brought, boats, ships and barges built, shields and weapons made ready, axes and pikes sharpened, swords and helmets polished, hauberks and spears polished, arrows and javelins sharpened, arrows trimmed, lance shafts prepared. When they had got everything ready, they took leave of their friends; with a favourable wind they set sail and made their way towards France. The arrived at the Somme in the Ponthieu and laid waste the entire region, burning the Vimeu,[361] the Amiénois and the churches of the Vermandois. They burnt the churches of Saint-Quentin, Saint-Médard and Saint-Martin, and in Noyon they slaughtered all the clerics including Bishop Emmo. From the cloths taken from the altars they made breeches and shirts; they burnt towns and killed men, violated women and captured booty. You would have heard children crying bitterly, men howling, women weeping. The pagans wanted to destroy and take everything; there was no one there to resist them. (229–82)

Four of King Louis's sons had laid waste the country.[362] The king always preferred Charles, his fourth son by another wife. He divided his land between the four sons, so that after his death there would be no strife. Lothar, the eldest, had as his share Rome, Tuscany and Lombardy, and whatever lay beyond the Great Saint Bernard Pass; all this was given to him as a fief. Louis had Maine[363] and he held Saxony and Germany. Pepin held Poitou and Gascony and Charles France and Burgundy. This Charles was Charles the Bald, who experienced much suffering and hardship. But after his father's death Lothar, the eldest and strongest, wanted to take everything off his brothers, refusing to tolerate them peacefully; in this way such a conflict arose between the two of them that the whole of France was laid waste. The two brothers fought against the other two and came came together in battle; they had as many men as possible come from all sides in order to plunder everything. Some of the men had gone forraging between Vézelay and Auxerre when the others arrived; then you would have seen the beginning of a battle with disastrous consequences. Near the town of Fontenay more than a hundred thousand were killed as a result; the flower of France perished there and many of the barons. In this way the pagans found the land devoid of men and easy to conquer. When they had destroyed the Vermandois and were all laden with booty, they went back to their ships and loaded them up with their booty. They sailed down the coast, going* from port to port. (283–324)

There was an abbey in Fécamp. There were nuns in it and they had abandoned it, departing because of the pagans and leaving in shame and anguish. The pagans destroyed everything, killed the inhabitants and took away the booty. Then they

---

[361] The manuscript reading here is Vignon.

[362] The reference is to King Louis the Pious, son of Charlemagne.

[363] Holden thinks that le Maingne here is a mistake for Allemagne (vol. 3, p. 295).

sailed around until they came to the Seine, which they entered; at the abbey of Jumièges they established themselves and their ships. For a long time there had been nine hundred monks there in a community; Saint Philibert founded it during the reign of Clovis.[364] Baltilde, Queen of France, who at that time had great power, created and established Jumièges, giving it lands and revenues. Because of fear and because of the reputation of Hasting, that enemy of God, the monks all fled and abandoned the church completely. The pagans set fire to the town and destroyed the abbey. From there they went to Rouen, where they remained; they destroyed the city completely and found a great deal of booty there; they burnt houses, shattered cellars, killed men and robbed churches. From Noyon to Saint-Denis, from Chartres to Paris, there remained no town or dwelling which was not set on fire or burnt to a cinder. They entered the abbey of Saint-Geneviève, captured booty and then burnt the abbey. Wherever they could find booty, they took it to their ships on the shore. The peasants went into the woods and stayed there as long as they could. The priests were distressed and they took the relics to other lands, taking missals, psalters, gospel books and censers and leaving nothing behind which they could carry; they gladly went wherever they could find peace. What they could not take with them they hid and buried in the ground. The relics and holy objects which used to be in Normandy the clerics secretly carried a long way away, as best they could. Monks, priests and clerics took flight and the pagans destroyed the churches. They sailed round Normandy and Brittany as far as the Mee,[365] and destroyed and devastated the regions of the Cotentin. They captured and laid waste Valognes and set fire to it out of spite, because it had been held against them. But it could not be defended; there were few knights there and no help could be expected. (325–88)

In Le Ham* there was a wealthy abbey, well situated and well equipped. Hasting the robber destroyed it; he took away its possessions and then set fire to it. In Saint-Marcouf, on the river, there was a wealthy and affluent abbey; at that time the region surrounding it was called Nantus.[366] Hasting and Björn destroyed it, robbed it and then set fire to it. Regouminie and Abilant and the castle of Garillant – Abilant is situated beneath a harbour; he would go straight there,[367] the castle was very strong and the region very fertile, with fine woods and a fine river. The man who first built it and who constructed the castle was very wise and

---

[364] St Philibert (*c.*608–*c.*685) founded the abbey of Jumièges in 654, on land given to him by Clovis II. He later founded the monastery of Noirmoutier on the island of Heriou (Poitou). He also founded monasteries for monks at Quincay (near Poitiers) and Luçon and for nuns at Pavilly.

[365] The Mee is the name of an area of Brittany occupying the frontiers between the county of Nantes and the counties of Rennes and Anjou to the north and the Vannetais to the west.

[366] For this information about Le Ham and Saint Marcouf see L. Musset, 'Monachisme d'époque franque et monachisme d'époque ducale en Normandie: le problème de la continuité', in *Aspects du monachisme en Normandie (ive–xviiie siècles* (Paris: Vrin, 1982), pp. 55–74 (p. 68). Due to his local knowledge, Wace is given the benefit of the doubt by Musset concerning the details he provides.

[367] In v. 402 the reading of the first part of the line is corrupt and, probably as a result of this, the sentence beginning in v. 399 is unsatisfactory (in the phrase *sus aire port* in v. 401 *aire* probably represents a place name).

courtly; it is now called Mont Hagneiz. Hasting came there, destroyed it and set light to it. He set fire to the abbey of Visaire, which was equipped with every amenity. He captured Meliant and pillaged it, and when he had plundered it he set fire to it, doing the same to La Tollete and Saint-Andreu, which at that time was a place of high standing. Bruschamport, Paillart and Montebourg and the castle of Cherbourg were destroyed by the powerful Hasting, by him and the men from his region.[368] In a number of places the ruins are visible which the Saracens created in Aurigny and Jersey, Sark, Herm and Guernsey, and they sailed upstream until they reached Brittany . . . as far as the Mee and his companions; there in Brittany he came to a stop.[369] (389–428)

They all sailed up the Loire, laying everything waste right and left, until they reached Saint-Florent. Then there were some sad and unhappy people! They moored their ships on an island; they set out from there and returned there. They ransacked both sides of the Loire, coming and going about their business,[370] destroying and demolishing towns and causing burgesses and peasants to take flight. They returned to their ships and set out from their ships, carrying to them everything they found. They destroyed Touraine and Tours and made their way to Orléans. In Anjou, the Auvergne and Poitou the devastation and destruction wrought by Hasting, as we know very well, remained visible for a long time. I take books as my witness that from Flanders to Gascony, just as in the direction of the setting sun, where the sea runs round the edge of the land, there was no castle or old city, burg or ancient town which did not experience Björn's treatment and which Hasting did not destroy, or take such a ransom as he himself sought. (429–55)

Björn was evil and Hasting was evil; each man was filled with wickedness. When France had been entirely destroyed and their fleet was fully prepared, Hastings heard talk of Rome and heard it greatly praised, for at that time no city in the whole world was so wealthy. Hasting said he would go to Rome and make Björn King of Rome; through Rome Björn would have the whole world and through Rome he would conquer everything. They came straight to their ships, intending to set sail with all haste. They departed from Nantes in Brittany and sailed round the whole of Spain, passing by Genoa. They rowed and sailed a great deal; at night they came to the port of Luni,[371] just as fortune decreed. Luni was a city in Tuscany, near the sea and close to Sarzana. Because it was well situated,

---

[368] For discussion of the proper names in vv. 399–418 see Holden, vol. 3, pp. 251–52. Mont Hagneiz is a hill above the valley of the Saire and Visaire was the former name for the abbey of Licornet near Barfleur. The other names have been identified, but, as in the case of the information concerning Le Ham and Saint-Marcouf (see note 14), Wace's references can be taken seriously.

[369] The apparent lacuna after v. 426 makes this passage difficult to interpret.

[370] Andresen, supported by Holden, suggests for *comment afere* the reading *comme a fere* 'like a fair'.

[371] Luni was an ancient city in the Gulf of La Spezia, near Pisa. At one time a prosperous port, it fell into decline when the Roman empire came to an end. Prudentius mentions a Viking raid, which took place around 860 and which could have been the one mentioned by Wace and before him by Dudo and William of Jumièges. See van Houts, *The Gesta Normannorum Ducum*, I, pp. 24–25.

very well built, well equipped and well placed, a beautiful city in a beautiful region, it was called Luni [Moon] and compared to the moon. Just as the moon exceeds and outdoes the stars in brightness, radiance and beauty, so that none matches it in any way, thus the city called Luni was nobler and more beautiful than any city in the country or known to be near it. But after Hasting had destroyed it, it deteriorated and declined, so that it was reduced to nought and virtually all ruined. (456–96)

In the bishopric's church, which had great authority within the town, matins had begun and were being conducted in such a way that some lesson or other was being read by one of the young clerics. In the middle of the reading he stopped and uttered something he was not supposed to say:

'A hundred ships are coming to Porto Venere, it seems to me.' The clerics asked: 'What are you saying? You have not been paying attention.'

'A hundred ships are arriving at the Porto Venere, I tell you.'

'Look at the scripture!' they said. And he said again what he had said.

'A hundred ships are arriving at Porto Venere, it seems to me.' He said the same thing a fourth time and could never say otherwise; he could not prevent himself from saying it. This was considered to be prophetic because in the morning, when they rose, they found Björn's fleet.[372] (497–520)

Hasting looked at the town and thought he had found Rome. The inhabitants of Luni were terrified when they saw the pagans; they saw a large number of masts, sails, men and ships. They all went inside the city, abandoning all the open land around it. The count gathered his men together and the bishop did the same. Hasting was a man of great cunning and full of trickery. He saw that the city could be defended easily and that it was fortified and capable of being held. He saw that he would not have it by force and would not take it by force; if he did not capture it by ruse, he would never enter it by force. He began to think up some trickery; he sent word to the bishop and to the clerics that he had no wish to do any harm. He had done too much harm and repented of it. He had not come to do harm, but he had experienced a storm and a contrary wind, which had driven him to that land. He was upset that he had come there and did not know where he was; he had been lost at sea. If he were in good health and had a favourable wind, he would not be there long, but he was suffering greatly and could not make a journey; he was greatly in need of rest. He asked for nothing from them except to be allowed to buy food and the peace to come and go and to buy food. He was very much afraid he would die and wanted to become a Christian; he could not regain his health by any other means. That was his opinion and he was certain of it, since he had done a great deal of harm in France and wanted to do penance for it. They thought he was telling the truth and wanted to save his soul. They agreed that he could stay and pledged his safety. He could buy food and drink, and if he wished to receive baptism they would baptize him willingly

---

[372] The allusions here to Porto Venere may go back to an eleventh-century Latin gloss in one of Dudo's manuscripts (from Jumièges), which seems to identify Luni with Portus Veneris and which contains the nucleus of this prophecy (see Dudo, trans. Christiansen, p. 184 n. 89, and the *GND*, I, p. 24 n. 1).

and receive him willingly. In this way the peace, which was inauspiciously given, was granted. (521–72)

The scoundrel was feigning illness. He had stained his face and countenance and was complaining bitterly about pains in his body and his head, saying that he was hurting all over. His skin was constantly pale and livid, he was constantly lying face down or on his back, constantly falling asleep and waking up, constantly stretching and rolling on his stomach. God, if only his death agony had really taken him! In that way the trickery would have ceased. He stretched out his arms and wrung his hands; everyone who saw him thought he was on the point of death. How would anyone who heard the wretch yelling and saw his antics, how he ground his teeth and waved his arms, stretched and bent his legs, constantly sobbing and yawning, wrinkling his nose and rolling his eyes, how would anyone who had seen him thought that the scoundrel would recover? Even those who knew him and were aware of the deception, hearing his moans and his cries and seeing his behaviour, feared that his soul was departing, that he would never get up again and that his death agony, which was showing itself in so many ways, had taken him. Why more can I go tell you? He kept on asking to become a Christian and had himself taken to the church, as if he could not walk. The bishop addressed him, the bishop made the sign of the cross over him, the bishop baptized him, the bishop anointed him with holy oil. The count came to the baptism, acted as his godparent and held him at the font. When the baptism was over and the scoundrel left the font and was dressed in his garments, he said:

'If I recover, I will certainly do honour to this place and on many a day you will benefit because of me. But I am weak and have a great deal of pain. I do not expect to live long, my heart is not healthy or in good condition; I do not expect to live long. But if I die, in God's name I ask you to prepare a burial-place for me in this church. I wish to lie there; the place is dear to me. Perform this service for my body exactly as one does for a Christian. I will be saved, I feel sure.' (573–628)

Neither the bishop nor count made a good decision; they allowed the scoundrel to perpetrate his evil deception. Then he had himself carried to his ship very carefully and smoothly. He did not stay there seven or eight days; rather the next day, the following night, Hasting summoned his barons, Björn and all his companions. In secret he recounted his trickery and plans to them and they told him he was acting wisely and that the plan would work. They laid him out on the bier, with his sword at his side and his hauberk on. O God, how sad that sudden death did not take him! Then the inhabitants of that land would have been rid of him. The scoundrel was covered in a silk sheet as if he were dead. Then suddenly there was a great deal of noise and shouting, and much weeping and wailing. They would not have made such a great noise if they had really seem him dead. That night, and then again in the morning, the pagans made a great noise, as if each of them had seen his father, his son, his daughter or his brother dead. With their hauberks beneath their broad tunics and their swords beneath their cloaks, they carried Hasting to the city gate on the bier. Then you would have heard the pagans yelling and weeping with all their might. Those inside were deceived by the great display of grief they had witnessed; they had the gates opened for them and admitted those who wanted to enter. In order to gather the people together, they had bells rung everywhere. The older and the younger clerics came, carrying crosses and censers and all running up gladly; they felt pity for those who were weeping and came there on foot with great humility. They were not aware of their trickery. The bishop and the clergy, and the count and his barons, were there, as if they had all been sent for; they all came running and no one stayed behind, as if it were for a holy relic. They all came running up for the sake of the others, feeling great pity for those who were weeping. They carried the body to the church; it would have been better for it to have remained outside. It was a great misfortune that they were not aware of the trickery. The senior clerics sang the office. This was a prelude for the great evil that was to befall them; they would have been better to confess, for they were very soon to die. The bishop sang the Mass and a great many pagans were there. (629–92)

When the time came to carry the bier, from which the body was to be buried, Hasting jumped up from it, and with his sword drawn uttered a yell. With the first blow he dealt he cut off the bishop's head, and he cut off his godparent's head as if he were a vile beast. The pagans, all with their swords drawn and their cloaks thrown off their shoulders, ran to close the door so that no one could escape. They slaughtered the wretches just as a wolf slaughters lambs, when it manages to get into a fold without the peasant noticing; it tears out the throat of sheep, ewes and lambs, large and small. The pagans did just the same with the unfortunate Christians. They killed the bishop and the count and so many of the others that it was impossible to count them; then they spread throughout the town, running from one dwelling to another. When the pagans had captured Luni, they thought they had taken Rome. But when they realised they had been deceived and made a mistake, they were all filled with wrath. They went through the whole region and left no possessions or booty there; they demolished walls and churches. The ruins can still be seen; pilgrims on their way to Rome can clearly see them. The pagans loaded all the possessions into the ships and destroyed the surrounding region. They decided to leave and return to France, going back by the same routes as they had come;[373] what they had had on their right, on the way back they had on their left. Björn set off with his ships, I do not know whether to Scythia or to Hungary, and Hasting came to the King of France and took up residence with him. The king, on the understanding that he would maintain peace and defend him against other peoples, gave him Chartres and the Chartrain, which he had in his power at that time. Hasting remained there for a long time, and France had been at peace for some time when Rou arrived in Rouen, bringing men from the north; they were called Normans because they had been born in the north. (693–750)

---

[373] The sense of v. 734 seems clear, but the line is corrupt.

BIBLIOGRAPHY

THE WORKS OF WACE: TEXTS AND TRANSLATIONS

The *Roman de Rou*

Andresen, Hugo, *Maistre Wace's Roman de Rou et des ducs de Normandie, nach den Handschriften von neuem herausgegeben*, 2 vols (Heilbronn: Henninger, 1877–79). Reviewed by:

W. Foerster, *Zeitschrift für romanische Philologie*, 1 (1877), 144–59 (vol. 1 only reviewed).

H. Nicol, *Academy*, 27 March (1880), 236–37.

G. Paris, *Romania*, 9 (1880), 592–614.

H. Suchier, *Literarisches Centralblatt für Deutschland*, 8 (1877), 249–52 (vol. 1 only reviewed).

Bouquet, M., 'Chronique française de Normandie', in *Recueil des historiens des Gaules et de la France*, 24 vols (Paris: Desaint), XIII (1886), pp. 220–56.

Brosnahan, Leger M. N., 'Wace's Chronicle of the Normans: A Translation with Introduction and Notes', unpublished dissertation, Harvard University, 1957.

Burgess, Glyn S., *Wace: The Roman de Rou* (St Helier: Société Jersiaise, 2002). Contains, in addition to the material reprinted in the current volume, the text of A.J. Holden's edition.

Gaudy, Franz F. von, *Der Roman von Rollo und den Herzogen der Normandie, von Robert Wace, normannischen Dichter des zwölften Jahrhunderts, nach der Ausgabe von Friedrich Pluquet metrisch bearbeitet* (Glogau: C. Flemming, 1835). A translation of Pluquet's text into German with some passages abbreviated.

Holden, Anthony J., *Le Roman de Rou de Wace*, 3 vols, Société des Anciens Textes Français (Paris: Picard, 1970–73). This edition is translated in the present volume. It is also reprinted in Burgess (see above).

Lepelley, René, *Guillaume le duc, Guillaume le roi: extraits du Roman de Rou de Wace, poète normand du XIIe siècle, présentés et traduits* (Caen: Centre d'Études Normandes, 1987).

Malet, Sir Alexander, *The Conquest of England from Wace's Poem of the Roman de Rou, now first translated into English rhyme with the Franco-Norman text after Pluquet, and the notes of Auguste Le Prévost, Edgar Taylor, F.S.A., and others* (London: Bell and Daldy, 1860). A translation of the battle of Hastings episode with Pluquet's text (corresponding in Holden's edition to Part III, vv. 5543–9340).

Meyer, Paul, *Recueil d'anciens textes bas-latins, provençaux et français*, 2 vols (Paris: Vieweg, 1874–77), II, pp. 291–97. An edition of the opening 336 lines of Part III with variants.

Palgrave, F., *Le Romant des ducs de Normandie* (London, 1828). Contains an edition of 1,258 lines of the text, abandoned when the editor became aware of Pluquet's edition; concludes at Part III, v. 1338, of Holden's edition.

Pluquet, Frédéric, 'La *Chronique Ascendante des ducs de Normandie* par Maître Wace', *Mémoires de la Société des Antiquaires de Normandie*, 1 (1824), 444–57. Provides an edition of the *Chronique Ascendante* (this item gave this section of Wace's text its name).

──────, *Notice sur la vie et les écrits de Robert Wace, poète normand du XIIe siècle; suivie de citations extraites de ses ouvrages, pour servir à l'histoire de Normandie* (Rouen: J. Frère, 1824). Contains extracts from the text of the *Rou* (pp. 23–64). Reprinted in the following item (pp. vii–xxii).

──────, *Le Roman de Rou et des ducs de Normandie par Robert Wace, poète normand du XIIe siècle; publié pour la première fois, d'après les manuscrits de France et d'Angleterre; avec des notes pour servir à l'intelligence du texte*, 2 vols (Rouen: E. Frère, 1827).

Taylor, Edgar, *Master Wace: His Chronicle of the Norman Conquest from the Roman de Rou, translated with notes and illustrations* (London: William Pickering, 1837, repr. New York: AMS, 1975).

See also the items below by Duncan and LePetit.

Other works

Roman de Brut, (i) ed. by Ivor Arnold, 2 vols (Paris: Société des Anciens Textes Français, 1938–40), (ii) trans. by Judith Weiss with a reprint of Arnold's text (Exeter: Exeter University Press, 1999, 2nd ed. 2002).

Conception Nostre Dame, ed. by W. R. Ashford (Chicago: University of Chicago Library, 1933).

Vie de sainte Marguerite, ed. by (i) Elizabeth A. Francis (Paris: Champion, 1932), (ii) Hans-Erich Keller (Tübingen: Niemeyer, 1990).

Vie de saint Nicolas, ed. by Einar Ronsjö (Lund: Gleerup; Copenhagen: Munksgaard, 1942).

OTHER IMPORTANT FRENCH TEXTS

Chronique des ducs de Normandie, par Benoît, publié d'après le manuscrit de Tours avec les variantes du manuscrit de Londres, ed. by Carin Fahlin, 3 vols (Uppsala: Almqvist & Wiksells, 1951–67).

L'Estoire des Engleis by Geffrei Gaimar, ed. by Alexander Bell (Oxford: Anglo-Norman Text Society, 1960; repr. New York and London: Johnson Reprint Corporation, 1971).

Le Roman de Troie par Benoît de Sainte-Maure, publié d'après tous les manuscrits connus, ed. by Léopold Constans, 6 vols, Société des Anciens Textes Français (Paris: Firmin-Didot, 1904–12).

WACE'S PRINCIPAL LATIN SOURCES

Dudo of Saint-Quentin. (i) *De moribus et actis primorum Normanniae ducum auctore Dudone sancti Quintini decano*, ed. by Jules Lair (Caen: Société des Antiquaires de Normandie, 1865), (ii) *Dudo of St Quentin: History of the Normans*, trans. by Eric Christiansen (Woodbridge: Boydell Press, 1998); references in the present volume are to the translation.

Orderic Vitalis, *Historia ecclesiastica*. *Orderic Vitalis: The Ecclesiastical History*, ed. and trans. by M. Chibnall, 6 vols (Oxford: Clarendon Press, 1969–1980).

William of Jumièges, Orderic Vitalis and Robert of Torigny, *Gesta Normannorum Ducum* (*GND*). (i) *Guillaume de Jumièges, Gesta Normannorum Ducum*, ed. by Jean

Marx (Caen: Société de l'Histoire de Normandie, 1914), (ii) *The Gesta Normannorum Ducum of William of Jumièges, Orderic Vitalis, and Robert of Torigni*, ed. and trans. by Elisabeth M. C. van Houts, 2 vols (Oxford: Clarendon Press, 1992–95) (references in the present volume are to this edition and translation).

William of Poitiers. *The Gesta Guillelmi of William of Poitiers*, ed. and trans. by R. H. C. Davis and Marjorie Chibnall (Oxford: Clarendon Press, 1998).

OTHER LATIN WORKS

The Brevis relatio de Guillelmo nobilissimo comite Normannorum, written by a Monk of Battle Abbey: edited with an historical commentary by Elisabeth M. C. van Houts, in *Chronology, Conquest and Conflict in Medieval England: Camden Miscellany XXXIV* (Camden Miscellany, fifth series, 10, 1997). Reprinted with an English translation in Elisabeth M. C. van Houts, *History and Family Traditions in England and the Continent, 1000–1200* (Aldershot: Ashgate, 1999), pp. 1–48 (references are to this edition and translation).

The Chronicle of Battle Abbey, ed. and trans. by Eleanor Searle (Oxford: Clarendon Press, 1980).

Chronica monasterii de Hida iuxta Wintoniam, in *Liber monasterii de Hyda*, ed. by Edward Edwards (London: Rolls Series, 1866), pp. 283–321.

Eadmer of Canterbury. (i) *Eadmeri Historia novorum in Anglia*, ed. by Martin Rule (London: Rolls Series, 1884), (ii) *Eadmer's History of Recent Events in England: Historia novorum in Anglia*, trans. by Geoffrey Bosanquet (London: Cresset Press, 1964).

Geoffrey of Monmouth. *The Historia regum Britannie of Geoffrey of Monmouth I: Bern, Burgerbibliothek, MS. 568 (the 'Vulgate' Version); II: The First Variant Version, a Critical Edition*, ed. by Neil Wright (Woodbridge: D. S. Brewer, 1985, 1988).

The Carmen de Hastingae proelio of Guy of Amiens, ed. and trans. by Frank Barlow (Oxford: Clarendon Press, 1999).

Henry of Huntingdon. *Henry, Archdeacon of Huntingdon: Historia Anglorum, The History of the English People*, ed. and trans. by Diana Greenway (Oxford: Clarendon Press, 1996).

Simeon of Durham. *Historia regum*, in *Symeonis Monachi opera omnia*, ed. by Thomas Arnold, 2 vols (London: Rolls Series, 1882–85), II, pp. 3–283 (esp. pp. 179–85).

William of Malmesbury. *William of Malmesbury, Gesta regum Anglorvm: The History of the English Kings*, ed. and trans. by R. A. B. Mynors, completed by R. M. Thomson and M. Winterbottom, 2 vols (Oxford: Oxford University Press, 1998–99). All references to William of Malmesbury are to the *Gesta regum Anglorum*.

STUDIES

Anderson, Carolyn B., 'Double Vision: Historiographers, Chroniclers, Romances and the Invention of Royal Character, 1050–1377', unpublished dissertation, Stanford University, 1992. *Dissertation Abstracts International*, 59 (1993), p. 3206A.

———, 'Narrating Matilda, "Lady of the English," in the *Historia novella*, the *Gesta Stephani*, and Wace's *Roman de Rou*: The Desire for Land and Order', *Clio*, 29 (1999), 47–67.

———, 'Wace's *Roman de Rou* and Henry II's Court: Character and Power', *Romance Quarterly*, 47 (2000), 67–82.

Andresen, Hugo, 'Über die von Benoît in seiner normannischen Chronik benützen Quellen', *Romanische Forschungen*, 1 (1883), 327–412, 2 (1886), 477–538.

———. 'Zu Wace's *Rou*, Bd. II 50 v. 511 und 529', *Zeitschrift für romanische Philologie*, 12 (1888), 525–26.

Archer, T. A., 'The Battle of Hastings', *English Historical Review*, 9 (1894), 1–41, 602–08.

Arnoux, Matthieu, 'Classe agricole, pouvoir seigneurial et autorité ducale: l'évolution de la Normandie féodale d'après le témoignage des chroniqueurs (Xe–XIIe siècles)', 98 (1992), 23–28.

Baist, G., 'Zu Wace, *Roman de Rou*, 3 Teil 3079–99', *Romanische Forschungen*, 1 (1883), 439–41.

Becker, Ph. Aug, 'Der gepaarter Achtsilber in der französischen Dichtung', *Abhandlungen der philologisch-historischen Klasse der Sächsischen Akademie der Wissenschaften*, 43, 1 (Leipzig: S. Hirzel, 1934). See pp. 46–50.

———, 'Die Normannenchroniken: Wace und seine Bearbeiter', *Zeitschrift für romanische Philologie*, 63 (1943), 481–519.

Belletti, Gian Carlo, 'Il sogno di Arlette (Le *enfances* di Guglielmo il Conquistatore nel *Roman de Rou* de Wace)', in *Incroci i lingue e di culturale nell'Inghilterre medievale* (Alessandria: Edizione dell'Orso, 1994), pp. 29–55.

Bédier, Joseph, 'Richard de Normandie dans les *chansons de geste*', *Romanic Review*, 1 (1910), 113–24.

Bémont, Charles, 'Wace et la bataille de Hastings: correction au vers 7816 du *Roman de Rou*', *Romania*, 39 (1910), 370–73.

Bennett, Matthew, 'Poetry as History? The *Roman de Rou* of Wace as a Source for the Norman Conquest', in *Anglo-Norman Studies V: Proceedings of the Battle Conference 1982*, ed. by R. A. Brown (Woodbridge: Boydell Press, 1983), pp. 21–39.

———, 'Wace and Warfare', in *Anglo-Norman Studies XI: Proceedings of the Battle Conference 1988*, ed. by R. A. Brown (Woodbridge: Boydell Press, 1989), pp. 37–57. Reprinted in *Anglo-Norman Warfare: Studies in Late Anglo-Saxon and Anglo-Norman Military Organization and Warfare*, ed. by M. Strickland (Woodbridge: Boydell Press, 1992), pp. 230–50.

Bennett, Philip E., 'L'Épique dans l'historiographie anglo-normande: Gaimar, Wace, Jordan Fantosme', in *Aspects de l'épopée romane: mentalité, idéologies, intertextualité*, ed. by H. van Dijk and W. Noomen (Groningen: Egbert Forsten, 1995), pp. 321–39.

Bezzola, Reto R., *Les Origines et la formation de la littérature courtoise en occident (500–1200)*, 3 vols (Paris: Champion, 1958–63). See esp. vol. 3, part 1, pp. 150–207.

Blacker, Jean, 'Wace's Craft and his Audience: Historical Truth, Bias, and Patronage in the *Roman de Rou*', *Kentucky Romance Quarterly*, 31 (1984), 355–62. This article was published under the name Jean Blacker-Knight.

———, '"La geste est grande, longue et grieve a translater": History for Henry II', *Romance Quarterly*, 37 (1990), 387–96.

———, *The Faces of Time: Portrayal of the Past in Old French and Latin Historical Narrative of the Anglo-Norman Regnum* (Austin: University of Texas Press, 1994).

Bliese, John R.E., 'Leadership, Rhetoric, and Morale in the Norman Conquest of England', *Military Affairs*, 52 (1988), 23–28.

Boüard, M. de, 'A Propos des sources du *Roman de Rou*', in *Recueil de travaux offert à M. Clovis Brunel – par ses amis, collègues et élèves*, 2 vols (Paris: Ecole des Chartes, 1955), I, pp. 178–82.

Braet, Herman, 'Le Songe de l'arbre chez Wace, Benoît et Aimon de Varennes', *Romania*, 91 (1970), 255–67.

Bréquigny, Louis-Georges Oudart Feudrix de, 'Notice du *Roman de Rou et des ducs de Normandie*', manuscrit de la Bibliothèque Nationale 6987; autre coté 7567[2]: manuscrit de la Bibliothèque de l'Arsenal, intitulé au dos, *Roman de Rou*', *Notices et Extraits des Manuscrits de la Bibliothèque Nationale*, 5 (1795), 21–78.

Brial, Michel-Jean-Jacques, 'Robert Wace, chanoine de Bayeux, historien-poète', *Histoire Littéraire de la France*, 13 (1869), 518–30.

Broadhurst, Karen M., 'Henry II of England and Eleanor of Aquitaine: Patrons of Literature in England?', *Viator*, 27 (1996), 53–84.

Brosnahan, Leger M. N., 'Wace's Use of Proverbs', *Speculum*, 39 (1964), 444–73.

———, 'A Propos du vers 3 de la "Seconde partie" de *La Geste des Normanz* par Wace', *Romania*, 87 (1966), 247–66.

———, 'A Collation of Wace's *La Geste des Normanz*', *Manuscripta*, 16 (1972), 83–97.

Buttry, Dolores J., 'Contempt or Empathy? Master Wace's Depiction of a Peasant Revolt', *Romance Notes*, 37 (1996), 31–38.

———, 'Maistre Wace: romancier malgré lui', unpublished dissertation, University of Pittsburgh, 1997. *Dissertation Abstracts International*, 58 (1998), p. 4290A.

Capefigue, B., 'Notice du *Roman de Rou ou des ducs de Normandie*', in *id.*, *Essai sur les invasions maritimes des Normands dans les Gaules* (Paris: Imprimerie Royale, 1823), pp. 410–22.

Carpenter, B. F., 'The Life and Writings of Wace', unpublished dissertation, University of North Carolina, 1930.

Cazauran, Nicole, 'Richard sans Peur: un personnage en quête d'auteur', *Travaux de Littérature*, 4 (1991), 21–43.

D'Alessandro, Domenico, 'Analisi del descrittivo nell'opera romanzesca di Wace', *Annali dell'Istituto Universitario Orientale: sezione romanza*, 33 (1991), 205–16.

Damian-Grint, Peter, 'Truth, Trust, and Evidence in the Anglo-Norman *estoire*', in *Anglo-Norman Studies XVIII: Proceedings of the Battle Conference 1995* (Woodbridge: Boydell Press, 1996), pp. 63–72.

———, '*Estoire* as Word and Genre', *Medium Aevum*, 66 (1997), 189–99.

———, *The New Historians of the Twelfth-Century Renaissance: Inventing Vernacular Authority* (Woodbridge: Boydell Press, 1999).

De Boer, C., 'Un Cas de critique de texte', *Neophilologus*, 1 (1916), 224–25.

Douglas, D. C., 'Companions of the Conqueror', *History*, 27 (1943), 129–47.

Du Méril, Édélestand, 'La Vie et les ouvrages de Wace', *Jahrbuch für romanische und englische Literatur*, 1 (1859), 1–43. Reprinted in *Etudes sur quelques points d'archéologie et d'histoire littéraire* (Paris and Lepizig: A. Franck, 1862), pp. 214–72.

Duncan, Jonathan, 'Wace, the Jersey poet', *The Guernsey and Jersey Magazine*, 2 (1836), 88–95, 162–68, 229–35, 359–64; 3 (1837), 20–27, 86–91, 155–60, 217–20, 288–90; 4 (1837), 29–33, 92–96, 166–72, 223–30, 287–91.

Eley, Penny, and Philip E. Bennett, 'The Battle of Hastings according to Gaimar, Wace and Benoît: Rhetoric and Politics', *Nottingham Medieval Studies*, 43 (1999), 47–78.

Foulon, Charles, 'Wace', in *Arthurian Literature in the Middle Ages: A Collaborative History*, ed. R. S. Loomis (Oxford: Clarendon Press, 1959), pp. 94–103.

———, 'Le *Rou* de Wace, l'*Yvain* de Chrétien de Troyes et Eon de l'Etoile', *Bibliographical Bulletin of the International Arthurian Society*, 17 (1965), 93–102.

Francis, Elizabeth A., 'Note sur un terme employé par Wace, avec quelques observations sur la chronologie de ses œuvres', in *Mélanges de linguistique et de littérature romanes offerts à Mario Roques*, 2 vols (Bade: Editions Art et Science; Paris: Didier, 1953), II, pp. 81–92.

Freeman, Edward A., *The History of the Norman Conquest: Its Causes and its Results*, 6 vols, 3rd ed. (Oxford: Clarendon Press, 1877–79).

Gouttebroze, Jean-Guy, 'Exclusion et intégration des Normands Hasting et Rollon', in *Exclus et systèmes d'exclusion dans la littérature et la civilisation médiévales* (Aix-en-Provence: Publications du CUER MA, 1975), pp. 299–311.

——, 'Le Diable dans le *Roman de Rou*', in *Le Diable au Moyen Age (doctrine, problèmes moraux, représentations)* (Aix-en-Provence: Publications du CUER MA, 1979), pp. 213–34.

——, 'Henry II Plantagenêt: patron des historiographes anglo-normands de langue d'oïl', in *La Littérature angevine médiévale: actes du colloque du samedi 22 mars 1980* (Angers: Hérault Imprimerie Édition, 1981), pp. 91–105.

——, 'Pourquoi congédier un historiographe, Henri II Plantagenêt et Wace (1155–1174)', *Romania*, 112 (1991), 289–311.

Hacquoil, Marleen, 'Wace, his Literary Legacy', unpublished thesis, University of Ottawa, 1991.

Haskins, Charles H., 'The Materials for the Reign of Robert I of Normandy', *English Historical Review*, 31 (1916), 257–68.

——, *Norman Institutions* (Cambridge: Harvard University Press, 1918).

Holden, Anthony J., 'L'Authenticité des premières parties du *Roman de Rou*', *Romania*, 75 (1954), 22–53.

——, 'De Nouveau le vers 3 du *Roman de Rou*: à propos de deux articles récents', *Romania*, 89 (1968), 105–15.

——, 'Nouvelles remarques sur le texte du *Roman de Rou*', *Revue de Linguistique Romane*, 45 (1981), 118–27.

Hollister, C. Warren, *Monarchy, Magnates and Institutions in the Anglo-Norman World* (London: Hambledon, 1986).

Holmes, Urban T., Jr, 'Norman Literature and Wace', in *Medieval Secular Studies: Four Essays*, ed. by W. Matthews (Berkeley and Los Angeles: University of California Press, 1967), pp. 46–67.

Hormel, Hermann F., *Untersuchung über die Chronique Ascendante und ihren Verfasser* (Marburg: Elwert, 1880).

Houck, Margaret, *Sources of the Roman de Brut of Wace* (Berkeley: University of California Press, 1941).

Jirmounsky, M. M., 'Essai d'analyse des procédés littéraires de Wace', *Revue des Langues Romanes*, 63 (1925), 261–96.

Keins, J. P., 'Zur Social und literarische Stellung des Dichters Wace', *Archivum Romanicum*, 16 (1932), 515–20.

Keller, Hans-Erich, 'Wace als Mehrer des französischen Wortschatzes', *Zeitschrift für romanische Philologie*, 68 (1952), 401–14.

——, *Etude descriptive sur le vocabulaire de Wace* (Berlin: Akademie-Verlag (Deutsche Akademie der Wissenschaft), 1953).
Reviewed by:
F. Lecoy, *Romania*, 76 (1955), 534–38.

——, 'Lettre à A. J. Holden au sujet du *Roman de Rou*', *Romania*, 78 (1957), 405–07.

——, 'Wace et les Bretons', in *Actes du 14e congrès international arthurien* (Rennes: Presses Universitaires de Rennes, 1985), pp. 354–70.

——, 'The Intellectual Journey of Wace', *Fifteenth Century Studies*, 17 (1990), 185–207.

——, 'Le Mirage *Robert Wace*', *Zeitschrift für romanische Philologie*, 106 (1990), 465–66.

——, 'Wace', in *Medieval France: An Encyclopedia*, ed. by W. W. Kibler and G. A. Zinn (New York and London: Garland, 1995), pp. 969–70.

Keller, W. L., 'Maistre Wace, eine stylistische Untersuchung seiner beiden Romane Rou und Brut', thesis, Zürich, 1886.

Körting, Gustav, *Über die Quellen des Roman de Rou*. Inauguraldissertation (Leipzig: Fues's Verlag, 1867).

——, 'Über die Aechtheit der einzelnen Teilen des *Roman de Rou*', *Jahrbüch der romanische und englische Literatur*, 8 (1867), 170–207.

Krappe, Alexander H., 'Le Songe de la mère de Guillaume le Conquérant', *Zeitschrift für französische Sprache und Literatur*, 61 (1937), 198–204.

Langille, Édouard, '"Mençunge ou folie?" Commentaire sur la mise en "romanz" de Wace', *Dalhousie French Studies*, 39–40 (1997), 19–32.

La Rue, Gervais de, 'An Epistolary Dissertation upon the Life and Writings of Robert Wace, an Anglo-Norman Poet of the 12th century', *Archaeologia: or, Miscellaneous Tracts Relating to Antiquity*, 12 (1796), 50–79.

——, *Essais historiques sur les bardes, les jongleurs et les trouvères normands et anglo-normands*, 3 vols (Caen: Mancel, 1834). The chapter on Wace is found in vol. 2, pp. 143–87.

Leckie, R. William, Jr, *The Passage of Dominion: Geoffrey of Monmouth and the Periodization of Insular History in the Twelfth Century* (Toronto, Buffalo and London, 1981).

Lecoy, F., see H.-E. Keller, *Etude descriptive*.

Legge, M. Dominica, '*Clerc lisant*', *Modern Language Review*, 47 (1952), 554–56.

LePetit, Jean, 'La Normandie sous les premiers ducs d'après le *Roman de Rou*', *Art de Basse-Normandie*, 63 (Caen, 1974). A translation of Part III, vv. 2823–3240, with commentary.

——, 'Guillaume le Bâtard depuis son avènement jusqu'en janvier 1047: traduction en français moderne du *Roman de Rou*', *Art de Basse-Normandie*, 70 (Caen, 1976–77). A translation of Part III, vv. 3241–684, with an historical commentary by Paul Fichet.

Le Prévost, Auguste, *Supplément aux notes historiques sur le Roman de Rou* (Rouen: E. Frère, 1829).

Liebermann, F., 'Eine Quelle für Waces *Roman de Rou*', *Archiv für das Studien der Neueren Sprachen*, 108 (1902), 380.

Lim, Ilkyung Chung, 'Authorial Interventions in Wace's *Roman de Rou*', unpublished dissertation, Purdue University, 1996. *Dissertation Abstracts International*, 57 (1997), p. 3012A.

——, '"Truth" and the Normans: Wace's *Le Roman de Rou*', *Romance Languages Annual*, 8 (1997), 46–50.

Lorenz, Fr. W., 'Der Stil in Maitre Wace's Roman de Rou', thesis, Leipzig, 1885.

Louis, René, and Michel de Boüard, 'La Normandie ducale à travers l'oeuvre de Wace', *Annales de Normandie*, 2 (1952), supplément IV–V; 3 (1953), supplément VI–VII.

Lyons, Faith, '*Clerc lisant* and *maître lisant*', *Modern Language Review*, 56 (1961), 224–25.

Marx, Jean, 'Les Sources d'un passage du *Roman de Rou*', in *Mélanges d'histoire offerts à M. Charles Bémont par ses amis et ses élèves à l'occasion de la vingt-cinquième année de son enseignement à l'École Pratique des Hautes Études* (Paris: Félix Alcan, 1913), pp. 85–90.

Mathey-Maille, Laurence, 'L'Écriture des commencements: Le *Roman de Rou* de Wace et la *Chronique des ducs de Normandie* de Benoît de Sainte-Maure', in *Seuils de l'œuvre dans le texte médiéval*, ed. by E. Baumgartner and L. Harf-Lancner (Paris: Presses de la Sorbonne Nouvelle, 2002), pp. 79–95.

Norgate, Kate, 'The Battle of Hastings', *English Historical Review*, 9 (1894), 41–76, 608–11.

————, 'Wace', *Dictionary of National Biography* (Oxford: Oxford University Press, 1973), vol. 20, pp. 404–05 (originally published 1899).

Paradisi, Gioia, *Le passioni della storia: scrittura e memoria nell'opera di Wace* (Rome: Bagatto Libri, 2002).

Paris, Gaston, 'Wace, *Roman de Rou*, hgg. von Andresen', *Romania*, 9 (1880), 592–614.

Payen-Payne, James B. De Vinchelez, *Wace, and the Roman de Rou*. Occasional Publications, 4 (London: The Jersey Society in London, 1913).

Pelan, Margaret, *L'Influence du Brut de Wace sur les romanciers français de son temps* (Paris: Droz, 1931, repr. Geneva: Slatkine, 1974).

Philpot, J. H., *Maistre Wace, a Pioneer in Two Literatures* (London: Methuen, 1925).

Pohl, Theodor, 'Untersuchung der Reime in Maistre Wace's *Roman de Rou et des ducs de Normandie*', *Romanische Forschungen*, 2 (1886), 321–50, 543–631.

Prentout, Henri, (i) 'Les Sources de Wace pour l'histoire des ducs'; (ii) 'Les Sources de la conquête d'Angleterre', *Bulletin de la Société Jersiaise*, 10 (1923–27), 24–27, 27–31 (appendices to the item 'Dévoilement d'une pierre commémorative à Maistre Wace', pp. 16–24).

Raynouard, F. J. M., *Observations philologiques et grammaticales sur Le Roman de Rou, et sur quelques règles de la langue des trouvères au douzième siècle* (Rouen: Edouard Frère, 1829).

Rechnitz, F., '*Fenestre* dans le *Roman de Rou*', *Romania*, 40 (1911), 91–93.

Rollo, David, *Historical Fabrication, Ethnic Fable and French Romance in Twelfth-Century England* (Lexington: French Forum Publishers, 1998).

Round, J. H., 'Wace and his Authorities', *English Historical Review*, 8 (1893), 677–83.

————, 'Mr. Freeman and the Battle of Hastings', *English Historical Review*, 9 (1894), 209–60. Reprinted in *Feudal England: Historical Studies on the Eleventh and Twelfth Centuries* (London, 1896, new ed. 1964), pp. 258–321.

Sandqvist, Sven, 'Remarques sur le texte du *Roman de Rou*', *Revue de Linguistique Romane*, 43 (1979), 287–308.

Sayers, William, 'The *jongleur* Taillefer at Hastings: Antecedents and Literary Fate', *Viator*, 14 (1983), 79–88.

————, 'OFr *s'esterchir*: Horse Rearing and Rearing Horses', *Romanische Forschungen*, 106 (1994), 217–24.

Schirmer, Walter F., and Ulrich Broich, *Studien zum literarischen Patronat im England des 12. Jahrhunderts* (Cologne and Opladen: Westdeutscher Verlag, 1962).

Schneider, O., 'Die Verbalform bei Wace'. thesis, Halle, 1908.

Schultze-Busacker, Elisabeth, *Proverbes et expressions proverbiales dans la littérature narrative du moyen âge français: recueil et analyse* (Geneva and Paris: Slatkine, 1985).

Stuip, René, 'La Conquête de l'Angleterre dans la littérature française du XIIe siècle', *Rapports-Het Franse Boek*, 58 (1988), 123–31.

Suchier, H., 'Zur Handschriftkunde: Ein Bruchstück des *Roman de Rou*', *Zeitschrift für romanische Philologie*, 21 (1897), 225.

Tomchak, Laurie S., 'Wace's Work: Patronage, Repetition and Translation in the *Roman de Rou*', unpublished dissertation, University of California, Irvine, 1983. *Dissertation Abstracts International*, 44 (1984), p. 3380A (includes a translation of the *Chronique Ascendante*).

Tyson, Diana B., 'Patronage of French Vernacular History Writers in the Twelfth and Thirteenth Centuries', *Romania*, 100 (1979), 180–222 (esp. pp. 193–99).

Van Houts, Elisabeth M. C., 'The Adaptation of the *Gesta Normannorum Ducum* by Wace and Benoît', in *Non nova, sed nove: mélanges de civilisation médiévale dédiés à Willem Noomen*, ed. by M. Gosman and J. van Os (Groningen: Bouma's Boekhuis,

1984), pp. 115–24. Reprinted in E. M. C. van Houts, *History and Family Traditions in England and the Continent, 1000–1200* (Aldershot: Ashgate, 1999), pp. 115–24.

——, 'The Ship List of William the Conqueror', in *Anglo-Norman Studies X: Proceedings of the Battle Conference 1987*, ed. by R. A. Brown (Woodbridge: Boydell Press, 1988), pp. 159–83.

——, 'Wace as Historian', in *Family Trees and the Roots of Politics: The Prosopography of Britain and France from the Tenth to the Twelfth Century*, ed. by K. S. B. Keats-Rohan (Cambridge: Boydell Press, 1997), pp. 104–32. Reprinted in E. M. C. van Houts, *History and Family Traditions in England and the Continent, 1000–1200* (Aldershot: Ashgate, 1999), pp. 103–32. Reprinted above, pp. xxxv–lxii.

Vielliard, Françoise, 'Deux historiens du XIIe siècle, Guillaume de Saint-Pair et Wace', *Revue de l'Avranchin et du Pays de Grabville*, 78 (2001), 325–52.

Warren, F. M., 'Features of Style in Early French Narrative Poetry', *Modern Philology*, 3 (1905–06), 179–209, 513–39; 4 (1906–07), 655–75.

Wheeler, Edd, 'The Battle of Hastings: Math, Myth and Melee', *Military Affairs*, 52 (1988), 128–34.

Woledge, Brian, 'Notes on Wace's Vocabulary', *Modern Language Review*, 46 (1951), 16–30.

INDEX OF PLACE NAMES

Names are listed according to the form used in the translation. Old French spelling, when it differs from modern usage, is indicated in brackets (forms preceded by a semi-colon refer to the inhabitants of the place or region concerned, e.g. Belesmeis 'those from Bellême'). References, which are to line numbers in Holden's text, are complete except in cases where the number of occurrences is particularly large (complete references are found in Holden's index of place names, vol. 3, pp. 283–306). Where appropriate, cross-references are provided to the Index of Personal Names. Some locations are difficult to identify and identifications here differ in some cases from those given in Holden's index. See the notes to Holden's edition (vol. 3, pp. 169–253). For further information on the place of origin of William the Conqueror's companions during the Conquest of England (III, vv. 8329–707) see E. van Houts, 'Wace as Historian', reprinted above, pp. xxxv–lxii.

CA = *Chronique Ascendante*; App. = Appendix.

(Seine-Maritime). River, place and county. *See* Robert, Count of Eu.

Eure, river, II 476.

Everwic, III 19. Earlier name for York.

Évrecin (Evrecin), II 2686 (Avrenchin in the text), III 3789, 4807. The region around Évreux.

Évrecy (Evrecié), III 4028 (Calvados).

Évreux (Evreues, Evreus, Evroes, Ewreues), II 569, 602, 606, 2686, 3993, 4145, 4152, 4245, 4254, 4302, 4358, 4373, III 917, 3288, 3789, 4857 (Eure).

Exmes (Oismes), III 963, 2227, 2253, 3353, 5136 (Orne). *See* Hiémois.

Falaise (Faleise), III 2256, 2823, 2896, 2899, 3374, 3383, 3704, 3713, 4321, 5147, 8417 (Calvados).

Fécamp (Fesamp, Fescamp, Feschamp), *CA* 230, 248, 279, II 1356, 1503, 1509, III 706, 734, 793, 1836, 2213, 2285, 2549, 2749, 2986, 4557, 6758, 8675, App. 325 (Seine-Maritime).

Ferrières (Ferreres), III 3254, 8365. Ferrières-Saint-Hilaire (Eure). *See* Henry of Ferrières and Walkelin of Ferrières.

Ferté, III 8577. Ferté-Frénel or Ferté Macé (Orne).

Flanders (Flandres, Frandres), II 396, 1158, 1792, 1820, 1891, 2173, 2178, 2182, 2188, 2214, 2188, 2222, 3313, III 1843, 4498, 4783, 6249, 6252, 7957, 10308, 10318, App. 448. *See* Arnulf I and Arnulf II, counts of Flanders.

Fontenay (Fontenei), III 4147, 8646. Saint-André-de-Fontenay (Calvados).

Fontenay (Fontenai), App. 313 (Yonne).

Fontevrault (Frontevalt), III 10289 (Maine-et-Loire).

Fougères (Felgieres), III 8363 (Ille-et-Vilaine).

Foupendant (Folpendant), III 3712. *See* note 200.

France, *CA* 6, 25, 45, 163, II 5, 229, 236, 256, 462, 468, etc. *See* Gaul. *See* Herbert of Senlis.

Frisia (Frise), II 321, 974. Region of The Netherlands and Northern Germany. *See* Radbod of Frisia.

Gacé (Gacié), III 8528 (Orne).

Gael, III 6371, 8494 (Ille-et-Vilaine). *See* Ralph of Gael.

Garillant, App. 400. Place in the Cotentin.

Gascony (Gascoingne, Gascuinne), *CA* 100,

II 839, III 24, App. 92, 295, 448. *See* Aquitaine.

Gâtinais (Gastineiz, Vastineis), II 748, III 4798. Region of Loiret.

Gaul (Guale), III 43. Earlier name for France.

Gebus, III 34. Earlier name for Jerusalem.

Genabés, III 39. Earlier name for Orléans.

Genêts (Genez), III 9536, 9540 (Manche).

Genoa (Genne), App. 473 (Italy).

Germany (Alemaigne, Alemaine, Alemaingne, Alemainne, Germainne, Germannie), II 1661, 3205, 3486, 3551, III 26, 662, 1380, 10145, App. 177, 294. *See* Allemagne.

Gerberoy (Gelberoi), II 3033 (Oise).

Gien, III 4803 (Loiret).

Gisors (Gisorz), III 2569 (Eure).

Gloucester (Gloëcestre, Glouecestre), III 1360, 7729, 11414 (Gloucestershire). *See* Robert of Gloucester.

Glos (Gloz), III 8538. Glos-la-Ferrière (Orne).

Gournay (Gornai), III 8455. Gournay-en-Bray (Seine-Maritime). *See* Hugh of Gournay.

Gouvix (Goins, Goïnz, Gouid, Gouniz), III 8523 (Calvados).

Grandmesnil (Grenstemaisnil), III 8437 (Calvados).

Great Saint Bernard Pass (Mongeu, Mongieu, Muntgieu), II 4206, III 3039, App. 291.

Greece (Grece), III 30, App. 88, 158. *See also* Pelasge.

Gué Berengier, III 3825, 3842. Place near Argences.

Guernsey (Guernerui), App. 424 (Channel Islands).

Guildford (Gedefort, Geldefort), III 4702, 7431 (Surrey).

Hainault (Hainon; Hanoiers), II 322, 4144.

Hampshire (Hontesire), III 7731.

Harcourt (Herecort), III 8639 (Eure).

Hasdans (Haudas), II 460. Probably Les Damps (Eure).

Hastings (Hastingues), III 6477, 6688, 6690 (East Sussex).

Herm (Erin), App. 424 (Channel Islands).

Hertfort (Herfort), III 7713 (Hertfordshire).

Hiémois (Oismeis, Oismés, Uimois), II 2688 (MS Orliens), 4136, III 3367, 3791, 3819, 4830, 5139, 11175, 11318. The region around Exmes (Orne).

Holy Peace (Sainte Pais), III 5387, 5388,

5392. Church in Caen; also called All Saints.

Holy Sepulchre (Seint Sepulcre, sepulcre), III 2926, 3136, 3168, 3197, 3210, 9728.

Humber (Honbre, Humbre, Hunbre), river, III 1247, 1263, 6643, 6646, 7147, 7201, 7238, 7741. River in north-east England.

Hungary (Hongrie), App. 738.

Huntingdon (Hontedone), III 7720 (Cambridgeshire).

Ister (Ester), river, App. 171. Earlier name for the Danube.

Italy (Itaire, Ytaire), III 31, App. 89. Used here as an earlier name for Lombardy and Pulia.

Ivry (Urinié), III 8575. Ivry-la-Bataille (Eure).

Jersey (Gernesi, Gersui, Gesui), III, 2770, 2771, 2775, 5302, 5305, App. 423 (Channel Islands).

Jerusalem (Jherusalem), CA 27, 214, III 34, 2925, 2933, 3135, 3152, 3160, 3209, 3229, 9238, 9661, 9685, 9689, 10122, 10130, 10163, 10301, 10319. See also Gebus.

Jeta, App. 188. Ancient region of Europe south of the Danube; land of the Getae.

Jort, III 8481 (Calvados).

Judea, III 37. See Palestine.

Jumièges (Jumeges, Jumieges), CA 296, II 399, 400, 403, 416, 1701, 1756, 1889, App. 333, 341 (Seine-Maritime).

Kaer Ebrac, III 20. Earlier name for York. See Eborac and Everwic.

Kent, III 4668, 7712, 7819, 7821, 8748, 9211.

La Fesse, III 9907. Place near Le Mans.

La Haye (La Haie), III 8571. La Haye-du-Puits (Manche).

Laigle, III 8459 (Orne). See Engenulf of Laigle.

Laison (Leison), river, III 3794 (Calvados).

La Lande, III 8585, 8589, 8591. La Lande-Patry (Orne). See William Patrick of La Lande.

La Mare, III 8422. Place in Normandy.

Lande Porrie, III 11221. Forest around Yvrande (Orne).

Langres (Lengres), III 2995, 9729 (Haute-Marne).

Laon (Leum, Leun, Lion, Monleüm, Mont Leum), II 1691, 2161, 2170, 2179, 2268, 2352, 2462, 2586, 2658, 2780, 3025 (Aisne).

La Tollete, App. 415. Place in the Cotentin.

Lassy (Lacié), III 8471, 8527 (Calvados).

Le Ham (Liham), App. 389 (Manche).

Le Hommet (Homez), III 8513 (Manche).

Le Lièvre (Luvres), III 3577 (Calvados).

Le Mans CA, 172, III 4193, III 1533, 1538, 1635, 1706, 4302, 4389, 5014, 5047, etc. (Sarthe). This list includes examples in which the terms Mansel and Manseaux are translated as 'the inhabitants of/those from Le Mans'. See also Maine, which is not always clearly distinguished from Le Mans.

Le Molay (Le Molei), III 8647 (Calvados). See Viez Molei.

Le Pallet (Peleit), III 6369 (Loire-Atlantique).

Le Pin (Les Pins), III 8434. Le-Pin-au-Haras (Orne).

Le Plessis (Le Plaisseïz, Le Pleisseïz), III 3621, 3757, 4203. Le Plessis-Grimoult (Calvados).

Le Sap, III 8538. Le Sap-André (Orne).

Les Biards (Les Biarz), III, 8468, 8499 (Manche). See Avenal of Les Biards.

Les Damps (Haudas), II 460 (Eure). See Hasdans.

Les Loges, III 8549 (Calvados).

Les Oubeaux (Onebac), III 8619 (Manche).

Lieuvin (Liesvin, Lusvin), II 2687, III 3790, 4808, 5166. The region around Lisieux.

Limousin (Limozin), III 4236.

Lincoln (Nichole), III 7723.

Lindsay (Lindesie), III 7723. A region of Lincolnshire.

Lingèvres (Lingievre), III 4212 (Calvados).

Lisieux (Lisewis, Lisieues, Lissieues, Luixuies), II 569, 2483, 2687, III 1053 (Calvados).

Lithaire (Lutehare), III, 8421 (Manche).

Loire (Lere), river, App. 429, 435.

Lombardy (Lombardie, Lumbardie, Lunbardie), III 31, 663, 1979, 1985, 3039, App. 89, 290. See also Italy.

London (Londres, Lundres), II 2312, III 17, 1266, 1273, 1277, 1338, 1356, 4694, 5505, 6741, 6755, 6763, 6900, 6901, 6959, 7016, 7017, 7025, 7712, 7825, 7900, 7901, 7907, 8860, 8974, 10341, App. 83. See also New Troy and Trinovant.

Longueville, II 1236. Place near Rouen.

Lorraine (Loherainne), II 3164.

Northumberland (Norhonberlonde), III 7200.

North Wales (North Guales), III 22. *See* Venedocia.

Norway (Norwegue, Norwerge), III 1709, 1824, App. 124, 186a.

Norwich (Norwiz), III 7716 (Norfolk).

Nottingham (Notinkehan), III 7722 (Nottinghamshire).

Noyon (Noion, Noions, Noon), III 4780, App. 274, 355 (Oise).

Odiham (Odiam), III 5456 (Hampshire).

Orbec, III 8536 (Calvados).

Orléans (Orliens), III 39, 4798, App. 442 (Loiret). *See* Genabés.

Orne (Ogne, Olne, Ongne), river, *CA* 166, III 3817, 4146, 4150, 4153, 5170, 10897.

Orval (Oireval), III 8511 (Manche).

Ouilly (Oillié), III 8529 (Calvados).

Our Lady (Notre Dame), II 1310, 2015, 3073. Church in Rouen.

Pacy (Pacié), III 8525 (Eure).

Paillart, App. 417. Place in the Cotentin.

Palestine (Palestina), III 37. Earlier name for Judea.

Palus Maeotis (Palu Meotida), App. 187. *See* Azov, Sea of.

Paris (Pariz), II 469, 561, 564, 568, 598, 606, 610, 618, 755, 1535, 1554, 1682, 1799, 2455, 2507, 2560, 2657, 2729, 2730, 2736, 2838, 3116, 3117, 3119, 3122, 3204, III 29, 670, 4971, 9638, App. 87, 356. In II 469 the region around Paris is called Parisie. *See* Lutetia. *See* Hugh, Count of Paris.

Passais (Passeis, Passeiz, Passoiz), II 2696, 4133, III 4244, 5005, 5041, 9645, 10738 (Orne).

Pays de Caux. *See* Caux.

Pelasge (Pelarge), III 30, App. 88. Earlier name for Greece.

Peleit, III 6369. Place in Brittany, probably Le Pallet near Nantes.

Perche, II 4135, III 4799. *See* Rotrou of the Perche.

Peronne (Perune), III 2162 (Somme).

Perrières (Praeres), III 8531 (Calvados).

Pevensey (Penevesel), III 6608 (East Sussex).

Picquigny (Picheingnié), II 1915 (Somme).

Pirou, III 3134, 8424 (Manche).

Poitiers (Peitiers, Petiers), *CA* 32, II 1551, 1568, 1570, 1574, III 5009 (Vienne).

See Ebles II and William III, counts of Poitiers.

Poitou (Peitou, Petou; Peitevins, Peitevinaz), *CA* 100, 298, II 1585, III 24, 1006, 4228, 4236, 4410, 8664, App. 92, 295, 444. *See* Aquitaine.

Poix (Pohiers, Polut), II 4144, III 7655. Poix-de-Picardie (Somme). *See* note 133.

Pont-Audemer (Punt Audumer), III 3533 (Eure).

Pontefract (Pontfrait), III 6673, 6675 (Yorkshire).

Ponthieu (Pontif), II 1842, 2925, III 4782, 4905, 5620, 5628, 5649, 6173, 6357, 8665, App. 267 (Somme). *See* Guy, Count of Ponthieu.

Pontoise (Punteise), II 3173, III 2557, 2585 (Seine-et-Oise).

Pontorson (Punt Orsun), III 2606 (Manche).

Port, III 8480. Port-en-Bessin (Calvados).

Portchester (Porecestre), III 10335 (Hampshire).

Porte Arthur (Artur), III 11300. Gate in Caen.

Porte Belvoisine, II 3192. Gate in Rouen.

Porte Milet, III 10896, 11319. Gate in Caen.

Porto Venere (portum Veneris), App. 505, 509, 513. Town near Genoa.

Portsmouth (Portesmue), III 1065 (Hampshire).

Pré de Bataille (Prez de la Bataille), II 1516.

Presles (Praels), III 8522 (Calvados).

Provins (Provinz), III 4785 (Seine-et-Marne).

Reading (Raduignes), *CA* 143 (Berkshire).

Regouminie, App. 399. Place in the Cotentin.

Rencesvals (Rencevals), III 8018. Site of the battle in the *Song of Roland*.

Reviers, III 8483, 9399 (Calvados). *See* Richard of Reviers.

Rheims (Reins), III 4779 (Marne).

Rhine (Rin), river, II 2994.

Risle (MS Lille, Lisle), river, III 4178, 4180 (Eure).

Robec (Roobec), river, III 367.

Rome (Romme, Rume), *CA* 137, III 663, 1382, 1391, 1392, 3043, 3054, 5469, 5485, 7932, App. 466, 467, 468, 522, 718, 728. *See* Matilda, Empress of Rome.

Rothoma, III 41. Earlier name for Rouen.

Rouen (Roem, Roen, Roent, Ruem, Ruen), *CA* 62, 199, 245, II 408, 419, 422, 464,

INDEX OF PERSONAL NAMES

Names are listed according to the form used in the translation. Old French spellings, when they differ from modern usage, are given in brackets. References, which are to line numbers in Holden's text, are complete except in cases where the number of occurrences is particularly large (complete references are found in Holden, vol. 3, pp. 261–82). Some individuals cannot be identified with certainty (for discussion of difficult cases, see the notes to Holden's edition, vol. 3, pp. 169–253). For further information on William the Conqueror's companions at Hastings, see the article by E. van Houts, 'Wace as Historian', reprinted above, pp. xxxv–lxii.

CA = *Chronique Ascendante*; App. = Appendix.

Goles, III 3652, 4208. Fool who warns William the Conqueror of impending danger.

Gonthier (Gohier), III 2465. Knight killed by Waryn; son of William of Bellême.

Gonthier (Gohier) of Aulnay, III 8465, 10935, 10939, 11065. Supporter of Robert Curthose.

Greeks (Grieus), III 3075.

Grimout of Le Plessis, III 3621, 3757, 3758, 3777, 4203, 4209, 4223. Norman knight who revolted against William the Conqueror.

Gunhild (Gunnil), III 1377, 1378, 1391. Daughter of Cnut and wife of Emperor Henry III.

Gunnor (Gonnor, Gunnore, Gunor), CA 237, III 236, 249, 611, 619, 621, 633, 650, 651. Wife of Richard I.

Gurim (Garin), II 68, 131, 157, 183. Brother of Rou.

Guy (Gui, Guion), III 1842, 3595, 3599, 3609, 3776, 4173, 4181, 4187. Son of Reginald of Burgundy and cousin of William the Conqueror.

Guy (Gui, Guoin), III 4905, 5628, 5653, 5661. Count of Ponthieu.

Gyrth (Guert), III 4673, 6802, 6903, 6940, 6985, 7019, 7041, 7043, 7045, 7049, 7056, 7057, 7181, 7197, 7203, 7225, 7295, 7300, 7835, 7854, 7864, 7879, 7890, 7891, 7907, 7918, 7923, 7960, 8819. King Harold's brother.

Gytha (Gite), III 5575. Wife of Godwin and mother of King Harold.

Haimo (Haim, Haimon, Hamon), III 3620, 3775, 3943, 4021, 4025, 4036, 4039, 4040, 4047. Lord of Torigny; called Longtooth (as Denz).

Hardret (Hardrez), III 4061. Norman knight who revolted against William the Conqueror.

Harold (Herou, Heroult, Herout), II 1776, 1782, 1784, 1789, 2869, 2880, 2897, 2913, 2917, 2987, 3067, 4150, 4153. King of Denmark.

Harold (Heraut, Herout), III 4631, 4647, 4695, 4713. Harold I, King of England.

Harold (Heraut), III 4673, 5566, 5579, 5581, 5607, 5613, 5625, 5639, 5642, 5653, etc. Harold II, King of England.

Harthacnut (Hardekenut), III 1377, 1390, 4622, 4625, 4629, 4721, 4723. Son of Cnut and King of England.

Haschier, III 9637, 9642. Supporter of William the Conqueror's son Henry.

Hasting (Hastaim, Hastain), CA 296, II 5, 13, 14, 412, 472, 473, 480, 488, 492, 499, 502, etc. Viking leader.

Hawise (Haïs, Hawis), III 263, 1402, 1422. Daughter of Richard I and wife of Geoffrey of Brittany.

Helias (Elie, Helie), III 9703, 9707, 9745, 9747, 9749, 9755, 9771, 9794, 9795, 9901, 9978, 9987, 10009, 10025, 11109, 11123. Helias of La Flèche, Count of Maine.

Henry (Henri), CA 136, 147, 197, 198, III 177, 4510, 5318, 9155, 9161, 9359, 9380, 9391, 9397, etc. Henry I, King of England.

Henry (Henri), CA 7, 17, 34, 65, 70, 89, 94, 97, 108, 110, 136, III 172, 185, 5317, 11431, 11435. Henry II, King of England.

Henry (Henri), III 179, 5318, 11431. Henry the Young King, son of Henry II.

Henry (Henri), II 1600, 1606, 1613, 1622, 1643, 1661, 2994, 2997, 3009, 3153. Henry I, King of Germany.

Henry (Henri), III 1380. Henry III, King of Germany.

Henry (Henri), III 2523, 2531, 2533, 2543, 2545, 2579, 3286, 3520, 3771. Henry I, King of France.

Henry (Henri) of Ferrières, III 8365. Norman knight who fought at Hastings.

Henry (Henris), II 1506. Bishop of Bayeux.

Henry (Henris), II 1926. One of those who assassinated William Longsword.

Herbert, III 5050, 5059, 5078, 5080, 9714, 9731, 9733. Herbert II, Count of Maine.

Herbert (Hebert) of Senlis, II 1325, 1536, 1552, 1555, 1683. Called Herbert of France in II, 1555.

Herluin (Heloïn, Herloïn), II 1793, 1795, 1798, 1806, 1812, 1818, 1824, 1826, 1835, 1862, etc. Count of Montreuil.

Herluin (Herloïn, Herluïn), III 6006. Herluin of Conteville, stepfather to William the Conqueror and father of Odo, Bishop of Bayeux, and of Robert, Count of Mortain. *See* Odo FitzHerluin and Robert FitzHerluin.

Holy Saviour (Saint Saveir), III 3942. Used as the battle-cry of Ranulf of Briquessart.

Hubert Paynel (Paienals) of Moustiers, III 8500. Norman knight who fought at Hastings.

Matilda (Mahelt, Maheut), III 4502, 5338. Daughter of Baldwin V of Flanders and wife of William the Conqueror.

Matilda (Mahelt), III 10139. Daughter of Malcolm, King of Scotland, and wife of Henry I.

Matilda (Mahaut, Mahelt, Maheut), *CA* 110, 118, 120, 136, III 11437. Empress of Rome, daughter of Henry I and mother of Henry II.

Maurilius (Maurile), III 4555. Archbishop of Rouen.

Michael (Michiel) of Baynes, III 4572. Son of Archbishop Malger.

Muriel, III 6004. Sister of William the Conqueror and wife of Odo au Chapel.

Nebuchadnezzar (Nabugodonosor), III 95, App. 29. King of Chaldea.

Nigel (Neel) I of Saint-Sauveur, III 1088, 1470, 1511, 1524, 1532, 1545, 1556, 2610, 2641, 2670. Vicomte of the Cotentin.

Nigel II of Saint-Sauveur, *CA* 157, 164, III 3589, 3619, 3773, 3939, 4084, 4101, 4125, 4130, 4169, 8355, 8493. Vicomte of the Cotentin; called Falconhead (Chief de Faucon) in III 4129.

Nicholas (Nichole), III 2283. Son of Richard III and abbot of Saint-Ouen in Rouen.

Nicholas (Nichole), III 11274. Knight from Caen.

Norman(s) (Normand, Normant, Northman), *CA* 43, 46, 55, 57, 99, 205, II 430, 431, 432, 437, etc.

Norwegians (Norreis, Norroiz), III 6667, App. 237.

Odo (Ode, Odun), III 270, 1436, 1444, 1451, 1479, 1537, 1677, 1697, 1705, 1794, 1797, 1803. Odo II, Count of Chartres.

Odo (Ode, Odon) FitzHerluin, III 5989, 6163, 7356, 8107, 8115, 9173, 9207. Half-brother of William the Conqueror and Bishop of Bayeux.

Odo (Odes, Odon), III 4790, 4904. Brother of Henry I, King of France.

Odo au Chapel (Yon al chapel), III 6003. Son-in-law of William the Conqueror.

Olaf (Colan), III 1709, 1820. Olaf II, King of Norway.

Olenoiz, App. 184. Scandinavian people. *See* Ortenoiz.

Oliver (Olivier), III 8017, 8935. Roland's companion in the *Song of Roland*.

Ortenoiz, App. 123. Scandinavian people. *See* Olenoiz.

Osmund (Osmont), II 1362. Blinded by William Longsword.

Osmund (Osmont), II 2063, 2070, 2171, 2265, 2291, 2297, 2302, 2337, 2357, 2361, etc. Tutor to Richard I.

Otto (Ote, Oton), II 3153, 3155, 3166, 3185, 3188, 3250, 3306, 3311, 3370, 3385, 3416, 3429, 3465, 3496, 3551. Otto the Great, Emperor of Germany.

Papia (Pavie), III 1854, 3404. Second wife of Richard II.

Pepin, App. 295. Son of Louis the Pious.

Philip (Phelipes), III 5294. Philip I, King of France.

Poitevin(s) (Peitevin(s), Poitevin(s), Poitevinz), II 938, 1018, 1022, 1576, III 4235, 7659. Inhabitants of Poitou. *See* William the Poitevin.

Popa (Pope), *CA* 300, II 592, 1289. Wife of Rou and mother of William Longsword.

Radbod (Rembaut), II 321, 328, 330, 338. Duke of Frisia.

Rainald (Renaut, Roinaut), II 468, 476, 511, 514, 543, 549, 561, 563. Count of Paris.

Rainer (Regnier) Long Neck (au Lonc Col), II 322, 342, 343, 348, 352, 355, 359, 360, 365, 376, 379, 386, 389, 395. Count of Hainault.

Ralph (Raol) of Conches, III 7580, 7587. Lord of Tosny and son of Roger of Tosny.

Ralph (Raol) of Gael, III 6371, 8494. Breton knight who fought at Hastings.

Ralph (Raul) of Tosny, III 1471, 1473, 1513, 1525, 1569. Vassal of Richard II.

Ralph (Raol) FitzOgier, III 11167. Knight from Caen, father of Thierry.

Ralph (Raol) Taisson, III 3849, 3862, 3875, 3879, 3897, 3914, 4051, 4829. Ralph I of the Cinglais, vassal of William the Conqueror.

Ralph (Raol) Taisson of the Cinglais, III 8489. Ralph II of the Cinglais, fought at Hastings.

Ralph (Raul), II 2153. Norman nobleman.

Ralph (Raol), III 11273. Knight from Caen.

Ralph (Raoul, Raul) Torta (Torte), II 2835, 2839, 2849, 2857, 3090, 3097, 3098, 3106, 3107, 3113. Louis IV's provost in Normandy.